D1083635

THE DEVELOPMENT OF
ENGLISH HUMOR

PARTS I AND II

THE DEVELOPMENT OF ENGLISH HUMOR

PARTS I AND II

By LOUIS CAZAMIAN
Formerly Professor at the Sorbonne

AMS PRESS, INC.
NEW YORK

Cambridge University Press, London, N.W. 1, England

Reprinted with the
Permission of
DUKE UNIVERSITY PRESS

AMS PRESS, INC.
New York, N. Y. 10003

1965

MANUFACTURED IN THE U. S. A.

CONTENTS

Part I.

From the Early Times to the Renaissance

Part II.
The Renaissance

Part I

From the Early Times to the Renaissance

FOREWORD TO PART I

CHAPTERS I-V of this volume incorporate the substance of lectures delivered at the University College of Wales, Aberystwyth, on the Aberystwyth Lectures Foundation, during the Session 1929-1930.

Humor is not the privilege of any country or any time. In its broadest connotation, it is an aspect of thought, or an aesthetic category. The present inquiry is not concerned with that general object. Humor is essentially concrete; it has its roots no less, and more, in the originality of national groups, than in the faculties of the abstract human being. Its growth may thus be regarded as part and parcel of the moral life and mental progress of a people; and it is studied here as such. Even so, however, the question arises of the influences which that development may have felt from abroad; and the problem of the connection between Medieval French and Middle English humor has had to be recognized.

The notion of humor explained in the first chapter, and upon which the whole argument is based, made it inevitable that the investigation should be practically restricted to literary texts. It is only in words that the duality of intent which we regard as characteristic of humor in the precise sense can be aptly expressed. The diffused humor which reveals itself through art and life is commonly merged in the indiscriminate field of the comic—fun, amusement, drollery pure and simple, from which it is not easily distinguishable.

Modern renderings have been given of the Old English or Old French texts quoted, and those from Middle English authors, with the exception of Chaucer, have been modernized.

Our thanks are due to Professor Emile Legouis, of the Sorbonne, who has looked over our manuscript and offered several suggestions; to Professor A. Koszul, of the University of Strasbourg; to Professor Emile Pons, of the Sorbonne; and to the staff of Columbia University Library, New York, through whose unfailing kindness the experience of a year as visiting professor in an American college has proved no less convenient for purposes of study than it was delightful.

February, 1930

CHAPTER I

THE OLD ENGLISH PERIOD

I. Humor and the English Temperament

SUBJECTS have their fates, and it would be vain to ignore the heavy doom that besets all disquisitions upon humor. The very word is enough to raise hopes which are surely and sadly to be disappointed. Shall then that single matter be excepted from the universal curiosity and hunger of scholarship, because to treat of it seriously is the unpardonable sin against artistic fitness, and to treat of it in a manner that suits the argument is to baffle the aim of serious inquiry?

Let it be our initial confession of faith that the austere pleasure which can arise from the disinterested quest for truth will prove enough to sustain us on our way. Indeed we cannot serve two masters at once. If our minds and hearts are lured away by the sprite that beckons to us, with an arch smile just showing on ever so slightly mocking lips, all is lost. Let us, then, brace ourselves for the ordeal. We start on our pilgrimage, buoyed up only with the expectation to understand, perhaps, a little better, the origin and the progress of a mental attitude which has grown to be one of the major features of the modern British genius.

For our purpose is strictly historical; and this is another shrewd blow to the hopes which probably still lurked in the background of our thoughts. Speaking of humor as a pure essence, apart from time, one is naturally led to describe, to show it forth, from the wealth of the most telling, the most persuasive examples. The audience that does not relish the analysis may thus at least find some comfort in the illustration. But history is our hard taskmaster. If the psychologist or the aesthetician has a conscience to save, what shall we say of the historian? There is no earnestness comparable with his. The question here is not to explain humor, but to trace it through the stages of its development. Nor is this all: we are to follow that course from the beginning only as far as the seventeenth century. This means that the matter we shall be dealing with must often yield but a poor reward for our labor. Modern humor hardly came into its own till the Renaissance; prior to that time the mental complexity which it requires was not very widely diffused. The investigator of origins has to make the most of mere symptoms; and the instances we shall quote may on occasion seem rather thin. Moreover, a short survey of some seven centuries can but take in the generalities of the subject, with the support of few concrete proofs.

Still, enough has perhaps been said to chasten expectation. After all, there would be no excuse for the inquirer and the inquiry if the special possibilities of the subject were finally reduced to nought. Such a disaster we are not quite ready to face. How could a man profess to treat of humor unless he had his little share of a sense of it; and enjoying that common privilege—a privilege truly democratic—how could he deprive his audience, when the occasion arose, of the modest gratification to which they would naturally look forward? Let the problem be treated just plainly: it would be hard luck if the examples produced were robbed of the flavor that may yet linger about them. Beyond that, we should be imprudent to trust the assumption that a study of humor must somehow be humorous.

One thing has to be stressed at once. By "humor" is meant here, not every kind and aspect of the comic, but a province within that empire. Shifting and loose as the value of the word has undoubtedly become again, it was rather more precise and restricted for a period of time; and at the center of its widened range nowadays there does persist a core of that more solid and specialized connotation. Upon this we take our stand; on that basis we shall persistently build. Are we thus at all straining matters, and running counter to one of those currents of language which it is wiser not to try to stem? The case, in all fairness, seems different. However commonly the word may be abused, the ground in logic and fact for the continued existence of its narrower use has not disappeared. To many, no doubt, humor is simply what causes laughter.[1] But to the majority of those who speak or write more reflectively, there is no humor unless a peculiar shade is superadded to the bare quality of the comic. One sees very good reason for not losing a distinction founded in the sense of a special aesthetic category, and, more surely yet, of a distinct psychological attitude. When the growing self-analysis of the modern mind, from the sixteenth to the eighteenth centuries, produced the proper notion of humor, language in order to name it stamped an older word with a new value. The idea thus evolved was no illusion; and no development of thought since that time has been able to blur the outline of the thing, even if the edges of the word have been worn out in common talk or unguarded criticism.

What that more precise notion is most of us know clearly enough, although we may fight shy of the necessity to define it. All things considered, we should lose more by trying to run away from a definition than we shall do by committing ourselves to one. Let us then say simply that we make a thing humorous by expressing it with a certain twist, a queer reserve, an inappropriateness, and as it were an unconsciousness of what we all the time feel it to be. This is a merely formal description; but form offers the safest way of approach to such an elusive spirit as that of humor. In the form, we shall see, much of the spirit is entangled, and to be caught. You can superadd some quality of humor to almost every subject in that way; but needless to say the method is most natural, and works best, when applied to themes which in themselves possess more or less of the value called "comic," that raises laughter. This is why the humorist is primarily a man with an eye for the potential fun of life; but the fun in which he specializes is that which consists in being apparently impervious to fun.

A kind of mastery over one's feelings is thus among the conditions of humor; but that repression, that negative power

[1] This is the view set forth or implied in the only work dealing historically with English humor: A. G. L'Estrange's *History of English Humor* (London, 1877); in the various anthologies of humorous texts; and even in most philosophical and literary studies of the subject, such as Max Eastman's *The Sense of Humor* (New York, 1922). Mr. J. B. Priestley's attitude, in his *English Humour* (London and New York, 1929), is substantially like our own.

is not of course sufficient; along with it there must be a positive virtue, the shrewdness that perceives the actual paradoxes of experience, and the agility that allows one to think on two different planes. It is hardly necessary to add that the working of the method thus described can be interpreted in terms of aesthetic theory. A word as to those implications, psychological and philosophical, will not be amiss here. Why should we use at all that queerly twisted mode of expression? Because our instinct, then our experience and art teach us that by its means we secure a whole range of effects: first, a special shade of the ludicrous, arising from the inverted manner itself, as every student of laughter knows; so that the comedy of life, thus shown forth, assumes a double, a richer, an intensified virtue, there always being more point in aesthetic enjoyment, up to a certain limit, when it demands our co-operation, and does not yield all its flavor at the immediate moment of tasting. Next, the trick of inversion is naturally bound up with a mood in which the stimulus of unexpectedness is cared for, sought after; the humorist joins hands with the artist who gives us the pleasure of a refreshed world; and just as the artist must take his stand upon facts as they are before he bathes them in an idealized light, the humorist reaps the benefit of his startling slyness through the concrete realism of his manner; the more objective his picture, the more vividly does the soul of his subjective intent flash out. Thus the surprise of humorous treatment rejuvenates the commonplaces of actuality, and from its mere fun there tends to radiate the suggestion of a topsy-turvy universe. Now topsy-turviness for its own sake is one of the most profound desires, as it is one of the most soothing values, of art and thought; it has always been longed for by mankind, driven and vexed under the iron laws of things; there is a delicious release in extravagance; and the deepest poetry and philosophy are thus gradually involved in the modest method of inverted presentment; they have an affinity with it, and flourish upon it.[2] With that ultimate background of humor we

[2] We have worked out this view of the subject in "Pourquoi nous ne pouvons définir l'humour," *Revue germanique*, 1906; reprinted as "Le Mécanisme de l'humour," in *Etudes de Psychologie Littéraire* (Paris, 1913); and in a short survey of the psychological problem against the background of the English intellectual temper, *L'humour anglais* (Paris, 1942).

need not be further preoccupied at present; some aspects of it, at least, will claim our attention as we proceed.

More to our immediate purpose are the elements which enter into the moral attitude of the humorist. A supple sense of the actualities of things and a command of his own reactions are his major gifts. Now it is remarkable that these two mental traits are among the outstanding features of the English, as revealed by the original life and manners of their land. Let it be far from us to suggest that England or rather Great Britain has a monopoly of humor: other nations possess their full share, and humor indeed is as old as civilization. But it is no mere accident that a name should have been found for it, and that it should have first grown to a realization of itself, on British soil. There are reasons in the nature of things why the wrong impression should have been created, and often expressed, that humor was a birthright of the British. It is not; but they evince in their constitution a somewhat special affinity with the temper of humor. A sense of the actualities of things they have ever displayed pre-eminently; the concreteness of their thought, their "mental materialism," and that intuitive perception which goes at least some way to extend their grasp of the practical over the field of the spiritual, are justly noted characteristics. Again, their faculty of withholding the normal flow of their impressions, their cool-blooded taciturnity, the subdued tone of their outward life, and that reserve which stretches all the way from the captaincy of their souls to pure sluggishness and to the fear of giving themselves away, have struck the foreign observer at all times. It would thus seem that, after all, the nation which first grew aware of the distinctive nature of humor was singled out for that discovery by a particularity of genius, and that to study the development of modern humor in England is to trace it on the chosen ground where the character of the race was to lend it the earliest and the richest fecundity. Whether that grace of nature has clung to the children of the blood, and followed them even to their overseas settlements, is a question that a little acquaintance with the United States and the Dominions enables one to solve.

It is a far different problem that will engross our attention through this first part of our inquiry as a whole. When did that special fitness of temper begin to assert itself? If humor has such deep roots in the very being of the English people, how is it that their earliest literature shows but slight traces of it? How can we account for its scarcity during the Anglo-Saxon period? And what interpretation are we to put upon the disturbing facts and probabilities which seem to point to French influence as having most to do with the rise of Middle English humor?

Problems are indeed writ large over each and every period in the development which we are attempting to follow. The history of English humor falls roughly into three phases, each of which has its predominant issue to settle. The first is that with which we shall be concerned throughout this series of lectures. From the early times to the Renaissance, the main point is to explain the apparent lateness in the growth of English humor, and to apportion their respective shares in that becoming to the two nations whose cultures and languages lived on the same soil after the Norman Conquest: England and France. The second period, from the middle of the sixteenth to the end of the seventeenth century, shows us the word "humor" undergoing a process of specialization, which gradually brought it to denote the attitude of the humorist in the modern sense; and the difficulty is to follow that subtly graded change of meaning. The third period, from the beginning of the eighteenth century to our day, is the final stage; then it was that the word and the attitude were completely fused, and, the self-consciousness of humor being achieved, individual variations upon the common theme had a free play. Of the three main questions, the first is the most difficult to solve; our data then are most scattered, our impressions most tentative. On entering upon that piece of research, let us express a sense of diffidence, only too sincere and too fully justified.

II. The Old English Period

Of humor, properly so called, we find very little indeed in the remnants of Anglo-Saxon literature. It has been often remarked that there is none in *Beowulf*—a deficiency that will cause us little surprise, if we remember the central mood of the poem, the inspiration out of which it grew, whether the collective or the individual elements in the authorship be more emphasized. The tone is pitched in such a key that humor, it must be confessed, would have to be handled very adroitly not to sound a jarring note. The theme of *Beowulf* is high and solemn. At the present day that beautiful epic appeals not in vain to the idealism and to the pride of racial origins; and a halo of almost religious veneration has developed around a text, in which it has been not unreasonably surmised that the self-sacrifice and death of the Saviour may have been dimly adumbrated. But the modern mind is no less irreverent than it is sentimental; and in spite of all the effort lavished by scholars and by the authors of academic textbooks, in order to make *Beowulf* the lay Bible of the Anglo-Saxon youth, it is undeniable that most students refuse to take it very seriously. Fine and grand as it is, its appeal is extraordinarily remote; its setting, its mental horizon demand of us an adaptation more difficult than is required for instance by the Homeric poems. And so, to one imagination that is genuinely fired by the tale, there are not a few that are tickled and prompted to a rebellious reaction. The number of unpretentious and not unkind parodies which the student of today has grafted on the poem, is significant.

Meanwhile the learned specialists mount a vigilant guard and enjoin us not to desecrate the text with disrespectful interpretation. The greatest *Beowulf* scholar, Klaeber, is positive in his warning: "In such a gloomy atmosphere there can be no room for levity, fun, or humour. Passages which to modern readers might seem to be humorous were certainly not so meant by the Anglo-Saxon author."[3] Instances follow; but strange to say, the texts as to the misleading appearance of which our authority is thus bent upon warning us are not those which our own sense of humor might perhaps find most dangerous. The great scholar's feeling of incongruity is stirred by possible implications that remind us of Charles Lamb's remarks about the jokes of the schoolmaster. Other spirits will be led astray at

[3] *Beowulf*, ed. Fr. Klaeber (Boston, 1936), introduction, p. lxi.

other places. No less a commentator than Clark Hall finds a "grim specimen" of "unconscious humour" in line 1545, "where the sea-monster sits on the hero, and draws her sword";[4] a grotesque image assuredly, did we not remember that those monsters in *Beowulf*—crosses as they are between heathen fiends and Christian devils—are endowed with half-human features and attributes. It would be easy to discover parallel examples—such as the passage in which Beowulf lies in wait for Grendel and the fiend is represented as much surprised at the reception he meets with. In a modern setting the remark would have been hardly possible without a flickering smile; there is nothing here to suggest any such intention. Or: "he [Grendel] became affrighted in soul and spirit, but he could get away no faster for all that."[5] After Grendel's death, when the terror and the danger are over, we are told that "the older courtiers turned back, and many a young [man] from the joyous journey, to ride boldly from the mere on horses—warriors on steeds";[6] and the fiend's mutilated limb being on view, "many a retainer, valorous of mood, went to the lofty hall to see the curious wonder."[7] Here are boldness and valor cheap indeed, after the event. Only children would fail to perceive the inappropriateness in the situation and the words. But is not a certain childishness of spirit the very feature of the poem? The temptation is to be resisted once more, when the hero himself relates the final episode of the fight: "I could not keep him [Grendel] from going—the Creator did not will it. I did not stick to him, the deadly foe, well enough for that—the fiend was too preeminently strong at going."[8] The man who wrote that had not the slightest twinkle in his eye.

Indeed Klaeber thus far is absolutely right. Of full humorous intent we have nothing in those texts, or similar ones. All we could speak of would be "unconscious humour," as Clark Hall does; and the phrase—a misleading set of words—should deceive no one; the essence of humor is to be conscious, instinct with a purpose, even if the development of the hint

[4] *Beowulf*, tr. J. R. Clark Hall (London, 1911), introduction, p. xxxii.
[5] *Ibid.*, ll. 753-55.
[6] *Ibid.*, ll. 853-55.
[7] *Ibid.*, ll. 919-21.
[8] *Ibid.*, ll. 966-71.

brings out more than the speaker was clearly aware of when he spoke. To endow a person with unconscious humor is simply a polite manner of saying that he conspicuously lacks a sense of it. We are here indulging in a cheap sort of game, that of systematic anachronism; we are taking a leaf from the book of the parodist; with interpretation, properly so called, this has nothing to do; and to interpretation it is time that we should return.

The history of all early literatures bears witness that the epic tone in itself does not exclude an occasional or a frequent humorous relaxation; and we know that the joy of battle and the triumph of victory have often enough in medieval poetry struck fierce notes of mocking and defiance. Might we not catch in the earnest mood of *Beowulf* a momentary gleam of that spirit; and might not that spirit be set off by that sense of relativity, that amused expression through repression, which is the saving grace of a humorous intent? If we look at the text closely enough, we shall find something of the kind, and passages in which the purpose of speech is pitched at least in the broader key of humor.

Ironical understatement is an elementary form of the inversion which all humorists practice; tested psychologically, it is akin to humor, and the next thing to it, so near, indeed, that a definition of the field must not leave it out. The trick of an expression obviously too low for the object, without any seeming awareness on the speaker's part of that error in valuation, runs through the whole development of our subject; and we thus have here one of its most central as well as most primitive roots. The manner agrees particularly well with the reserve of temperament, the distrust of profession as compared with action, with which most observers have credited the English character. It has been even possible to say that just as understatement is typical of the English, that converse and equivalent trick, overstatement, or systematic and transparent exaggeration, is a favorite process in American humor.

Now we have some understatement in *Beowulf*. It would much exceed our sense of reality to pretend that the following passages were irresistibly funny; but that a certain grotesqueness of inversion is there dimly sought for, and brought about by a conscious turn of style, is very probably no illusion. For instance, we read that "a chief of the Geats severed one of them [the sea-monsters] from its life, from its conflict with the waves, so that the hard war-arrow stuck in its heart: it was the slower in swimming in the waves, since death took it off."[9] Here the irony is colored with hatred and insult; and a similar motive peeps out in the remark about the fearful dragon, which determined to keep watch over the treasure, and, the narrator adds, "not be one whit the better for it"—as events will show.[10] A shade further in slyness of understatement can be detected through the hint thus thrown out: "the Scyldings folk never used treachery in those days";[11] or through Beowulf's scornful words to Unferth: "I have never heard such contests, such peril of swords related about thee. . . . In truth I tell thee, son of Ecglaf, that Grendel, the frightful demon, would never have done so many dread deeds to thy prince, such havoc in Heorot, if thy heart, thy spirit, were so warlike as thou sayest thyself. But he has found out that he need not too much dread the antagonism, the terrible sword-storm of your folk, the Victor-Scyldings."[12]

The last instance is of special interest. What comes out in it, more clearly than in the others, is the kind of insulting intent which consists in a reminder, affectedly though transparently toned down, of unpleasant facts. That such scornful irony was congenial to the Saxon temper can be no surprise;[13] we find plentiful evidence of the mood in Middle English poems where French influence is not at all conspicuous; and this is the sort of indirect statement to which relatively simple minds would first rise, the mental complexity required being prompted by the stimulus of fierce anger or hatred—emotions one naturally associates with a warlike race. It seems safer not to surmise that we have in these taunting words more than a germ

[9] *Ibid.*, ll. 1432-36.
[10] *Ibid.*, l. 2277.
[11] *Ibid.*, ll. 1017-18.
[12] *Ibid.*, ll. 583-96.
[13] The most typical example, with *Beowulf,* would be the *Brunanburh* poem in which the victors taunt the vanquished, and especially a traitor chief, Constantine, with ironical comments.

of the modern "flyting"[14]—a humorous exchange of huge opprobrious high-sounding abuse, a kind of serio-comic contest which flourished in the Scottish poetry of the sixteenth century. But we are on solid ground when we say definitely that such passages reveal the essential requisites of humor: a conscious restraint of speech, an appearance of unconsciousness that sets off a hint more forcibly, and a comic element, here resulting from the contrast between the actual meaning and the words.

Such tests are conclusive, provided we do not press them too far. A glimmer of indirectness in speech has broken through the tenor of the Saxon poet's single-mindedness; he has shown his kinship to us in one more respect; his soul, when all is said, was cast in a human mold. With all his primitiveness there was in him the perceptible germ of the duality of meaning which was to grow so luxuriantly in later ages. And that is about the nearest approach to humor we can find in *Beowulf*.

The rest of our literary survey may well be brief. No one would expect any humor from such poems as *The Wanderer* or *The Seafarer*. Of all moods, that of longing, regret, and moralizing is the most incompatible with the twist of sentiment, of thought, and style that humor requires; it is the essence of an elegiac inspiration turned to edifying uses to stake all on a direct communication of itself; the suspicion of a double meaning would almost necessarily be fatal to its appeal. The same or similar remarks would apply to the bulk of Anglo-Saxon literature. It is very generally didactic, with a moral or religious purpose; and that is the kind of impulse which, if not checked or subtly qualified, gives thought a fixed bent, sets it decisively toward a plain downright manner, deprives it of its inner suppleness and freedom. Now the Anglo-Saxon mind, generally speaking, would hardly entertain two ideas at a time; and subtle qualifying shades were mostly beyond its scope.

Our search indeed would be fruitless, had not the *Exeter Book* preserved for us a number of "Riddles," in which a rather different range of interest is brought into play. There is an

[14] The best-known instance is *The Flyting of Dunbar and Kennedy*. The verb *flitan* is of current use in Old English, with a range of connotation from actual physical wrangling to a rebuke in words; but the properly humorous sense appears to be of more recent date.

affinity, in the nature of things, between the method of the gnomic poet ingeniously working out his riddle, and that of the humorist on the formal side of his expression. Both hide their meaning and half reveal it through cleverly contrived hints; in either case the reader has to make a guess. The riddle can be too hard to solve; and there is ever a margin where humor overshoots itself, so that its assumed unconsciousness is mistaken for genuine. The pressure of their common aim drives the writer of riddles and the humorist to concentration and implication; with both, transposition is used to an aesthetic as well as to an intellectual end. In a modest way, the transferred thought of the riddle-maker is a germ of the complex many-sided meaning which will play in iridescent shades over the full-grown varieties of modern humor.

That the riddles of the *Exeter Book* are a joy forever, it would be too much to say. The most successful, from our special point of view, are at best like puns, on a clumsy plane of inverted images instead of words. Some are quite fine poems, in which a powerful imagination is at play; but the pleasure here is of a very different order, and indistinguishable from that which we should reap from a striking description in verse. For our purpose of pleasantry not much is to be expected from such jokes as the following—the word being the horn of a bull:

> I was once a warrior armed; but now a youthful thane,
> A hero bold, doth deck me round with silver and with gold,
> And bended wire bows; sometimes men caress me;
> Sometimes I to battle the willing comrades call.
> . . . .
> Ask what is my name?[15]

That is mild indeed. But as we study the riddles, we grow aware of some very interesting facts. To begin with, they do possess a vein of distinctly humorous flavor; but this is not in their purpose itself, in the puzzle which they laboriously construct; it is in the choice of their subjects, in their tone and manner, and to sum up this aspect of the question under one phrase, in their popular realism. On the intimate

[15] Riddle 15; tr. W. Clarke Robinson, *Introduction to Our Early English Literature* (London, 1885).

relation between realism and humor I shall have to dwell again presently; if the main root of humor lies in the most genuinely English temper, if humor is after all a growth of national and not of foreign origin in England, it is owing primarily to the realistic bent of the native English genius. But this is not all; the realism of the riddles is often free, and at times quite strangely free, from the relative narrowness of scope which the authority of aristocratic and religious influences has stamped upon the bulk of Old English literature. A new spirit, racy, spontaneous, audacious, coarse, peeps out here from under the earnest edifying tone which spreads itself everywhere else to such a remarkable tenor of meaning and expression. It is as it were the revelation of another side—a no less human side, one we should have been certain to find sooner or later—of the Anglo-Saxon mind. Not only do we meet with a number of riddles on the most common objects of country life, and share in the sympathy of the rustic imagination with the dog and the ox, the hens and the swine, the cowhide and the wine vat, the onion, the leather bottle, and the one-eyed garlic seller; but an undercurrent of extremely coarse suggestion—so coarse that horrified scholars have often succeeded in remaining unaware of it—runs through not a few.

This is enough to give us pause. The riddle had been from the oldest age of civilization a popular pastime as well as a refined exercise of wit. Its fortune with the Saxons has been traced to their love of metaphor and allegorical puzzles—a trait they shared with their Scandinavian kinsmen. But good Bishop Aldhelm, a Saxon of the Saxons, in his Latin enigmas, had tried to make plain the spiritual meaning of creation by entangling it in a pleasant maze of ideas and words. We have here no such thing, only a frank intimation of what a popular appeal could be in this kind of literature. These texts are an exception in fact, but not in right; they presuppose and dimly reveal a whole background. The Anglo-Saxon poets thus find themselves eventually united in a common paganism of instinct with the naïvely impudent genius of all early literatures. They lose the doubtful privilege of an exclusively monastic inspiration, with which their modern admirers had been too easily prepared to endow them. And this brings us to what should be the chief, as it will be the final, point in this part of our survey.

III. The Anglo-Saxon Problem

It would have been not a little unreasonable to expect that the mental life of the Saxons should have given rise to the most finely shaded kinds of humor. An age of civilization can express itself only in modes to which it is adequate; and all that we know of Old English culture from the time of *Beowulf* to the eve of the Norman Conquest precludes such a possibility altogether. The complete detachment from one's self and the expert playing with one's own frames of mind which full-grown humor requires are feats of which the Anglo-Saxons would be generally speaking incapable. But they were not exactly Barbarians. Their moral civilization offers interesting features, and in certain directions of imaginative strength or brooding aspiration they display a kind of refinement. To all practical purposes, they are the end, as well as the beginning, of a cycle in culture.[16] Intellectually, of course, they do not rise much higher than the labored ingenuity of the riddles. Still, it might not look at all absurd to credit them with the shrewdness of sense and the rough love of play which endowed other Germanic stocks, of approximately similar development, with at least elementary forms of humor.[17] The problem of their destitution in that respect has thus to be worked out in its own terms.

The most natural interpretation of the facts seems to be that the negative privilege is more apparent than real. It is very likely that the Anglo-Saxons had their own sense of humor. But it was not of the finest brand and would not recommend itself to the more exacting propriety of the clerics who were their spiritual guides and censors. That the Church, through the Middle Ages, was always more or less in conflict

[16] The poem of *Beowulf* "is highly sophisticated and aristocratic, essentially a courtly epic. It was no wild outpouring of adventure for the ears of the vulgar, but an elegant entertainment for a royal circle" (W. W. Lawrence, *Beowulf and Epic Tradition*, Cambridge, Mass., 1928, p. 4).

[17] Both the Eddic poems and the Sagas easily offer instances in point.

with the heathenish amusements of the people we know from many documents. In England, the fight began early—from the very first centuries of Saxon Christianity. The *joculatores* or *jongleurs,* the heirs of the Latin mimes, soon made their way across the Channel from the merry fields of France; a sure sign that in the elementary love of fun the companions of Alfred were not so deficient as has been generally supposed on the single evidence of their literature. The clergy themselves were not above succumbing to the attraction of the gleemen; again and again we find the Councils enacting that priests or even bishops shall not seek for relaxation in the regular company of those jesters; and the prohibition is enforced by the Anglo-Saxon canons of Edgar in the tenth century.[18] The jolly ecclesiastics could plead that by striking a bargain with the singers of levity they tended rather to minimize the evil; did not the Church through those ages find it more profitable to join in the saturnalia of the people on set occasions, the better to keep them within bounds? Words written by a divine, Thomas Cobham, in the thirteenth century, except from the general condemnation such *joculatores* as sang of epic subjects or recited the lives of the saints ("qui cantant gesta principum et vitas sanctorum");[19] so that we are to infer the scurrilous jesters knew how to change their note, when the necessity arose, and meet halfway the compromise which the Church desired. All that we need, in the present instance, is to suppose that the Anglo-Saxons were finally more or less submissive to the authority of their pastors; and in view of the vividness with which they realized the frightful powers of the fiends, or the sufferings of the reprobate, there is much substance in the conjecture. The faint outline of the moral idiosyncrasies which were to characterize the English people at most periods in its history, and to reach their typical form in the Victorian era, would thus be descried in its earliest infancy. The supposition is the more likely as the spontaneous effusions of the natural man need not have been expurgated or excised through actual censorship; the free utterances of the sinful were simply not honored with

[18] See E. Faral, *Les Jongleurs en France au moyen âge* (Paris, 1910), pp. 21-22.

[19] *Ibid.*, p. 44.

the treatment reserved for dignified themes; they were not written out, copied, handed round, and preserved. It is difficult at the present day to imagine what loving care and patience it took then to save words that pleased from oblivion, to register them among the manuscript texts, that is to say among the classics. The more popular inspirations would be given no actual record, even though they were transmitted orally for a long time; and the monks who acted as trustees for the interests of literature, amending with a few Christian touches all the works that savored too much of the pagan spirit, just ignored what was too low to be thus improved.

Are we then to set store by the impression that besides the records of the Anglo-Saxon mind which some lucky accidents have brought to our notice, there was a much broader range of mental life and of naïve expression, which has been entirely lost? The supposition rests on a solid basis of probability. The argument has never been put more cogently than by Professor W. P. Ker, in his remarks on *The History of the Ballads*. The ballad spirit, he points out, is as old as anything in humanity; yet our extant ballad forms can hardly be older than the eleventh century.

Where were the ballads before they were made? . . . An old civilization with an elaborate literature of its own came to an end in the eleventh century. . . . Part of the difficulty in understanding the former age, comes from the mere accident that so very little of its poetry has been preserved, and, in that little, so very much less of the popular unambitious sort. . . . But here and there in the earlier period we discover the same sort of popular tastes as are found much more fully represented in the later. There were the same comic stories; only, whereas the later Middle Ages got them in the easy form of fabliaux, and in large numbers, the earlier time has only preserved a few by turning them experimentally and as a sort of literary game into Latin verse. It seems a fair conclusion that the difference between the earlier and the later Middle Ages—e.g. between Anglo-Saxon and Middle English—is in some respects not as great as the existing remains would make us imagine. . . . It is pretty certain that beneath the difference there was the same kind of folklore. The ancient Germans knew the story of Big Claus and Little Claus, they had the same jokes as the fabliaux and the Decameron, though by the literary fashions and conditions of their time they were not encouraged to put these things in writing, and only did so occasionally and accidentally. Later, and mainly through the influence of France and the much less pretentious narrative forms of France, it was easier for folklore to get into literature.[20]

Those illuminating words throw light on the nature of our missing link. In that folklore, where stories that were later to become ballads, and humorous ballads, would play a conspicuous part, the more relaxed need of expression and instinct for literature of the Anglo-Saxons found a vent. How could they after all lack such an instinct and such a need? There never was yet since the world began a people wholly made up of prigs or of saintly ascetics; and the sad seriousness prevailing in the few Old English texts that we possess does not mean that the whole range of the Old English mind is contained in them.

It seems thus possible, on some such grounds, to define the relation in which the Anglo-Saxons stood to humor. They were neither brilliantly gifted nor quite destitute in that respect. Their mental equipment was such as rather to promise future fitness than to secure actual ability. Like most early races, they would be handicapped for humorous thinking by the violence of their passions, and by their general incapacity to be detached from the urgency of their own feelings and ideas. Again, they lacked the supple intellect which perceives subtle shades of meaning and likes to play with them. They would be wanting in the finer varieties of humor; while the coarseness of their taste would make their spontaneous revels, their outbursts of fun, a kind of horseplay and rough banter hardly reconcilable either with decency or with that modicum of neatness and point without which humor cannot find its proper style. As a result, whatever humorous dispositions they may have possessed have vanished from their records.

But over against those disabilities, they were well provided with the stuff out of which humor is made. Their literature affords abundant evidence of that rich fund of concrete per-

[20] W. P. Ker, *On the History of the Ballads, 1100-1500* (London, 1910), pp. 13-14.

ceptions, that sensitiveness to the distinctive qualities of things which is the source of a realistic frame of mind. The potential wealth of humor lies in the scattered evidence of vivid mental realization which most Anglo-Saxon texts give, and which the set habits of verbal rhetoric are powerless to hide. And if the Old English people had not the intellectual control of their inner life, their temperament was in other respects fitted by nature for the self-command of humor. Their seriousness, their very sluggishness were nearer to the requisites of properly humorous expression than was or could be the liveliness of southern peoples. It is a fact of common experience that the slow-minded nations have developed the most remarkable originality[21] in the field of humor. The actual possibility of the suspense and reserve which are the conditions of the humorist's attitude can be found in the still childlike brooding and wonder of the Saxon. It is not in the least a paradox to say that a sad and hesitating temper bears a greater affinity to real humor than does a lighthearted propensity to easy, explicit mirth. It was not by their seriousness that the Anglo-Saxons were paralyzed as incipient humorists, but by the clumsy stiff habit of mind that they were only very gradually learning to shake off.

As a conclusion, it would seem that the mystery of the obtuseness to humor with which the Saxon settlers in England have been charged and which is an irritating puzzle to their English descendants should be somewhat dissipated. Those forbears of the people that have been associated more than any other with the individualization of modern humor were not parted from them in that respect by an impassable gulf. They show us the promise and the means; the achievement was to come later. It took, for the promise to be fulfilled, the fostering influence of time, the action of spontaneous mental growth, and the stimulating and refining presence of the spirit which from the time of the Conquest was brought into such intimate intercourse with the silently ripening English genius—the spirit of France.

[21] One might instance *Don Quixote*—one of the world masterpieces of humor—and the *relatively* slow rhythm of the brooding Spanish mind.

CHAPTER II

MEDIEVAL FRENCH HUMOR

I. The French and Humor

HAVE THE FRENCH a sense of humor? Put the question to an Englishman, and the answer, if quite frank, will betray some hesitancy, not to say doubt. The French, he will say, have rather a name for pleasantry of a different kind; and when cross-examined as to what the difference is, he will perhaps reveal the idea at the back of his mind. He will point out that the Frenchman has wit, drollery, satire, and all the brilliant manners of raising a laugh; but that all the tricks of his cleverness are conspicuous, just as they may be successful;[1] they make him admirable and admired; but as humor they would fail because the Frenchman's fun is explicit and obviously self-conscious; you read upon his face the coming climax of the story, the point that is just going to be made; and when a man gives away the effect he is out to produce, what on earth could he have to do with humor?

That our English friend is right to some extent we have no intention of denying. Indeed, we believe that the main characteristic of humorous expression lies in its restraint, its apparent unconsciousness of value; and so the general temper of French pleasantry remains today, as it has always been, a little too explicit, in spirit and method, properly to deserve the label of humor. But we know from universal experience that such generalizations on national character are the most dangerous things, chiefly in what they pretend to exclude. How many exceptions do we not meet with every day to each single trait in the accepted notion of the Englishman, the American, the Frenchman? This is quite a case in point. Obviously,

[1] "French wit has about it a public air" (J. B. Priestley, *English Humour*, London and New York, 1929, p. 5).

there has always been some humor among the French; more or less, as the mood of thought, life, and letters changed with the times; at the present day humor has become an accepted and a very prevalent manner of expression in France. As for the Middle Ages, it is no paradox to submit that the French literature of the period offered rather more substantial proof of the prevalence of that manner than did the body of the literature in Middle English. Chaucer, needless to say, is the incomparable humorist, whose work both raises in its most acute form the question of French influence, and goes furthest to redeem for the English the primacy which they claim to have possessed at all times in the field of humor.

II. Their Medieval Record

One glance at the records of life and letters is enough to remind us that medieval France had a prominently merry side. Of course, almost every quality can be safely ascribed to the Middle Ages. Shall we say that they were chiefly epic and chivalrous; or tragic and somber; or mystic and dreamy; or again, quiet, happy, and sane; or lastly, bubbling over with fun? Yes, indeed; all five separately, or together. There perhaps never was a time when the comic and the serious things were more freely associated. The tones and values of life, as will happen with a relatively new culture, had not yet been sorted, classified, and assigned their proper places. However sad the world may then have been, or have had good reason to be, it thus assumes, to our minds, the stamp of a more spontaneous, a more unsophisticated gaiety. It could weep, no doubt, and suffered incredible ills; but we feel that it laughed with a better heart than we do now. And the feeling, thus qualified, is not wrong.

Medieval French religion acknowledged the claims of mirth unreservedly. The churches displayed grotesque carvings, and jolly festivals were held in the naves. The sacred dramas and the epic poems left room for familiar episodes. The fabliaux were oral traditions before they were texts. Every city had its fairs, with the mountebanks and clowns, and a large supply of comic performances—*jeux*, *soties*, and farces. It was in France that the *jongleurs* had their headquarters, enlivening castles and halls with their scurrilous songs; from the seventh or eighth to the fourteenth century, we see them spreading to Saxon or Norman England, and indeed everywhere. The goliards, disciples of the mythical bishop Golias, were an even more significant, because a hybrid kind; truant and itinerant clerics, welcomed by abbots and monks, they cheered the gloom of convents with their jingling rhymes and gave vent to a startling fund of irreverence and profanity.

Through the varied aspects of medieval France, there runs thus a broad vein of gaiety, mischievousness, and fun, of a free, popular, rather coarse type; not hidden and repressed, but displayed; very similar, however, to that underworld, a glimpse of which we seemed to catch under the austere surface of Old English life. The mirth of the crowd is pretty much the same everywhere; one tenor of spontaneous merrymaking, at all events, seems to have prevailed over Western Europe, in the cosmopolitan culture of the Middle Ages. But in so far as medieval France was concerned, how does the frequency of that holiday mood help us towards the solution of our problem, her positive or negative relation to humor?

We must here face a real difficulty. We have committed ourselves to such a definition that we cannot regard humor as coextensive with mere fun. Our notion implies an element of difference—a special restraint, resulting in some apparent unconsciousness of value. How largely is that characteristic present in medieval French manifestations of the comic spirit? There lies the whole question. Now, the test is a delicate one to apply; its working calls into play a factor of subjectivity, if not of arbitrariness. It may and will happen that the testing does not yield plain results. The quality of humor is not always pure and entire; every intermediary degree can be found, as is generally the case with moral or aesthetic categories. Our impressions, in concrete instances, will often be relative; through a fine gradation of shades, genuine humor is linked up with simple mirth. The dividing line cannot be drawn accurately.

Let us suppose, however, that the examination has been carried through to a conclusive end. The huge volume of laughter-provoking words, shapes, gestures, in medieval French life, art, and letters, is, generally speaking, too explicit to deserve the name of humor. It expresses the lighter-hearted, merrier temper of the French, their greater susceptibility to the joy of living—that national addiction to gaiety which remained, as far as the eighteenth century, their main feature in the opinion of the outside world, and formed a sharp contrast with the English, who, as Froissart perhaps said, and the Duc de Sully may have remarked, took their pleasure sadly.[2] In the majority of instances, the handling of the comic is more direct, plain, obvious than humor can put up with. The facts, at first sight, thus seem to bear out the verdict of our English friend: the cheeriness of France, in the Middle Ages as in later times, was too easily exteriorized and transparently revealed, to be identified with the proper type of humorous expression.

Shall we stand by that merely negative finding? We keep

[2] The famous saying attributed to Froissart, as to the English (who "se réjouissaient tristement selon la coutume de leur pays"), has so far baffled all attempts to trace it to an authentic source. It seems to have been first quoted as Froissart's by W. Hazlitt, in "Merry England," *New Monthly Magazine*, Vol. XIV, Part II (Dec., 1825), pp. 557-565; next by Rathery, in the well-known study upon "Les Relations Sociales et Intellectuelles de la France avec l'Angleterre," *Revue Contemporaine*, XX (1855); and by Emerson (*English Traits*, "Character," Boston, 1856)—in all three cases without a precise reference. M. G. Ascoli in his work on *La Grande Bretagne devant l'opinion française* (Paris, 1927), p. 33 n. 1, quotes the text with a very slight difference as Froissart's, and refers to Rathery. Meanwhile a different source had been assigned to the saying by Mr. W. Gurney Benham in his *Book of Quotations* (Section: Historical and Traditional): "The passage is not found in Froissart, but it seems to be derived from the Duc de Sully's *Mémoires*, written c. 1630, as follows: 'Les Anglais s'amusent tristement selon l'usage de leur pays' "; and this assertion is substantially repeated by Mr. J. B. Priestley in his *English Humour* (London, 1929), p. 2. The present writer has failed to find the text either in Froissart's *Chroniques* or in Sully's *Mémoires;* he cannot help wondering whether it might not have been coined by Hazlitt, who quoted much from memory and who would have more or less unconsciously summed up in those striking words a well-known reaction of French observers to the apparent moroseness of English pleasures. Distant equivalents for the phrase can be found, e.g., in the words of Deslandes, a French traveler in England at the beginning of the eighteenth century, which we shall quote (chap. v), or in those of Voltaire: "Le sombre Anglais, même dans ses amours, Veut raisonner toujours," "Les Originaux," III, xii). As, in a general way, from the Middle Ages, the French agreed that the English were melancholy, it is probable enough that Hazlitt may have thought of that national judgment, when writing an essay in which he gives the same appearances, on the whole, a different construction, and so been led to crystallize the French view in the so-called saying of Froissart. Our thanks are due to Mr. Priestley, Mr. Benham, and M. Ascoli, who have kindly answered inquiries and given the help of their suggestions.

our allegiance to our definition so long as we do not see any necessity to alter it. But two things are to be remembered. First, we may agree that the light-hearted, simple fun that gives itself away is not humor; but when all is said, it would be strange if we did not experience that the two brands existed side by side in quite a number of cases. They are not identical; but neither are they mutually exclusive. On the contrary, in some essential respects they show an affinity, and all things being equal call for each other. An eye for the comic is, after all, the best qualification of the humorist. We remarked that the most merry nations were not necessarily the richest in humor. That is true, in so far as they keep merry, and nothing else. But life sees to that, and the jester has a thousand occasions to chew the cud of bitterness. As soon as the more sober and serious mood is induced, over a background of simple fun, you may have humor. That is why there must needs be some in the vast merrymaking of a jolly people. From a mere consideration of probabilities, we can expect the broadest medieval farces to be often flavored with a humorous spice.

And next, we should not allow the problem to rest at that. What are those other species of the comic, with which humor is linked up? It shades off, on one side, into the mere irresponsible flow of animal spirits, and popular farce; on the other, into the artistic and intellectual elaboration of comic points. According as they share more in the quality of one or the other, we may call the intermediate varieties "humor of release" or "humor *de finesse*"—there being perhaps in English no equivalent for the latter phrase. Even where France had not much of the central brand to show, she might offer us a good deal of those slightly mongrel kinds.

A word in caution, however, is necessary. The distinction which we are making here has been put forward, in partly similar terms, by an acute critic, whose remarks serve our special end, provided they do not lead us away from a proper insistence on the element of consciousness which is an indispensable part of humor. Release, indeed; but along with release there must be some manner of restraint. The contrast which Mr. Edwin Muir[3] describes between the popular and the aristocratic humorist is a pregnant fact. It is true that in the course of time the former, generally speaking, came first, the latter next; and personally, one may prefer the earlier, fresher outpourings of the vein to the more sophisticated that followed. But the natural progress of humor was not its degeneracy; it became more and more tinged with consciousness and reflection, because its very attitude implied the seed of reflectiveness. To inoculate humor with thought and art was not to vitiate its principle; it was to develop it towards an inevitable consummation. Before there was thought in pleasantry, there was no humor. Falstaff looks thoroughly impulsive in his rollicking fun: while he is only so, he is farcical, not humorous. The humor comes in with the shrewd control over himself which the rogue manages to keep all the time; with his watching, and letting himself go only as far as he likes; with the cool judgment which adds a flavor of self-mockery to the absurdity of his pranks. At bottom humor is one; it always demands a background, so to say, a feeling of relativity, another plane of consciousness. In its wildest outbursts something still must be kept back. Even through the mood of the saturnalia, humor comes out, from mere anarchy or indecency, as soon as there is superadded to the release a perceptible awareness, a feeling of something in the situation, the words, the gestures, that is meant, implied, not expressed. The succession in time which Mr. Muir emphasizes is thus simply the gradual refinement of humor. On the other hand, we must acknowledge that

[3] "It [Mr. Joyce's] is a humour, too, in which extravagance is reinstated, after being banished for a long time as childish and contrary to mature taste. In primitive humour there is something outrageous, and the humorist not only discloses the foibles and indecencies of his audience, but flaunts his own, piling them up in a mountain and squatting upon it. This humour was an intellectual parody of the saturnalia. . . . It was a great emotional and intellectual release. . . . Later came the comic artist who in making his audience laugh retained a sober countenance, admitting no fellowship with the frailties and lusts which in describing he satirized or excused. This has been the fashion of the last three centuries, a polite fashion, in which the original flavour of humour was refined away. Comedy in this style amused men and made them resigned to their lot, thus fulfilling both a social and an ethical purpose; but it no longer gave them release. It was something different from humour in its first rude state, its means restraint and economy where originally they had been extravagance and grotesque abundance. Disregarding the fashion of centuries, Mr. Joyce has recaptured the boundlessness of primitive humour" (*Transition; Essays on Contemporary Literature*, New York, 1926, pp. 40-41).

indeed humor can be overrefined, and refined away. The greatest humorists—Chaucer, Cervantes, Rabelais, Shakespeare, Sterne, Lamb, for instance—have managed to fuse and unite the two strains into one; to preserve some of the freshness and raciness of popular humor, whilst pushing the elaboration and improvement of the method as far as they could go.

The distinction, thus qualified, will prove at once serviceable in the field of medieval French literature. France had much "humor of release"; but she had more "humor *de finesse*"; in this converse domain was her proper contribution to the common progress; there she was really a guide to European thought.

That she possessed an abundant literature of release is plain enough; it was just those expressions of a merry irreverent mood, which we briefly outlined above. The Middle Ages in essential respects lay stress on discipline and repression; mirth was then the outbreak of the pent-up forces; in it the voice of the natural man would be heard. The various authorities of religion, chivalry, the feudal system, courtly love were rejected in a mood of rebellion. The presence and activity of a similar mood we dimly felt under the surface of orthodox Anglo-Saxon life. Here, in medieval France, the revolt is patent, glaring. We have the texts, and can be edified.

In that literature of escape humor is often to be traced. We find the outstanding examples of it in the literary kind that was most narrowly subjected to the influence and conventions of the artificial, aristocratic world: the epic. The historians of the *chansons de geste* have pointed out how, gradually, what were mere gleams of irreverence became the very light of the picture, and the grand austerity of the *Roland* was changed into a mood of parody. We then have the *Pélerinage de Charlemagne,* in which the knights vie, not in feats of arms, but in bragging stories and "gabs"; and we have the *Moniage Guillaume,* the very soul and purport of which is the spirit of pleasantry.

The valorous knight, Guillaume d'Orange (Guillaume "au Court Nez"—au Courb Nez, hawk-nosed), is turning over a new leaf; he enters an abbey and must needs be a monk. The abbot is delighted, although the candidate to holy orders, as meek now as he was terrible, proves singularly raw in spiritual lore. "Can you read?" he is asked. "Yes, but without looking at the book." No matter: he will be taught. He is tonsored in due course, and the monastery is ransacked for a frock that will fit his giant limbs—to no purpose, as all are too short. A monk now, and one among his brothers, he is in spite of all looked up to by them, to his own undisguised satisfaction, not unmixed with threats, should they dare treat him as an equal. Indeed the haughty overbearing temper will not be repressed. Complaints and grievances are soon heard: Guillaume eats and drinks ravenously; when fed, he chases the other monks and strikes them. His clothes take up a tremendous lot of stuff, the brother tailor moans. The caretaker in charge of the victuals hobbles by on crutches: Guillaume has half killed him, has smashed the door of the food cellar open with a kick, and rifled everything. This cannot go on: the abbot and the monks lay their heads together; let Guillaume be sent on an errand of danger and trust: he shall go and buy fish at the seaside. Should he be attacked by robbers on the way (and everybody expects that he will), he must not defend himself with weapons, but only use flesh and bone, as befits a man of God. Guillaume goes, is duly set upon, and, tearing off a limb from a packhorse, kills all the robbers. He rides back to the abbey in triumph and takes his revenge on the monks. In another version of the story are some comic touches of a finer kind: on approaching the spot where the robbers are suspected to lie in wait, Guillaume asks his valet to show his pluck by singing, but the rogue's voice, for fright, chokes in his throat; as soon as the dangerous corner is passed, he wants to break out in valorous song, to his master's merriment. Guillaume finds, after a while, that he must not stay in the abbey; he never could, he remarks, save his soul if he did.[4]

That is all, no doubt, pitched in the key of release and parody. Fun is poked at the temporal and the spiritual lords at once, in their awkward association and resultant clash. The jokes are none of the most delicate, and often verge upon mere

[4] *Le Moniage Guillaume,* ed. W. Cloetta (Paris, 1906).

clownish horseplay: Guillaume in his anger seizes the abbot, throws him against the prior, who with the impact is thrust against a pillar and breaks his pate. Still, an element of genuine humor is diffused through the whole. It resides in the perceptible consciousness and restraint of the narrator, in his relative discretion and reserve. All is not plainly said, much is left to be gathered from the implications of the text. Some of the comic at least is not directly presented. Again and again the audacious and grotesque potentialities of the scenes, the characters, the gestures, the words are hinted at, suggested; and we feel that the author enjoys them to the full, but he does not let himself go, and chuckles where he makes us laugh.

Other instances might be adduced. But the early development of the "humor *de finesse*" is more characteristic of medieval France; upon it we should dwell at greater length. Of course, there is *finesse* of some kind wherever there is humor. Was not the restraint that qualified the release an intellectualization and a refinement of the mood? Conversely, there will be some release in the texts we shall quote next. The distinction, once more, cannot be made too hard and fast. However, it is another temper of pleasantry, and a different aspect of the French faculty of humor, to which we now turn.

III. Humor "de finesse"

In this new field we seem to perceive the working of a special affinity; and we are thus led to ask ourselves what might be, after all, the roots of humor, in the psychological and artistic temperament of the French.

The French are mainly—or are supposed to be—excitable, impulsive; they will not resist the prompting of their impressions, will give away their point in pleasantry. But will they indeed? Do the facts often answer to that much simplified image? A modern nation offers a wealth of characteristics and tendencies; there is a Northern type in France, as well as a Southern; among the provincial figures the Flamand, the Picard, the Champenois, the Lorrain, the Bourguignon, the Normand, the Breton show various modes and aspects of coolness, inwardness, self-possession. Can we forget the potential humor in Lyon, where "Guignol" expresses a fund of racy ironical satire; in Bordeaux, where the shrewd composure of the race need not be traced to an admixture of English blood? And even the much abused Southern temper can be so strangely cool, and quiet, with sudden flashes. The psychological possibility of humor is to be found everywhere in France; and more than ever at the present time, when the trials and experiences of an unmatched crisis have given the last touch to the sobering of centuries.[5]

But let us concede the point: the French, as far back as we can look into the past, did evince as a rule a more modest share than the English of the dispositions which we associate with the special reserve of humor. Still, failing the sluggishness and the self-command of the average Briton, were there not other tendencies, frequently or normally French, through which a spirit of restraint and a method of indirectness would develop in pleasantry, leading it towards the "humor *de finesse*"?

There were indeed; and these are the elements, native to the soil of France, out of which medieval French humor, or the main strain of it, did grow.

Of raciness, practicality, a realization of things—of the "realistic" temperament, akin to humor at the root—the French were never destitute. Some of them, no doubt, in all ages were carried off by the eagerness of their logic or the impetuousness of their passion; but the others kept their feet firmly enough on the solid ground of facts. There ever was a French shrewdness, akin to that of the British, though different; a special kind of clear-sightedness, with a tendency to shade off into an intellectual subtlety of perception—this being the bane, as we shall see, of French humor. The seed of skepticism, or even of cynicism, always grew and prospered more or less in France; and that lively refusal to accept conventional views passively, to take them for granted, was the spirit of much French mockery through all times.

[5] A typical French tennis star is thus described by an American paper: "The great Cochet, languid, unhurried, the antithesis of all popular conceptions of the Frenchman as impetuous and excitable. . . ."

Humor is distinctly on the increase among the present generation of French writers.

But what matters more is that the France of the past or the present shows us a rich vein of slyness—an untranslatable word, like the roughly though not exactly similar French term *malice*. Many were the tributaries to that general fund of disposition: the *esprit Normand*, the *goguenardise*, which crops up everywhere and assumes a different coloring in each new province, the hundred local varieties of the outwardly dull and secretly ironical rustic manner. And here indeed, the Southerner can be at one with the Northerner: his quick temper and his bragging mood leave him his ready, sharp sense of the hidden flaws of things, his bitingness of implied sarcasm and satire. The French intelligence, in life and letters, shows itself gifted, from the beginning, for indirectness of allusion through mental agility and the faculty of thinking two things at a time—of saying one, and meaning the other. Now such a double intent, if refined and abstracted into a pure clash of ideas or words, is just what is called wit; but so long as it remains in touch with the concrete, is enough nourished with fresh direct experience, it possesses a distinctly humorous flavor. What we mean by "humor *de finesse*" is simply the brand which bears the mark of an actively analytical mind, and is thus halfway to wit.

Through yet another of her gifts France was endowed with some kind of proficiency in the wider field of humor: her writers from the first disclose a power of artistic restraint, an instinctive sense of the additional vigor which economy of effort, discretion, sobriety impart to phrasing; and this vital intuition of the superiority of reserve in words would lead of itself to the implicitness which is the method of the humorist. There runs through the whole course of French literature a preference of suggestion to plain statement; *sous-entendu*—not only in satire, but in normal expression—is a national art. The generality of classical thought and style links up with this power of condensed and virtual meaning. That pleasantry should be cast in the same mold was inevitable; and from the first it was shaped by it. A pointed utterance would thus be sought so as to set off the comic; and in this value of point, the Southern Frenchman would even possess a sort of inborn advantage. Now point, just like mere terseness, tends to concentrated statements, that is to say, suspended and restrained. In this way again, the spirit and the technique of humor would begin to arise; humor would be present, in the first degree, as a sort of verbal felicity, enhancing the effect of pleasant contrasts cleverly and discreetly presented. It would live and breathe, so long as it were not lost in an excess of elaboration and ingenuity.

Thus it is that from the Middle Ages we can find, and do find in France, some national traits and tendencies that would make for the manner of slyness, closely akin to humor, which gives its distinctive quality to much satirical or comic French writing. The *esprit gaulois* of irreverence here merges in the *esprit français,* and it is the latter which is responsible for those expressions of the national temper.

In this domain it is possible to say that French literature, which developed first, set an example to other modern literatures; and here it is that medieval French precociousness could quicken the growth of Middle English humor towards a more definite artistic realization. Chaucer, in this field, will be heir to the teaching and to the practice of France; only, the disciple will improve upon his masters.

Looking through medieval French literature, we find much widespread evidence of that latent spirit of humor. Some instances, in roughly chronological order, will not perhaps be amiss.

The date assigned to the two versions of the *Moniage Guillaume* is the twelfth century. To the same century belong the Fables of Marie de France—who is herself, in this respect of early humor, such a significant link between the two countries: a French woman, writing in England, she translated an English original, derived from the Latin of the fictitious "Romulus," into the apologues of her "Ysopet." Through the neat and fine turn of her French, there develops at times a note of unmistakable humor, which seems, when it is heard, but the soul of her quiet archness. In her ninety-sixth fable, a scold has fallen into a river, and is carried off by the current. The laborers who witnessed the mishap rush downstream to seize her as she floats by; but the husband, who knows better, shouts a warning to them not to do it:

> Li Vilein lur a escrié
> Qu'il ne sunt mie bien alé:
> Contremunt la cuvient-il querre,
> Que là, la porrunt bien troverre. . . .
> A sa mort ne fist-ele mie
> Ce que ne volt faire à sa vie.[6]

That cycle of parody and satire, the *Roman de Renart*, belongs again to the twelfth century. Although it seems safer, according to the latest views, not to see in it the anonymous product of a mythical folk mind, but the work of a score or so of individual authors, it was the people of France who made the success of the *Renart*, and gave it its significance. We find more links with England here: not only does the cycle show the distinct influence of the North, of Picard and Walloon writers; but the French texts have English allusions, there are English branches, and various English offshoots from the same trunk are extant. The spirit of the narrative, in many places, is indistinguishable from genuine humor, through its subdued manner, its cunning roguery, its slyness of allusion, its fine unconsciousness of the mischief implied. One might instance the beautiful economy of effort and artistic restraint in the immortal *Jugement de Renart*, where the obvious human, feudal implications are quietly ignored. The climax is perhaps reached when Renart, found guilty of numberless crimes, and seeing the fatal noose draw quite near his neck, is seized with a sudden itch to take the cross and fight God's battles beyond the seas:

> "El non de seinte penitance
> Voeil la crois prendre por aler
> La merci deu outre la mer."[7]

[6] The peasant did call out to them
That they had taken the wrong course;
It's upstream they should look for her,
Only there might they find her. . . .
In her death she no whit could do
What she would not do when she lived.

[7] Episode I, ll. 1388-90 (ed. Martin).
"In the name of Holy Penance,
I wish to take the cross and go,
God be thanked, beyond the seas."

In the next century, the outstanding work is the *Roman de la Rose;* and if the first part, by Guillaume de Lorris, is pitched in a key very different from humor—a key of genuine moralizing relieved by lyrical freshness, by a dainty imagination, and much allegorical subtlety—the second part, by Jean de Meung, is one of the main repositories of medieval French humor. Not that the author's temper is not didactic; but his didacticism is aggressive, ironical; and being qualified by a strong dose of skepticism, leaves his mind that margin of freedom without which humor cannot live. The humorous note in Jean de Meung's lines is quiet, restrained; it is heard as an undertone of slyness and mockery, set off by the paradoxical, the unbelievable evenness and simplicity of the style. At the same time as the poet's face keeps perfectly unruffled, his tongue, so to say, is just perceptibly in his cheek. The deepest essence of that humor is the feeling—or rather, a full and clear realization, untinctured with emotional bitterness—of the relativity of things; and its method is an apparent unawareness of the effect which a momentary heightening of the color, a keying up of the artistic means, is bound to produce. Such is the potential comedy of the ravings of a jealous husband, in which there lives and breathes a perception of the ridiculous that goes much beyond what the countenance of the writer, if one may say so, does confess to; or the exquisite comedy of this curtain lecture, where a wife pleading for an exceptional measure of trust, which she claims to have deserved among all women, so artfully and artlessly gives away her point (lines 17,420 to 17,439, in Francisque Michel's edition):

"Ge voi toutes ces autres fames
Qui sunt de lor hostiez si dames,
Que lor maris en eus se fient
Tant que tous lor secrez lor dient.
Tuit à lor fames se conseillent,
Quant en lor liz ensemble veillent,
Et privéement se confessent,
Si que riens à dire ne lessent,
Et plus sovent, c'est chose voire,
Qu'il ne font néis au provoire:

Par eus-méismes bien le sai,
Car maintes fois oï les ai;
Qu'el m'ont trestuit recongnéu
Quanqu'el ont oï et véu,
Et tout néis quanqu'eles cuident.
Ainsinc se purgent et se vuident.
Si ne sui-ge pas lor pareille:
Nule vers moi ne s'apareille,
Car ge ne sui pas jangleresse,
Vilotiere ne tenceresse."[8]

The century of the *Roman de la Rose* gives us as well the satirical poetry of Rutebœuf; and while nothing is more French, how can we escape an impression that the true note of humor rings there again and again, in the sly roguery, the restrained archness, the constant understatement; even if the humor is instinct with a definiteness, a neatness of turn, a clever epigrammatic elegance which might no less deserve the name of wit? Let us watch the poet dealing shrewd blows, in his quiet way, to the much hated Friars:

Humilité a bien grandi,
Car les Frères sont les seigneurs
Des rois, des prélats et des comtes.

. . . .

Pour mieux Humilité défendre

[8] Ellis's free rendering in verse has made Jean de Meung, not inappropriately, read here much like Chaucer (ll. 17,293–17,308):

"Other men
Speak freely to their spouses when
In bed o'nights with them they lie,
Telling them all their privity
As openly, to say the least,
As though they shrived them with their priest.
All this I know for gospel truth,
Since I from their own mouths, forsooth,
Have learned things many a time when fain
Were they, in confidential strain,
To tell when all alone we've been
The secrets they have heard and seen.
But you would do me grievous wrong
Should you suppose that I belong
To women of such sort, for I
Ne'er blab or speak unseasonably."

Contre les attaques d'Orgueil,
Ont fondé deux palais les Frères. . . .[9]

The thirteenth and the fourteenth centuries were the great time of the fabliaux. Of that characteristic expression of the medieval French mind, but not of that mind at its best, it would be wrong to say that humor, in the precise sense, was an essential element. The comic purpose of the fabliaux is most often quite explicit; here indeed is the proper field of the *esprit gaulois*, and that is not an *esprit de finesse*, nor a restrained wit. The coarseness is thoroughly impudent, and truth to say, thoroughly unconscious; the satire is almost always too plain and blunt to be sly. The spirit of the fabliaux is that of popular fun; in this connection again, one might speak of release; and it is but rarely that a humorous note can be heard, in the reserve of statement or in the duality of thought. Still, we have something of both here and there, and a diffused *narquoiserie*, which occasionally crops up with an effect as of indirect presentment. Where discretion is to be found, it can be very efficient in its veiled implications. Chaucer will take more than a hint from the fabliaux; but how much will his art transform what he takes!

Do we not hear a ring of humor in the quick run of these ironical lines, with their even tenor, behind which we seem to catch a wink of the poet's eye? The theme is that of the deceived husband—a familiar one:

Cis fabliaus aus maris promet
Que de folie s'entremet
Qui croit ce que de ses iex voie;
Mès cil qui vait la droite voie,

[9] "La Bataille des Vices contre les Vertus; ou le Dit de la Mensonge."

Much has Humility increased,
For the Friars are liege lords
Of Kings, of prelates and of earls.
. . . .
The better Humility to shield
Against the onslaughts of Pride,
Palaces two the Friars have built. . . .

Doit bien croire sans contredit
Tout ce que sa fame li dit.[10]

One might quote as well from other tales: "La Borgoise d'Orliens"; "Le Cuvier"; "De deux Angloys et de l'anel," etc. But among all fabliaux the masterpiece in the field of humor is "Le Lai d'Aristote." There we are told how Alexander the Great forgot the pursuit of his ambitious schemes and the care of his glory in the love of a beautiful Indian woman. As his tutor Aristotle was warning him eloquently against her, she used her wiles and coquetry to put the philosopher in a ridiculous position of humility and obedience, riding on his back, and appearing to Alexander in that posture; when Aristotle had the wit to turn the occasion to the uses of wisdom by pointing out that if he himself at his time of life could not stand the lure of a woman, and was thus put to shame, to how much more dangerous extremities of folly would not a young prince be driven?

It was only in the fifteenth century that the French comedy of the medieval type reached its fully developed stage, with the great popular success of the farces. But the appeal of those plays, mostly of the rough and ready kind, was of the plainest and the most explicit; and it takes a masterpiece, the *Farce de Maître Pierre Pathelin,* to find a *finesse,* a restrained economy of statement, a concentrated power of realism and ridicule, which are equivalent to humor in method, and very much akin to it in effect. Comedy, of course, raises a special problem: dramatic presentment in itself demands that the provocation to laughter should be, in some degree, kept back and restrained, at the same time as it is put forth and stressed. There is an incipient reserve in the attitude of the comic playwright, since he shows us, not his reaction to his own characters, but his characters themselves. A minimum of indirectness, and so a minimum of humor, is thus implied in the very definition of comedy.

[10] "Du chevalier à la robe vermeille; de Montaiglon et Raynaud," III, 45.
This fable to the husbands shows
That he in folly gets involved
Who believes what his own eyes see;
But he that walketh the straight path
Must believe, and no mistake,
Whatever his wife does tell him.

But that admission once made, everything depends on whether the artistic restraint is reduced or not to that bare margin. The margin, in itself, is very little; a farce can be most explicit if the author, so to say, seems to point out all his own jokes, and if the jokes are exhausted in the act of perception, so that the laughter has no background. On the contrary, the comic force of a play partakes strongly of the characteristics of humor if it is rich in implicit elements, which are gradually realized and gathered. In that respect, *Maître Pathelin* is already an example of full-grown art: its effects are almost constantly potential. To say that it is very good comedy, and that its comedy is largely colored with humor, are thus two practically correlative propositions.

IV. The Medieval Promise

We should be in a position to conclude from this very brief survey[11] that medieval French literature can show us much humor of the finer kind; an intellectual and a literary growth the more remarkable as it developed spontaneously from the promptings of the national mind and its craving for expression.

Being thus very early in the field, at a time when modern European culture and modern thought were still mostly in their infancy, medieval French humor was able to encourage and stimulate a parallel growth in other national literatures—for instance, in that of England after the Conquest. How far that process of influence did actually take place is a question

[11] Only the fringe of the vast literature of medieval France has been touched, needless to say, in the above pages. Much material of a significant nature could be found in many other texts. See for example Mr. E. Vinaver's study of *Malory* (Oxford, 1929), where he brings out the contrast between Malory's unsuspecting earnestness and the vein of humor in the French romances which he followed: "There is reason to believe that the French Arthurian writers of the Middle Ages were awake to the difficulties of their theme and possessed the sense of humour which Malory so completely lacked. Even Chrestien's attitude towards his fantastic world was somewhat detached: a smile played upon his lips and there were touches of irony in his subtle psychological discussions. The attitude of the writers of the Cycle towards the tales of chivalric magic is often one of scepticism" (p. 65 n.). Again, the fifteenth-century work of Villon might be searched, not in vain, for evidence of an ironical realism, with a strongly humorous flavor. Still, enough has perhaps been said to throw some light upon the general characteristics of medieval French humor, with its two main types, one of which (the finer, of *finesse*) we find more interesting. Rabelais was to fuse the two strains into a wonderfully rich mixture.

that remains untouched and that must be discussed in each particular case on its own merits. So far as England is concerned, we shall try to give a general estimate of the relationship in the next part of our study.

On the other hand, as might have been expected, the bulk of the comic literature in France during the Middle Ages was of a type too explicit to come properly within a precise, and so a rather narrow, description of humor.

We have thus reason for saying that the literature of medieval France seemed to betoken the rise of humor as an important, perhaps a characteristic, attribute of French culture. Although humorous expression played some part in all the subsequent course of French literary development,[12] it must be acknowledged that the progress of thought in France did not justify that promise to the full. France so to say lost the empire of humor to England, as she was to lose her colonial empire in the eighteenth century. If we inquire into the cause of that relative failure, we shall find that the genius of France, in the decisive transition to the modern period, from the early sixteenth to the mid-seventeenth century, concentrated on the rational study of man and on the clear delineation of his general features, thus losing touch to some extent with the concrete and individual aspects of reality; just as the polished minds of Louis XV and his statesmen were to ignore the concrete claims of Canada and her "few acres of snow." Now, humor lives on the concrete; and its final development in England, from the sixteenth century onward, was to be very definitely based on its intimate association with individuality.

[12] A tentative list of markedly humorous French writers from the Renaissance to the end of the nineteenth century would include Rabelais, Molière, La Fontaine, La Bruyère, Lesage, Montesquieu, Voltaire, Beaumarchais, Balzac, Mérimée, Flaubert, Claude Tillier, Daudet, Taine, Jules Renard. Many more names could be added; and it is only in a quite relative sense that one may speak of a deficiency of humor in modern French literature.

CHAPTER III

HUMOR IN MIDDLE ENGLISH LITERATURE BEFORE CHAUCER

I. Merry England, English Seriousness, and Humor

IN THE ELEVENTH CENTURY William the Conqueror and his army possessed themselves of England. His companions were the Norman knights and soldiers, of originally Scandinavian stock, who had been thoroughly steeped in French culture by their prolonged occupation of a French land, Normandy; and a number of adventurers from various provinces of France. The supremacy of the invaders was fully asserted in all the fields of political, social, intellectual relationships, and the official language of England for three centuries was French; besides, a close intercourse was kept up between Norman Britain and French civilization, in the broader cosmopolitanism of the Middle Ages. Meanwhile, under the surface of the aristocratic life at court and in the castles and manors of the nobility there persisted the repressed but still vigorous originality of the Saxon people; and how, when the two strands were eventually united, the homely stuff counted for no less, and probably for more, than the brilliant inwoven threads, is matter of common knowledge.

From the special angle of our problem, what interpretation should we put upon those safely established data? It is tempting to read them in the light of a simple moral opposition. The Anglo-Saxons were a gloomy people; at least, they are regarded as such. On the other hand, the Norman invaders were undoubtedly instinct with a lighter spirit; and it is patent enough that the Conquest made a difference in the atmosphere of Britain. From the first years of the fourteenth century we begin to hear of "merry England,"[1] and it is not only in Chau-

[1] In the *Cursor Mundi*, shortly after 1300.

cer that we catch direct tones of her gaiety. The inference is then obvious: the Frenchified "Normands" brought mirth into England; the Saxon stock, reacting to that stimulus according to the law of its bent, produced the enemy of mirth and joy, Puritanism; a long struggle ensued, with various fortunes; and when after the spacious days of Elizabeth, in which life could still be sweet, the Puritans enforced their ascendancy, merry England was gone, although gleams of her joyous self would reappear at intervals. How English humor arose is thus made clear. If we take it loosely to be coextensive with laughter, we shall say that the Norman invasion was directly responsible for its growth, and that its modern development from the seventeenth century onward answers to the partial reassertion of merry England. If we entertain a more precise notion of humor, our point will be that its birth must be traced indirectly to the same cause, as after all there is no humorist without a sense of fun, and fun was a gift of the invaders; humor was born, in the words of a critic, when the austerity of the Saxon was fused with the mirth of the Norman.[2]

It would not be well advised to deny the soundness of the derivation altogether, in the face of the evidence that can be produced. But the simplicity of the argument, we hold, should be a good deal qualified and toned down. The process, assuredly, was much more complex; and it is not safe to link up those two psychological attitudes—humor on the one hand, puritanism on the other—with the distinct influence of either stock; nor are the two attitudes mutually exclusive, or even antagonistic. The mental diversity which runs through modern England cannot be, even roughly, identified with an opposition of blood or race. We take it that merry England need not have been of Norman origin; and conversely, there is quite

[2] Floris Delattre, "Les Origines de l'humour dans la vieille Angleterre," *Revue Anglo-Américaine*, April, 1927, p. 292. The evidence that links up merry England with old France has been marshaled with special ability by Jusserand (*A Literary History of the English People*, New York, 1906-9, Book II, chap. ii, sect. v, and chap. iv, sect. ii). See also W. H. Schofield, *English Literature from the Norman Conquest to Chaucer* (New York and London, 1906), pp. 323-26, 330-35; and G. H. MacKnight (ed.), *Middle English Humorous Tales in Verse* (Boston and London, 1913), Introduction.

as good ground to father humor upon the Puritan, as upon the jolly liver.

We have reason to believe, it was pointed out above, that the roots of a pagan, rough jollity were planted deep in the temper of the Saxons themselves; and it did not require the Conquest to make them laugh, although their untutored laughter may not have had an elegant ring. Was then the polished gaiety of wit, as distinct from coarse fun, introduced by the invaders? It certainly was, in so far as a more refined tone of living, thinking, and speaking did spread through the circles where the aristocratic influence prevailed. But the spirit of a whole nation is not changed in that way; and merry England was not a layer of distinguished geniality, laid on the body and mass of English life; it was a mode or an aspect of the English people itself, in which the lower classes had their full share, and which seemed to rise spontaneously from the national traditions and instincts. If the England of Chaucer's, or that of Shakespeare's, time was in part "merry"—an epithet the significance of which should not be overstressed—she owed it no less, and more, to the broadest elements, the popular ones, in her constitution, than to the derived and diffused example of a way of life communicated from abroad. Neither had Puritanism to assert itself as a reaction against mirth. England long before Chaucer's time shows us the symptoms of that mood, ranging from a sober reflectiveness to a melancholy disposition, which radiates from what are perhaps the strongest influences of the British land and sky and have stamped themselves indelibly on the character of the race. The inward turn and the preoccupation with a moral world, severely checking and limiting the appetites of the natural man, developed from within, as did the love of pleasure and of fun; the Puritans were neither more nor less native and national than the merry-Englanders; only they appear to have received more encouragement, after all, from the conditions and circumstances in which English civilization had to grow; and their relative victory was a case of a manifold personality organizing itself, when the time came for it to be stabilized, around what was in fact its most powerful tendency.

No doubt there was in England after the Conquest a different atmosphere; a strong impetus was given to the civilizing forces at work, and the temper of what was to be the English nation was not the same for the change. Stress has been justly laid[3] on the Southern light that seems then to have pierced into the dark and the chill of a distinctly Northern air. That a more genial tone was thus diffused through the life and mind of the Saxon people from the centers of Anglo-Norman influence it would be futile to deny; and that a sense of readier pleasantry was an aspect of the mood thus gradually awakened is highly probable. This greater liveliness of disposition would create a more vivid susceptibility to the claims of the comic, and so, some affinity, at least, with the frame of mind from which humor can be born. But we must remember, first, that this argument has reference to the broad condition of humor, not to humor itself; a mirth-loving person is not necessarily, in our view, a humorous one; and next, that the most indisputable symptoms of the bent which the English character, then in the crucible, was taking reveal the persistent strength of a serious and indeed a self-centered and brooding propensity. The mental bias which was to result in Puritanism is perceptible from the earliest period of the English Middle Ages; and the Conquest, while it gave opposite germs their chance, was powerless to sterilize the seeds from which Lollardism eventually developed. On the soil which the invasion of French culture had fertilized, Wyclif and Langland grew by the side of Chaucer; and it was in the fourteenth century that, from the long and hostile contact of the two nations[4] on the ravaged fields of France, there began to grow in the mind of the more Southern people a dim notion of the other's moral being, as a personality characterized by a stubborn, sad, fierce doggedness of silent purpose.

The image of a nation which is reflected in the eyes of its foreign observers may not be an ideal index to its genuine self; there are national idiosyncrasies in the judgment thus passed,

[3] By Professor Emile Legouis, in *A History of English Literature (650-1660)* (New York, 1926-1927), chap. ii.

[4] See M. G. Ascoli, *La Grande Bretagne devant l'opinion française* (Paris, 1927), pp. 37-48.

as there are in the reality that is being judged. Still, the idea of the English temper that was stamped upon the French by the repeated contacts of the Hundred Years' War is no negligible test of what that temper may have been in effect. England had no nearer neighbor than France, and none with whose life she then was, for better or for worse, more intimately associated. Now the French view of the English character, as seen by Froissart and his contemporaries, is a fairly vivid and distinct outline, in which cheerfulness has no apparent share.[5] The merrymaking of the English people, if we are to trust those witnesses, seems to have been mostly of the practical order, and to have consisted chiefly in good eating, hard drinking, and a robust attachment to creature comforts. All the other traits are rather serious, and more often than not show a kind of harshness. The British, we gather from the documents of the time, are a proud and a warlike race, with a fierce disposition; they are not so subtle mentally as the French, and can be cheated easily enough; but their shrewd sense of reality stands them in good stead, and somehow they manage to make good in the end. Used as they are to victory, they like to wage war upon the foreigner, whom they despise. Strong men they are and valiant soldiers, but unsettled in their plans and fickle in their moods; it is dangerous to rely upon them. Their land is wealthy, and their trade prosperous; but they cherish susceptible notions of their own rights, and are jealous of their kings. Their thoughts are self-centered; they evince a pessimistic or saturnine turn, and believe more readily what is evil than what is good.

That in such a moral physiognomy, where an average is struck, the combative features should be emphasized is only too natural, at a time when France was feeling the aggressive power of the English. Still, the impression thus created was not to be easily effaced, and in spite of the urgent motives which made

[5] Mr. J. B. Priestley, in *English Humour* (pp. 1-5), points out that the foreigners have most often failed to perceive the humorous flavor that is diffused through the life, words, manners of the British, and so have much exaggerated the moroseness of their character. Whatever one may think as to the latter point, the argument decidedly bears out our contention that whether in the distant or near past, there ever was a marked difference between English humor and plain visible gaiety.

him a political friend of England, Sully two centuries later was to express a substantially similar judgment.[6] We are not to forget, on the other hand, that Froissart draws a distinction between the two main classes of English society: the temper of the aristocracy, he points out, is not the same as that of the common people.[7] Yet, it may be safely taken for granted that the above outline is fairly accurate as a sketch of at least the more external aspects of a collective personality.[8] What the moral being thus delineated would be in itself and how it would appear in its own self-realization are different and more difficult problems. It is possible to say, however, that such a character must find its inner support in some energetic purpose and a tension of the will, so that the fickleness charged upon it by foreign onlookers should be rather interpreted as the shifting adaptation of a realistic, utilitarian instinct to varying conditions, and that its thoughts and feelings must be steeped in a habitual sense of the urgency of daily things and the difficulties of conduct. The tone of life that would ensue would be more subdued and inward, with a serious and slow, almost a melancholy hue, than it would be light and bright, expansive and gay.

A tinge of sadness, indeed, was already the most frequent and most characteristic hue of a national temper, upon which the inevitable alternation of sunshine and shade, of confident and active or diffident and pensive moods, would play as it does in all countries and at all times. A serious, sober disposition was settling as a permanent habit upon the most typical Eng-

[6] Sully, *Mémoires*, Livre XIV (Paris, 1822 ed.), III, 322-23.

[7] *Chroniques*, ed. Siméon Luce (Paris, 1869), I, 214.

[8] Not much store is, of course, to be set here by the more satirical aspect of the popular French judgment as to the English and their ways. Studying *La Paix aux Anglais*, a farce of the thirteenth century, M. Faral has described it as one of "la série extrêmement abondante des compositions satiriques dirigées par les gens de France contre ceux d'Angleterre. L'orgueil de ces derniers était proverbial, et on se plaisait à le mortifier. On disait qu'ils étaient ivrognes et menteurs; on les plaisantait sur l'origine de leur nom; on prétendait (moquerie qui les exaspérait) qu'ils étaient *coués*, c'est-à-dire munis d'une queue; enfin, on s'amusait à tourner en ridicule leur façon vicieuse de parler le français" (E. Faral, *Mimes Français du XIII*[ieme] *siècle*, Paris, 1910, p. 34). The converse ridicule of the French by the English was never wanting; but there is some ground to say that it developed chiefly after 1400. Till about that time the French, who felt superior in culture and were more precocious in sharpness of wit as in national feeling, had most of the satire in their hands. Agincourt decidedly turned the scales.

lishman; and that preoccupation with moral issues, engrossing the energy which other races spared for amusement or pleasure, took the form of a potential, an incipient, puritanism. The literature in Middle English gives on this point decisive evidence; to one Chaucer,[9] and to a few minds who through their expressions appear as more or less of a Chaucerian turn, we find an overwhelming number of personalities whose main bent is towards meditation or doctrine.

Those remarks would appear to restrict within narrow bounds the field of possibility open to humor in medieval England. But English humor has not only flourished on the psychological set of tendencies which might seem to be demanded by its superficial affinities with laughter. The argument that humor being somehow akin to mirth, only a merry bent of character will favor humorous expression, is found wanting by the crucial test of England. A study of Middle English literature bears out the proposition that into the complex product which humor is there entered very often, and to tell the truth more often, mental qualities that might have been thought alien to mere amusement, or hardly reconcilable with it.

If we look at the problem in itself, we shall be led to understand easily enough an association that is paradoxical at first sight. Just as the French found in their faculty of slyness and artistic restraint the means of an indirect and implicit phrasing which possessed all the value of humorous expression, the English developed an approach to humor, the approach most easy and congenial to many of them, in the reserve and self-control which a habit of inward brooding would nurse. Understatement was the soul of the few instances of elementary humor which we discovered in Anglo-Saxon literature. Now there is a touch of sadness in chronic understatement; it betokens a sort of depression. Let only the manner grow somehow conscious, and lend itself to intentional use with a view to the consequent effect, and you have humor. Or to put it more broadly: the humorist deals in self-restraint; so does the Puritan; and the modes of the restraint are not of course identical; but that there is an analogy and a natural passage from one to

[9] It should not be forgotten that Chaucer himself was very far from indifferent to moral issues.

the other is undeniable. The humorist has a shrewd sense of the concrete realities of experience; the Puritan cherishes a vivid inner realization of the natural man—of passion, desire, instinct, as the stubborn facts with which conduct must deal; he watches himself keenly, and history shows that he no less keenly watches everything else. The outside world being the field open to conduct, he sets a mighty store by the knowledge and the command of the outside world, and so the outside world is commonly given unto him. Humor essentially consists in a duality of meaning; and the serious reflective disposition of the English character, as it evolved to its final shape in the period between the Conquest and the Renaissance, laid so to say a background of serious pensiveness behind the more external and superficial mood of everyday. The presence of that background would produce effects similar to those which were created elsewhere by the intellectual sense of the relativity of things or by the sly purposive disguising of one's thought. Here again, the affinity would not work unless a more positive inducement were superadded; the Puritan would not necessarily be a humorist; as often as not, more often than not, he was not one; but let only the spark of self-criticism or self-detachment flash out, and his stiffened mood be enough relaxed to play momentarily with itself: the deepening of consciousness which a moral meditation of life had induced might spontaneously act in the same way as a duality of meaning.

In fact, and whether a puritanic temper be actually congenial to humor, or only not uncongenial, medieval English humor developed most often in personalities which were of a moralizing turn. It was not from "merry England" that the most normal type of humor grew; the jokes of merry England were perhaps better jokes, as they came more naturally; but for that very reason, the jokers cared less to assume the indirectness of humorous intent, and they are less certainly included within the definition of our subject. Chaucer is perhaps the outstanding exception; enough by himself, as art goes, to outweigh a world of contrary evidence; but our main concern is not art, it is the psychology of English humor. Surveying the field as a whole, one sees mostly writers who found their way to humor along a rather different track. Their humor was mostly inferior to his; but they were humorists still, and quite as significant individually; in the mass, more significant and typical. Out of the national synthesis in the making, the more average and normal English humor drew to itself such elements as it could feed upon; and what elements would it draw but such as, not being inassimilable, were most abundant? English humor is not a thing that grew apart; it is an aspect of the progress of the English mind; and the central organization of that mind controlled that of every one of its aspects. Even puritanism entered into the mixture, since puritanism was there and could not possibly be ignored. We shall be sufficiently mindful of the diffused French influence which we acknowledged, if we say that the example of French slyness and point may have been often the magnetism that called the liveliness of fancy into play, and awoke in the Puritan the glimmer of intuitive sense, out of which the full grace of humor grew.[10]

II. Instances from Literature

Humor in Middle English literature before Chaucer offers to us various modes and degrees of adaptation between the national temperament, then being shaped, and the humorous method, which we defined as slyness and indirectness of statement with an artistic or at least a conscious intent. Whether

[10] That view of humor as rooted no less, and more, in the seriousness than in the fun and high spirits of the English temperament may claim support from the pregnant words and self-analysis of William Hazlitt: "I do not see how there can be high spirits without low ones. . . . They [the English] have a way of their own. Their mirth is a relaxation from gravity, a challenge to dull care to be gone; and one is not always clear at first, whether the appeal is successful. The cloud may still hang on the brow; the ice may not thaw at once. . . . Our insular situation and character are, I should say, most likely to foster, as they have in fact fostered, the greatest quantity of natural and striking humour, in spite of our plodding tenaciousness, and want both of gaiety and quickness of perception. . . . Fielding and Hogarth. These were thorough specimens of true English humour; yet both were grave men. In reality, too high a pitch of animal spirits runs away with the imagination, . . . is inclined to take the jest for granted when it ought to work it out with patient and marked touches, and it ends in vapid flippancy and impertinence. . . . We seem duller and sadder than we are. . . . I conjure up the cheerful passages of my life, and a crowd of happy images appear before me. No one would see it in my looks—my eyes grow dull and fixed . . . the traces of pleasure, in my case, sink into an absorbent ground of thoughtful melancholy . . ." ("Merry England," *New Monthly Magazine*, Vol. XIV, Part II (Dec., 1825), pp. 557-565).

the instinct for slyness was of French origin, representing the contribution of a more sophisticated culture, or was rooted in the spontaneous gifts of the native writer, deriving for instance from the understatement of the old Saxons, we are in each instance unable to judge. The problem of course is too delicate and difficult to be susceptible of plain solutions. All we can say is that in a number of cases it does not appear unreasonable to conjecture that both formative influences had a share; the instinctive use of felicitous restraint in speech would come to some extent naturally; and then, the lesson and example of the French *trouvères* and *jongleurs* would tell its own tale. Most influential on the French side was probably the general tone and atmosphere of high-class life.

Let us frankly give up all attempt at a methodical grouping, the difficulties of which would be insuperable, and content ourselves with taking up the more important texts in, so to say, a progressive order, as they show a gradual approximation to genuine humor. It is hardly necessary to point out that this selection, made out of four centuries of an abundant literature, must be not only very tentative, but quite incomplete, and not a little arbitrary. A fuller and a more accurate study of the period would have to render their dues to the conditions of space and time, to distinguish between different regions, as for instance the South and the North of England, Scotland, and Wales; and try to follow the ups and downs of French influence, in that stretch of time as a whole, or within each century.[11]

The most popular things, in the free style of the French fabliaux and tales—which had quite a vogue, and were plentifully translated—fell under the ban of censorship, as they had done during the Anglo-Saxon period: "scarcely any representatives of humorous tales in English before 1400 are extant."[12] We know, however, that the jongleurs and the goliards flourished in England, were it only from the condemnations and censures passed upon them. The Latin form with which the

[11] In so far as the fourteenth century is concerned, those distinctions are ably surveyed by Mr. K. Sisam in *Fourteenth Century Verse and Prose* (Oxford, 1921), pp. xvi-xxix.

[12] J. E. Wells, *Manual of the Writings in Middle English* (New Haven, 1916), p. 177.

scurrilous songs of the vagrant priests were invested has allowed them in some cases to pass muster; and to the name of Walter Map were attached some of the best-known hymns in praise of Bishop Golias; well worth quoting, were it not that Latin texts are not strictly within our subject. Who could find fault with the dignified Oxford archdeacon if the other side of his personality, when given free play, was anything but orthodox? In that "Norman-Welshman," as has been remarked, lived one of the predecessors of Chaucer.[13] As far as we can judge, that literature of release was no less explicit than in France; but there often breathes in its impudence and irresponsibility a soul of humorous intent, quietly chuckling over the contrast between manner and matter, language and theme.

Some English fabliaux of the fourteenth century have come down to us; and none are of more vivid interest than the "Dame Siriz," and that shoot from the trunk of the French Renart, "The Fox and the Wolf." The "Dame Siriz" has all the brazen cynicism of the typical French tales. It treats the well-known theme, common to many ages and literatures, of the naïve woman whom an old hag wins to a lover's suit by frightening her with the sad case of a lady who was unkind and so was transformed into a bitch. The slyness in this piece, and the felicitous traits, full of gusto and verve, in the "Fox and Wolf," would tend to show that a Middle English audience could appreciate properly humorous elements in stories, the fun of which was rather, generally speaking, of the broad and easy kind. The same might be said of such older irreverent or topsy-turvy pieces as "The Order of Fair Ease" and "The Land of Cockaygne."[14] But most often, and even in cases where the French original was plain and inviting (as in the "Pennyworth of Wit"), the shamefaced English narrator manages to save the story from the final triumph of the vicious, so that the point itself is unwittingly given up or spoilt. Few are the texts in which the light-hearted cynical manner is caught and rendered with genuine efficiency. The fact is that

[13] W. H. Schofield, *English Literature from the Norman Conquest to Chaucer* (New York and London, 1906), p. 57.

[14] For a full treatment of the subject, see *Middle English Humorous Tales in Verse*, ed. G. H. MacKnight (Boston and London, 1913).

the resistance of the cultivated taste to such tales was in the fourteenth century becoming more open and confirmed, while the common people continued to relish them; and it is not difficult to see why the main stream of real English humor did not and could not flow in that ready channel.[15]

It is thus elsewhere that we must look for that main stream. No doubt, through the three long centuries from the Conquest to Chaucer, the Saxon peasants, artisans, or tradesmen, no less than the Norman barons, lawyers, or merchants, loved to hear funny stories; a fund of potential humor was thus accumulated in which we may conjecture that the livelier wit and mirth that had come from France raised the broad jokes of the native stock to a somewhat higher level of self-possession and piquancy of phrase. But if we look for symptoms of humor in contemporary literature, we find more often than not that the mood on which it is based bears the hallmark of a more characteristically English origin.

The insulting ironies and invectives of Layamon's *Brut*, mostly added to the speeches of his model (Wace), are almost as primitive in spirit as those taunts which we noticed in *Beowulf*. At the moment, a critic rightly points out, when Uther has fatally wounded Gillomar and slays Pascent, "the poet's voice has the very tone of the 'Ode to Brunanburh' ":[16]

On the head he smote him
So that he down fell,
In his mouth his sword thrust—
Uncouth his dinner—
So went the sword's point
In the earth beneath him.
And then spake Uther,
"Pascent, now lie there,
Now hast thou Britain,
To thy hand hast won it.
So is now hap to thee;

[15] M. Ascoli (pp. 37-38) has justly laid stress on the significant attitude of the Englishman, who ignores the Frenchman's broad hint, in Robert Gaguin's late fifteenth-century French poem (*Le Passe-Temps d'Oisiveté*, 1488).

[16] E. Legouis, in *A History of English Literature*, Part I, Book I, chap. ii, p. 5. See also the passage quoted by Jusserand, *Literary History*, Book II, chap. iv, sect. ii, pp. 220-21.

Therein death has come to thee;
Dwell shalt thou therein
With thy fellow Gillomar,
And well enjoy Britain.
To you I deliver it;
Ye twain may presently
Dwell in the land with us;
Nor dread ye ever
Who food will give ye."[17]

There is a note of restraint as well, a fierce duality of meaning, an understatement of exultation, just able to key down slightly the words of victory and of hate, in the patriotic songs of Laurence Minot.[18]

That is not much yet. And one may contend that irony has nothing to do with humor—although the two shade off into each other, and no doubt answer to one and the same broad mental attitude. The distinction between them has been chiefly emphasized under the influence of definite views as to the nature of humor and its so-called soul of sympathy, the truth of which our survey will bring us solid reason to doubt. But we next pass on to writers of greater significance for our purpose, because in them we plainly catch the affinity of English humor with the homely native spirit of realism allied to moralizing.

Who would expect humor from the heavily didactic manner of Robert of Brunne's *Handlyng Synne?* Here is the typical utterance of a medieval preacher, bent upon the endless and ever attractive task, the full explanation of the whole duty of man. Nothing could be more English than that treatise on the ten commandments and the corresponding sins, although it is founded on an Anglo-French work, William of Wadington's *Manuel des Pechiez*. Still, in that edifying stuff we find not a few episodes where a sly humor peeps out, as that tale (not

[17] *Layamon's Brut,* ed. Madden, II, 334-35, ll. 18,090–18,109.

[18] See the "Battle of Halidon Hill," ll. 11-16 and 57-61; the poem on Bannockburn, ll. 59-70; the poem marked XI, ll. 25-30; etc. (*The Poems of Laurence Minot,* ed. Joseph Hall, 1887). Another element of some significance, though only related to humor, and not exactly humorous, is the vigorous realism of the late thirteenth-century poem, *Havelock the Dane*, of which a critic has remarked that "the horse-play of *Havelock* . . . is similar to that found in Chaucer" (Prof. S. B. Liljegren, in *Litteris,* Vol. V, July, 1929, p. 13).

in the French original) "of the witch and her cow-sucking bag; and how a bishop failed to work her charm, because he did not believe in it." We seem to hear some dour Scots minister or some English country parson, with a twinkle in his eye, telling the story. The witch has hoodwinked the bishop and persuaded him that at the bidding of some magical words which she recites a bag flies out of the room and milks the cows; the holy man, in the enthusiasm of wonder, must needs try in his turn, and repeats the charm, but it does not work; and as he grows suspicious, the witch rises to a sublime height of appropriateness and humor. What you lack, she tells the bishop, is faith; believe in my words, pronounce them in the right spirit, and the miracle will happen. This is one of the first authentic notes of exquisite humor in English. The paradox of the situation, the mute eloquence of the inverted parts of teacher and taught, the fine essence of relativity and irony are set off by the economy and subdued tenor of the style.[19] An indefinable flavor of the same kind is diffused again and again through the naïve, familiar, and quaint equanimity of the moralist, who can suppress at will, and with no apparent effort, the expected reactions of his ethical sense. A foretaste of Chaucer's quiet smiling manner may almost be enjoyed there.

If we detect some humor in William Langland, shall we trace it to a spirit of mirth and affirm that its ultimate origin lies in the lighthearted, cynical gaiety of the Norman-French invaders? The question, thus put, answers itself. In mood, in inspiration, no work more genuinely expresses the national tendencies of the fourteenth-century English, as a synthetic race, than *Piers Plowman;* and its conscious borrowing from the properly French strain seems to be very slight. The author's temper is that of the man for whom moral issues are desperately prominent, and who cannot help concentrating upon them heart and soul. There never was a more entire earnestness. And yet, from the very Prologue, there dimly rises before our mind's eye the image of a storyteller with a power of grim, forcible emphasis, which does not preclude, and rather

[19] Robert of Brunne's *Handlyng Synne,* ed. F. J. Furnivall (London, 1901), the first commandment, pp. 19-21. The text belongs to the first years of the fourteenth century.

invites, the quiet glow of a just perceptible slyness. Whether Langland was one poet in three texts or three writers under one name we do not know for sure, although the thesis of a single authorship in *Piers Plowman* has been rather gaining ground; but the chief personality that lives and breathes in the main parts of the work evinces, when all is said, a self-possessed determination, a shrewd sense of the other side of things, and a turn for irony, although the tense seriousness no doubt stands in the way of a fuller humor. The poet knows how to suppress the signs that would reveal his own perception of paradox or absurdity; he is well aware of these, however; he catches them as they rise, and his subdued sense and enjoyment silently emanate from the reserve of the manner.

One might instance, besides the well-known apologue of the rats trying to hang a bell around the cat's neck,[20] such occasional flashes as the idea that when the angel of heaven condescends to speak, it is only in Latin—since common people, we are to remember, ought not to be told how to justify themselves;[21] or the words in passing about the pilgrims, with the finely managed anticlimax:

> They went forth on their way, with many wise tales,
> And had leave to lie all their lives after.[22]

Or the simple remark of other holy men:

They turned themselves into hermits, in order to have their ease.[23]

Or the truly effective touch that when Avarice hears the French word *restitution*, he guesses at once that it is another name for stealing;[24] and the episode of the palmer, who has been to all the shrines but who in his pilgrimages has never met a person called Truth (God the Father);[25] or the picture of the procession that accompanies to Westminster Lady Mead (Bribery) riding upon a sheriff "shod all new," while Falsehood sits upon a "sisour" (or deputy magistrate) "that trotted softly";[26] and so many more. Indeed, how could humor fail to crown, as a

[20] Prologue, ed. Skeat, ll. 146 *et sqq.*
[21] *Ibid.*, ll. 128-30.
[22] *Ibid.*, ll. 48-49.
[23] *Ibid.*, l. 57.
[24] Passus V, ll. 232-40.
[25] Passus V, l. 520.
[26] Passus II, ll. 163-65.

natural and essential bloom, the vigor of an imagination that caught so vividly, so racily, the concrete figure and picturesqueness of things; and how could an artist be dead to the potential comedy of life, who was enough of a realist to draw the picture of a tavern in London,[27] where Gula (or Gluttony), out for church and a shriving, irresistibly finds his way? With all the didactic bent, the bitter pessimism of heart and mind, and the total lack of artistic cleverness, we have here the indispensable and all-sufficing background: a sense of contrasts, supple enough for the writer to handle them objectively and to draw from them effects of implicitness; a fund of shrewd experience, conscious and free enough for him to take pleasure in the indirect presentment of a many-sided reality. Repressed and checked in almost every way, the essence of humor is still present and active; and its aroma is of an unmistakably national, English quality.

Very similar in its general characteristics is the spirit of broad humor displayed by the unknown author of *Patience*, that alliterative paraphrase of the Book of Job, whose connection with the other poems of the Cotton manuscript has roused so much interest among scholars, since *The Pearl* has been recognized as one of the jewels of the finest water in all literature. Here again, we have a homily, a moralizing aim never lost sight of; and yet, a strong realism, a concrete mental grasp of things imagined, called up, and shown forth with the full vivid wealth of their attributes; and a vein of sly, almost subtle amusement in the display of ponderous, grotesque, unseemly, startling images, which belongs to the raciest fund of popular English humor. Although the author's intimate acquaintance with French literature is regarded as certain, it is the Scandinavian influence that can be traced most strongly in the vocabulary and phrasing. Having before him the episode of Jonah, from the Vulgate, our poet, in the words of Sir Israel Gollancz, whose translation into modern English we are quoting, "transformed and amplified . . . the terse Biblical narrative, so that the story might vividly appeal to simple folk":[28]

[27] Passus V, ll. 314 *et sqq.*
[28] *Patience*, ed. Sir I. Gollancz (Oxford, 1913), Preface.

As a mote in at a minster door, so mighty were its jaws,
Jonah enters by the gills, through slime and gore;
he reeled in through a gullet, that seemed to him a road,
tumbling about, aye head over heels,
till he staggers to a place as broad as a hall;
then he fixes his feet there and gropes all about,
and stands up in its belly, that stank as the devil;
in sorry plight there, 'mid grease that savoured as hell,
his bower was arrayed, who would fain risk no ill.
Then he lurks there and seeks in each nook of the nave
the best sheltered spot, yet nowhere he finds
rest or recovery, but filthy mire
wherever he goes; but God is ever dear;
and he tarried at length and called to the Prince.

. . . .

Then he reached a nook and held himself there,
where no foul filth encumbered him about.
He sat there as safe, save for darkness alone,
as in the boat's stern, where he had slept ere.
Thus, in the beast's bowel, he abides there alive,
three days and three nights, thinking aye on the Lord,
His might and His mercy and His measure eke;
now he knows Him in woe, who could not in weal.
And onward rolls the whale through deep wild-seas,
through many rough regions, in stubborn will,
for, though that mote in its maw was small,
that monster grew sickish at heart, I trow,
and worried the wight. And Jonah aye heard
the huge flood as it lashed the whale's back and its sides.[29]

That is not the cynical fun or even the pert slyness of the French fabliaux; a world of instinct and temperament parts this rich, full, highflavored rejoicing in the grotesqueness of things holy, when humanized and realized, from the elegant hints of the "humor *de finesse*." The main origin and descent of English humor is here; and even when the refining has been done by Chaucer, and done again by the Addisons and the Sternes, the vein of the more typical English humorists will be rather in line with *Patience* than with the artistic restraint of the French pattern.

[29] *Patience*, ll. 268-82 and 289-302.

The same note can be heard in the poem on Christ's descent to hell, ascribed to the middle of the thirteenth century,[30] which has been called "the oldest English drama," although it seems more proper to regard it as a link between the English minstrels and their French rivals, whose *disputoisons* and *jeux-partis* they translated and imitated, and between the repertory of the English minstrels and the early drama, especially the morality.[31] The whole situation of the *Harrowing of Hell*, in which the Lord consents to argue with the evil one, on a plane of assumed equality and almost friendliness, is rich with a flavor diffused through all the implications of the dialogue. These are of course well known to every reader, and build up an exceptionally efficient background of sly, indirect allusions and drollery. How could one resist the exquisite naïveté of Adam's words, underlining what was the grim tragedy of the plot to hearts full of faith, and anticipating the use of understatement in so much modern humor:

> Lord, since then thou art come to us,
> Thou bring us out of this house.[32]

Or let us listen to the Lord's pleading with Satan:

> Satanas, he said, it was mine
> The apple that thou gavest him [Adam],
> The apple, and the apple tree,
> Both were made through me.
> How mayest thou in any wise
> Of other men's things make merchandise?
> Since then thou boughtest him with mine,
> With reason should I have him.[33]

But the York play on the same subject, whose relation to the poem is obscure, gives us over a much more ample canvas a more varied and a fuller display of genuine early humor. The author is visibly taking much pleasure in the fun of that extraordinarily vivid rendering of Christ's descent to hell, but

[30] W. Creizenach, in *Cambridge History of English Literature*, Vol. V, chap. iii, p. 46.
[31] F. J. Child, *ibid.*, Vol. V, chap. ii, p. 29.
[32] *The Harrowing of Hell* (Edinburgh, 1835), p. 12.
[33] *Ibid.*, p. 9.

he remains in full control of his amusement, and plays with the realistic, everyday, familiar human transcription of the tremendous episode which he gives us, in a spirit of freedom untainted by irreverence. The detachment of humor is there, in its incipient state; and the scene is enjoyed for its own sake, not only as a means of edification. The effects are not explicit, but, partly owing to the reserve which the subject would naturally command, discreet and virtual. When the demons complain to Beelzebub of the commotion and unrest that are set loose in Limbo by the coming of Christ, the chief urges them to use the strong hand; but Jesus breaks in against all opposition; and when Satan, the supreme leader, intervenes in person, Beelzebub retorts angrily:

> Aye, beat him sore, that is soon said,
> But come thyself and serve him so.[34]

The rest is as delightfully lifelike and quaint; but along with the quaintness, which is the reaction of our modern mind, we feel here the slyness of the medieval sense of humor. This is almost as finely managed as Chaucer's manner. And yet, the inspiration is definitely popular and national. The parallels one might point out with French *mystères* cannot alter our impression that this English rendering of a theme common to European Christianity in the Middle Ages is racy of the soil of England, as the French episodes were rooted in similar French instincts. A people does not learn to relish such things from the example set by another; they must be congenial and native to be at all possible.

To the cycle of early drama we might turn again, so as to share in the peals of laughter with which the Towneley *Play of Noah*[35] must have been received. But if Noah's wife is a shrew and her husband has to enforce his will with the patriarchal vigor of his fists, the whole theme and the treatment, we have to confess, are funny without being humorous in our sense of the term. That is broad farce, of a very explicit kind, al-

[34] K. Sisam, *Fourteenth Century Verse and Prose* (Oxford, 1921), pp. 205-6. For this part of the subject, see J. B. Moore, *The Comic and Realistic in English Drama* (Chicago, 1925).

[35] Sisam, *op. cit.*, pp. 185-203.

though there may be felt here and there a whiff of a better flavor—a passing sense of the contrast between the majesty of the biblical style and the familiarity of the modern rendering. Those gleams are rare: it is not humorously, but simply and wholeheartedly, that a farcical color is spread thick over the story of Genesis. And the comic interludes in the other plays of the series, while they show vigor, are hardly more significant for the purpose of our inquiry.

We are thus led to place our final emphasis on a very original and interesting poem, in which medieval English humor reached one of its most remarkable, as it was one of its earliest expressions. The author of *The Owl and the Nightingale* was probably that Master Nicholas whose name is mentioned at the beginning of the piece; and the latest evidence seems to throw the date of composition back to the end of the twelfth century, about 1180.[36] To our external knowledge, the life and personality of Master Nicholas are almost a blank; but how we penetrate, through his poem, into the mind of a singularly reflective, mature, and shrewd man! His theme in itself is almost a commonplace; but he has loaded it with a remarkably full intent, and the main allegorical purpose is worked out on several planes of symbolism. What the Owl stands for—the old religious poetry, a stricter mood of moral restraint, the spirit of Puritanism before its time—and what the Nightingale represents—the new love poetry, an early humanism, a softened ideal of conduct, with a touch of the modern spirit[37]—is a fascinating problem; while the skill with which a free scope is given to the expansion of the subject, though "neither the action nor the debate ever leaves the animal plane of being,"[38] is in itself a feat of art. But to our purpose, what matters most is the intuition here displayed of the exquisiteness of a relaxed, easy, and familiar simplicity, as the ground note upon which is raised a fabric of subtly humorous variations. The charm of the manner which was to be Chaucer's, and La Fontaine's, is

[36] H. B. Hinckley, "The Date, Author and Sources of the Owl and the Nightingale," *PMLA*, XLIV (June, 1929), 2.

[37] *The Owl and the Nightingale*, ed. J. W. H. Atkins (London, 1922), Introduction, p. lxxix.

[38] *Ibid.*, p. lxxx.

here distinctly adumbrated; a perfect tone and air of naïveté creates the very atmosphere of humor by spreading a constant sense of normality and naturalness. The whole treatment and the style savor of the implicit, and release an ever-fresh undercurrent of delicate suggestion and meaning. Even the self-revelation of the writer under a veil is turned to use as an element of humor. The sense of the relativity of things lives and breathes in the delicious fun of the Owl demonstrating, to her full satisfaction, the superiority of her song to the Nightingale's.

"I sing smoothly, with full melody and in loud tones. Thou dost regard every song as dreadful that is different from thy piping tones. As for my note, it is bold and masterful—much like the sound of a great horn; while thine is like that of a tiny pipe fashioned out of a weed unripe."[39]

The portraiture of the two birds, of the two characters, one might say the two moral types, has the plenitude and sureness of touch which have been reached only by the masters in the perennial comedy of humanity. Is the piece, as a whole, a satire upon the austerity of wisdom and against surly experience? Far from it; a philosophical impartiality is maintained throughout; and the winsome blithe spirit of the nightingale carries the verdict of every reader, like that of the birds which listen to the debate; but Master Nicholas knows better; and it is not the least of his ironical hints, conveyed between the lines, that the young and the brilliant will be given the prize, but that the old and the sad and the wise may still not have been in the wrong. The inspiration of a tolerant, charitable sweetness is here tinged with the sober pensiveness which is such a common attribute of the masters of English humor.

How does the poem stand in relation to French influence? Of course the subject belongs to the fertile category of the debates, with which the French *trouvères* were particularly associated; but its particular kind, the fable or animal theme, is one whose special home was perhaps in England. It seems difficult to believe that such a subtle achievement, such a sure design and sense of suggestion, may not have been taught by

[39] From the modern rendering in the edition of the text by J. W. H. Atkins, *ibid.*, pp. 157-58.

the more finished examples of French skill; here, surely, is the spirit of *finesse* active; but the derivation from Southern models, which was long regarded as certain, does not rest on actual evidence; and the traces of French influence in the poem itself are but slight.[40] Altogether, it may be safer to say that *The Owl and the Nightingale* is already a synthetic work, like that of Chaucer two centuries later; it testifies in a striking way to the cosmopolitanism of the twelfth century; it embodies a general stimulation of thought and art, the source of which can be definitely laid in the culture of France; at the same time, it welds that more refined and conscious spirit into an original whole with a solidly English inspiration; and the humor, which is the essence of the fresh delightful novelty in the manner, while it owes something to French *finesse,* is more distinctly of a national quality; it reveals, at that early date, the fusion of the French and the native strains into a product where the foreign elements are no longer alien, but turned into part and parcel of a different collective personality, a new genius.[41]

Those features seem to foresketch the eminent artistry of Chaucer; and the perspective of Middle English literature leads up to him, the greatest humorist, as the greatest writer, of medieval England. But Chaucer is of a class apart, and must be studied by himself.

To sum up, there indisputably was an important French influence upon the development of English humor in the medieval period before Chaucer; it was not, however, of the kind which has been more than once implied or defined; it should not be regarded as the awaking of a new faculty, the direct and full shaping of a mental attitude after a foreign model. It was formative rather than creative. The latent possibility of humor was there; the keener spirit of French pleasantry, the more precocious instinct of French artistic restraint stimulated and to some extent guided the growth. But the process was controlled from the first by the imperious law of the original temperament which was evolving with the self-consciousness of

[40] H. B. Hinckley, *op. cit.*

[41] It has been as well pointed out, with good reason, that the early thirteenth-century *Ancren Riule,* besides its serious intent and highly devotional feeling, shows not a few distinct intimations of humor.

England; and the national elements assumed the leading part almost at once; the properly English traits of character were reflected in the mode and manner of English humor. As the development went on, it grew more apparent that the fund of serious, and not that of merry, disposition would have more to do with the duality of meaning which humor implies, than the cleverness and agility of the French mind. Was Chaucer the supreme, the outstanding exception? The problem can no longer be evaded; and we shall devote to it the next stage in our inquiry.

CHAPTER IV

CHAUCER'S HUMOR

I. "My Wit is Short"

EVEN AFTER THE VEIN of English humor has been followed through the preceding centuries, as it crops up here and there, and the contribution of France to its development has been recognized, its broad and full emergence in the work of Chaucer comes upon one with the suddenness of a miracle. Here humor is no longer a momentary gleam, a lucky accident, or at best an incipient disposition, gathering strength into some distinct flashes. For the first time in the history of English literature, perhaps of all literature, it is the soul and essence of an artist and his art.

It was not so from the beginning of Chaucer's self-expression. Penetrating studies have been written[1] on the gradual change in his manner, from the uncertainties of his early apprenticeship to the sure, firm aim of the writer who has found himself. Stages can be marked out in the dropping of convention and the fastening on the truth of personality. Humor grows with the personality and the truth, from the *Book of the Duchess*, the *Parliament of Fowls*, to the *House of Fame*, where it breaks in decidedly upon the solemnity of a high theme, and the *Legend of Good Women*, where its demands become so exacting that the poem has to be left unfinished, because its subject and a humorous disposition agree too ill together. Even when the matter is still borrowed, as in the *Troilus and Criseide*, the treatment transforms it by pitching it in a comic key. Critics are agreed that the *Canterbury Tales* are the complete revelation of a genius which brings all its materials under the resolute law of an original design. Here Chaucer's mastery is supreme, and his humor displays all its freedom and

[1] Especially by Professor Emile Legouis (*Chaucer*, 1910).

range; it is no loss to concentrate our short survey on this single work, the scope of which is so varied and ample that from it no characteristic note is missing.

Chaucer's humor is a way of thinking, an attitude to life; it possesses that background of moral correspondences and affinities which is not exactly the same with all humorists—for the correspondences are supple, the affinities are not binding—but which tends to be more or less present in all, and the variations of which answer to the varieties of the humorous manner. Chaucer's position in humor is a normal and a central one; he has not consciously worked out, one feels, all its implications, he has not realized all its philosophy; but his inmost self is saturated with it, and in that habit of mind he truly moves and has his being. His busy thought has gathered in the facts of life, analyzing and distilling them, and the quintessential product now impregnates each element of his consciousness. Subtle and rich is the flavor; but it yields its secret to the intuition born in us of our own experience; we know that aroma, it is the very spirit of the relativity, the diversity, the unreasonableness of things. A pragmatist would say that the philosophy of humor was pluralistic; and indeed it is made up of the acceptance of the stubborn contradictions which our endeavors in all fields fail to eradicate, and there is no greater enemy to humor than the passion of unity. An acceptance not inert, since it is lively, and may be ironical; not insipid, since it is pungent, and the pungency may even shade off into bitterness; but the natural outcome of which is a tolerance, a readiness to understand, almost to sympathize; a broad genial humanity, if not necessarily, as has often been said, a tenderness and a love.

Chaucer, from the mental watchtower whence he surveys the world of his time, has taken in all the varieties and the absurdities; he has noted the discrepancies of character, the perverse individualities of creatures, the shiftings of principle and conduct, the clash of reality and appearance. His intelligence is reconciled with the relativity of things; and his eye quietly looks for the contrast, the opposition, the other side of the face and the soul, the tears in happiness, the smile in misery; to all the unaccountable habits of men and of fate he responds with the suppleness of the mind which no single formula has enslaved; and as his reaction is free and easy, it is immune from the pain of disappointed expectations or jarred principles; his sense of the novelty and the freshness in daily happenings supplies him with an intellectual amusement, a pleasure of satisfied curiosity; the comedy of mankind offers itself fully to him; and his sensibility not being engrossed by the grievances of the naïve or the weak, his mood preserves its softer quality, the fellowship, the sympathy, the pity, which will rise in a normal consciousness from the mere sight of the human drama.

No more is needed to give that philosophy of universal tolerance and mellow wisdom its glow of appealing gentleness; the sight of the unlimited error and misfortune that so intimately mingle with the infinite fun of life elicits the smile that is not unkind, the irony that accepts and forgives. A warm radiance emanates from the dramatic presentment which might be serene but might be cold; and the all-embracing genius of Shakespeare by the side of Chaucer's will seem mysterious and unresponsive in its more powerful equanimity. The mind that took up and displayed the images of youth and love and honor and cruel fate which combine in the "Knight's Tale" into such a gorgeous tapestry of feudal pomp and destiny had possessed itself of the most lucid spirit which the wise have ever learnt from life; but the wisdom was quick and feeling as it was thoughtful. If modern humor comes with Chaucer into its own, it is because on the apparently limited scale of a still early age, from a contact with the world which was in fact singularly varied and broad, he evolved the very soul of modern humor. The name of "humor" he had not yet, although he made use of this word in its current fourteenth-century sense;[2] and so the self-realization of the attitude in his mind could not be complete;[3] a degree

[2] Representing a physical state associated with a corresponding tendency of mind. See C. R. Baskervill, *English Elements in Jonson's Early Comedy* (Austin, Texas), 1911.

[3] The words which Chaucer uses in order to denote his idea of comic inventiveness, are none the less interesting:

> "Touchinge this cherl, they seyde, subtiltee
> And heigh wit made him speken as he spak. . . ."
> ("Somnour's Tale," ll. 582-583).

The association of "subtlety" with "high wit" is significant. The "churl" has been devising a form of retaliation which is an experiment in practical humor.

further of conscious deliberateness will be added from the time when the notion of a special mode of reacting to life has crystallized around a name. But it can be doubted whether Chaucer lost more than he gained by that still relatively primitive standpoint of his art; humor with the moderns, as its method has become so clear, is liable to grow mechanical; and the margin of loose, unconscious intent, previous to humor's final coming of age, favors the retention by the humorist of the virtue of spontaneousness. That, however, short of the fullest lucidity of purpose, Chaucer was very much alive to the original manner of his pleasantry, it is no less essential to emphasize.

The instinct of relativity which is the soul of humor is reflected in its method; it will say one thing and mean another thing; or rather, it will bring out more forcibly what it does not actually say, adding point to a suggestion by its very indirectness. Just as its matter lies in contrasts, its manner is an inversion, a transposition. The tragicomedy of life is thus shown forth with no apparent sense of its quality. Now slyness is the name given to the underhand conveyance of values, especially comic; and slyness indeed is next of kin to humor; it is as it were its outward transcription and figure. The humorist from the first has been sly; he has staked his success on his seeming naïveté or sluggishness of mind.

It is a remarkable fact that not only should Chaucer have possessed so largely the spiritual background of humor, but that his keen intuition should have revealed to him the virtue of its characteristic method. We know that the countenance of the poet bore the stamp of that absorption which seems to betoken a mind turned all inward upon itself, indifferent to the fascinating varieties of things—those varieties which in fact humor feeds upon. Let us listen to the words of mine host, addressing the silent member of the company:

> . . . "What man artow?" quod he;
> "Thou lokest as thou woldest finde an hare,
> For ever upon the ground I see the stare.
> Approche neer, and loke up merily."
> . . . .
> "He semeth elvish by his contenaunce,
> For un-to no wight dooth he daliaunce."[4]

[4] Prologue to *Sir Thopas*, ll. 5-8 and 13-14. The meaning of "elvish" is

While Chaucer was drawing that sketch, what could he be but keenly aware of the several planes of thought on which he actually lived? By not refusing his sanction to that incomplete figuring of his mood, he allows us to infer that the oversimplified image did not clash with his main purpose. He knew that it served his turn to look "elvish." He went even beyond that degree of self-consciousness; he grasped the nature and the meaning of the mask which the humorist must wear, and let us see that he saw through it by now and then peeping from under it. His readers might after all believe that a sober, serious countenance was a transcription of his whole inner being; humor is not only compatible with a pensive bent, but bears a genuine affinity with it. What shall we say, however, to the pretense of a weak understanding? The poet's frequent insistence on the slowness and shortness of his "wit" lets us into the secret of an artlessness, which is not properly speaking the cloak of art; it is the art itself.

> "My wit is short, ye may wel understonde. . . ."[5]

The trick was not uncommon among the French *trouvères;* it was part of the stock in trade of feigned humility, in poetry as in love; to some extent, we have here a matter of tradition and form; but the way in which Chaucer acquits himself of that perfunctory gesture charges it with a totally new significance. What we find in his words is the seeming mental sluggishness of the humorist grown so conscious, felt to be so useful, so vital that he must needs be constantly calling our attention to it. The hint, he feels, will not give him away, but rather arouse some unwary reader to a more lively attention, play the part of a twinkle in the poet's eye: is not the mask, on occasion, mistaken for the face, and does not mine host accept "Sir Thopas" as a serious romance? Never was naïveté more sly than that of Chaucer; but never was the appearance of naïveté turned to more fertile or more delightful uses. And so perfect is the imitation of naïveté that it is not entirely an imitation; the

"absent-minded, engrossed in distant cares"; and that of "daliaunce," "gossip, pleasant demeanour, favour." Here, as everywhere else, we quote from Skeat's text (London and New York, 1909).

[5] Prologue, l. 746.

mood of simple-mindedness which best serves the purpose of humor has grown so habitual that the mind really lives it and does not only play with a mere pretense; at the same time as it indulges in the sophisticated perception of its own deceit, it tastes the pleasure of looking at things in an unsophisticated light. The quaintness of Chaucer's poetry is not entirely an illusion, the inevitable anachronism of our modern reaction to an earlier and a very different mode of thinking; it is the genuine gift of a man who has retained the freshness of youth in mature, disillusioned experience.

Thus it was that in the plenitude of his artistic powers Chaucer turned instinctively to the pageant of English life, and from its variety, with no other object, on the surface, than the picturesqueness of contrasted figures, called up the wide, manifold scene of the *Canterbury Tales.* His deeper purpose was at work in the choice of this topic; and the treatment was shaped by a free, broad touch, with no apparent effort, to serve its turn. Doubly strengthened by a concrete philosophy—a temperament of mind rather than a set of ideas—and by a clear intuition of its own psychological process, Chaucer's humor is so rich and full that it reaches at one stroke a stage of development far beyond that of his own time. His art will be lost by his successors, and will have to be rediscovered; no one before Addison, except Shakespeare, will equal the delicacy of its shades, and no one before Sterne will add substantially to its background. From the eighteenth century to our own day, the progress of consciousness has inevitably endowed humor with a new depth and a further wealth of materials; the increased self-knowledge of modern man has enlarged the possibilities of humorous expression, and given a sharper edge to that sense of moral contrast upon which humor lives. Sterne extended its scope to the subconscious personality, Lamb found in a more supple psychological detachment the means of freer and madder pranks. The humor of our age is heir to a much vaster range of potential effects. But the form of Chaucer's humor can hardly be improved upon; it is perfect, within its limits and of its kind.

II. Chaucer's Range

For the very reason that Chaucer's humor is so subtle and pervasive, to illustrate it with examples is not easy; it is diffused almost everywhere, and although it will have its moments of greater density, its manner of gentleness and bland, genial irony hardly allows of those outbreaks which supply the critic with a wide choice of typical passages. Moreover, the works of Chaucer are much better known than those of other Middle English writers; a fair acquaintance with the *Canterbury Tales* can be taken for granted. It may be permissible in this case to rely more upon allusion than on quotation.

From the opening sketches of the Prologue, the sense of a singularly attentive and sure manner grows upon the reader. Things are said quietly, with ever so slight a tremor of consciousness, and over the canvas that a leisurely hand fills with full-length portraits of men and women there plays ever so discreetly a lambent flame of irony through the smiling light. Every statement is made in such a way as to create a feeling that all its force and virtue is not spent at once; a portion is more subtle and releases itself more slowly; it comes out in the pause of attention, while the thought lingers still in our minds; and that constant reserve of phrasing, that habit of meaning a little more than one thing at a time, builds the most general and most elementary impression of humor. Upon that common ground the moments of more definite quality stand out; but it is the even tenor of that just perceptible discretion and slyness that contributes most to the atmosphere of the poem.

Is that tone always present? The exceptions are very few, and fewer than one might expect from the subjects of the tales or the nature of the speakers. Chaucer, no doubt, took much care to relieve one note by another and to prevent monotony; his cleverness in the grouping of the themes is conspicuous; but the temperament of humor was too strong and would come out through the most definite trend of pathos or moralizing. Is it quite sure that the artist, in those cases, was not aware of its coming out? We have good reason to believe that Chaucer's subconscious instinct had few secrets to which his lucid mind was not a party. In the "Knight's Tale," while the narrator seems bent only upon the creation of dramatic suspense and the raising of a fine fabric of noble episodes, we feel all along that on a deeper plane his interest and his sympathy are tinged with a wistful and pitying amusement. The sentimental and mournful tale of the Man of Law is broken in upon here and there by some jarring notes, which would be inexplicable if the countenance of the poet, with just the ghost of a twinkle in his eye, was not dimly discernible behind that of the speaker. The didactic treatise of Melibaeus would be a psychological impossibility if some subtle signs did not intimate a purpose not of seriousness but of mockery. The frequent and dull quotations, for instance, are obviously handled with a keen perception of the pedantry and irrelevance of most edifying texts. The contrast between the Monk's physical and moral person and the tragic stories which he so perfunctorily relates is the main element in our latent sense of impropriety and insincerity. The fun about the "Pardoner's Tale" is that this homily on the deadly sins preached with such glaring lack of genuine faith and piety is no worse than another sermon would probably be; while the mind of the preacher dwells in characteristic fashion on the realities that appeal to him. The Clerk's story of Grisildis would remain in our memory as a purely touching interlude, did not the irrepressible humor of the poet break out in the ballad at the end. Such gleams and flashes are to be found in the Squire's and the Franklin's tales; the Parson's lengthy disquisition winds itself out over a background of feigned resignation and genuine impatience, called up by the host when he begs the holy man to be short. Even the Prioress, in her pretty, self-conscious affliction at the sore fate of the poor murdered child, reveals too much of her mincing, coquettish ways not to stir a delicate sense of comedy in the reader.

Those are the portions of the poem where the undercurrent of humor might most naturally have been interrupted. That it is never so for long is a very significant fact. At the other extremity of the poet's range, we find the stories and passages of undoubted jollity and merrymaking. Here it is that our study would linger most complacently if we agreed with the unrestricted meaning so often attached to the word *humor*. But the rollicking farce which takes up a large part of the *Canterbury Tales* is not in our view their best claim to be recognized as humorous. It is not the farce itself, anyhow, that is the humor.

The free, coarse adventures related in the Miller's, the Reve's, the Shipman's, the Somnour's tales, for instance, raise an irresistible laugh, or amuse us even while they ruffle our notion of decency, provided that notion is not too exacting. But what then? Like the French fabliaux, the stories of that kind in Chaucer are mostly quite explicit. Nothing, apparently, is kept back, and we surrender to the force of a broad current of fun that whirls us off our feet and carries us onward in triumph. There is the release of the mind from the seriousness of life, the joy of irresponsibility and primitiveness, the salutary sense of the rebellion and the saturnalia of character, the occasional fit of drunkenness which the ancients regarded as part of the hygiene of a sane man. That Chaucer aims at those effects, and achieves them, is sure. But is there nothing else? Has not the writer, so to say, his tongue in his cheek? Do we not feel that over and above his obvious meaning, he holds back something less definite, another part of his moral and artistic intent, which steals into us gradually and silently? There is a humorous lining to the farcical stuff of those tales. They appeal to the natural and the unpretentious being in us, no doubt; but our thoughtful and more subtle part is not left unsatisfied. In the history of literature it has almost always happened that the enormities of common writers were farce, whilst those of great writers were humor. We might have expected it; how could the obscene, the gross, the absurd recommend themselves to deep and refined minds, unless the grossness and the absurdity were invested by them with their own inner depth and refinement? Aristophanes, Rabelais, Shakespeare are cases in point; Chaucer is no exception. Not only are the broad stories enriched, again and again, with touches of a different order, where the wealth of observation, the knowledge of character, a picturesque realism are drawn upon; but the broadness and the coarseness themselves serve more ends than appear on the surface. The poet sometimes has through them his fling at us, as in the prologue to the Miller's tale, where he warns the reader, if he feels squeamish, to pass over what is coming—a sly trick which Sterne and many others have since used; how shall we kick against the author's cynicism when he has an accomplice in ourselves? Or there is the aesthetic irony of the contrast between the dignified occasion, the careful speech, and the unseemly subject. Or more generally still, there is the active presence of a spirit of paradox: the restraint and discretion of the manner imply a conscious purpose, and that purpose, under the circumstances, cannot possibly be other than the purest and most philosophical irony. The imperturbability of the artist, by effecting a transposition of style, creates the very condition of humor; and at the same time his meditative mind, justifying that inversion in its own terms, places before us the staring fact of our animality; a fact to be laughed at rather than wept at, the wise in all times have generally agreed.

Most often, however, the comedy which is offered us lies in the middle region between the incongruities of our physical being and the higher discords of the moral world. Chaucer then finds the materials of his humor in the rich field of character. The *Canterbury Tales* abound in satire, ordinarily gentle, upon occasion more harsh; and what gives to the satire the special quality of humorous art is the restraint of the style, the subdued manner, the slyness and implicitness of the hints. The most sober degree of satire is very near pure realism, without of course being one with it; and the quiet method of the portraits in the Prologue, the close firm touch of the hand which feels and probes all their features, is guided by a motive where the instinct of psychological truth unites with the artist's joy in the quaintness of individuality. A thrill of recognition and amusement stirs through those wonderful pages; but it is checked, controlled by a master purpose, and the reward of that self-possession is the heightened pleasure of humor. How each of the men and women who figure in the inimitable company is penetratingly, caressingly delineated, and what fine essence of shrewd curiosity, fearless intelligence, genial sympathy breathes in the whole work of the painter, is universally recognized. All through the development of the poem the study of character is kept up, either in the local prologues where so much lively, suggestive talk is exchanged, or in the tales themselves; and the spell of that supple analysis, which lights up the weaknesses and the contradictions of each and all, without embittering our sense of life, would never be broken were it not for the few instants when the artist is infected by the medieval disease of conventional moralizing, and we listen incredulously to the self-revelation of the Pardoner or of the Wife of Bath—the poet substituting himself for them, and describing them through their own mouths in his own words.[6]

What wealth of comedy and humor we enjoy in the moral and social satire of Chaucer's great work every reader knows. Women come in for a full share of the satire, but the treatment of this theme is different from what we find in the "Roman de la Rose" and the fabliaux. Who could resist the inimitable slyness of:

> "Leve brother Osewold,
> Who hath no wyf, he is no cokewold.
> But I sey not therfore that thou art oon."[7]

Or:

> "Mulier est hominis confusio;
> Madame, the sentence of this Latin is—
> Womman is mannes Joye and al his blis."[8]

And who could stand the magnificent impudence, the high color, and the loud prattling of the Wife of Bath, and not be aware of the cruelty that lives at the heart of her selfishness? But when all is considered, the feminine sex is spared much of the savage indictment which was almost the rule with the compatriots of Jean de Meung. And again, what an incomparable gallery of half-ecclesiastical rogues Chaucer has given us! But the passion and the vehemence of Langland's satire are here toned down by the sense of relativity, the worldly prudence

[6] The Pardoner's Prologue; the Prologue to the Tale of the Wife of Bath.
[7] The Miller's Prologue, ll. 43-5.
[8] "Nun's Priest's Tale," ll. 344-46.

of the poet, and altogether by his humor. He shows us many abuses, hints at more; he never actually commits himself with the Lollards.

Parody is indirect, implicit satire; its cuts off the formal criticism and pointing out of faults; it holds a mirror—a more or less distorting mirror—to things, and lets their image be their own censure. There is a strong affinity between that method of apparent abstention and a humorous turn of pleasantry; most humorists will, at least in passing, try their hand at parody. Chaucer has presented us with a fine example of the manner in "Sir Thopas"; so successful that, as will happen with the best of both humor and parody, it has deceived unwary readers; it deceives mine host in the poem. The close imitation of the themes and style of the degenerated epic romances is maintained very cleverly just one key above, or below, that of the real thing; and those plainer hints which the professional humorist throws out to his audience, those signs of his playful intent—the raising of the eyebrows, the quick flash of the eye, the pouting of the cheek—or, on the contrary, the supernatural quiet and impassiveness of the speaker's countenance, are here represented by sudden sallies of irreverence or absurdity which should at once edify us:

> And I yow telle in good certayn,
> He hadde a semely nose.[9]

Nothing can be more modern in spirit, more expert in artistic handling, than the whole piece; while the unruffled seriousness of genuine humor is preserved all through, the special trick of parody is practiced with a fine tact, the features of epic style being reproduced not without a slight twist, just enough to deform them and make them comic. A mischievous absurdity plays pranks with the set paraphernalia of armor, setting, description, and narrative. Among the wild beasts of the forest run "the buck and the hare";[10] among the romantic herbs grows nutmeg "to put in ale."[11] Sir Thopas runs away from his giant when he sees him; after which, due praise is given in

[9] "Sir Thopas," ll. 17-18.
[10] *Ibid.*, l. 45.
[11] *Ibid.*, l. 52.

the conventional words to his "fair bearing."[12] The spirit of parody is diffused through many other tales, as in that of the Nun's Priest, a delightful mock-heroic variation on an episode of the French *Roman de Renart*, where it must be confessed that Chaucer has admirably developed the suggestions of the theme and enriched it with all his finer and more lively fancy:

> O destinee, that mayst not been eschewed!

the poet cries out, when the Fox has seized Chauntecleer.

> And on a Friday fil al this meschaunce.
> O Venus, that art goddesse of plesaunce,
> Sin that thy servant was this Chauntecleer,
> . . . .
> Why woldestow suffre him on thy day to dye?
> . . . .
> Certes, swich cry ne lamentacioun
> Was never of ladies maad, whan Ilioun
> Was wonne. . . .
> . . . .
> But sovereynly dame Pertelote shrighte,
> Ful louder than dide Hasdrubales wyf,
> Whan that hir housbond hadde lost his lyf,
> And that the Romayns hadde brend Cartage.
> . . . .
> O woful hennes, right so cryden ye,
> As, whan that Nero brende the citee
> Of Rome, cryden senatoures wyves.

And the sudden sly characteristic touch:

> Now wol I torne to my tale agayn.[13]

The story was never more gloriously raised to the magniloquence of heroic lore, nor was the roguish irony ever more patent without ceasing to be implicit. But even in the most serious tales, the mood of parody is lurking, as is that of humor. Chaucer cannot bear with the pedantry of logic or "rhetorick"; he forestalls Rabelais in his poking fun at scholastic thought or

[12] *Ibid.*, l. 121.
[13] "Nun's Priest's Tale," ll. 518-54.

speech. Hardly any text is ever quoted in the *Canterbury Tales*, but with that intent. The tale of Melibaeus, and even that of the Parson, are probably to be read in that light.

It might be useful, as it would not be uninteresting, to study Chaucer's humor under many more of its aspects; to point out, for instance, how wide its range is, from the finest, most delicate shades, and a spirit of nonchalant good-natured slyness which reminds one of La Fontaine, to brazen effects of effrontery, miracles of cheek, and downright jokes that resemble what is generally regarded as typical forms of American humor:

"But first,"

says the Miller,

"I make a protestacioun
That I am dronke, I knowe it by my soun."[14]

Or this, of the "Doctor of Physick":

In al this world ne was ther noon him lyk
To speke of phisik and of surgerye,
For he was grounded in astronomye.[15]

Even puns put in an occasional appearance.[16] The possibilities of understatement, that ancient trick, are not ignored:

If that he faught, and hadde the hyer hond,
By water he [the Shipman] sente them hoom to every lond.[17]

And as for the physician,

His studie was but litel on the Bible.[18]

Enumeration, that besetting sin of medieval literature, is turned into a fresh source of comic effects by the use Chaucer makes of it. He will create a sense of mechanical and funny exaggeration through the mere virtue of a repetitive series, each term of which is in itself quite innocent:

[14] Miller's Prologue, ll. 29-30.
[15] Prologue, ll. 412-14.
[16] "Somnour's Tale," l. 514 ("ars-metrik" and "arithmetic").
[17] Prologue, ll. 399-400.
[18] *Ibid.*, l. 438.

Wel knew he the olde Esculapius,
And Deiscorides, and eek Rufus,
Old Ypocras, Haly, and Galien,
Serapion, Razis, and Avicen;
Averrois, Damascien, and Constantyn,
Bernard, and Gatesden, and Gilbertyn.[19]

One might instance as well the many distant places to which Chaucer's knight had been, and where he had fought, always with honor; a worthy man, and quite unable of a brag; but is not the soul of bragging, Chaucer hints, implicit in all the literature of knightly prowess? Was ever any record of valor *quite* truthful?

At Alisaundre he was, whan it was wonne.
. . . .
In Lettow hadde he reysed and in Ruce,
No Cristen man so ofte of his degree.
In Gernade at the sege eek hadde he be
Of Algezir, and riden in Belmarye.
. . . .
This ilke worthy knight had been also
Somtyme with the lord of Palatye
Ageyn another hethen in Turkye:
And evermore he hadde a sovereyn prys.[20]

Shall we not confess that a thrust is made here, behind an almost uncannily bland manner, at the most approved style of the romances, in which the palm of valor is won, with unfailing ease, by one hero after another?

Never was it more plain than in Chaucer's practice that irony is not parted from humor, as a common opinion has it, by the whole distance between secret spite and charity; that irony is in fact a variety of humor, with a range of fine intermediary shades. The humorous intent, in the portraits of the parson and the ploughman, resides in the sheer idealism of such descriptions; it is no more here than the faintest aroma, but its presence is felt nevertheless; to set up such figures as living facts is an irony in itself.

[19] *Ibid.*, ll. 429-34.
[20] Prologue, ll. 51-67.

Conversely, the close relationship between humor and realism has been often emphasized, and we have taken it for granted. It is written large over the whole stretch of Chaucer's inspiration and art. But that the two artistic attitudes are after all distinct, and not in a constant proportion to each other, is no less plain. The passages and moments where realism is stressed, in the *Canterbury Tales*, are often those where the humor recedes into the background; one purpose, growing more marked, may become exclusive of the other. The portraits of the somnour and the reve, for instance, are masterpieces of realistic intensity; but their sheer forcefulness makes them almost tragic.

III. His Originality

Is Chaucer's mastery of humor a pure gift of individuality? Or shall we trace it to some general influence; and in the latter case, with which of the major elements in fourteenth-century England shall we connect it more largely: with the French strain of intellect, literature, and art, or with the English strain of shrewdness, instinct, and concreteness?

That the miracle of personality has most to do with it, and that Chaucer's humor is primarily the exception of genius, it is safe to say. The conditions being what they were, the man might not have appeared who was fit to make the most of them. Still, a share must be granted to the "milieu"; and leaving out the question of actual causes and origins, it is at least important to try to determine which aspect of early English culture Chaucer's humor chiefly represents.

The evidence in favor of the French derivation and descent is impressive. It has been said by an exceptionally keen critic that Chaucer's very mind was French.[21] His *finesse* is indeed closer to that of the best medieval French authors than to any model in his own country. He displays an exquisite sense of measure and sobriety, qualities which the French taste was naturally hankering after and evolving, while they were abnormal in England, and very rarely to be found in whole works of art. His general discipleship to French literature is well

[21] Emile Legouis, *Chaucer*, p. 49.

established; from the special angle of humor, do not his poems evince an acquaintance with the fabliaux and with at least English branches of the *Renard;* and did he not study—perhaps translate—the *Roman de la Rose,* in which Jean de Meung had poured out the lavish flow of his satirical irony?

Chaucer's humor is certainly modeled to a large extent on the pattern of the humor *de finesse,* which French literature had developed before him. He is the decisive, the supreme test of the bond of kinship between fourteenth-century English culture and the older civilization of France; whatever that culture owed to that civilization, Chaucer exemplifies and illustrates to a signal degree. His humor is involved in that all but universal debt of his mental being; how could it not be, when it is only the subtle expression of that being itself? But just for the reason that Chaucer's humor is the essence of his personality, it would be wrong to say that it is French, because his personality, when all is considered, remains pre-eminently English.

The latest evidence has tended to weaken the reliance placed on such facts as the French origin of his surname.[22] As far back as one century and a half before the poet's birth—a much longer span than the time required for full actual naturalization—his stock appears as English. His heredity was normal in the middle class of a nation which was growing to the sense of its spiritual independence. His selection of the English language as a medium points to a consciously national purpose. Machaut and the other French writers with whom he can be more especially connected in his lifetime could give him no humor, since they had none. Chaucer's humor developed with the maturity of his original powers; neither the French nor the Italian phase in his career had much to do with that development; his humor found itself gradually, but reached its full vigor in the last and supreme work where a purely English subject gave his art ample scope for the expression of English life and thought. The humor that is the highest distinction of the *Canterbury Tales* is the flower of Chaucer's self-realization as a national poet of England.

The matter and even the manner of his pleasantry are no

[22] J. M. Manly, *Some New Light on Chaucer* (New York, 1926).

doubt very often derived from France. But the temper of his humor, or of his method in handling those comic elements, and of his whole reaction to life, does not need to be explained by a fictitious French descent. There never was in France before Chaucer a humorist like him; there never was one in England either, but a deeper affinity to humor was in his time fast becoming a trait of the English character. He took many and invaluable lessons from his French masters; but in the field of humor, as in most other fields, he improved very much upon their example. The free use he made of broad stories shows that there was in his constitution what is called a rather Gallic vein of frankness, with a touch of cynicism; but the same vein can be found in the most distinctly English literature down to the eighteenth century and beyond; Victorian reticence is after all an exception. The sap of rich realism and supple shrewdness which nourished his humor was of native racy flow. He announces the breadth of the Elizabethan drama and the subtlety of modern English humorists, much more than he does stand as an heir and disciple to Jean de Meung, or Eustache Deschamps. Not only through his more vigorous intuition of the virtue that resides in concreteness, through his wonderful sense of life, but through his humanity and his genial tone of feeling, he is as a humorist in line with his English successors, not with his French predecessors. It is assuredly a fallacy to say that humor implies an element of tenderness or love; the association is perhaps a sentimental illusion of critics, chiefly English; but that the ring of Chaucer's humor was English in its predominantly sympathetic note who could deny?

Altogether original, raising the fabric of his personality upon the very suggestions and data which he made his own, Chaucer is a national writer, though one in whom the French affinities of the English genius are seen most strongly and widely.[23] Solitary in his greatness, he stands apart from his contemporaries, and above them—how much apart and above as a humorist, the story of the next century and a half will show.

[23] When all is said, Chaucer bears witness to the still profoundly cosmopolitan spirit of the fourteenth century. The question whether his art and mind are more English or more French should not be pressed too far, as it is almost an artificial issue.

CHAPTER V

ENGLISH AND SCOTTISH HUMOR AFTER CHAUCER

I. The Anticlimax

TO PURSUE THE HISTORY of English humor further than Chaucer's time, and only as far as the beginning of the Renaissance, is to face an almost unrelieved anticlimax. The end of the fourteenth, the fifteenth, and the early sixteenth centuries can offer us nothing that compares with the *Canterbury Tales* in breadth, delicacy, and subtlety of humorous art. Still, the logic of the subject has to be obeyed, and its demands are plain: in the field of humor, as in that of general thought, the Renaissance is a decisive turn. There, if anywhere, a pause must be made. One step more, and we are caught in a fresh tangle of problems. It was during the Renaissance that under the stimulus of a quickened consciousness the self-realization of humor actually began, with the definite support of a name. So thorough was the process of reaction that the new mental attitude could seem to bear but a slight indirect relation to the old. No progress is more complex and involved than the one which from the age of Shakespeare to that of Addison and Sterne refashioned English humor on a basis of individual expression. That is another stage in a long story, and one upon which we shall gather strength to venture next. Meanwhile this part of our survey may well come to a close with the period, not barren but of relatively inferior fecundity, which preceded the new birth.

Chaucer was recognized in his own lifetime as the leading poet of the age; his most eminent contemporaries and successors professed admiring and respectful allegiance to him. But no one singled out the outstanding originality of his genius as a value worthy of praise or imitation.[1] The absence of a word to denote that special quality, and the dearth, for centuries, of minds that could equal Chaucer's advanced standpoint in the conscious sense of humor are the main causes of that strange unresponsiveness. A few critics, no doubt, among the earliest, though not earlier than the sixteenth century, mention his "pleasant vein" and his "delightsome mirth"; but nothing more is meant here than a general or a common spirit of pleasantry. Indeed the broader aspects of the comedy in the *Canterbury Tales* could hardly pass unnoticed, even when they were not thought worthy of particular praise; but the finer and the properly humorous elements took much longer to be recognized. It was only in the eighteenth century that Chaucer's readers, then possessed of a name for the mental attitude of which he had been the first absolute example in English, awoke to his significance in that regard; and it was only after the middle of the nineteenth century that something like justice was meted out to his extraordinary achievement as a humorist.

In the age that saw the close of his career and that which immediately followed it the very writers who seem to us of greater interest with respect to the continuation of humor did homage to him in curiously irrelevant ways. "Moral" Gower, in the first edition of his *Confessio Amantis*, praised Chaucer as before all the poet of love. These are the words of Venus to the author:

> "And greet well Chaucer when you meet,
> As my disciple and my poet:
> For in the flower of his youth
> In sundry wise, as he well could,
> Of ditties and of songs glad,
> The which he for my sake made,
> The land fulfilled is overall."[2]

[1] Full light has been thrown upon the subject by Professor C. F. E. Spurgeon in *Chaucer devant la critique* (Paris, 1911). Of special interest in this respect are pages 146-53 and 195-202 of her work. They remain to this day the most substantial contribution towards a study of English humor in its historical development.

[2] *Confessio Amantis*, Selections, ed. G. C. Macaulay (London, 1900-1901), ll. 2,940 *et sqq*.

With Hoccleve and Lydgate, discipleship to their master was a proud obligation. But how strangely do the stresses fall which they lay upon his features! Hoccleve in the *Regement of Princes* depicts a benign, almost an edifying Chaucer; and the image of his genuine benevolence is thus warped by its one-sidedness. Lydgate is better aware of the complex nature of his patron's genius, and mentions his "fresh comedies" no less than his "piteous tragedies"; but what shall we say to this summing up of the case? Chaucer has written poems

> Of great morality,
> Some of disport, including great sentence.[3]

Among the Scottish poets, Henryson comes nearest to a perception of Chaucer's unique gift, since he pays him the compliment of linking up with his work a poem not unworthy of his humor, *The Testament of Cresseid*. But the author of the *Kingis Quair* associates Chaucer with Gower:

> Unto the hymns of my masters dear,
> Gower and Chaucer, that on the steps sat
> Of rhetoric, while they were living here,
> Superlative as poets laureate
> In morality and eloquence ornate,
> I recommend my book in lines seven,
> And eke their souls unto the bliss of heaven.[4]

And rhetoric is again the key-word of Dunbar's praise:

> O reverend Chaucer, rose of rhetorik all,
> As in our tongue one flower imperial,
> . . . .
> Thou bearest of poets the prize royal.[5]

While good bishop Gavin Douglas follows suit: "venerable Chaucer" is a "heavenly trumpet," "in eloquence balmy,"

> Milky fountain, clear strand and rose royal
> Of fresh invention.[6]

[3] *Fall of Princes* (Oxford, 1924-1927), I, ll. 246-47 and 344-45.
[4] *Kingis Quair*, st. 197.
[5] *The Goldin Terge*, st. xxix.
[6] *King Hart*, ll. 7-12.

No distinct perception appears to have dawned of the singularly keen, supple, and profound spirit of humor through which Chaucer stands out, in single eminence, among his predecessors and contemporaries. And yet, the writers whose words have just been quoted had all more or less a humorous strain in their constitutions. The sluggishness of their realization and response is an illuminating fact, and one which, taken in conjunction with all the evidence that can be adduced from the literature and manners of that age, makes the issue quite clear.

The progress of English humor did not stop short at Chaucer. But it continued on another plane, and along rather different lines of development. Chaucer's creation in that field had not only been supreme; it had been exceedingly precocious and exceptional in more respects than that of time. The intellectual detachment which it evinces betokened a maturity of reflection much beyond the stage which all but a very few minds of the period could reach. The playing with the shades of character and with the contrasted aspects of life in the master's works answered to a subtlety of thought and a clearness of artistic purpose which none in England had yet shown, or would show for a number of years. Moreover, the subtlety of Chaucer's humor was cast in a mold which, while it was not foreign, did not answer to the central and most normal type of English disposition and temperament. It embodied all the heritage of French *finesse* which the influence of an imported culture and a personal affinity of temper could make assimilable; it was as French as the genuine spontaneous activity of an English mind can be without ceasing to be English.

Too modern and clear-sighted, too subtle and conscious in its shading, too French in its slyness, Chaucer's humor was not only inimitable, it was at first almost unintelligible to vastly the greater number of his compatriots. It remained in abeyance as it were, enclosed in works whose fecundity was to be gradually released, as a potential treasure to be discovered by a distant posterity. Meanwhile the broader development of English humor went on as the growth of a mental gift which the English genius was putting forth from its instincts, and according to the dispositions that were its own. The lesson of Chaucer's example was for three centuries as if it had not been. On the basis of that meditative reserve and seriousness, and of that racy realism, which were the more special qualifications of the English for a restrained original tone in pleasantry, the vein of spontaneous humor which had been shown by the predecessors of Chaucer remained productive. Its fecundity seems but poor by the side of Chaucer's brilliant achievement; but it was nourished from the more average temper of the race, and its refining, when it was done, would be more genuine for not being too precocious. How that refining took place from the sixteenth to the eighteenth centuries, and how finally modern English humor grew upon a psychological root quite different from Chaucer's subtle intellectual analysis, is a separate, and a difficult subject in itself. Over that prospect we may cast a tentative glance and adumbrate its outline, before we have done.

II. Gower, Hoccleve, Lydgate

Gower was Chaucer's contemporary, but died a few years after him, and may be regarded as the first of his successors. Standing by the side of his greater friend as a more average and representative figure, he is, however, curiously less alive to the national issue in language; the bulk of his French and Latin works exceeds that of his English poems. No fourteenth-century writer was more steeped than Gower in the influence of France; but the grace of temperament was wanting, and he captured little from the more elusive values of the literature and the spirit which he studied. Whatever humor he possessed was not of the kind which French examples could have encouraged. That very much, in that line, should not be expected from him how could one doubt, as soon as one reads his own account of the plan and object of his Trilogy:

Since every man is bound to impart to others in proportion as he has himself received from God, John Gower, desiring in some measure to lighten the account of his stewardship, while yet there is time, with regard to those mental gifts which God gave him, amid his labours and in his leisure composed three books for the information and instruction of others, in the form which follows.[7]

[7] Translated from the Latin by G. C. Macaulay, in *Selections from the "Confessio Amantis"* (Oxford, 1903), pp. xi-xii.

That solemn didacticism was the common attitude of the Middle Ages, and Gower fulfils his pledge to the letter. We read the first hundred lines of his best work, the *Confessio Amantis,* with a sense of thickening despair; the agility of mind, the self-detachment that humor implies cannot possibly live in that clumsy, explicit heaviness of purpose, thought, and style. But what is this? Has not the glimmer of a twinkle stirred in those dull eyes?

> For often, if one heed but took,
> It's better to wink than to look.[8]

as the fate of Actaeon testifies. We read on: the sins of hearing are discussed after those of sight, and we relapse into downright moralizing. Gradually, however, there steals into us a fuller sense of the habit and demeanor of the mind that is thinking aloud in our hearing. Worthy John Gower is no humorist; still, he is not quite the pedant and the preacher; there is in him a fund of observation and shrewdness, and he can see the other side of a subject; more than that, he can hint at it, and his plain tone then tingles with a sort of subdued liveliness. There is a piquancy in the neat wording of his wisdom; and much will be forgiven him because he knows how to smile at himself. The advice which, in the poem, Venus gives the grey-haired author lacks Chaucer's dexterous light touch; but shall we deny it a pleasant turn of sincerity, mixed with wistfulness and that reserve of statement which is the soul of humorous expression?

> My son, if thou be well advised,
> This toucheth thee; forget it not:
> The thing is turned into: "it was";
> That which was of yore green grass
> Is withered hay by this time.
> Therefore my counsel is that thou
> Remember well that thou art old.[9]

Against him should be reckoned the many occasions when his theme gave him a chance, and which he let slip by. But what then? He was not out to improve those opportunities. And there was in him that seriousness of intent, that genuine pre-

[8] Book I, ll. 383-84.

[9] Book VIII, ll. 2433-39.

occupation with moral issues, which is the bent of the Puritan. The background of reflection upon life, and of sober sadness, is there; the man and the writer are of the type that grows and flourishes most naturally in the England of the fourteenth, as in that of the nineteenth century. Does that background by itself, as we thought we could say it did, create a possibility, a potentiality of humor? It seems to do so really, and the test answers well enough in the case of Gower. Born as he was to be not merry but grave, he is led by his meditative mood itself to a sense of interiority, a duality of mental planes; that things are relative and diverse he knows, since character and conduct are to be adapted to them as such; and withal, he has his share of the racy, concrete perception which book knowledge may kill, but which the study of life nourisheth. As a result, he says not a few things, quietly, that mean more than they look on the surface. He is like that king of Hungary whom he mentions, who "thought more than he said."[10]

That is but the initial, elementary stage of a progress which in Chaucer reaches its full consummation. But we are here nearer the central temperament of English humor.

With Hoccleve, the situation may well look even more desperate. In his *Regement of Princes*, a personality is revealed: that of a man, like Gower, of a serious, moralizing turn, who in the declining years of his life draws on his experience for the benefit of others. His words breathe the brooding sadness, almost the anxiety, of a pessimistic mood; and his utterance, sincere as it is, seems the naïve outpouring of a primitive mind when compared with Chaucer's. His modesty outdoes that of his master and runs to an awkward excess: "I am as lewd [ignorant] and dull as is an ass."[11]

Shall we take him at his word? To do so would be imprudent. Hoccleve's naïveté is superb; but it cannot be as thorough as it appears, since he has such a shrewd eye for reality and gives us such telling picturesque sketches of the manners of his time. Might there not be a touch of slyness in that intense presentment, the vividness of which the author seems hardly to feel, and which keeps on the same tenor un-

[10] Book I, l. 2106.
[11] Ed. Furnivall (London, 1892-1925), p. 139, st. 552.

perturbed? We should be inclined to believe there might be, when in the praise of Chastity we come across the episode of the Roman lady whose husband had a bad breath and who did not know that he had, as she lacked the necessary standards for comparison. Does there not flit a passing light in the author's eyes, when he writes: "Full few men had she kissed, as I guess." We think we see a wink, and are confirmed in our impression as we read on:

> To find many such is full difficult;
> Let us await well when the wind is south
> And north at once,

before we look for them.[12] Such moments are rare, and Hoccleve, assuredly, is no humorist. But he is not the dull ass he pretends to be. Everything points to the presence in him of a sort of virtual humor, made up of a pithy knowledge of things, just enough alive and conscious to be half "actualized" at times, but too much repressed by a heavy didacticism to become fully actual. Common sense is another name for that humor in the rough, and the men who keep to that stage simply do not make us laugh; but they have in them the root of the matter, and from the root the flower some day will grow.

Lydgate introduces us to his *Fall of Princes* in words which hold out very little promise of better things. His aim, he says, is to survey the great catastrophes of fortune, "beginning at Adam and ending with King John taken prisoner in France by Prince Edward."[13] He claims to follow in Chaucer's footsteps; but alas, the difference to us! How light was the master's touch, how ponderous is that of the disciple! How little he seems to have learnt of the virtue there is in leaving unsaid whatever one can spare to say! With him we feel back in the Middle Ages again. Still, Lydgate is not always painstakingly dull. It is not only that he will take a leaf out of Chaucer's book and complain of the emptiness of his purse, or, like a thirsty monk, lament the drying up of Bacchus's fountains, whence inspiration used to flow; there seems to have been not a little truth of fact in those complainings, and the truth some-

[12] P. 135, st. 536.
[13] Book I, Prologue.

how interferes with the humor. His self-depreciation, again, on the ground of dullness, compares unfavorably with Chaucer's, as there speaks in it, or we are tempted to hear, the accent of genuine modesty, which, while it redounds to the credit of Lydgate's character, does not further such humorous purpose as he may have had. But in his earlier works, *The Temple of Glass, Reason and Sensuality,* there does arise a certain liveliness from the freer play of a more spontaneous fancy—as in the dialogue between the author and Diana, and the chaste goddess's vivacious, realistic faultfinding with Venus.[14] A faint glimmer we have here at best, just enough to feel sure that under the mediocrity of an all-too-plain meaning, a current of virtual humor has not ceased to flow. And as Lydgate in other respects is typically English, with a love for nature, a reverence for woman, a vein of national feeling, there is in him, altogether, a representative quality, which may explain the high esteem in which he has been held by good judges of their own literature. No doubt, he is a fair specimen of the early fifteenth-century Englishman; and it must be confessed that if there is in him the matter of shrewdness, the fit manner to set it off is singularly lacking.

III. Scottish Writers; Skelton

From England, indeed, the main stream of literary humor seems then to have passed into Scotland. It was north of the Tweed that poetry and the arts flourished most brilliantly at the end of the fifteenth and the beginning of the sixteenth centuries. Through their intellectual vigor and gift of telling expression, Henryson and Dunbar are Chaucer's most worthy successors, as the *Kingis Quair* is unmatched in the south for its lyrical fervor and charm.

Is there a distinctive quality in Scottish humor? Of course there is. The Scots themselves are positive on the point, and they have some right to be heard, as have assuredly, on their respective grounds, the Welsh and the Irish. But the trouble begins when that special flavor is to be described. You must not ask each people to justify their claim; they will be content

[14] Ernst Sieper (ed.), *Reason and Sensuality* (London, 1901-1903), ll. 3315, *et sqq.*

with pointing out that theirs is "good" or "genuine" humor; conversely you must not ask them as to the value of their neighbors' brand: they are no less ready with a triumphant answer that it is bad. For example, the English have it that Scottish humor is of the broadest kind. Dunbar and the writers we are coming to would certainly seem not to clash with that verdict; but can anything be more broad than the popular English tales and fabliaux of the fifteenth century? The Scotsman's view as to the English is no less definite, since the Southron, he holds, has no humor at all. The post-Chaucerian period is not such as to make that opinion glaringly untenable; but the rest of the world, on the evidence of other ages, persists in crediting England with a creative faculty in the field of humor, and even merges the separate claims of Scotland and Wales in that of the larger unit. Indeed the national aroma of humor is like the specific smells which everyone will agree upon within the herd or the tribe, and no one will agree upon without. Our first or second cousins are not in that respect much nearer to us than distant races. If we are to believe the citizen of New York, the Londoner is proudly and sluggishly humorless; but listen to John Bull, and hear what *he* has to say on the subject of American pleasantry. Humor no doubt being intimately bound up with national character, that character must be felt in the inner determinations of humor; but this holds only of its finer and more subtle shades; the form, the essential trick of the humorist, is roughly speaking much the same everywhere. It would be tempting to try to study the special dosing of elements which gives some substance to the claim of absolute originality each British group will put forward in that domain; but the research would be most difficult, the matter being most elusive; and perhaps a foreign observer may be excused if he goes by the opinion of the world in general. The world, which has digested the separate individualities of England, Scotland, Wales, Ireland, and has learnt to speak of Great Britain, insists on speaking, as do the British themselves, of the English language and literature; and since our inquiry bears almost exclusively on literary expression, we may have some reason for keeping to our ready-made label of "English humor."

All the greater Scottish poets of the period we deal with are under the spell of Chaucer's influence. But in a most remarkable way, they are not indebted to Chaucer for their humor. This is a native growth, racy of the soil, and the vein of which, with them, answers to the more popular tone of their inspiration. To the English master they go for the example of the conscious art and dramatic management in which his practice is so easily superior to that of his time. As was pointed out above, they seem hardly to be aware of his most original merit.

Henryson, when all is considered, is not an exception. Through the depth, the meditative quality, the background of his humor, he is the only writer of the age who can be mentioned in the same breath with Chaucer; but however large his debt to him, he owes more to himself and to Scotland. Inferior in delicacy, subtlety, suppleness, and in the range of humorous expression, he is perhaps superior in one respect—that of the sense of tragic irony which instils such a modern and romantic flavor into the philosophical bitterness of his greatest poem. Some of his traits and hints display an almost Chaucerian slyness; but the spirit of humor with Henryson is fed by a more concentrated purpose of moral reflection; it is nearer the normal temper of the British mind. A thoughtful pessimism in the *Testament of Cresseid* sustains the vigorous movement of the firm, full, grand style. Such are the theme and the mood that the tone of the piece must be mainly pathetic and instructive. It is not of the *Canterbury Tales* that we think here, but of William Hogarth, and his "Progresses."

Nearer than Chaucer to the popular heart as he is in his most elaborate poem, Henryson shows a closer sympathy with the instinct of rough merrymaking in the huge irrepressible fun of *Sum Practysis of Medecyne*. Chaucer's fabliaux seem tame by the side of that Rabelaisian outburst, where the coarser realism of a more primitive and Northern culture pours itself out. But Henryson has a vein as well of a finer and gentler kind: *The Garment of Good Ladies*, *The Reasoning between Age and Youth*, *Robyn and Makyne*, the *Fables*, etc.; here, the neat, nimble cleverness of Chaucer's manner is often caught.

A deft point is made out of the experience of the lover who did not catch the tide of opportunity:

> The man that will not when he may
> Shall have not when he would. . . .[15]

With Dunbar, we revert to the characteristically broad vein that does appear to be, at least in older Scotland, the national brand of humor. Our poet's comic verve rushes forward with such impetuosity that one might expect to see him swept off his feet by the torrent which he has let loose. Nothing can exceed the Rabelaisian gusto with which the "Two Married Women and the Widow" converse on the theme of their conjugal experiences. We have here, of course, a quality of temperament, an individual gift, the gushing invention of impudently realistic fun. There is a genius in that, the genius of popular raciness. But however racy, a manner is not necessarily humorous. A fishwoman's hot argument with a customer is a pleasure for the gods; but in order that humor, properly so called, be injected into the rich mixture, the lady must be able to control her fury and her glibness of tongue with a sense, however relative, of artistic restraint. The originality of Dunbar resides in the remarkable self-possession of his most fiery invectives. He keeps a cool head and a clear judgment all the time. Everything is explicit in the "Two Married Women," no doubt; but that's just it: more is explicit than there ever was in actual talk or in actual life; what we have here is the poetry of exaggeration, and that overstatement which is similar, in most respects, to the opposite process of understatement. The humor that mixes with the farce lies in the fantastic and pretended unawareness, on the author's part, of the wild improbability of his own tale, and in other elements, such as the amazing wealth of picturesque words, or the grotesque impudence of the indecency. The final effect is very amusing and high-flavored; but the colorful episode does not eclipse the much more finely shaded art of Chaucer in the character of the Wife of Bath.

Dunbar's manner is mostly of that type; on occasion it is touched with a more subtle essence; but the grim physical hor-

[15] *Robyn and Makyne,* ll. 91-92.

ror, symbolizing moral corruption, that rises to a powerful effectiveness in "The Dance of the Sevin Deidly Synnis," tends to replace and dispel the humor altogether. Here again, as in Henryson's *Testament of Cresseid*, we are come down to the bedrock of moral faith and the sense of sin. The poet is so clearly aware of it that at the end, with a masterly skill, he shifts us back into humor at one stroke: Mahoun (or Mahomet, the Devil), to crown the doings of the day, has wished for a "Highland pageant"; and a messenger fiend, shouting the war cry of the clans, has soon gathered about him a crowd of harsh-voiced Highlanders:

> Those termagants, in rags and tatter,
> Full loud in Gaelic began to clatter,
> And croak like raven and rook;
> The Devil so deafened was with their yell,
> That in the deepest pit of hell
> He smothered them with smoke.[16]

The best-known pieces in that style—as the one called for short "The Tournament," "The Flyting of Dunbar and Kennedy," "The Feigned Friar of Tungland," etc.—stir up much the same kind of interest and humor. There is still a beautiful central calm in the mind of the poet, amid a stormy whirl of tremendous abuse; but when all is said, the range is not very wide, nor is the humor of the finest. Release is the label that would best cover most of that brand; and it was to be Rabelais's privilege to endow release with a rich mental background. Great as Dunbar is undoubtedly in his satire, his method as a comic writer is too explicit. He is the first to hold his sides, and that is not the most approved method of humor:

> Such comfort to my heart it wrought,
> With laughter near I burst.[17]

Not the least efficient of his characteristics, on the contrary, is his wonderful talent for writing in verse; all along, the metric regularity and brilliancy of the stanza underlines, confirms the sense of a measured and deliberate expression. That such scurrilous matter should be put into those correct, neat, inevitable

[16] "The Dance of the Sevin Deidly Synnis," the end.

[17] "The Justis betwix the Talzeour and the Sowtar," ll. 101-2.

lines greatly furthers our impression of a conscious purpose, and of humor.

After Dunbar, Scottish poetry loses much of its very high quality; the work of Bishop Gavin Douglas shows a falling off in vigor, as it is animated no doubt by a more gentle spirit. Humor with him is most often a pleasant gleam that lights up the moralizing and the allegory of his verse. The poet in the *Palace of Honour* meets Diana hunting with the virgins of her train:

> . . . but few I saw with Dian hunt.[18]

He is arraigned before Venus: has he not sung a ballad on the evil doings of false love? The worthy bishop, in that embarrassing predicament, turns his knowledge of law to good use:

> "Madam, ye may not sit into this case,
> For ladies may be judges in no place."[19]

Besides, he is a "spiritual man," and must be tried by his own ecclesiastical court. The hero of *King Hart*, being wounded with an arrow, is handed over to Dame Beauty to have his wound dressed; but the more she tries to cure it, the worse it becomes. These are innocent pieces of slyness, not very original indeed, but genuine; and they suit well the temper of the man; their gentleness is a relief, after the crude force of so much stronger verve. *King Hart,* as a whole, is an arresting poem, in which the mood of reflective detachment, not unmixed with a mild playfulness, is closely akin to the essence of much modern humor, without perhaps freeing itself quite enough from a didactic intent to allow of a thorough identification.

A vigorous irony is once more to be tasted in the earnest, heavy poems of David Lyndsay, who one century and a half after William Langland gave a Scottish counterpart to *Piers Plowman* in his character of John the Common Weal *(The Satire of the Thrie Estaitis).* But Lyndsay's satirical animus is instinct with the spirit of the Reformation, and he belongs already to the new age.

[18] *Poetical Works,* ed. J. Small (Edinburgh, 1874), p. 14, ll. 26-27.
[19] *Ibid.,* p. 27, ll. 17-18.

We find ourselves on English soil again with the work of Skelton; and we are reminded once more of the danger that lurks in too definite views of national characteristics; if Scottish humor was often broad, what shall we say to Skelton's? But the vitality of his verve is not second even to Dunbar's. The animation, the flow of spirits that put life into all that he writes have their source in the liveliness of a fancy brimful with the fun of things. Not the most philosophical, not the most refined fun, certainly. Our poet finds his delight in all the wide range of easy amusement, from pure farce to jolly satire and self-mockery. The rhythm of his mirth is inseparably mingled with the skipping measure of his most typical lines, in which the nimbleness of quick, flashing, prancing thoughts is invested with the ironical jingle of sonorous, almost macaronic rhymes. To write verse in that style is to laugh at one's reader and at one's self; and the humor of the laugh is that it should be associated at all with the dignified garb of poetry. This contrast, this paradox is the essence of Skelton's art; and the soul of burlesque is diffused through all his work—as the free paganism of the jolly priest was the triumphant humor of his life. Do we not breathe the flavor of parody in that strangest paraphrase of Catullus's elegy, the *Book of Philip Sparrow?*

> When I remember again
> How my Philip was slain,
> Never half the pain
> Was between you twain,
> Pyramus and Thesbe,
> As then befell to me:
> I wept and I wailed,
> The tears down hailed;
> But nothing it availed
> To call Philip again,
> Whom Gyb our cat hath slain. . . .
> I sighed and I sobbed,
> For that I was robbed
> Of my sparrow's life.
> O maiden, widow and wife,
> Of what estate ye be,
> Of high or low degree,

Great sorrow then ye might see,
And learn to weep at me!
Such pains did me fret,
That mine heart did beat,
My visage pale and dead,
Wan, and blue as lead;
The pangs of hateful death
Well-nigh had stopped my breath.[20]

And is not the enthusiastic, rapturous realism of that most extraordinary paean of praise, *The Tunnyng of Elynour Rummyng,* a skit upon the fossilized traditional language in which the courtly poets would describe the lady of their love?

But that the joy of picturesqueness, the pleasure there is in striking outline and character could raise Skelton's realism and his humor to a higher plane of artistic intensity, who could doubt who knew for instance the portrait of Riot, in *The Bowge of Courte?*

IV. The Modern English Temper

We thus bring our survey to a close on the eve of the Reformation and the Renaissance. From Chaucer's exquisite delicacy and subtlety we have dropped to a more modest level of vivacious, broad, and fanciful realism. But this was the solid level on which English humor could spontaneously develop; there it was founded in the wide instincts and temperament of the people.

Literature, properly so called, is the best, the safest index to the development which we have attempted to follow. Had it been possible to extend our study beyond its moderate limits, confirmation might have been sought for the views presented above in evidence of a more or less different kind. As soon as the spiritual life of the English people is tested in its various aspects, from the end of the fourteenth to the middle of the sixteenth centuries, it can be easily understood how and why the period which followed Chaucer's death was not indeed one of actual decay in the domain of humor. Documents of all kinds about that relatively modern period are more numerous; and

[20] Alexander Chalmers, *The Works of the English Poets* (London, 1810), II, 290.

from two classes of them in particular some idea may be formed of the part which a taste for the comic was playing in the everyday thoughts of the nation. One is the outpouring of the common mind in "humorous" pieces, and in the ballads[21]—those creations, not of the crowd, but of the popular singers, the heritage of several centuries, but in which the fifteenth can perhaps claim the largest share. The other is the carvings, full of a grotesque fancy, which we notice in the cathedrals and churches of the time.

If our notion of humor were of the looser and freer sort, such documents would have been to us of a significance not second to that of the major writers. But we have committed ourselves to a stricter notion, and the element of implicitness in pleasantry is a condition of the mental attitude which it is our object to trace. Now, that implicitness is rather an attribute of reflective thinking, and hardly to be found in the forms of expression that leave only very little to the interpretation of the reader or spectator. It is a fact that the comic verve which gives itself vent in the ballads or the church carvings is very generally too explicit to afford us direct evidence of the presence and activity of the proper spirit of humor.

What those documents should encourage is the impression that the life of the English people, after all, was normal, as measured by the standards of balanced human feelings everywhere. The already prevalent tone of seriousness or even sadness which the foreigner would notice should be interpreted in the light of those qualifying facts. The character of the English nation had by that time developed most of its ripe and modern features. The gravity and even moroseness would

[21] For the humorous pieces, see the list in J. E. Wells, *Manual of Writings in Middle English* (London and New Haven, 1916), p. 180 (the list covers the period later than 1400). See as well Schofield, *English Literature from the Norman Conquest to Chaucer* (New York and London, 1906), pp. 323-35 (remarks are made on the period from Chaucer's death to the Renaissance); and G. H. MacKnight, *Middle English Humorous Tales in Verse* (London, [1913]). For the ballads, see F. J. Child, *The English and Scottish Popular Ballads* (Boston, 1882-1898), e.g., in Part IX (numbers 266-305): "King Edward the Fourth and a Tanner of Tamworth" (273), "Our Goodman" (274), "The Friar in the Well" (276), "The Wife Wrapt in Wether's Skin" (277), "The Farmer's Curst Wife" (278), "The Jolly Beggars" (279), "The Keach in the Creel" (281), etc.

strike the observers from abroad; but the English who drank their wine in a silence which the French visitor naturally regarded as gloomy[22] had bright patches of mirth in the piebald cloak of their moods; they could be rowdy or blithe, their spirits would at times be exuberant, they knew how to crack jokes and spring a heavy, or a jolly laugh. The note of merry England is still part and parcel of the tones of those centuries. The latent disposition to humor had its roots in that complex mingling of a sober pensiveness with shrewd and lighter-hearted impulses.

The day was to come when the original temper of the English would express itself more fully in an original manner of stressing the contrasts of life. But the necessary mental preparation had not yet reached a sufficiently advanced stage. Humor in its indubitable, complete state was yet the privilege of a minority; the instances of its finished perfection were very few. Time was needed to make the attitude quite self-conscious and bring it within the reach of many minds, though not of all. To this decisive growth, the Renaissance and the Reformation were equally to contribute; both stimulated the initiative and self-reliance of the individual man. Under their combined influences the vitality of the humorous instinct was spurred from a dormant to an active state; the affinities of natural genius which were to give England a primacy in that field were revealed and confirmed. For the fulfilment of that destiny, it was indispensable that the English temperament and the higher method of humor should be reconciled as it were in a mutual adaptation. Chaucer's art was not the pattern after which the adaptation could be generally effected; and modern humor was re-created on the basis of a psychological tendency that answered

[22] The words of Deslandes, a Frenchman who traveled in England at the beginning of the eighteenth century, are typical of the remarks which many of his compatriots must have made before him: "Il n'est point à mon avis de spectacle plus comique que celui de quinze ou seize buveurs qui s'enivrent posément. . . . Des personnes austères, avec un maintien affecté et des manières pesantes, passent douze heures de suite sans se dire un seul mot. Les bouteilles se succédent les unes aux autres, et elles ont une éloquence naturelle qui persuade les convives. Il n'est point besoin de les exciter au plaisir; une résolution ferme de s'enivrer est le motif gracieux qui les anime" (p. 251; the account of Deslandes was published in 1717). We are indebted for this quotation to M. G. Ascoli's *La Grande Bretagne devant l'opinion française au XVIIe siècle*, Vol. II (Paris, 1930).

to the most typical feature of the English mind: its stubborn individuality. Such was the main issue in the next period, from Shakespeare and Ben Jonson to Addison, when a word, which originally denoted a passive bent of temper, most alien to the supple detachment of the humorist, went through one of the most fascinating transformations in the history of language, growing to mean the very thing which it would have seemed least fitted to imply.

Part II

The Renaissance

FOREWORD TO PART II

TWENTY more years have seen the world once again shaken, and grievous encroachments upon the quiet of the spirit. The theme of humor seemed at times singularly inopportune; but already in our mellowing remembrance tragedy is fused with a sense of contrast, with the ironies of fate; and is not that mixture the essence of a humorous mood?

Still, events have been too much for the ambitious initial scheme; it has had to be cut down, so that the survey practically ends with the Restoration. What follows, a period that is the heyday of English humor full grown, is sketched only in so far as it shows us the humorous mind at last becoming conscious of itself and formulating its own attitude.

The indispensable references are given in the footnotes. No attempt is made to set up a general bibliography of the vast subject of humor, or of English literature as viewed from that special angle.

April, 1950

CHAPTER VI

THE RENAISSANCE, THE REFORMATION, AND HUMOR

I. The Two Trends

THAT THE RENAISSANCE should have been the decisive stage in the development of English humor can only be regarded as natural. Such a relation would be expected between the period when the English genius came of age and the growth of a mental attitude in which some permanent features of that genius are surely reflected. During the years that elapsed between the early sixteenth century, when the revival of learning began in England, and the outbreak of the Civil War, not only did humor, as an original mode of pleasantry, show increasing vitality, but it almost reached a degree of self-realization. That it still did fall short of the supreme achievement marked by lucid awareness can be traced to an obvious cause: the condition on which the discovery of its own identity was dependent—the finding of an individual name for itself—was not yet completely fulfilled.

It might have seemed a logical, as it was a tempting, object for the present inquiry to follow that process of self-discovery to its very end, in the eighteenth century; and such indeed was at first the intended scope of the second part. But the matter proved too abundant, and the limit had to be set earlier—before the end of the seventeenth century. The crowning touches which the Augustan period brought to the consciousness of humor as a distinct instrument, along with the final display of its possibilities by the humorists of the classical age from Addison to Sterne, must thus be left for some other survey, planned out on independent lines.

As has been explained in the Foreword to Part I, the investigation must be practically restricted to literary texts. "It is only in words that the duality of intent which we regard as characteristic of humor in the precise sense, can be aptly expressed. The diffused humor which reveals itself through art and life is commonly merged in the indiscriminate field of the comic—fun, amusement, drollery pure and simple, from which it is not easily distinguishable."[1] Still, the intention was at the start, as far as possible, to follow the broadening out of the humorous vein in the thought of England as part of the intellectual progress of the people and in terms of that progress. That aim has not been given up, but the attempt has had to be somewhat narrowed down. It became obvious, as the Elizabethan period was reached and the expressions of the national mind were growing much more plentiful, that if all documents were to be considered, nothing less than the psychological history of a people, watched from a particular angle, was involved. All the extant traces of that vast process would have had to be studied and sifted. The task exceeded the energy of a single inquirer. While humor, therefore, is here considered in its natural connection with the major movements of the age, it is continuously investigated only through its most suggestive symptoms, those of greater significance, in that field of literature. Altogether the present work assumes its definite purpose as a study of the evolution of literary humor, with only a general background of collective psychology. It is hoped that the aesthetic development thus sketched out may yet possess some reliability, as the central and main thread in a tangled web.

English humor during the Renaissance period developed along two main lines, one answering to the humanistic, the other to the popular inspiration and influence. As time went on the difference between them grew less visible, and they were finally united in one progress. It may not be superfluous, however, at the start to give a brief sketch of their characteristics.

The spirit of humanistic humor was widespread enough, as a light, thin atmosphere; it appeared in a concentrated form only with a small number of exceptional minds—writers and

[1] See above, p. 1.

thinkers, more highly cultivated and refined. Socially speaking it was aristocratic; it prevailed in the circles of the court, the nobility, the families of leisure, including part of the middle class, and of course the universities, though it would find enthusiastic disciples among self-made men of low origin; it opened itself easily to outside influences and was in close contact, not only with the classics but with foreign literatures, especially those of Italy and France. Its activity was felt cumulatively in the shaping of a tradition, treasured by a series of literary humorists; these were mainly responsible for the discovery of the tone and manner that could best express a certain mental attitude, which they intuitively perceived, though no name was given to it. The nearest approach they could have made to a description of it would probably have been to call up the most famous model of irony, that of Lucian. It may seem at first sight that this was the very core of the intellectual advance that gave English humor its full scope and self-consciousness; but the humanist example did not play the decisive part; it acted as a complementary factor, though a very important one.

The popular energy, though less conspicuous, was the predominant force. It appears to us as a psychological trend much more widely diffused, and actually common to all the ranks and classes, though it would be seen more clearly in men and women who had not felt the influence of culture. It had its roots in the inborn tendencies of a majority of the nation, arose naturally from their temper and from the turn which they would give to their jesting. Shrewdness here, raciness, and a sly way of not unduly displaying even one's sense of fun had more to do with the flavor of the product than art and ingenuity. Here humor indeed sprang from the instinct of a nation, from an all but universal need; it satisfied the native cravings of a cultural group. Life and literature did equally, then as now, show an unlimited number of individuals in whom a more or less developed germ of that faculty could be discovered. The humorous manner in this respect is a collective creation; as a set of empirical habits and rough patterns of thought and speech it embodies a peculiar reaction to life in which the genius of a people is expressed. Similar discoveries, of course, could be, and have been, made by other nations.

To the latter element in the development of modern English humor, the main share must be assigned; when all is said, the essential originality of English humorists lies rather with it. It is owing to its influence that humor preserved a store of vitality which saved it from the risk of becoming a mere trick, an artifice of style. Its presence is felt in the quality of naturalness, the full advantage and the full charm of which a humorous manner tries to keep by all means, even while an inevitable self-consciousness dwells at its very heart. Thanks to it the English critics have often had a right to lay stress on the spontaneity of humor, a feature which is never quite genuine, but the visible absence of which is at once detrimental. To it again is due the cordial acceptance of things as they are, whatever their oddities, that usually reflects the temper of a people in touch with life at all the points of its personality.

The former influence must be largely credited with the aesthetic process through which a technique of pleasantry was evolved, that kept its self-command perfectly, and did not say things, but hinted them; that creation taking place with the help of the popular instinct, which co-operated all through, but chiefly in the light of a cosmopolitan heritage, classical and foreign. We are here in touch with the more lucid and artificial aspect of English humor; we come across the series of the philosophical, satirical, and artistic humorists. A kindly undertone, with these, is no indispensable constituent of their manner; while a majority perhaps have it, we miss it in not a few. Conversely, an actual duality of meaning and the complete repression of one's dominant mood are decidedly, here, necessary characteristics of the humorous attitude; the psychological fact that the presentment is indirect, and so to say transposed, comes out with its full effect; and we draw nearer to the contiguous domain of irony with which humor of this kind, more intellectual and dry, largely overlaps.

When those two trends had merged into one, modern English humor was full grown, with all its wealth and the whole range of its effects. Still, in individual humorists down to the twentieth century it remains possible to trace the secret predominance of one or the other. The humanistic spirit savors more of Mediterranean influences, the popular vein is more directly heir to the Saxon derivation of the English genius. In Shakespeare the fusion was first signally achieved; and yet, if we contrast him for instance with most of the university wits, his contemporaries, he stands primarily not only as a synthetic and conciliatory writer but as the supreme representative of one tradition, the more deeply rooted—the tradition of the national originality in pleasantry.

II. The Renaissance

What the Renaissance was as a broad intellectual influence is so generally known that it may be taken for granted. We have here only to ask ourselves how far such an influence can have acted, favorably or unfavorably, upon the growth of English humor.

It seems clear enough, as soon as the issue is raised, that a movement whose outstanding traits were the enthusiasm of rediscovered beauty and an impassioned thirst for knowledge can hardly have had, in so far as it obeyed those impulses, a fostering effect upon the progress of the humorous attitude. The latter implies detachment and a duality of mental planes; while the consequence of zeal, whatever its object, is single-mindedness. The fervor of the artist or the scholar, in itself, leaves hardly any scope to the spirit of relativity, since it seeks eagerly for the sense of fulfilment in joy or in truth; its excess will be dogmatism or pedantry—the very opposites of humor.[2]

If, taking a wider view of the subject, one surveys the social aspects of that expanding time, the Renaissance appears as well in conflict with the aims and method of the humorist.

[2] A feature of the Renaissance influence, related to those, which would run counter to the development of humor, is the overemphasis which the grammarians and schoolmasters taught, in imitation, as they thought, of the rhetoric of the ancients. Style could not be too explicit or too intense, and the deliberate repetition of one idea in varied forms was regarded as the mark of good writing (R. Pruvost, *Robert Greene et ses romans*, Paris, 1938, p. 27). Humor on the contrary demands a dense, implicit manner. The further refinements that were prompted by the intellectual cravings of the time and that led eventually to Italianism, Euphuism, the vogue of conceits, etc., acted we think, if a balance is struck, rather as favorable influences (see below, chap. vii, sect. iv).

That age was flushed with the intoxication of maturing youth and of unbounded hopes; it pushed impatiently forth towards a newly enlarged world, which called for the initiative of explorers, soldiers, and merchants; on all sides it held out prizes which the nations, like individuals, vied with one another in seeking. Now a sense of material or political success, while it thrills the citizen and the statesman, is a stimulus mainly to the expansive powers of personality; the roots of the humorous instinct are in the more sober activities of experience and reflection. It grows when the limits of possible action have been reached and its data have become familiar, when having taken stock of life, the ripening mind withdraws into itself.

Still, all things considered, the Renaissance did much to favor the tendencies of which a bent to humor is made. In the very eagerness of desire and exertion, men's personalities were quickened; even the impassioned allegiance to an ideal of beauty stirred them to a more intense realization of their own selves. The discovery of a new and a fuller scale of values was tantamount to a vitalizing of the soul; the average mind looked out with a bolder curiosity over the universe of facts or of ideas. It is a commonplace of intellectual history that modern individualism should be traced back to the Renaissance. Now, too intimate or too direct a connection cannot be established between the independence of private judgment and that paradoxical originality of thought which is called humor. The humorist reacts to things in a way which reverses the process of normal, stereotyped reaction: his peculiar attitude can flourish only where the rules of conformity are not too binding. Humor would thrive in an atmosphere that released everyone's idiosyncrasies and thus fostered fresh observations and thought.

That the liberated personality of the modern man did most often run riot is a general aspect of the age, artistically viewed. The prevalence of the baroque in art and literature is almost coextensive with the period of the Renaissance. From the free play of imagination and fancy, shot with the impulses of an adventurous intelligence, there arose in the various fields of self-expression the ardors, refinements, whimsicalities, and excesses which are so typical of the time. An ambitious straining after brilliancy is discernible in most characteristic products of the mind of the English Renaissance; everywhere a search for the new and intense put the humdrum safety of plain lines and unsophisticated language in jeopardy. Literary fashions like Italianism, Euphuism, conceits, "metaphysical" poetry can be matched by analogous symptoms in architecture, painting, decoration, gardening, manners, and dress. The baroque taste is thus connected by deep-laid affinities with that energy of mental realization and that zest for fresh experience, of which humor is, on a different plane, a no less conspicuous sign. Moreover, such excesses would naturally prompt to action the craving for a healthy balance, which is the very soul of satire and comedy. The humorist, as a castigator of exaggerations, would not be short of opportunities in an age when intellectual individualism was rampant.

Further than that one should not be prepared to go. The recent fortune of the epithet "baroque," now applied freely to the whole development of Renaissance art and literature, might well involve us in a measure of confusion. There still lingers about the word the atmosphere of its former, more restricted, sense, in which ideas of oddity and whimsicality were almost exclusively predominant. Now in grotesqueness pure and simple, unconscious effects easily shade off into at least half-conscious ones; and the refinement in intensity, which along with the ardor and the exuberance is a frequent characteristic of the Renaissance, would tend to suggest that the lucid self-command implied in that artistic awareness should normally prompt our conjecture of a spice of intention, a willing exaggeration, a spirit not very distant from the soul of humor. If one followed that line of inference to the end, all the fanciful display which is spread out in the works of the period, whether literary or artistic, would be claimed for the domain of humorous or semihumorous expression. That would be, to say the least, a very dangerous conclusion. A genuine seriousness of purpose, often colored with religious zeal or emotional fervor, is deeply embedded among the motives of most typically baroque writers and artists. It is only when we have reason to doubt that entire seriousness, and for instance when the effort of strained modes of expression appears more or less automatic and perfunctory, leaving some room for the possibility of a self-mocking intent, that the question will indeed arise of the presence of subdued parody. All the Renaissance baroque is not to be annexed at one stroke to the field of the potentially humorous; but in Euphuism, for example, in the conceits, even in metaphysical poetry, we shall have to try to look for the modicum of humor compatible with a manner that apparently precludes the very idea of it.

Indeed, the heyday of the individual is just the background against which our theme should be viewed if the development of "humor" must be studied, as seems obvious at first sight, in its interrelation with the fortune of the theory of "humors." No doubt, the Renaissance spirit encouraged indulgence in the vagaries of temperament; and those vagaries, naturally enough, imparted a more actual, a more striking significance to the old doctrine of tempers and their physiological causes. It took some prevalence of oddities and whims for Ben Jonson to come out with a consistent thesis, that the comic writer was the champion of sanity against crooked "humorous" propensities—a modernized form of the classical notion of comedy. But while the study of humor, in its precise meaning, is inseparable from the tangled history of the name which was eventually specialized to connote it, other psychological elements than the traditional belief in "humors" did enter into the mental growth which we are trying to follow. The problem particularly associated with Jonson will not be lost sight of, and the contribution of his own or his contemporaries' ideas to the gradual realization of a special manner of pleasantry will be given due heed. However, a wider view must be taken of the relation between that process and the general influence of the revival of learning.

A prominent aspect of the latter movement was the increased complexity of thought. Startling prospects were opening on every side. At the same time as a distant past was being raised from the shadows and flooded with a brighter light that made it real and alive, the boundaries of the known world receded again and again over the surface of the earth and throughout the stellar spaces. The fresh acquisitions of knowledge, now superadded to the familiar data of the Middle Ages, modified them, corrected them, but did not destroy them. The modern and the medieval points of view were incorporated with each other through a series of compromises that underwent constant revision. Such momentous readjustments could not be effected in a short time; the old persisted by the side of the new. The mind of the sixteenth and that of the early seventeenth centuries are thus made up of different layers, and that essential heterogeneity goes a long way to explain the strange contrasts of the age, the conflicts to which so many divided souls bear witness. To a greater extent than in Italy and in France, literature and thought in England, true to the conservative instincts of the nation, preserved then the substance and the forms of the preceding centuries. The very facts would thus teach men a lesson in relativity. From the contradictions of ideas there resulted, not unbelief, but a modified way of believing in which a touch of skepticism can be detected. The mental world of an Erasmus or a Montaigne is to be accounted for in that way. A subtle shade of difference had sunk into the heart of things. The faith to which men clung was seen against a background of change that altered it in perspective; the present of culture linked up with the distant past of classical antiquity, and broke away from the more recent precedents of the Middle Ages. If we remember that humor thrives on mental complexities, that contrasts are its food, and that a duality of mental planes is the law of its being, we shall better understand how the Renaissance could give a decisive impulse to an instinctive growth, which had been so far but slow, irregular, and tentative.

One last remark may not be the least important. The temper of the Renaissance was not evenly and constantly that of fervent zeal and glowing optimism. From the difficulties of the adjustment that was to be made there arose, soon enough, all the shades of anxiety, doubt, or despair. The "pale cast of thought" is often conspicuous on the personalities of men who were "sad" in the Elizabethan sense, and sometimes in the modern sense as well. It is generally recognized that a perceptible darkening of prospects and moods set in with the end of the sixteenth century; and that the early seventeenth, in spite of a comforting assurance, secured at last, of political and national stability, owed some of its peculiar features to a soberness of tone and manners that, with representative thinkers, inclined not a little to melancholy. The age of Shakespeare's *Sonnets*, of *Hamlet* and *Lear*, of Donne and Marston, of Burton and Browne, had surely in its making a vein of reflection tinged with disenchantment; it could brood over problems of the flesh and the spirit, of good and evil, of life and death, until the joyous flush of a youthful civilization seemed gone. While the hope and the pride of national success were still paramount, a sense of frustration was already in the air.

Now it is a fact, though it may be superficially a paradox, that a serious temper is more conducive than a light one to the rich and interesting varieties of humor. Whatever promotes the growth of the inner life furthers the possible development of that other plane of meditative thinking, in relation to which our daily experience assumes the quality of a contrast, comic or tragic. Here again, the feeling of relativity, the very soul of humor, arose from the deepening of consciousness. As compared with the rosy world of childhood and youth, that of a reflective maturity is instinct with a silent significance; from it there radiates an ironical or pathetic comment upon early illusions. A survey of English literature, at the first glance, shows us that the vein of humor runs broadening out through the later Renaissance period, with sharper and finer shades as the seventeenth century comes upon the scene.

On the whole, therefore, it is safe to assert that the Renaissance in England did favor the development of humor much more than it may have checked or retarded it. The positive influence of the revival of learning upon that discreet but significant vein of thought should be traced less distinctly to the eagerness and the zeal, to the high aspirations and the lyrical fervor, which are the obvious aspects of the movement, than to some secondary attributes and side issues; it acted rather indirectly than directly. Essential, in that particular respect, were the intellectualization of moods, the new complexity of even average minds, the conflicts created, and the recoil from unguarded enthusiasms. In one way only could the influence be more direct: among the classical writers who assumed a refreshed appeal, Lucian was to be found, a great master of irony and humor; and to him, as to Aristophanes, the humorists of the English Renaissance were frequently indebted. Other certain or possible debts to Germany (Grobianism), France (Rabelais, Montaigne), Italy (Castiglione, Ariosto), or Spain (Cervantes) will be examined in due course.

Whether indirect or direct, the influence of the new learning stirred to life especially the more subtle spirit of humor. It would encourage a manner of pleasantry in harmony with the modern refinement of the mind; under its stimulus the properly humorous technique, the method of reserve and aptly managed implicitness would develop from the explicit and clumsy farce of the later Middle Ages. In vain had Chaucer been pointing the way; it took the mental progress of the sixteenth century to create the conditions in which a slyness equal to his own could cease to be the privilege of a few. With the Renaissance should be definitely associated the first of the two complexes of facts and tendencies which we are going to study —that to which we shall tentatively assign the label of "the humanist contribution." When a balance is struck, however, it may be finally found that the main body of English humor, not excluding its delicate shades, owed more to the raciness of a genius both native and national. Shakespeare was the greatest English humorist of the Renaissance; his work is shot through and through with its influence; but Shakespeare's creative power, in this special field as in all others, is spontaneous and independent, not derivative.

In this very respect, however, the fecundity of the Renaissance reasserts itself. That great revival was a central force; it was felt in all the provinces of intellectual life, and even stimulated the national vitality and consciousness. But the Renaissance, if it is to be coextensive with the growth of England's self, must not be regarded from too acute an angle; it is to be viewed in its real perspective, as a mental and social, no less than a literary, transformation, the roots of which strike deep into all the developments of the previous centuries. It thus appears no longer as the rediscovery of classical literature, but as the birth of modern Europe.

III. The Reformation

Can the dramatic change that took place at the same time in the religious life of England be related in some similar way to the progress of humor?

It seems hardly possible, at first sight, to assign it any but a negative influence upon such an object. Whatever view one may take of the Reformation on the spiritual plane, it assuredly brought about, on the psychological one, the concentration of a purpose that braced itself up towards a stricter practice. This is not a mood that will conduce to the lighter relaxations of the mind. A glance at the history of manners will apparently confirm the impression. The most significant aspect of the new faith in England was Puritanism; and the Puritan made a name for himself as the archenemy of laughter. He hated and denounced it in daily life no less than in the theater; a morose cast of features was the approved symbol of the tension within. The whim of a minority, Puritanism radiated out more or less over the temper of most. The national character itself thus received a stamp of grave earnestness, which was to remain for more than three centuries marked enough to be held as distinctive. The seriousness of the English, a byword among foreign observers, was traced by nonplussed visitors either to the climate or to the fact that having changed their faith, and still nursing a sense of reform, they needs must be more than normally conscious of their religion. In so far as humor is bound up with the spirit of mirth, one would be prepared to find that it had lost more than it gained by the rapid extinction of "merry England." The process could hardly work out differently. A vigorous dogmatism of the ethical kind will lay such stress on one prominent set of values that the perception of any other set, for instance that of the comic—will become very difficult. The spiritual crisis through which the English people went in the sixteenth century hardened its fiber, and so must have deprived it of some mental elasticity.

But other facts soon assert themselves. To begin with, "merry England" died harder than is generally thought, and the student of manners finds himself confronted with symptoms of its stubborn persistence in later ages, down to the Victorian period. Indeed, the diversities of human nature reappeared under the strain of an endeavor that meant to purify and unify it. Even the Puritan did not shake off the natural man; repression still left the banned tendencies a secret existence, which would break out on occasion. In his more easygoing companions, ethical zeal did not attempt an impossible mutilation of instincts; it sought for a compromise, which left all the tolerable elements among them some measure of free play. Between the godly and the ungodly there ever was a wide range of intermediate shades. In the very age when the new fervor of Protestant zeal was at its warmest, there did not cease to be a large demand for "cakes and ale." As a result, the spirit of mirth and the blitheness of a pleasure-loving disposition never grew so rare that the roots of comedy in the national temperament should dry up. The austere citizen might shake his fist at the playhouse; he even could have his way and shut it up for a while; but on a broader view of the period he is seen to have failed. The comic Muse was never more flourishing in England than during the century and a half that followed the Reformation, if the time—less than a score of years—during which the theaters were closed is left out of account.

This, of itself, would make one wonder whether after all the Reformation might not have exerted some favorable influence upon the perception of comic incongruities; and one way or another, the student is bound to fall back on the conclusion that it did. The vigor of English life was in no wise impaired by a religious change that braced up character and gave it a sharper edge. A close attention to the details of conduct did not tend to blur out the lines of the concrete world; it made them more definite. It is a trite remark that the spirit of Protestantism, far from slackening men's hold upon actual facts, strengthened it to such good effect that the Puritan found prosperity in the path of virtue. Realism as a bent of mind is first cousin to a practical turn; and on nothing will humor thrive more than on a realistic bent.[3] The firmer ethical will which was induced, at least in principle, by a stronger sense of individual responsibility would stimulate the perception of the inevitable conflict with the world and with one's self, and bring into stronger relief the forces and objects among which man, as a free agent, has to struggle. No less direct is the inner connection between humor and a full-grown individuality of temper—such an individuality as must arise from a revolution that placed the spiritual fate of each man in his own grasp and made his own judgment in matters of faith his chief guide. Here the Reformation and the Renaissance meet on the same plane; they both favored the self-assertion of the individual.

But the more obvious point is that, provided the wealth of natural tendencies is not hopelessly impoverished, a sane austerity of outlook will be rather favorable, in itself, to the growth of a reflective type of humor. Moral earnestness here links up with the intellectual seriousness which we stressed when surveying the aspects of the Renaissance. The Puritan spirit, by darkening man's prospect, by making the issue of spiritual life or death more dramatic, and by prompting the inner activity of self-examination, contributed to the deepening not only of the conscience but of the psychological consciousness itself; it increased the mental complexity and the faculty of thinking on two different planes which enter so largely into the constitution of humor.

The humorist, even when he merely plays on the surface of life, strikes out for himself, leaving the beaten track and the familiar landscapes. By reversing the process of expression, he creates a pregnant strangeness of outlook, where the data of experience assume the aspect of paradoxes. To venture upon such a course demands a possession of one's own thought and a solid personality, confirmed inwardly, proof against the disturbing effects of intellectual solitude. Originality is an erratic impulse; indulged exclusively, it will drive a thinker away from recognized bearings; it will make him wild, unintelligible.

[3] In fact, among the more prominent English or Scottish Reformers, many show in their writings a keen knowledge of the practical world, a sense of the oddness of life, and a gift of humorous expression. See below, chap. viii, sect. vii, n. 55.

In order to readjust the threatened balance, compensatory forces must ever be at work, piecing up and strengthening the ties by which our farthest sallies remain connected, were it only at long distance, with the fast positions of common certainty. Humorous individualism spells at least some moral independence, an actual responsibility of the man within. Interiority of some kind is the mental condition of humor. Now such a bent was the inevitable outcome of the process which the character of the English people underwent in the decisive century from Luther to Cromwell, when it acquired its final cast of features. Then did the Englishman conquer the captainship of his own soul.[4] Many kept from the ordeal an austere, a somewhat morose, brooding disposition; but in the sobered mood of the national mind there developed at the same time a pondering, reflective, noncommittal attitude, an expectancy and a reserve, in one word a relativity of thinking, which harmonized with a concrete perception of things, a habit of seeing the object itself, and both sides of the object.

Those tendencies together provide just the rough constituents of humor. If to them is added a sharper eye for the oddities and the contrasts than the majority of observers can claim, a measure of supple freedom under the mask of sluggishness, the man is marked out who will seize upon that material, instinctively shape and polish it, giving it the quiet glow that is outshone by the flash of wit but outlasts it, leaving with us a permanent gleam of suggestive significance.

[4] As to the captainship of his body, and that phlegm which is at least the physiological basis of humor, a word has been said in the first part of this study (Part I, chap. i). The major influences on this plane would be, of course, blood and climate. That the predominant element after all is not the physical but the intellectual one, an obvious remark may tend to show. All the main strands that went into the making of the English nation were of Northern stock. From the eleventh century, when the last invasion took place, the influences of the British land and the British climate were active, finally molding the temper of the race. The Englishman, ethnically speaking, was complete long before the Renaissance. Yet it took a more advanced stage in his mental progress to make him develop, as a normal feature, an actively humorous faculty. No doubt, humor in psychological tendencies and oral expressions must have antedated a good deal the emergence of the humorist in literature. Still, it is possible to say that if the sluggishness of the race, a feature of very long standing, prepared the ground for modern English humor, a moral maturation, the decisive aspects of which were the Reformation and the Renaissance, was necessary before that disposition could be brought to a head.

It would thus seem that there may have been some natural lack of affinity between the lighter, more explicit varieties of comedy and the inwardness of an ethical bent; but humor, properly so called, fares differently under the same test. The self-control of the humorist is very often, in common experience, associated with a staid, or even a saturnine, disposition. The spiritual decision by means of which England in the sixteenth century chose the religious form of her national life and set up for herself an ideal of sober earnestness did not check the ripening growth of her humorous gifts; on a balance being struck, it decidedly furthered the process. We can safely conclude that modern English humor owed at least as much to the Reformation as it did to the Renaissance.[5]

Under the combined influences of the Renaissance and the Reformation, the English genius quickly matured; it developed the exuberant vitality and the expansive youthful force which are revealed in the brilliant literature of the Elizabethan era. Involved in that progress was a clearer realization of its own powers. The method of humor, still used instinctively, began to assume the quality of a consciously handled instrument. Before the final stage could be reached, however, and humor, as a distinct category in aesthetics, could enjoy the common privilege of a separate name, the more lucid analysis of the Restoration and the Augustan age had to be brought to bear upon the less sophisticated product of Reformation gravity and Renaissance ardor.

[5] The sixteenth century, and chiefly its earlier half, owed to the combined effects of the Renaissance and the Reformation a peculiar atmosphere that could act favorably upon the growth of humor: the widespread sense of a legitimate, almost a necessary, reticence, a duality of meaning and purpose. The elite of scholars and reformers were taking strides in many directions ahead of the common man; they felt in possession of knowledge or truths which it would be possible to popularize only by degrees; they realized that outside the circle of the initiated, a disguised manner of speaking or writing was a natural precaution. Along with the frequent use of apologues, a tendency to humorous presentment would ensue. Even the forcible directness of most reformers left room for the tendency to work in.

CHAPTER VII

THE HUMANIST CONTRIBUTION

I. A Survey of the Field

IN HUMOR, as in other fields, the hundred years that followed Chaucer's death were to England a time of stagnation or relative decay. After the exquisite slyness of the *Canterbury Tales,* even the powerful and brilliant manner of Skelton—who prolonged the transition period into the first decades of the sixteenth century—looks very broad indeed. The task of the new age was to recapture the gift of *finesse* and reconcile it with the racy vigor of the native temperament. In the glowing furnace of the Renaissance the fusion was effected. A compromise was thus reached between a spontaneous realistic verve, the roots of which were as old as the originality of the English genius, and a fine reserve, a well-bred economy and delicacy, which could hardly be reached except through culture.

Culture was the contribution of the humanists; and examples of the most accomplished method of humor were offered at the same time by two eminent writers, one foreign but a cosmopolitan, the other English, united one to the other by a complex web of mental affinities. The mind of Erasmus, like that of Sir Thomas More, was steeped in the literature of antiquity; and their subtle handling of suggestive understatement can be traced in particular to the lessons of Lucian, the Greek master of irony.

From Italy as well there came a little later the refining influence of culture and the ideal of a self-possessed courtly behavior. Castiglione's *Cortegiano,* in Hoby's translation, brought home to several generations of would-be gentlemen the superiority of a polished wit and of a nice discretion in the management of the comic. The earliest formula of that seeming unconsciousness of effect which sums up the trick of humor can be found as early as 1561 in Hoby's *Courtier*.

The inspiration of humanism runs through the work of English writers who were definitely spurred to expression by the enthusiastic love of classical models. The brand of humor associated with the scholars, from Udall, the schoolmaster, and the "University Wits" to Sir Philip Sidney, the nobleman and knight, on the whole shows the predominance of a somewhat similar vein; here again the tone of pleasantry is colored by the knowledge of pre-existing patterns.[1]

Lastly, in France and in Spain the Renaissance had been awaking, directly or indirectly, a spirit of critical reflection. Rabelais, Montaigne, and Cervantes wrote in the light of a bolder reason that did not fear to take itself as the test and measure of all things. Their works are pervaded by an atmosphere of humor, unequally diffused and mixed with various elements. To trace their several influences on the English literature of the late sixteenth and early seventeenth centuries is by itself a sufficient piece of research, with which the hands of a student might well be full. We shall only try to define the temperaments of those great writers as humorists, and in a tentative way to sum up their possible contribution to an English development that does, one way or another, bear some affinities to their intellectual attitude.

It may seem illogical to examine first the influence that arose to work upon the instincts of the people, and next the spontaneous development of those instincts, governed by a tradition of long standing. One generally deals with the permanent, before one passes on to the transitory, causes. The reason why that order is followed is not only that it answers to a kind of dramatic progression, the stronger and more decisive factor being considered last; but even if chronology is given its due, there is much to be said for what one may call here the ante-

[1] That the humanistic influence, derived from the ancients, at times grew diffused enough to join, and merge in, the wider stream of popular pleasantry, can be shown by such collections as *Merry Tales, Witty Questions and Quick Answers* (1567), which "draws distinctly from literary sources, from Diogenes Laertius, Aesop, and Plutarch," with the consequence that "there is a corresponding decrease in vigour and effect" (F. O. Mann, Introduction to *The Works of Thomas Deloney*, Oxford, 1912, p. xxii).

riority of the Renaissance. In humor as in other fields, it took the initiative; and the rebirth of Chaucer's *finesse* under the stimulus of the humanists from More to Lyly might have proved in that respect of overwhelming importance, finally shaping the growth of literary pleasantry. Yet, just as on the stage the influence of Seneca and the imitation of ancient models, after doing what they could, were eventually pushed into the background by the rise of the native school of drama, so Shakespeare, the supreme humorist no less than the greatest dramatist of the age, drew his inspiration mainly from national sources. After the dynamism of the Renaissance had made itself fully felt, the last word belonged to the temper of the people. In humor and more widely in drama, the work of Shakespeare, eked out as it is by a powerful body of evidence from that of his direct predecessors and contemporaries, is the conclusive token of a successful national reaction; a synthesis indeed, in which the leaven of humanism was incorporated, but the vitality of which was due to its unfailing contact with the natural impulses of the English genius. It is a normal course to study the reaction after the action.

II. Erasmus, More

The life and the personality of Erasmus are related to England by so many links that we must not exclude him altogether from our survey. The *Praise of Folly* and the *Colloquies* are repositories of a fine, discreet humor, more often than of open, pungent satire. Such a complete mastery of the humorous method, although it owed something to the example of Lucian, must be seen primarily as the gift of temperament. Erasmus's essentially modern mind had gathered to the full, from an early age, the disillusioned wisdom of experience. To him the relativity of things was an intimate perception. A cautious, self-contained thinker, he steered clear of definite entanglements with either side in the great religious quarrel of his time; and although his veiled hints or slashing epigrams were doing mainly the work of the Reformers, he never actually fell into line with them. A supple, shrewd intelligence was thus allowed to play freely around the rich incongruities, the wrongs, and the absurdities of the world; and although the mockery at times has the audacity and some of the rankness of Rabelais, we are rather as a rule reminded of Lucian's keen, unruffled manner; or a gentleness of touch, the ghost of a lambent smile on features that play the comedy of simplicity and unconcern to perfection, call up the memory of Chaucer. An exquisite mixture of Dutch stolidity, French acuteness, and English realism, seasoned with individual wit, was thus offered to the international circle of scholars and to the cultivated public of Europe. That Erasmus was indebted to England for the beginning of that devotion to Greek studies that made him the leading light of the Renaissance is common knowledge; but the seed of humor was laid deep in his nature, and not of English sowing. That he was widely appreciated in England is no less certain.[2] His *Praise of Folly* could be enjoyed in the Latin text by practically all educated readers of either sex, before the English translation of 1549.[3] Owing to a mere accident, the book was written under the roof of his friend Thomas More; one cannot help investing the fact, however, with a special significance.

This delightful treatise is a triumph in the art of disguised expression. The fiction that Folly speaks is by itself an efficient means of implicit fun.[4] All values being upset, there develop both a comic contrast and a no less pleasant confusion between topsy-turvydom and normality; while ever and again the paradox releases its ironical soul: the hint of its actual truth, which convention and custom had obscured. The trick at the most superficial level creates a bewildering uncertainty; "I knew that none of you was wise enough, or rather enough foolish—I mistake, wise enough, not to agree with me." But at its deepest, the purport of the book is the radical irrationality of life. Through the light, irresponsible tinkling of Folly's bells, there are heard rich undertones, hints that start adventurous trains of thought. The finest, the subtlest humor of the following

[2] The pedagogic treatises of Erasmus and even his *Colloquies*, were used as textbooks in most English schools all through the sixteenth century (R. Pruvost, *Robert Greene et ses romans*, Paris, 1938, pp. 51-52).

[3] *The Praise of Folly. . . .* Englished by Sir T. Chaloner (London, 1549).

[4] For the social and psychological background of this treatise, see B. Swain, *Fools and Follies during the Middle Ages and the Renaissance* (New York, 1932).

centuries, the audacious slyness of Sterne, the elusive detachment of Lamb, are all adumbrated in that searching analysis of the madness that goes by the name of reason. Under the indulgent smile that hardly leaves the author's imagined face lurks a cool, clear-sighted pessimism; four centuries later the art of Anatole France will live on no other fund of cynical philosophy; but here the grace of an almost poetical fancy, some of the jolly mirth of Aristophanes, at times soften the deadly Lucian-like irony. The tone rises, at the end of the first part, to a noble, enthusiastic picture of the bliss that dwells in the self-forgetfulness of genuine faith—a passage one would like to link up with the influence of More upon his friend; and the lesson is conveyed, in no indirect words, that true Christianity is more akin to folly than to human wisdom. All through, the ease and economy of the manner cannot be bettered; each word tells, and the genius of implicit raillery hovers over everything.

No more fertile leaven than Thomas More's *Utopia*[5] was cast into the seething mind of the Renaissance; and no more attractive pattern of gentle humor guided the mental forces that were shaping the English instinct of that special mode in self-expression. The book was widely read—was it not, as the title of the English edition of 1597 puts it aptly, "a most pleasant fruitful and witty work"? Indeed, it has the winning quality of charm; the more so to us as the quaintness of Robinson's English still enhances More's invention and subdued raillery.

The raillery and the free play of imagination are of course a transparent veil for the deep earnestness of a generous mind. So serious is the social and human purpose that it breaks out repeatedly into impassioned though controlled utterance; and those direct appeals to the reader's sense or sensibility are chiefly frequent in the second part. In the first the atmosphere of humor is almost unbroken. The emotional germ of the work is More's indignation at the sight of an oppressive and cruel world, his longing for the sweet reasonableness of a just

[5] Probably written in 1515-1516, published in 1516; soon had a second edition (1518), which is the standard Latin text; translated into English by Ralph Robinson in 1551.

order. But inherent in his thought is the stubborn lesson of experience, the clear perception of the thousand and one obstacles in the path of progress. The conflict of desire and resignation is transcended by the wisdom of the sage, who clings to a simple faith in man. But the two clashing intuitions, that of the security of hope and that of its fragility, are ever preserved and held before his consciousness; their mutually destructive force is the motive power that gives animation to the book; and their duality creates the two mental planes, from one to the other of which the pranks of humor are constantly shifting. The idea of relativity is thus the subtle soul of the whole treatise; an idea in which the intellectual position of the Renaissance is, as it were, contained. A sudden enlargement of all limits had accompanied the great revival; the classical antiquity was a distant golden background to the schoolmen's narrow certainties; after the discovery of a new continent the frontiers of the known had melted into the possibilities of the unknown. But scholarship assigned as many bounds as it raised expectations. The essence of ancient learning was reason; and reason taught the unreason of all things. Opinions differed, and the prophets had always been outnumbered by the fools. While More keeps quietly the tenor of his way, hinting at the stupidity of war, at the fearful excesses of legal punishments, sketching out his sensible community, he knows, and makes no mystery of it, that he is casting pearls before swine. There never was such an aftertaste of pessimism to a Utopia. "For it is not possible for all things to be well, unless all men were good. Which I think will not be yet these good many years."[6] And how can a shrewd thinker, fed on the marrow of ages, ward off the sting of self-criticism? "While that I go about to remedy the madness of others, I should be even as mad as they."[7]

Still, slyness has its way, soothing the disappointment of fond hopes and enlivening the glamor of persistent dreams. Hythloday's relation was so convincing that a professor of theology, we are told, wanted to rush at once to the Utopian land. Unfortunately, through some oversight no one had

[6] Arber's *English Reprints* (London, 1869), p. 65.
[7] *Ibid.*

thought of inquiring about the way. More instinctively makes use of that matter-of-fact precision of detail which instils a scientific aroma into the fancies of humor. Did Hythloday say that the river Anyder was five hundred paces broad? No, the report is not correct; he spoke, in fact, only of three hundred paces. Who can resist the evidence of such candor? Of course, a community of goods would imply dreadful consequences; it would destroy "all nobility, magnificence, worship, honour, and majesty, the true ornaments . . . as the common opinion is, of a commonwealth"; but, More quietly remarks, "many things be in the Utopian weel public, which in our Cities, I may rather wish for, than hope after."[8] Swift will appropriate several of the tricks whose efficiency is here demonstrated: each of Gulliver's successive voyages begins with the same display of familiar, technical normality; the language of the Utopians adumbrates that of Brobdingnag. More's "Printer" apologizes to the Reader for not yet giving him a key to the mysterious words he quotes; "but I trust, God willing, at the next impression hereof, to perform that, which now I cannot . . . , to exhibit perfectly unto thee, the Utopian alphabet. . . ."

All through the delightful little book a soul of gentle irony is present and active or makes its distant influence felt; and more or less plainly the author confesses to an admixture of fun in seriousness, for which, wanting a name, he uses the labels ready at hand. The tone is first of all set by Hythloday, the worthy teller of the tale—the thin cloak under which More hides himself and through which he is not unwilling to be descried: "All things that you said," Hythloday is told, "were spoken so wittily and so pleasantly."[9] But the same temper—as luck will have it—prevails with the Utopians: "The people be gentle, merry, quick, and fine-witted."[10] They feed their humor on the proper food, being "delighted with Lucian's merry conceits and jests";[11] and they have "singular delight and pleasure in fools. . . ."[12]

The affinity of humor with kindliness—one that being natural, but by no means necessary, asserts itself very often but not

[8] *Ibid.*, p. 162.
[9] *Ibid.*, p. 55.
[10] *Ibid.*, p. 118.
[11] *Ibid.* p. 119.
[12] *Ibid.*, p. 126.

always—is here illustrated, as in Chaucer's work, and if anything even more plainly. The charm of More's manner is largely made up of a sweetness that seems ingrained in a simple, modest, loving temperament—a simplicity the more attractive as it is bright with the sharpest sense of things; the light vein of mirth, inseparable as it is from the deeper thought of the moralist, is of a piece as well with the gentle disposition of the man, whose affection for his friends and cheerful family life are revealed through many an episode or hint.

III. Italy and Castiglione

Modern English humor is the rich amalgam of two main elements: a delicate slyness, a *finesse*, of which Chaucer was already a brilliant master, the secret of which was all but lost, to be gradually recovered; and a vein of racy realism, which had cropped up again and again in the literature of England from the earliest beginning. The latter is truly a national strain of purely indigenous growth; and though many writers managed to make excellent use of it in their search for literary effects, it was peculiarly rife in the spontaneous expressions of the people. Although the development of the former was partly natural, bound up indeed as it was with the progressive refinement of English mental life, it owed something at the same time to influences from abroad. While the wealth of the concrete world was to the British, from the first, an intuition, an experience, and a treasured possession, they could be with profit trained to a dexterous slyness in the handling of comic hints. With Chaucer the examples of a lucid, shrewd perception of humorous values may be traced to the lesson of French artistic detachment and adroitness. But France was not the only country where culture had been growing relatively faster than in England and whose temper bore perhaps a quicker affinity to intellectual nimbleness. Italy, in both these respects, was at least on a par with France; in most fields the initiative of the new departures that by their interrelation make up the Renaissance belonged to Italy. It is no surprise to the student that Italian models should have played a part in stimulating the growth of English *finesse* and loosening the various complexes that still commonly tied it up in the sixteenth century.

Of course Italian literature from an earlier period had a humorous tradition of its own. Although Pulci's *Morgante Maggiore* (1488) was the first signal example of the modern burlesque, more important than the parody is its manner—a quiet good-natured tone, an apparent unawareness of any disrespectful intention. The method was used at practically the same time to very good purpose by Boiardo (*Orlando Innamorato*, 1495) and shortly afterwards, not quite so efficiently perhaps, by Ariosto in his more famous *Orlando Furioso* (1516). But even Ariosto's poem was not translated into English before the end of the sixteenth century. The lesson of its gentle, discreet raillery, among more brilliant merits, may not have been lost upon individual writers, who read it in the Italian original, until Sir John Harington's translation (1591) made it quite accessible; still, the development of English humor during the central part of the Renaissance period can hardly be regarded as materially indebted to it. The case is altogether different with B. Castiglione's prose treatise, *Il Cortegiano* (1528), which Sir Thomas Hoby's translation (1561) made at once, and for several generations, actually popular in England.

Everything contributed to heighten the appeal of that work to men whose minds obeyed the promptings of the Reformation no less than those of the Renaissance. Attractively written in a lively style of dialogue and anecdote, the *Courtier* is a staid, moralizing survey of a subject, the education and manners of a gentleman, that was uppermost in the thoughts of all men with any social pretension. While showing some slight traces of Italian freedom, it more than justified itself to the most exacting readers by its transparent honesty and genuine refinement. How its description of the accomplished man of the world entered into the very ideal of late sixteenth-century England and nourished the teaching of moralists, pedagogues, and poets from Ascham to Spenser deserves an inquiry by itself. Our object is only to emphasize a single aspect of the theme: the stress laid on the characteristic manner of well-bred, courteous pleasantry.

Sir Walter Raleigh's pregnant preface to the modern reprint of Hoby's *Courtier* has aptly described the indebtedness of Elizabethan comedy to the whole school of Italian writers, among whom Castiglione is the most brilliant, who "shaped the dialogue for argumentative and dramatic purposes."[13] The debt with which we are here concerned, though more restricted, is no less essential. Hoby's graceful, easy English matches to perfection the matter of the Italian treatise; and the whole work breathes a spirit which encourages politeness, attention to others, the suppression of self. Such tendencies, and especially the last, have an aesthetic bearing. Just as good manners will repress the selfish display of the natural man, well-educated persons will have a fondness for understatement. We cannot then wonder that in the Second Book, devoted to the proper way of jesting, a doctrine should be taught which sets in full light the superiority of the more subtle and more implicit varieties of the comic. Something must be left to the reader or the audience; even when counterfeiting people for the sake of creating a laugh, the proper way is to be discreet, "always keeping the estate of a gentleman, without speaking filthy words, or doing uncomely deeds, without making faces and

[13] A passage is so close to our point in this chapter that it must be quoted in full: "At the time when Hoby's *Courtier* was published, and during the ensuing years, the favourite characters of our native Comic Muse were Ralph Roister Doister, Diccon the Bedlam, Huff, Ruff, Snuff, and Grim the Collier of Croydon. The speeches that she best loved were loud lies and vain boasts; her chosen actions were the frustrated clouting of old breeches, the rank deceits of tricksters and parasites, the rough and tumble of clown, fools and vice in villainous disorder. Yet this same English comic stage was soon to echo to the wit of Beatrice and Benedick, of Rosalind and Orlando. The best models of courtly dialogue available for Lyly and Shakespeare were to be sought in Italy: not in the Italian drama, which was given over to the classical tradition, but in just such natural sparkling conversations as were recorded in the dialogue form of Italian prose. And of these the best are to be tasted in *The Courtier*. It matters little if the English courtly dramatists be found to have taken none of their many jests from Castiglione; without appropriating passages from his book they might yet learn his dramatic verisimilitude, his grace and polish of manner, to use it for their own ends. So that Castiglione, Bembo, Aretino, Gerazzo, Pasquier, Speroni, and many others of those who shaped the dialogue for argumentative and dramatic purposes, may fairly claim a place in the genealogy of English comedy" (*The Book of the Courtier* . . . , with an Introduction by Walter Raleigh, London, 1900, pp. lxxxiv-lxxxv).

antics, but frame our gestures after a certain manner, that whoso heareth and seeth us, may by our words and countenances imagine much more than he seeth and heareth, and upon that take occasion to laugh."[14] Both understatement and overstatement are tricks to be recommended, "as when to increase or diminish, things be spoken that uncredibly pass the likelihood of truth."[15] Indeed there is "an honest and comely kind of jesting that consisteth in a certain dissimulation, when a man speaketh one thing and privily meaneth another." An example suggests itself naturally, "when with a grave and dry speech in sporting a man speaketh pleasantly that he hath not in his mind. . . . There is like unto this manner a certain witty and kind dissimulation, when a man . . . that is wise maketh semblant not to understand that he doth understand."[16]

The last pieces of advice have brought us near enough to the central trick of humor—the severing of the normal link between meaning and expression in jokes. But we get still nearer as we proceed: "There be certain other jests that be patient and spoken softly with a kind of gravity."[17] And finally: "Beside these respects he that will be pleasant and full of jesting, must be shaped of a certain nature apt to all kind of pleasantness, and unto that frame his fashions, gestures and countenance, the which the more grave, steady and set it is, so much the more maketh it the matter spoken to seem witty and subtil."[18] This passage is the sure token of a decisive intuition; not only is a serious bearing in jests recommended, but the reason for it is explained: such an attitude sets off the joke, makes it appear "more witty and subtle." Now, wit and subtlety are the two chief virtues which Castiglione is never weary of praising. So a serious countenance, whatever the time or place, should be preserved in pleasantry because it will sharpen the point and increase the efficiency of the joke. In other words, the humorous method, all things being equal, is of superior value to the more explicit manner. At that early date (1561 for Hoby's translation), the how and the why of

[14] *Ibid.*, p. 162.
[15] *Ibid.*, p. 179.
[16] *Ibid.*, p. 183.
[17] *Ibid.*, p. 184.
[18] *Ibid.*, p. 190; these words are spoken by a Mr. Bernarde. Of course Quintilian had said something to the same effect (see chap. iii).

humor are thus clearly presented to English readers—readers who, before the book lost its hold on the public, were exceedingly numerous and included the elite of several generations. Only the words which Shakespeare will put in Falstaff's mouth: "a jest with a sad brow,"[19] will show as sure a grasp of the inner process of humor. After those two revealing statements, more than a century will pass before the acute analysis of Addison gives proof of a critical realization at all comparable.

No doubt the progress of humor is not primarily to be measured in terms of the full consciousness or the adequate description of its method. Although a genuinely humorous intent is necessarily aware of itself, some degree of spontaneousness is implied in the creative activity of the humorist; the greatest period of English humor will be the eighteenth and the early nineteenth centuries—the time when a fully realized perception of the manner is still balanced by the freshness of the discovery, by some wonder and some uncertainty as to the nature of the thing itself; whilst with the staleness and sophistication of our own age, for instance, humor has lost something of its vitality. It was not the gradual revelation of a trick that made humor a leading constituent of the English genius; but the general progress of thought, the more supple and assured sense of original mental power, and the growing awareness of a special mode of pleasantry, linked up with a peculiar attitude of the mind, with a subtle detachment and a mastery of instinctive reactions. Castiglione's analysis was by no means the guiding light by which the development of English humor actually took place. But by emphasizing the essential importance of self-restraint in refined pleasantry, it very probably stimulated the growth of the manner and helped it towards that realization of itself, but for which it would not have acquired its name, the badge of its definite individuality. The Italian critic's widely read treatise must have contributed to further that half-conscious wish for the coining of a new word, or for the stamping of an old one with a new meaning, which

[19] *2 Henry IV*, V, i, 92.

was the active permanent impulse at the back of the evolution of the term "humor."[20]

IV. Lyly and Euphuism

It would be tempting here to adduce in a body the so-called "University Wits" as likely representatives of the humanist influence. But the facts do not allow of any such simple argument. The writers who are thus usually labeled would not, from our point of view, be necessarily grouped together. Humor, indeed, is a wonderful test of temperament, a searcher of secret instincts and deep-laid tendencies. Genuine as must always have been the effect of a university education upon impressionable minds in their young years, some of their powers would escape the controlling influence of classical culture; and among such, none more naturally than a stubborn raciness rooted in a national fund of concrete realism. No doubt with such writers as Lyly or Sidney and, less obviously, with some of their contemporaries, a distinguished shade of humor can be traced to the atmosphere of the schools and to the spirit of humanism; in all those writers the Renaissance made itself felt so overwhelmingly that it reached the very sources where comic invention originated. But even in what regards Sidney, the refinement of the scholar failed to neutralize all the germs of innate realism, as the *Arcadia* plainly shows. And when we come to a Nashe, although his works do bear the plain mark of a university schooling, they must be classed unhesitatingly, in so far as humor is concerned, among the products of the popular inspiration.

The relation of John Lyly to humor is not easy to define. To say bluntly that he was a humorist may well take a reader's breath away. He had in his constitution many trends that would simply clash with the very purpose of humor. The moral seriousness of his *Euphues* is not all a pretence; he was sincerely aware of the values that go to the making of the earnest life. He was not indifferent, either, to the conditions

[20] "Humor" is never used, in fact, for "pleasantry" in Hoby's English text. According to the Oxford Dictionary the first example of the word in that sense dates back only to 1682. The subject will be dealt with at length in a further part of this inquiry.

of success, literary or social, and knew when a misplaced joke could lose a writer the favor of the Court. At the same time, his nature was spontaneously prone to a gentle play of wit, and a subtle atmosphere of raillery wraps up the greater part of his work. Comedy, before he turned to writing for the theater, was to him an instinct, which he obeyed sometimes frankly, more often in elusive, indirect ways. Of the comic flavor that enlivens most of his writings, the quality in general is so discreet and the method so reserved that it can broadly be assigned to the category of humor.

But Lyly's outstanding literary characteristic is his "Euphuism"; and what are we to make of such a feature? To associate humor with it seems at first a rank paradox. The pedantry of labored devices, of far-fetched similes, is of course a major trait of the Euphuistic style; it forces language into channels of convention and artifice; its stiffness is as distant as possible from the mental freedom in which the humorist lives and has his being. Only the total lack of a sense of humor could apparently account for such an aberrant phase in the history of literary fashions. No wonder if the only recognized link between attitudes so glaringly contrasted should be that the Euphuist did often prompt comic writers to triumphs of not unmerited satire.

Still, we must set full store by the fact that the popularizer —though not the creator—of that style, John Lyly, was in other respects a shrewd critic of affected manners; that his work shows a thousand proofs of a delicate perception of the comic. Such psychological evidence cannot be lightly dismissed; the same mind must have been active at the back of all its expressions. Could Lyly's awareness of excess, of the ridiculous and the grotesque, have been completely paralyzed by the fanaticism of the faddist, or by the ambition of the pushing writer? That awareness, even repressed, must have been obscurely present.

If, turning to the *Euphues,* we reconsider the problem from that angle, it assumes a new aspect. Between Euphuism and humor some analogies can be discovered after all. In the psychological world, as is well known, very few incompatibilities are really binding. But that is yet short of the truth; from one of those terms to the other, partial affinities establish a possible field of contact. Both are sophisticated tricks of expression and imply a duality of meaning. The motive for the duality is, on the face of it, very different: humor is free, Euphuism seems to be tied, a slave to a stubborn, desperate earnestness. But is it indeed? A serious countenance has sometimes been a mask. Is it inconceivable that Lyly's tongue, when he wrote his most extravagant stuff, may have been more or less in his cheek? He might be innocent of any irony at first, but who will assert that he was to the end? Could he be so impervious to some major artistic values, and blind to the extreme affectation of what he was penning? A conjecture it must all remain; but who will insist that passages such as the following were written without an inner reserve, the ghost of a mocking intent, and did not share, to any degree, in the quality of subtle mystification?

But as the Cameleon, though he has most guts, draweth least breath, or as the Elder tree though he be fullest of pith, is farthest from Strength; so though your reasons seem inwardly to your self somewhat substantial, and your persuasions pithy in your own conceit, yet being well weighed without, they be shadows without substance, and weak without force. The bird *Taurus* hath a great voice, but a small body; the thunder a great clap, yet but a little stone; the empty vessel giveth a greater sound than the full barrell.[21]

Or again:

The filthy Sow when she is sick, eateth the Sea-crab, and is immediately recured; the Tortoise having tasted the Viper, sucketh *Origanum* and is quickly revived; the Bear ready to pine licketh up the Ants, and is recovered; the Dog having surfeited, to procure his vomit, eateth grass and findeth remedy; the Hart being pierced with the dart, runneth out of hand to the herb *Dictamum*, and is healed. And can men by no herb, by no art, by no way, procure a remedy for the impatient disease of Love?[22]

Assuredly, the conjecture must not be pressed too hard. Literature is before all a matter of experiments. Lyly tried his

[21] *Euphues*, Arber's edition (Westminster, 1900), p. 45.
[22] *Ibid.*, p. 61.

hand at Euphuism in order to score a hit, and he scored. What he was doing, others had done, and he never thought that he was going much further. While straining every nerve to gather ingenious similes from natural lore, he must have been engrossed by the excitement of the hunt; relishing the quaintness of his instances, he need not have felt that they were funny as well. The sense of fun is essentially relative. It has suffered extraordinary eclipses. Again and again, preciosity in language and style has run to unbelievable excesses; what will not a would-be wit do, speak, or write, what will he not swallow and digest, just to stand among the elect? The readers who liked Lyly's affectation, the writers who imitated it, took it, we are to presume, seriously. The awe with which classical rhetoric was invested in seminaries of learning, haloed round many extravagances of that kind; a special scale of values, in the minds of masters and pupils, attached to the exercises and declamations of the schools. The compilers of the old bestiaries had not been critically inclined; their gullibility knew no bounds. Even to the cultivated few, the limits of the wonderful in the sixteenth century were uncertain. Lastly, Euphuism does not reside only in comparisons; it is an elaborate manner, the essence of which would be symmetry or rhythm; and this is not comic, unless pushed, as often happens, to obvious exaggeration. Still, the pleasure with which such conceits were handled by the writer and that with which the reader enjoyed them may not have been usually unmixed; and in that complex of feeling, a tickled sense of their probable absurdity would not be at all out of place.

Such is, all things considered, our final impression. Euphuism was decidedly not humor, but did not run counter to the mood whence humor is born, and it developed in some respects on a similar basis. Along with a desire to strike and dazzle through the brilliance of verbal display, it implied a quaintness of invention and an obscurely mystifying intent; the whole mixture being maintained in a serious key by an additional influence, the professed and unfeigned wish to edify and to instruct. It was a game of fancy and words, largely but not completely earnest, in which the author himself tasted a flavor not unlike that of secret comedy, but whose success with the uncritical public emphasized only its conceited cleverness and eclipsed its undercurrent of amused bravura. Being partly an equivalent of, or a substitute for, humor, it might lead up, in a way, to the real thing—not simply through the channel of reaction, negatively, but positively as well. From the aesthetic point of view, it gave style a lesson in deferred, indirect meaning and conscious artifice; it experimented in *finesse,* and was a training for the prospective humorist—as soon as he could liberate himself from the spell of his own preposterous pranks.

That Lyly was able thus to get free, even in his *Euphues,* is a reasonable assumption on the strength of his whole record as a man and as a writer. His plays have genuine and charming touches of humor. They breathe a spirit of discreet comedy, suitable as well to the scholar in him as to the courtier, the moralist, and the humanist; his object is "to breed soft smiling, not loud laughing."[23] That seemly, delicate mirth is in keeping with the graceful, somewhat unsubstantial originality of those works. The few attempts at a more popular kind of fun (as in *Midas* or in *Mother Bombie*) are not happy; they lack real robustness and verve; their roots are not in the fund of national raciness, in the realistic instincts from which Lyly had cut himself loose, but rather once more in classical tradition and the example of Plautus. Altogether different is the atmosphere of light merriment in *Campaspe,* a play full of genial quaintness; or the character of Pandora *(The Woman in the Moon),* an ironical sketch of a woman ruled by the stars, whose patroness is fickle Cynthia; or again, the delightful scenes between Venus and Vulcan *(Sapho and Phao).* It is not only in such episodes that Lyly's intellectual, imaginative sense of the comic really expresses itself, but all over those classical plays, where a kind of youthful amusement arises from the actuality lent to famous, legendary themes and persons. We feel carried along by the easy flow of a good humor, enlivened with a properly humorous spice, the source of which is the pleasure the scholar enjoys in calling to life again the heroes,

[23] Prologue to *Sapho and Phao,* in R. W. Bond (ed.), *Complete Works of John Lyly,* Oxford, 1902.

the gods, and the grotesque figures of story. No frame of mind could be more typical of the Renaissance.

As a disease of the fashionable taste, the wide success of Euphuism created an atmosphere unfavorable to the development of humor, whose breath is sanity. But it contributed something to mental progress, a condition of all intellectual growth; it encouraged subtlety and taught writers to play with expression, while preserving an inner freedom of intent. From Euphuism to humor the way is long and not straight; yet the passage could be made easily enough: it just took writing the same stuff in a spirit of slight self-mockery, instead of pure, stiff pretentiousness. The disillusioned Euphuist, if a humorist, will be a competent one. Shakespeare was to illustrate the change most markedly. The author of *Euphues* seems often ready to effect it; and although he never takes the decisive step, he wraps up his display in a manner that somehow awakes the suspicion of a hidden purpose. Was he not thinking of himself when he described his young hero as "merry but yet so wary"[24]—the wariness, indeed, in this field more than disguising the mirth? The phrase, which is primarily meant of moral behavior, would not badly fit his own attitude, all through the egregious performance which a twinkle of slyness so felicitously relieves now and then.

V. Greene, Sidney, Peele

The case of Robert Greene is rather different. The temperament of realism was in him; it broke out again and again, especially during the latter part of his career. He might have been an early representative of the national, popular vein of storytelling, a direct predecessor of Deloney. His manner, when free and spontaneous, is no less picturesque than that of Nashe; and of that rich sense of concrete comedy, humor is naturally no mean part. Well may the "Cony-Catching" pamphlets, *A Quip for an Upstart Courtier*, *The Blacke Bookes Messenger*, claim an ethical purpose: the spirit of jollity is alive there and jogs on as it can with its strangely uncongenial fellow. In Greene's plays the fun wells up here and there from a genuine spring. Of outstanding interest, in that respect,

[24] P. 33.

is *Friar Bacon and Friar Bungay* (1589?).[25] The mind that reveals itself there is English to the core, with a fresh perception of the flavor of country life, a sense of pure, noble womanhood, and an instinctive dislike of cheap, unnatural exaggeration: the modern reader is almost inevitably led to suspect that the obvious imitation of Marlowe's *Doctor Faustus* is discreetly tinged here and there with the spirit of quiet parody—just as *Alphonsus* is perhaps a sly skit on *Tamburlaine*. It has been pointed out that Miles the poor scholar, and to a less extent Ralph the "King's fool," in *Friar Bacon,* adumbrate the clowns of Shakespeare.[26] Greene's dramatic humor, though not abundant, shows a sympathy with life and a respect for the essential decencies that would tend to heighten its representative, national quality.[27] Again, a delicate liveliness will crop up in the novels: the pleasant story put in the mouth of Chaucer *(The Mourning Garment)* has little of the coarseness of Boccaccio; and the heroines in *Mamillia* or *Gwydonius* possess some of the sprightly charm, as they show all the unblemished honesty, of a Portia. But those features of Greene's work are largely neutralized by inferior aspects of classical or Italian tradition, the source of which seems to lie in the intoxication of ill-digested humanism. His Euphuistic style is stiffer, more clumsy, and even more artificial than Lyly's. His surrender to the demons of rhetorical or of didactic writing thus very often plays havoc with his undeniable gifts. There are few touches of humor in the more ambitious part of his output. The conflict of his ill-adjusted tendencies and the repression under which in certain respects he labored can be guessed at times, when his mischievous mood indulges in a parody of the very patterns which he had so submissively made his own. He pokes ironic fun at Euphuism;[28] while the conventions of

[25] Less stress is to be laid in that respect on *James the Fourth,* although the humorous vein, and an undoubtedly national one at that, crops up here and there in the play, with the clowning of Slipper for instance, and more markedly, in the Induction, with the delightful figure of Bohan, whose Scottish slyness might almost be described as "pawky."

[26] R. Pruvost, *Robert Greene et ses romans* (Paris, 1938), p. 563.

[27] When all is said, perhaps too much is made of Greene's humor by both G. E. Woodberry and C. M. Gayley in their very suggestive essays on his "Place in Comedy" and on *Friar Bacon,* in *Representative English Comedies from the Beginning to Shakespeare* (New York, 1903).

[28] In *Menaphon;* R. Pruvost (ed.), *op. cit.,* pp. 364-65.

courtly love and of Petrarchism are very successfully burlesqued in *Francesco's Fortunes.* When a final balance is struck, Greene's interesting contribution to the growth of English humor turns out slighter than it might well have been.

Not so Sir Philip Sidney's. A writer of such exquisite culture and high principle, no less refined in his tastes than he was scrupulous in his life, would be expected to have staked all on a straining after heroism and beauty. But although his zeal sometimes outran his discretion, as when he wrote to the Queen to dissuade her from a French marriage, his moral eagerness had nothing priggish about it; he knew how to unbend, the more so as the austerity of his heart and thought was unfeigned; and a lambent humor enlivens the serious, didactic eloquence of the *Apology for Poetry,* as well as the romantic fancy of the *Arcadia.* There hovers in the background of those works a charm of youthful, well-bred gaiety; and as Sidney's wit possesses the virtue of reserve, it is spiced with the implicitness of the properly humorous method. In the *Apology* the playful spirit breaks out here and there, as at the beginning and at the end; but it crops up in between through a sly, offhanded detachment, not unmixed with the conscious superiority of the man of the world, who can look down upon the professional vehemence of the literary hack. Congreve, one hundred years later, was to strike a somewhat similar note. The pleasantry here is not unworthy of the *finesse* of Erasmus; it takes distinctly after the newly recognized pattern of the humanist manner.

The leaven of delightful humor in the *Arcadia* is richer. It is as it were the efflorescence, the smile of a naturally charming imagination. A touch of pleasantry seems but the necessary ingredient of an accomplished tale. The ease and the simplicity are so convincing that they carry along with them the many tricks of language—the conceits, repetitions, parallelisms, puns, the traces of Euphuism, all the signs of a juvenile intoxication with words. But those excesses never run riot; a fine sense of measure, the discipline of a spontaneous art which is only another name for the inborn poise of temperament, subdue the mannerisms and keep the style sweet. As in *Love's Labour's*

Lost, the atmosphere of which the *Arcadia* sometimes recalls, we are aware that the exuberance of fancy is not its own end: the mind that revels in it sees beyond and through it. And into the world of idyllic freshness a balanced instinct of truth will bring elements of ironical realism; by the side of the princes and the fair ladies a compensatory impulse sets Damoetas, "the most arrant doltish clown." His wife Miso, his daughter Mopsa, are worthy of him; and the whole family, used as a foil, is the occasion of well-bred amusement that rarely commits itself to open satire. The note of Sidney's humor is almost always the reserve of a fine discretion. The doggerel poem in praise of the beauties of Mopsa lapses at times, no doubt, into the broad fun of a popular ballad; and this is one more reminder of the fact that Sidney's aristocratic temper was in no wise—as readers of *Astrophel and Stella* know—cut off from the full-blooded humanity of his time. We have realistic touches of deliberate farce: Damoetas "looks like an Ape that had newly taken a purgation."[29] Realistic, as well, and explicit is the episode of Dorus's courtship of Mopsa.[30] Still, the usual tenor of Sidney's wit is that of delicate hints and light innuendoes; here again, he belongs to the posterity of Erasmus and More. A typical instance, among many others, would be the passage where good old Kalander naïvely remarks that the world is aging, and things not getting better.[31] Even Damoetas, in his clumsy attempts to rise above his animal nature, is handled with not uncharitable irony, and his character looks at times like an altogether gentler sketch of Shakespeare's Caliban. And the playfulness is fused with a graceful invention, tender episodes, a chaste imaginative ardor, and the strokes of manly heroism, into the unique charm of that lovely romance.

George Peele, who loved Sidney and mourned over him so feelingly, had a vein of gentle satire in his constitution; no humor can be discovered in the graceful fancy of *The Arraignment of Paris;* but there is a good deal in *The Old Wives' Tale* (1595), where the conventions of romances are mocked

[29] Edited by Feuillerat (Cambridge, 1912), Book I, chap. xiii, p. 87.
[30] II, ii, 154-58. [31] I, x, 60.

with a light, implicit touch. The method of the parody—subtle and discreet—somewhat reminds the reader of Chaucer's *Sir Thopas:* a self-possessed irony handles exaggeration and over-statement to very good purpose. Rather excessive claims have been made for the originality and significance of Peele as a humorist.[32] Still, it is possible to agree that through his naturally refined manner he stands in a favorable contrast to much of the horseplay of the age; and that his humor, not being an additional motive but an essence incorporated in the whole work, is of a high artistic quality. The humorous streak in Thomas Lodge is quite as pronounced. The charm of his *Rosalynde* is conscious and smiling, though simple and fresh; and the lively passages between the heroine and her friend Aliena have a quality of sprightliness, enhanced by reserve and tact, that reveals the essential soul of sly, indirect pleasantry. Shakespeare's Rosalind will owe her namesake more than a name.

To look for humor in Christopher Marlowe would be proverbially a paradox: he set his pitch very far from the "conceits" of "clownage,"[33] and whatever may be thought of his full responsibility for the comic episodes in *Doctor Faustus,* they are but broad farce.[34] The comedy in the *Taming of a Shrew* is more genuine, but his association with the play mere conjecture. Marlowe's genius, vehement, lyrical, impassioned, had not learned to unbend and to smile at its own eagerness.[35]

[32] F. B. Gummere in C. M. Gayley, *Representative English Comedies from the Beginning to Shakespeare*, pp. 341-44.

[33] Prologue to *Tamburlaine.*

[34] The case is slightly different with Kyd's almost equally powerful and very popular drama, *The Spanish Tragedy* (acted 1588); an exceptional feature of the play being that no attempt whatever is made to relieve its tragic atmosphere by means of farce or comedy, unless a passing smile can be roused by the words of the Boy in III, v, and some sinister irony detected in Pedringano's losing battle with the hangman (III, vi). A flicker of grim irony, again, did probably light up for the groundlings Hieronimo's half insane "Hieronimo, beware! go by, go by!," which seems to have appealed so much to their sense of absurdity (III, xii, 819). And what phrase but "dramatic irony" could express the horror of the final episode, when in front of the actually stabbed bodies of their kith and kin, the spellbound spectators go on listening to Hieronimo's frantic outburst—a situation to be paralleled only from the records of the "Grand Guignol"?

[35] A word has been said above of the grounds upon which Nashe is to be studied rather with the literary expressions of the popular vein. Chapman's comedies will be part of the survey of humor in Elizabethan drama. The order

VI. France—Rabelais and Montaigne

During the later Elizabethan age and all through the seventeenth century, a substantial influence was exerted in England by three great foreign writers—Rabelais, Montaigne, Cervantes—whose personalities and works, otherwise very different, can be brought together in their relation to our subject. A distinctly humorous vein being with all three a more or less recognized element, they must not be excluded from this survey. But any attempt at assessing their actual contributions to the development of English humor with fulness and precision would be out of place here; the matter is so rich and intricate that it must be left to the specialist. All we can do is to try to estimate the impulse which each of those writers had in him to communicate, and which, broadly speaking, it is certain that he did communicate in the long run. Although that stimulus was spread over a long period—Rabelais antedated Montaigne by a half century; Montaigne, Cervantes by some years—and continued well beyond the final limit we have set to this study, it has seemed possible, for convenience' sake, to view jointly three distinct waves of influence which followed one another at intervals, and which, while they overlapped, can be regarded as contemporary only in a relative sense.

In so far as the growth of English humor is concerned, that Montaigne and Cervantes should be associated with the "humanist" tendency will probably seem natural enough. But that, in the same respect, Rabelais should be connected also with the same current, rather than with the complementary tide of popular realism, may well rouse some surprise. It is obvious that whatever view is taken of him, from this tide he cannot be wholly separated. Still, all things considered, the purely grotesque element in Rabelais is not the most pregnant aspect of his personality or of his message; the comic verve with

here adopted rests on the evidence of inner characteristics and affinities, the value of which is only relative. The cross sections thus established through the body of literature cannot be absolutely clearcut, and some overlapping, with a measure of arbitrariness, is inevitable. In the following section the stimulus given by Rabelais will be mentioned under the label of humanism, although the quality of his verve smacks so richly of the popular inspiration. On the contrary the *Grobianus*, while distinctly academic in its origin, will be regarded as one of the influences that fed the current of realistic English humor.

which his work is instinct has a soul of subtlety and of thought; and when the long wave of his influence in England culminated at last, that climax took place in the work of Sterne—the most quintessential and the shrewdest of English humorists.

Gargantua and the successive parts of *Pantagruel* were published between 1532 and 1564. Rabelais was to wait for an English translation till 1653. During some hundred-odd years the impact of his audacious imagination was received in England only by such readers as were able to approach him in the French text, or indirectly, and more widely, through that aura of vague significance which unread books have been known to possess and to which vicarious impressions and rumor are the keys. One way or another, we know on reliable authority that the first recorded mention of Rabelais in England occurred between 1567 and 1579, and that by the end of the century his influence had been powerfully felt.[36] Thenceforward he was to remain a permanent force in the background of English literary consciousness.

Rabelais's obvious motive and object is the joy, the delightful preposterousness of enormity. The characteristic method of his humor is overstatement. This, on the face of it, puts him in a different class from that of the subtle humorists, who play finely with the reserve of an expression pitched below the key of actual meaning. But Rabelais has an astonishing range; his fondness for the gigantic is the outward dress, the plain symbol of an inner wealth of free intent; the break with the normal scale of familiar experience signifies and introduces the independent movement of a mind untrammeled by use and wont; he is no more fully satisfied with the material size of his heroes and the hugeness of their world than Shakespeare is with the bulk of Falstaff. His robust coarseness is of a piece with his policy of exaggeration; by ignoring the common rules of reticence, he frees our instincts from mental convention and forces us to ask ourselves whether our system of moral values is not so fragile that a mere magnifying of proportions would upset it. All those pranks and fooleries of an apparently frolicsome imagination are controlled by a singularly cool brain; the han-

[36] See Huntington Brown, *Rabelais in English Literature* (Cambridge, Mass., 1933).

dling of unbridled fancy is masterly in its reserve; it never goes in any direction one inch further than the watchful, lucid sense of paradox and effect will advise.

One of the main aspects of the paradox is the apparent unawareness of verbal intoxication; Rabelais ever and again revels in an orgy of language. The concrete world pours itself out with its untold wealth, and the abundance of words, running parallel with that of things, even exceeds it. At the heart of the display reigns the sly spirit of realistic humor, posturing as an impassibility akin to that of the scientist. The diversity of creatures and the multiplicity of their names are facts which an observant mind, respectful of what exists, will fully take into account. This mode of the mock objectivity of the humorist finds its first signal example in the author of *Pantagruel;* and Sterne, two centuries later, will be its chief modern adept.

Meanwhile, the inner soul of significance is released; through innumerable hints the satire works itself out. The cloak of pedantry is worn only as a means of showing up pedantry itself; the stress laid upon words sets off a keen hunger for things; a thousand arrows pierce the ponderous conventions of medieval thought. The rebellious eagerness of the Renaissance pitilessly pursues the clumsy ghost of scholasticism. At bottom, in essentials, the message of Rabelais is not unlike that of Montaigne; with a more impassioned, a more single-minded ardor, that of a rationalism still almost immune from the wistful sense of intellectual relativity. How could such a bold, aggressive lesson be conveyed but under disguise? Prudence is the motive of the constant repression that sets upon the work of Rabelais the stamp of light-hearted, playful unreason; and the events of his life more than justify that caution. So he thinks, he writes ever on a double plane; and the humorous flavor of an inverted presentment, of a farce rich with philosophical comedy, is present everywhere.

As noted above, one of Rabelais's outstanding traits is the very frank emphasis laid on the physical aspects of human life, in a spirit, not of bitter humiliation and disgust as was to be the case with Swift, but of easy, genial, almost triumphant jollity. Of course such innocent though bold grossness was a clever cloak for an intellectual irreverence that played its more dangerous game under cover. But the epic breadth of Rabelais's peculiar cynicism answers to a geniune bent of his temper; it reveals a willing acceptance of the facts, all the facts, of living as a condition, not unwelcome, of man's unchecked development. The complete admission of animality is thus pregnant with a much richer meaning than would emanate from the rather coarse contrasts it directly produces; flouting the decencies liberates a silent protest against the narrowness of social ethics; stressing the body, in the heyday of the mind-intoxicated Renaissance, is a timely reminder of our dual nature. Both suggestions are indirect, and humorous. We have good reason to believe that Shakespeare knew something of Rabelais;[37] and indeed the artistic growth that created Falstaff may have been indebted to the magnetic stimulus of Gargantua's figure.[38]

It would be an obvious distortion of the facts to describe Montaigne's attitude as that of a humorist.[39] Bent on exploring in himself the strange ways of man, his purpose is set and serious, nonchalant as his manner may be. And while Rabelais will laugh outright, because laughter is "le propre de l'homme," it is but rarely that the author's imaginary features, conjured

[37] A book called *The Historie of Gargantua* appears in the Stationers' Register for December 4, 1594; probably a chapbook based on the legend and showing that it was then common property (J. Lindsay's Introduction in *The Metamorphosis of Aiax . . . by Sir John Harington*, ed. by Peter Warlock and Jack Lindsay, London, 1927).

[38] Among the writers who testify to the early influence of Rabelais in England, Sir John Harington deserves a special mention here. His acquaintance with "Rabbles" is certain, since he refers not only to him but to his work very precisely. Harington's *Metamorphosis of Aiax* (1596) bears all the marks of the humanist spirit, and of imperturbable humor. It is a learned, witty, mythological treatise upon a realistic theme: the advantage of improving the unsavory condition of privies by the simple device of the water-closet—the author's invention. While the propaganda is serious, the successful effort to keep the subject on a consistently dignified plane is an example of the mock-heroic method. At the same time, the implications of the manner link it up obviously with the popular strain. Harington's translation of the *Orlando Furioso* into English verse (1591) creates another association between his name and the general progress of humor. See the modern reprint of *Aiax*, edited by P. Warlock and J. Lindsay, and the latter's introduction, where the suggestion is made that Shakespeare may have alluded to the book in his revised *Love's Labour's Lost*, V, ii (Costard's words).

[39] The *Essais* were published in 1580 and 1588 (the third book). Florio's translation, ready in 1599 and probably seen by many, came out in 1603; the second edition is dated 1613.

up by us above the pages of the *Essais,* will wear even a flickering smile. Still, the book is enlivened with the flavor of something that, if it is not humor, is very nearly akin to it. The inner earnestness has nothing pedantic or dogmatic; it is all tempered with watchful self-diffidence, with the freedom of a cool, shrewd mind. And Montaigne's favorite theme will be naturally seasoned with a spice of amusement. At once the keynote is struck; "surely, man is a wonderful, vaine, divers, and wavering subject: it is very hard to ground any directly-constant and uniforme judgement upon him."[40] From the wealth of examples which illustrate that ever-reiterated text, there emanates a rich, concrete sense of the infinite diversity of our nature. A sober comedy plays itself out before us; in the experience either vicariously borrowed from books or gathered by the writer through life, much is quaint, with much that is absurd, touching, shameful, cruel; while first and foremost, human opinion appears in the prodigious range of its contradictions. Quiet and composed as the survey is, there lurks in it a shade of philosophical irony. The author stands at the center, inquisitive and tolerant; not detached, not indifferent indeed, but proof against the raw impulses of indignation or anger. His even tone cannot hide the gusto with which he dwells on the most surprising vagaries of custom and manners; but there is no room for more than a discreet tinge of enjoyment; the desire for truth, sure as it is to be baffled in the universal relativity of judgment, is too eager and subtle to be contented with the tickling sense of the ludicrous; and the desire for a rule of living, for the modest maxims of empirical wisdom, is too pressing to relax for long. The comedy ever shades off into a subdued drama of thought.

That storehouse of ethical and psychological suggestion was to be tapped by the later Elizabethan dramatists and by Shakespeare himself. In the field of humor no more precise indebtedness can be traced. But it is safe to say that the *Essais,* after the printing of Florio's translation, and possibly for some years before, were in England a leaven of mental and moral

[40] Reprint of John Florio's translation (The Tudor Translations: London, 1892-1893), Book I, chap. i, p. 16.

suppleness, a manifold illustration of the complexity of nature, eked out with a lesson in the effectiveness of an honest, objective attitude to human facts. The example was one of freedom and self-mastery in a thinker's reaction to life; of a sincere, reflective art, pitched in a sober key of intellectual animation. It would act as an antidote to sourness, pedantry, fanaticism; it would direct the study of man towards the fascinating variety of creatures. Though not humorous in itself, it would indirectly foster the growth of humor. Others besides Burton were to reap the benefit of its easygoing catholicity of interest and sympathy.

VII. Spain and Cervantes

In various ways English literature had felt the influence of Spain before the days of Cervantes. Shortly after 1550 Don Hurtado de Mendoza's lively study of Spanish manners, *Lazarillo de Tormes* (1554), stimulated the spontaneous taste of the English public for picaresque fiction. It was translated by David Rowland as early as 1567, had two new editions before 1600, six more before 1700. But that vein of piquant realism, whose contribution to the development of humor is of great importance, rather belongs to the other main current: the stream of tendencies that derive from, or link up with, the popular spirit.

With *Don Quixote* (first part 1604, second part 1614), we come to the most outstanding modern example of genuine humor on the continent of Europe before the time when the influence of English models could be felt abroad. England did respond first to the brilliant success of the book in the country of its birth; the *History of the Valorous and Wittie Knight-Errant, Don Quixote of the Mancha,* containing the first part, was published in 1612;[41] the very next year the *Knight of the Burning Pestle* testified to the immediate effect of the sugges-

[41] The translator was Shelton. The probability is that his work, from 1607, when it was begun, to 1612, was consulted in manuscript by his literary friends. J. Fitzmaurice-Kelly regarded it as possible that Shakespeare might have had a hand, with Fletcher, in a lost drama, *The History of Cardenio,* based on an episode of *Don Quixote,* and performed in 1613 at the Globe Theatre (Introduction to a reprint of Shelton's translation, in The Tudor Translations, 1896).

tion on the quick minds of Beaumont and Fletcher; the second part was added in 1620. If the full tale of the numerous editions and of the various translations is taken into account, it becomes clear that the masterpiece of Cervantes is woven in with the very woof of the psychological and literary movement out of which fully conscious humor was growing. That story has been told.[42] One point must be briefly emphasized: the affinities through which *Don Quixote* appealed at once to the instincts that lay at the very root of English humor.

On an outside view, the method of Cervantes is very similar to that of the burlesque. The more obvious comic elements in his book belong to the technique of parody—one that the general public is always ready to welcome. The grotesque features of the hero's craze and of his repeated clash with hard realities struck the early readers with a keener edge than they did later generations. It was not only in France that the work was hailed at once as the most funny satire of a world then going or gone, but the memory of which was yet fresh. The literature of chivalry had not disappeared, and the ideal of superhuman straining after a grand nobility of purpose and deed was dying hard in the contemporary novel. In that respect the appeal of *Don Quixote* hardly falls in with the more refined tradition of humanist culture; it runs close to the broad, strong impulses of that bourgeois, practical criticism of medieval values which accompanies the emergence of modern civilization. And the central trick of humor, the serious presentment of laughable things, is very simply and naturally called for by the inevitable tactics of parody—the raising of silly absurdities to the plane of dignity—which obtains through the whole story of the distempered Knight's misadventures.

More essential are the traits by which the sad fate of Don Quixote chimes with latent deep-laid susceptibilities in the national English character. One set of those tendencies is purely experimental and practical. The Knight-errant will fly in the face of facts. His brain secretes chimeras, and he has stubbornly

[42] It has not proved possible to consult A. H. Mayor's dissertation: "Cervantes, with Especial Reference to Don Quijote in English Literature until 1781," 1926, Princeton University Library; mentioned by Huntington Brown in *Rabelais in English Literature* (Cambridge, Mass., 1933), p. 46 n. 2.

ignored the lesson of things as they are. A refusal to learn at the school of experience is to the more matter-of-fact genius of England the sin against the Holy Ghost; that a mature hidalgo should egregiously suffer from the ailments of the lunatic, the dreamer, and the logic-chopping man with a system—all of them tilters against windmills—is enough to rouse the laughter of gods and men. There was a very special titillation in such a sight to the early seventeenth-century forbears of John Bull; the absurdity of it was to them exquisite. To the author of *Hudibras,* fifty years later, the great Puritan attempt at a godly system of government and life looked just as ineffably ridiculous. After all, a good deal of England was, and is, ruled by the spirit of Sancho; the trusty squire has found there in many respects his real, not imaginary, island kingdom.

But the genius of England is not all empirical and practical; in its complex making there do enter tendencies which seem the very reverse of those but which are reconciled with them through a wider intuition. Don Quixote, after all, is no less at home than Sancho among the English; with them sentiment, imagination, dreams keep their appeal in the teeth of matter-of-fact wisdom. The very extravagance, the whimsicality of Don Quixote gradually endeared him to English hearts, as to the hearts of most reflective readers then or since.

His obstinacy under the blows of disaster stirred the chords of admiration and sympathy for an idealism that would not yield. Here the deeper essence in the masterly creation of Cervantes is reached by a perception that, blurred and obscure at first, soon grew clearer, and before the seventeenth century was over, already colored the common notion of his hero. Don Quixote was thus identified with a generosity of purpose and a fondness for the innocent hobbies of disinterested minds, in which some characteristic preferences of the national English genius had been expressing themselves. From an object lesson in the grotesqueness of a perverse craze, he became the patron saint of all the "paladins" floundering in daily life. His spiritual brothers or cousins stand out in such prominence through modern English literature that the affinity is eloquent: Sir Roger de Coverley, Parson Adams, Uncle Toby, the Vicar of

Wakefield, Mr. Pickwick—representative figures each; and all, around which the greatest humorists have allowed their creative fancy to play, take more or less after him. To that extent the influence of *Don Quixote* would appear to be central in the development of modern English humor. But it is not so much a matter of influence as of parallelism, affinity, and likeness. The national instinct of England discovered itself in an indulgent, loving tolerance for the eccentricities of beings who refused to acknowledge that only safety mattered and that there was safety in common sense. The feeling revealed some of the most profound preferences of a people that was staking so much, at the same time, in other fields, on the necessity of exploring the will of nature and obeying her laws. The smiling affection that the modern man feels for Don Quixote helped to bring to a head a fondness for sentiment that has stamped most of English humor with kindliness, and persuaded English critics that unless there is cordiality, there can be no humor.

CHAPTER VIII

THE POPULAR VEIN

I. A Survey

ENGLISH HUMOR is part and parcel of the national character, and permanent features of a collective mind can hardly be traced to a passing intellectual influence, were it even as wide as a movement or as prolonged as a whole age of thought. Though the humanist contribution was paramount in refining the peculiar manner of pleasantry which England, like many other nations, was gradually mastering, that manner had its main roots more deeply and broadly in the instinctive genius of the whole people; it derived not only from the Renaissance but from a distant past. The popular tradition was the principal origin of English humor. For centuries that heritage of shrewd implicitness in fun had lain dormant, or developed slowly, obscurely; its tentative displays were mostly clumsy, and often coarse; but they were alive with the spontaneous sense, the ready intuition that a laugh roused in that way did somehow more naturally suit the quiet temper of a people who disliked, even in a joke, the open pretense of jesting.

Thus resting on a wider basis of national character and life, the popular tradition, nevertheless, played at first but a secondary part in literature properly so called. Most of its expressions were given no written form, or only an ephemeral one. Its surviving records are incomplete and disconnected. An attempt to follow its historical development fully and closely would involve a baffling inquiry into the manners, the daily talk, the moods, and amusements of the people themselves; it would in fact be equivalent to a study of the growth of English thought, as revealed, not in its supreme, but in its rather undistinguished achievements. Such histories of the common man, regarded as the real foundation of a civilization and a culture, have often been advocated in principle, and the method has actually been carried into practice; indeed the interpretation of the past in all fields more and more approximates to this point of view. But until that extremely wide domain has been fully explored and mapped out, it would be premature to try to survey the intellectual life of the multitude under one of its most elusive aspects, that of humor. We have to pitch our effort in a much more modest key and to be content with a limited object: that of catching the reflection of the popular instincts in literary works whose authors were, for various reasons, more directly in touch with those instincts, or influenced by them. Without ever forgetting that the current of thought which we now attempt to follow was a collective fact, we shall endeavour to seize it and to illustrate its characteristics through individual examples.

II. Ballads, Satirical Pieces, Roguery, Jestbooks

A word has been said of the relation between the ballads and humor in the first part of this inquiry.[1] Further study since then has brought me to reconsider the subject, with the result that I would not at the present time lay quite the same stress on the relative inferiority of the comic inspiration in that field. Although the average quality is not high, some touches are excellent, and the significance of the material as a whole is plain: the signs of a natural gift are there clearly apparent. The same judgment may be passed upon other literature of the popular, anonymous kind: the satirical poems, the rogue stories, and the jestbooks. In all, a spontaneous instinct, a fund of natural ability, are present and active; when the occasion arises, they will as often as not hit upon the very manner of humorous expression.

The concision, the economy of the ballads, that adds so much poignancy to their pathos can set off just as well a sly hint or a roguish intent. Their manner of repetition and the piquant adaptation of the refrain to changing aspects of the theme are efficient means to serve an ironical purpose. Al-

[1] Part I, chap. v, sect. iv.

though love, sentiment, patriotic and warlike emotions, the wonder and pity of dramatic events are the most frequent motives, the sense of the fun of life crops up again and again as an irrepressible impulse, however dark the background of civilization may be which those poems generally suggest. And that sense is sometimes communicated with the reserve and detachment, the neat turn of phrase of the genuine humorist.

Other examples can be quoted than those which have been already mentioned. There is a world of quiet, sly philosophy in the smiling banter of "Take thy auld cloak about thee."[2] The mood of parody in "The Turnament of Tottenham"[3] seems light and irresponsible enough; but how cleverly managed the verve is, and how scathing the brazen-faced irreverence of the tripping meter! The deftness of "King John and the Abbott of Canterbury"[4] could hardly be improved upon. On a somewhat similar theme "The King and the Millar of Mansfield"[5] shows the sureness of conscious art in many of its strokes. "The Dragon of Wantley," obviously more modern, but probably no later than the early seventeenth century, with some broad touches, is a brilliant display of ingenuity in satire, whose buffoonery manages to preserve a sober face in its antics. The soul of humor that breathes through those pieces has its being, as ever, in a lively perception of the comedy of character, in a free acceptance of the relativity of things, and in the discretion of manner which goes so far to make us aware that more is meant than is said.[6]

[2] Percy's *Reliques* (Everyman's Library: London and New York, 1906), I, 190.

[3] *Ibid.*, p. 296 *et passim.*

[4] *Ibid.*, II, 124.

[5] *Ibid.*, II.

[6] *Wit and Mirth: or Pills to Purge Melancholy; being a collection of the best Merry Ballads and Songs, Old and New, etc.*; by Thomas d'Urfey; 6 vols., London, 1719-1720. That a good many "merry songs" are not quotable, goes without saying. J. A. Froude, a very competent Victorian, though an exceptionally vigorous mind, thought as much; and he singled out for special praise, on account of the author's "discretion," the mildly funny piece called "Gossips mine." "I select it," he pointed out, "as being capable (which most of them are not) of being printed without omissions" ("Essay on *The Commonplace Book of Richard Hilles*," *Fraser's Magazine*, Vol. LVIII, Aug., 1858, pp. 127-144). We may as well give a few lines from a poem which has so signally passed muster; it is indeed a good example of the more polished form of popular humor, although the theme is none of the most delicate. The "gossips" are drinking at some alehouse. Quoth one to the other:

A burlesque note is manifest in several of those poems; and although burlesque, as an art, was hardly to flourish till the seventeenth century,[7] the breaking up of medieval ideals or conventions, such as chivalry or courtly love, was of course no mean tributary to the gathering stream of humor. But the sixteenth century instances of English parody mostly belong to the literature of refinement and scholarship. "Nothing is clearer," Dr. Kitchin says, "than that the best products of our wit were the result of schooling in the classics."[8] Another possible incentive to the humorous is the satirical spirit; the two inspirations run close to each other and at times intermingle, although their courses remain separate. Well could satire be instinct with the rough vigor and the raciness of the popular mind, at a time when the deepest emotions were stirred by the religious conflict; and the social discontent that had been simmering from the fourteenth century, breaking out now and then, was fed by the gradual disruption of the old relations between the classes. The powerless grievances of the common man against the privileged orders and the professions, when not too bitter, would find a vent in humor. "The London Lackpenny"[9] is at an earlier period a very significant example of popular satire enlivened with a humorous flavor. The subject seems an echo from *Piers Plowman:* it is "Meed" indeed that everywhere checks the bewildered course of the poor countryman wandering in the maze of London town; but if lack of money, from a crushing handicap in a law suit, grows

---

"Would God I had done after your counsel;
For my husband is so fell;
He hateth me like the Devil in hell;
And the more I cry the less mercy."

To which pat comes the answer:

"Margaret meek said, so might I thrive;
I know no man that is alive
That give me two strokes, but he shall have five.
I am not afeard though he have a beard."

The subject of humor, needless to say, is in that literary kind of very wide, and international, application.

[7] "Leaving monkish forms of mimicry and ribaldry aside, there is scarcely any tolerable parody after *Sir Thopas,* till we reach the age of dramatic burlesque in the age of James I" (George Kitchin, *A Survey of Burlesque and Parody in English,* Edinburgh, 1931, pp. x-xi).

[8] *Ibid.,* p. x.

[9] Probably early fifteenth century; no longer attributed to Lydgate.

to be the obsessing doom of the socially inferior in all the walks of life, the tone is not that of denunciation and wrath; the subtle blend of naïveté and slyness that characterizes a rustic's manner is caught to perfection; simplicity and good nature are the more efficient for not being entirely feigned, and the tale with its subdued manner, its restrained irony, is rich with the very essence of comedy.[10]

In the great satirical age that came in with the latter years of the sixteenth century, the humanistic spirit and the popular verve were often fused. But, when all is said, the world of satire and that of humor are different; and from our point of view it will be possible to keep those elements apart. Nashe and Dekker, for instance, will be studied, not as critics of their age, but as humorists; and the same rule will be applied further on to Lodge, Hall, Jonson, and Donne.

The "literature of roguery" cannot be assigned exclusively to the popular inspiration. It was variously in contact with the humanist influence; and its inner purpose, in some respects, may even be called aristocratic. An eager desire to be acquainted with low life and outlawry has ever been more or less a feature of the cultured and socially respectable. Stories of "villainy" have always appealed to a very large audience; so presumably, among the number, to the virtuous. But except in periods of marked sophistication, like the beginning of the eighteenth century, that curiosity hardly went the length of actual sympathy; the thrilled or shocked readers would feel the fascination of the theme and pass on to something else with a sense of having glimpsed a submerged world, which it was better not to probe too deeply. The writer of a rogue story, in the more precise meaning of the phrase, saw things differently; his tale "regards rascality with humour, or explains it as the result of social environment."[11] Now in that humorous tolerance there is the seed at least of a fellow-feeling; and the common man, with his modest portion of the

[10] Two signal examples of early burlesque with a genuinely humorous element are *The Court of Love* (late fifteenth or early sixteenth century), and under Henry VIII, *Cock Lorell's Bote,* a burlesque of the *Ship of Fools* (see below, sect. iv).

[11] F. W. Chandler, *The Literature of Roguery* (Boston and New York, 1907), chap. i, pp. 1-2.

rewards of life, will be more likely to feel in that way; he will enter more readily into the convention that literature may ignore some aspects of the moral code, especially, of course, those that concern private ownership. At bottom, the complacent picture of roguery has a tinge of potential rebellion; it is an outlet for a repressed sense of inequality and unfairness. The rogue, moreover, will more often than not move in undistinguished circles, and the tone and the language of the tale are naturally colored by its surroundings. Be this as it may, the wide success of those stories, their atmosphere, and the features of their humor would assign them a place rather among the products of the popular vein.

The most interesting kind of rogue literature, the picaresque novel, has been defined as "the biography (or more often the autobiography) of an antihero who makes his way in the world through the service of masters, satirizing their personal faults, as well as their trades and professions."[12] The influence of the fountainhead of the whole kind, the Spanish *Lazarillo de Tormes* (1556), translated by David Rowland in 1576, can already be traced in England through the latter part of the sixteenth century, and the picaresque spirit must not be left out of account in a study of Elizabethan humor. But its action, when all is said, was not essential in that field; and as its major development took place well after 1600, continuing into the eighteenth century and giving rise to the modern novel of manners, it may be passed over here very briefly. All we have to do is to try to trace the inner relation between the picaresque spirit and the method of humor.

It has been pointed out that in fact humor remained very generally, to the end, one of the elements of the rogue story, although some writers, for instance Defoe, dispensed with it in the eagerness of their realistic and moralizing intent. Some sort of latent affinity must thus be looked for and will be easily discovered. The picaresque kind is all suffused with a subtle essence of parody; the attention that the romances of chivalry gave to highborn knights, noble feelings, and great deeds is here systematically granted to persons of mean birth,

[12] *Ibid.*, p. 5.

realistic doings, and very prosaic motives; the story now has no longer a hero, but an "antihero"; the contrast in itself will tickle our sense of fun. A picaresque novel rests upon a reversal of ordinary values; the social scale which was implicit in the traditional story, with its setting and choice of characters, is now quietly put aside; the reader's mind receives just the pleasant stimulus of surprise, which is so often the immediate cause of laughter. Humor indeed, whatever its object, always works by the apparent and paradoxical abdication of our power or willingness to judge normally of things. The "judgments" that in the present instance abdicate are the ethical ones; and the seeming disappearance of the sense of right and wrong creates the silent absurdity which is, one way or another, at the source of humor.

Jestbooks are another kind of literature that testifies to the popularity of tried and safe incentives to laughter. But it is only in a wider sense, indeed in a loose one, that funny stories, comic repartees, and bons mots necessarily belong to the category of humor. In fact, the numerous pamphlets which have survived and purport to be repertories of mirth are to our taste sadly disappointing; very naturally so, since the joke that can be registered and quoted, out of its own atmosphere, must draw from the most superficial or the grossest sources of the comic. Genuine implicitness, the reserve of expression, a subtle soul of relativity, the discreet suggestion of a thought-provoking paradox can hardly be included in a few lines. Wit of no very distinguished order, or buffoonery are the ordinary staple of those collections.[13] One of the most famous of the later series,

[13] A much fuller treatment of the subject, with bibliographies, will be found in the *Cambridge History of English Literature*, Vol. III, chap. v, and Vol. IV, chap. xvi, both by H. V. Routh. We quote from the former, as to a representative collection, "the earliest English jest-book, . . . in print by about 1526 under the title of *A. C. Mery Talys.* This miscellany covers practically the same ground as the *Fabliaux*, treating of the profligacy of married women, the meanness and voluptuousness of the priesthood, the superstition and crassitude of the peasant, the standing jokes against feminine loquacity and obstinacy, the resources of untutored ingenuity and the comedy of the fool outwitted by the knave. All the tales are narrated with a pointedness and simplicity which show how well English narrative prose had learnt its lesson from Latin. Some of the anecdotes, to modern taste, are merely silly or obscene. But a certain number, following in the footsteps of the Latin *Facetiae*, harbour a sense of wit and subtlety beneath apparent crudity" (p. 93). Stress is usefully laid here upon the

to which an individual name is attached, *Tarlton's Jests,* is no better than most. The great actor's flat nose and his "disposition to squint" must have counted for much in his unfailing hold upon the crowd, who as we know from contemporary witnesses burst out roaring as soon as he opened his mouth, or before. The saving virtue in Tarlton was his faculty of self-criticism; that he could crack a joke at himself is the sign that after all the soul of humor was in him. Some of his jests reveal a shrewd mind, a quiet fund of observation, the deft handling of the rough wisdom that is gathered from life. In his way he must have contributed to the schooling of the audiences that were to relish the much better pranks of Shakespeare's clowns. But indeed F. O. Mann's remark[14] that the tradition of the jestbook leads up to the realistic novel points the right way. Realism, rather than true humor, is the spirit of that literature, and it is in regard to this that its historical interest is to be assessed.

As a conclusion to that very brief survey, the wide diffusion of books, tracts, and poems whose avowed purpose was to create a laugh shows that the temper of the early Renaissance in England was not unduly austere. In that normality of reaction to the comic the people themselves shared, like the cultured classes. While the scholars and the humanists, the disciples of Lucian, Erasmus, and More, would sharpen the expert strokes of their wit, the man in the street enjoyed as ever, but rather more willingly than during the darker medieval times, the robust play of an inborn sense of fun. The materials for humor lay thus everywhere in the stronger and bolder posses-

fact, never to be lost sight of, that even with the most popular expressions of English mother wit, the schooling in "pointedness" and "finesse" came directly or indirectly from the classics. But the slyness at the back of all was native. A case can be made out for this proposition not only from the *Hundred Merry Tales,* mentioned above, but from *The Sackful of News,* 1557, etc. Of all those stories F. O. Mann says: "There are few or none that seem to have a definitely literary source, and yet in many cases they are told with an art that has perhaps never been excelled in the history of the written joke. The story of the Welshmen in heaven is related *with a satirical reserve and malice* that shows how completely the art of simple jest was understood by these writers of earliest Tudor English" (italics our own) (Introduction to *The Works of Thomas Deloney,* Oxford, 1912, p. xxl). This story, we may add, fully deserves that praise through its humorous terseness.

[14] Deloney's *Works,* Introduction, pp. xxi-xxiii.

sion of themselves and the world, which the abundant life of the Elizabethans prompted and allowed. Of humor worthy of the name there is not much in the outpourings that have come down to us; the quality of the pleasantry is often cheap and coarse, and what is a more grievous sin from the aesthetic point of view, it is most often quite explicit. But the vigor, the invention, the fund of spirits are there; occasionally we detect a reserve, a self-command in the managing of a joke, a slyness that will sharpen the arrow by pretending not to see that it is one. These are the sure seeds of future developments; and in individual works, which must be now examined, they strike one more forcibly.

III. Morals and Interludes; John Heywood; Early Comedy

The humanist influences cannot be excluded from a study of humor in English drama before Shakespeare. At hardly any point in the field would such a summary dismissal be possible. The main emphasis, however, may be laid on the instinct for comedy of the native English genius. While the refinement, most often, must be traced to foreign sources, chiefly classical or French, the comic invention, the racy realism, the sly indirectness, usually not unmixed with a taste for broad or coarse jokes, have their roots in the home soil. The national temper, in its spontaneous search for expression, might not be averse to blunt, explicit farce; but it had within itself the seed of better things, whenever an inborn sense, an intuitive presentiment guided the writer to methods that leave something unsaid and rely upon the power of a meaningful tacitness.

From the very beginning English religious drama had shown a tendency to relax into comedy, where the unmistakable note of humor would crop up.[15] Full light has been thrown on the whole process of that development.[16] In the fifteenth century we shall only mention the Wakefield Plays, with the

[15] See Part I of the present work for the earliest instances in the thirteenth and fourteenth centuries (chap. iii).

[16] See C. M. Gayley, "Historical View of the Beginnings of English Comedy," in *Representative English Comedies, from the Beginnings to Shakespeare* (New York, 1903); and J. B. Moore, *The Comic and Realistic in English Drama* (Chicago, 1925).

famous *Prima* and *Secunda Pastorum;*[17] and among the Coventry Plays, the *Pageant of the Shearmen and Tailors.* The mothers whose children are threatened by Herod rise to the occasion with admirable gusto:

Third Woman:

Sit he never so high in saddle,
But I shall make his brains addle,
And here with my pot-ladle
  With him will I fight.
I shall lay on him as though I wood were,
With this same womanly gear. . . .[18]

This may seem broad enough. But the unknown author must have enjoyed the picturesque scene thus briefly called up, and in the serious, solemn atmosphere of the story, the welcome flavor of familiarity—a parody with enough reserve not to destroy our sense of human relief. And we know that all through the next hundred years the realistic and the comic in their natural association enlivened those edifying works. With the Morals and the Interludes, that feature grew even more significant. "It was through the Morals rather than the Mysteries that realistic comedy may be said to have escaped finally into an independent existence for its own sake."[19] In spite of the strongly didactic purpose of those works, "the Vice, or Vices, always tended to become merely mischievous characters —and after that, merely comic characters."[20]

A few examples will suffice. In *Mankind,* too much has perhaps been made of the devil Titivillus and his grim fun; the play bears the strong stamp of classical learning, and the

[17] C. M. Gayley thought he perceived in the Wakefield Plays the personality of a "distinctive poet-humorist" ("Historical View," p. xxvii), who, A. W. Pollard says, "as an exponent of a rather boisterous kind of humour had no equal in his own days" (*The Towneley Plays,* Introduction, p. xxii). His masterpiece, Gayley adds, is the *Secunda Pastorum:* "It stands out English and alone, with its homespun philosophy and indigenous figures—Mak and Gyll and the Shepherds—its comic business, its glow, its sometimes subtle irony, its ludicrous colloquies, its rural life and manners, its naive and wholesome reverence" ("Historical View," p. xxviii). With those judgments it is still possible to agree, and they rightly emphasize the national quality of that remarkable humor.

[18] *Fifteenth Century Prose and Verse,* with an Introduction by A. W. Pollard (London, 1903), p. 270.

[19] J. B. Moore, *The Comic and Realistic in English Drama,* p. 45.

[20] *Ibid.,* p. 65.

lapses into humor, though genuine enough, are kept within somewhat narrow bounds.

Mundus and Infans, an Interlude whose title points as well to scholarly authorship, is suffused at times with the charm of a quaint simplicity that cannot have been unconscious.[21] A discreet smile hovers on the staid countenance of didacticism, and in an almost pure allegory, with unlimited application, the "local color" of London, the allusions to familiar places are pleasantly realistic touches.

Hyckescorner has unmistakable humor in plenty. We catch in it a rebellion of instinct and natural mirth against the repression of a faith too strictly bound up with the fear of hell. The naughty characters speak with a strangely genuine and free voice. Let us hear Imagination, who has been told of heaven:

> What, syr, above the mone?
> Naye, by the masse; then sholde I fall soone!
> Yet I kepe not to clymme so hye,
> But to clymme for a byrdes neste,
> There's none bytwene eest and weste,
> That dare therto ventre better than I![22]

A Rabelaisian note of frank, almost pagan, naturalism more than once rings out between the accents of perfunctory orthodoxy; and that slyly double inspiration is the source of what we may well call "humor of release." *Nice Wanton* shows us the same conflict, with a similar mixture of stiff doctrine and subdued longing for the freedom of instinct. Release and humor appear in flashes, when the pranks of the truant boys appeal to us more than they should. The play, as a whole, remains edifying and explicit.[23]

In the English humorous literature of the sixteenth century a writer of Interludes, John Heywood, stands out eminently; with the unknown author of the *Secunda Pastorum* and Sir Thomas More—of whom, significantly enough, he was a close

[21] J. M. Manly, *Specimens of Pre-Shakespearean Drama* (Boston and London, 1897), Vol. I.

[22] *Ibid.*, ll. 969-74

[23] Among the surveys which have been made of those texts, the nearest approach to a consistent study of their relation to humor is still to be found in C. M. Gayley's "Historical View of the Beginnings of English Comedy," 1903, quoted above.

friend—he is worthy of being placed in that respect among the successors of Chaucer. To Chaucer, as to More, he was certainly indebted; and it may be regarded as established that he owed occasional inspiration or suggestions to French fabliaux and farces. His work, more generally, bears the impress of humanist affinities and influences. Still, his vigorous originality remains unimpaired and is thoroughly English. The spiritual resemblance which links him up with Chaucer, and which, it must be confessed, would set the two writers apart in the tradition of earlier English literature, is the freedom of the artistic spirit. The fact that Heywood, like More, and of course like Chaucer, was a Catholic, is not perhaps on that account entirely negligible. For the first time, critics have pointed out, English comedy with him stood on its own ground and ceased to be dependent on the didactic purpose from which it had seemed its function to provide a relief.

That detachment harmonizes well with the inner sense of relativity which is the soul of humor. Its appropriate method Heywood divined, or disengaged, from the practice of Chaucer, Erasmus, More, and the French. In spite of those examples, his re-creation of the manner may be regarded as a creation. It is only in the eighteenth century that the humorous attitude grew to be so clearly realized and its characteristic signs so familiar, that one may think of it as lying within the potential reach of all and transmitted bodily from one writer to another. The humorists of the eighteenth century were no longer innovators in technique; each of the masters only added the individual shades of his own temperament to the common store. The case was very different in the early sixteenth century; imitation then implied not only a gift, but a divination.

Heywood's expert handling of the method is the more remarkable. His store of realistic observation is racy and popular; he sets it off with a perfectly cool, objective manner, the slyness of which only peeps out in the willing unguardedness of some overstatement—in an unnecessary touch of precision, an unlikely fit of naïveté. The Pardoner of *The Foure P. P.* has his tongue in his cheek:

> Give me but a peny or two pens,
> And as sone as the soule departeth hens,
> In halfe an hour, or three quarters at moste,
> The soule is in heven with the Holy Ghost.[24]

The four cheats, with their professional tricks and their rivalries, are worked off against one another in masterly fashion. The short, neat, deliberate lines carry the dialogue admirably; and through their ironic rhythm, with their often exaggerated rhymes, they hark back to Skelton and point forward to Samuel Butler. The innuendoes are at times very free, but the responsibility for the coarseness need not be put upon French models, as English precedents are not lacking. What might be traced to France is the *finesse*—that is no moral excuse, but certainly heightens the aesthetic effect—and the deftness with which so many of the jokes are turned.[25] Let us hear the Pardoner again:

> Here is an eye-toth of the Great Turke;
> Whose eyes be ones sette on thys pece of worke
> May happely lese parte of his eye-sight,
> But not all tyll he be blynde outryght.[26]

The play drops to a much lower level at the end. In the more even quality of their art, and their almost unfailing liveliness *The Pardoner and the Friar*, and *A Merry Play between John John the husband, Tyb, his wife, and Sir John, the Priest* are on a somewhat higher plane; we have there no longer farces, but comedies of manners, and an exquisite talent for expression. The critics who insist that a genuine humorist must have a kindly heart will be at pains to digest the hardness of Heywood's wit. But he has charming touches of freshness; his children are merry and convincing. The best of his humor may perhaps be found in his *Play of the Weather*, where it reaches a philosophical significance and is wholly founded on a realization of relativity.[27]

[24] In Manly, *Specimens*, I, ll. 147-50.

[25] The *Farce de Maître Pathelin* was translated into English as early as 1535.

[26] Manly, *Specimens*, I, ll. 538-41.

[27] *A Parable of the Spider and the Fly*, which Dr. Kitchin pronounces not to be a parody of the epic manner *(A Survey of Burlesque and Parody in English)*, might well be one after all. See R. G. Bolwell, *The Life and Works of John Heywood* (New York, 1921), p. 136.

That recognized landmark in the development of comedy, *Ralph Roister Doister,*[28] is less essential from the point of view of the present study. It is a pedagogue's masterpiece, with an unmistakable classroom atmosphere, duly deferential to the models of Terence, and still, not devoid of observation, verve, and humor. Its roots are in English soil and it looks forward to the achievements that are coming. The humanist influence in *Gammer Gurton's Needle*[29] is less prominent, and the native invention, the humorous realism more original. Here we have sheer farce, but rich with the flavor of country life; the rustic quaintness of much of the language, the ballad-like homely measure of the fourteen-syllable line serve efficiently a comic purpose that is intensely aware of itself. The plot moves naturally forward, the dialogue is lifelike, and in spite of the many broad touches the general effect is one of sureness and discretion. We are reminded, not of Plautus or Terence, but of some merry Dutch picture, modern and shrewd in its naturalistic gusto. The man who wrote it had in him, even more certainly than Udall, the root of the matter—a quiet grasp of the fun of everyday things and the sense of proportion that can view one's amusement against the background of experience as a whole. There is the temperament of humor, as well, in the subplot of Richard Edwards's *Damon and Pythias,* with a polished reserve in the irony and some happy realism of a popular tone.

But Henry Porter's comedy, *The Pleasant History of the Two Angry Women of Abington* (1598), is certainly of no less significance. The "Barkshire" humor of Dick Coomes, emphasized in the full title, is far below the standard which Shakespeare's clowns had then been already setting up; of Nicholas Proverbs, the less said the better; and it must be confessed that the play is broad, with a rather slow movement. Several scenes, however, appeal irresistibly even to a fastidious sense of humor; while the country atmosphere, the pleasant picture of rustic life, and the realistic studies of character are worthy of the best English tradition. The quiet satire, not

[28] By Nicholas Udall; acted about 1540.

[29] By "Mr. S.," variously identified; published in 1575; probably written much earlier.

unkind but tolerant, and the fun that bubbles up from many situations link up with the series of attempts on the comic stage over which Chaucer's clear-sighted, supple, and detached genius seems to preside.

IV. Grobianism

In its rise and development "Grobianism" was inseparable from the humanist spirit; its implicit aim was to indicate a value—the refinement of manners and feelings—which is generally associated with a scholarly ideal. Indeed the affinity was more materially expressed: Dedekind's Latin satire, the *Grobianus* (1569), in spite of its German translations could of course be known in England by but a minority of cultivated readers until it was rendered into English verse at the beginning of the seventeenth century. For his method, moreover, Dedekind had been indebted to Erasmus's *Praise of Folly*. Still, when stock is taken of the influence which Grobianism, as a literary theme and movement, can have exerted on the growth of English humor, it is to be classified rather with the signs of the national and popular inspiration in that field. The case is an old and familiar one, that of a foreign impulse received, assimilated, and organized by a nation in conformity with its own genius and preferences.

Through the humanist contribution, English humor had felt the refining force of the Southern, the Mediterranean spirit —that of the classical literatures, of France and Italy. Germany had taken an active share in the work of the Renaissance; but it was not finally her erudite zeal that did most to further the progress of humor in England. It was those aspects of her temperament that would naturally harmonize with the realism and the robust liveliness of Saxon England. A seriously moral purpose, lying at the root of a satirical impulse, and a keen interest in the concrete world would chime in with the mood of the common Englishman. The two elements were differently mingled in the outstanding German satires of the age—the book of *Till Eulenspiegel*,[30] Brant's *Narrenschiff*

[30] In *Owle Glasse*, a version of the Eulenspiegel stories, "Owle-glasse is a grotesque lubberly hero, a practical joker of magnified dimensions" (F. O. Mann, Introduction to *The Works of T. Deloney*, Oxford, 1912). See F. W. Brie, *Eulenspiegel in England* (Berlin, 1903).

(translated into English as the *Ship of Fools* by A. Barclay in 1509), and the *Grobianus*;[31] in the first a popular vein, the rebellion of country people against the superior airs of the citizens, was predominant; in the second and the third, the preoccupation with conduct; but in all three a racy realism and the full possession of the varied scene of life created an animated relish for concrete details that would almost of itself lead to humor.

Although the fortune of the *Ship of Fools* in England is a fascinating theme for the specialist, it concerns our present purpose less than that of Grobianism. Dedekind's poem was an object lesson in the power of the indirect method of presentment; through its trick of "inverted precept" it shamed gross, boorish manners by making a deliberate description and eulogy of them. The principle was the apparent upsetting of all the values of behavior. Now the essential manner of humor is just that inverted tone. The often coarse but vigorous fun of the *Grobianus* was nothing else than the saturnine amusement that lurks behind the unruffled surface of irony, with an element of robust familiarity and realism that made it rather more genial. Its example would thus act as an artistic suggestion and tend to bring the sense of the method to clearer consciousness in unawakened minds; the more efficiently, as in the field of everyday behavior the rights and wrongs are safely and universally settled, so that the indirectness of the presentment would not fail to be caught and deciphered, even by the least attentive peruser.[32]

But the deepest chord that the theme of Grobianism struck in the instincts of English readers, when the satire was made more accessible by a translation (*The School of Slovenry*, 1605), was one which Dedekind had probably not meant to be touched at all, in his clearer intention, at least. By a paradoxical but a natural shifting of the main stress, a satire written to deride rude, selfish manners gradually turned into a derision of all artificial strains in behavior. There was after all a kind

[31] This symbolic name was first used by Brant in the *Narrenschiff*.

[32] See C. H. Herford, *Studies in the Literary Relations of England and Germany in the Sixteenth Century* (Cambridge, 1886); and E. Ruhl, *Grobianus in England*, 1904.

of sincerity, a freedom about the unconventional examples at which the finger of scorn was being pointed; the critic's mock admiration of the boor could shade off into a genuine sympathy. A preliminary condition was that the brute should no longer be a public nuisance; and this was very simply brought about: he was becoming an exception, while the affected fop tended to be the rule. In the England of the early seventeenth century such unfeeling rudeness as that which the original *Grobianus* denounced was already abnormal at all the levels of decent society; so there remained hardly any point in the denunciation. To dwellers in large cities, on the contrary, and to men and women swayed by the influence of a court, the real temptation was vanity, sophistication, snobbery of thought and language. Besides, the English mind had always harbored a sentimental fondness for a rough candor of manners and speech, and the type of the plain, freedom-loving individual was ever popular. Simplicity, at bottom, had a secure and a permanent place in the national scale of values. A satire that ridiculed departures from simplicity would be enjoyed by practically all readers, whether the excesses laughed at were within their reach or above their means.

So Grobianism in England became a vent for the vindication of sheer human nature. Dekker's free adaptation of Dedekind, *The Gull's Hornbook* (1609), clearly shows the change of emphasis and testifies as well that he was aware of it. His "gull" makes feeble attempts at first to be a cad; but he soon develops into the more shining and likely figure of an affected coxcomb. In *Grobiana's Nuptials,* an Oxford skit of 1640, the transformation is complete; the rancor of cynical dons against the fopperies of the unacademic world expresses itself freely.

Two masters of humor occupy conspicuous places on the line of literary descent from Grobianism and its method. One is Samuel Butler, the author of *Hudibras,* whose admirable portrait of his cantankerous hero is done after the manner of Erasmus and of Dedekind, but rather with something of the latter's coarse energy. The other is Swift, who may be regarded as the modern writer in whom the indirect mode of satire came finally into its own.

Great as their genius was, neither Butler nor Swift is perhaps in the most central and the most characteristic vein of English humor. And indeed the influence of Grobianism must not be exaggerated. It was by no means decisive in starting any process of development. The growth in which it inserted itself had begun long before and was going on along other lines. But it was chiefly responsible for one of the most approved modes of ironical humor: the inverted satire of pretended praise. The transparent duplicity of the *Grobianus* would be more popular, and so more widely effective, than the subtle and discreet innuendoes of Erasmus. The tradition was to bear its perfect fruit in Swift's *Directions to Servants.* It thus stands, not at the main fountainhead, but at the source of a tributary to the principal stream; and its prolonged success, to which Roger Bull's belated verse translation (*Grobianus, or the Compleat Booby,* 1739)[33] bears witness, undoubtedly schooled the verve of realistic satire in the systematic trick of inversion.

V. Nashe

In the perspective of Elizabethan literature Thomas Nashe cannot be viewed apart from the influences of his university education, of his prolonged contact with humanist examples. He was soaked in the Latin writers, knew Lucian,[34] admired Erasmus, whom he styles "superingenious," Sir Thomas More, whom he significantly calls "merry,"[35] and Sir Philip Sidney. He shows an acquaintance with Chaucer, with the *Grobianus;* and his fondness for Rabelais, whose echo is to be heard again and again in his work, was founded on some affinity of temper. Although in his quarrel with Harvey he enjoyed the advantage of a free lance, fighting, as he thought, a mere pedant, he cannot himself be cleared of his adversary's fault; his complacent display of learning will be at times singularly heavy. Still, his undeniable gift of humor found vent in ways that would hardly suggest discipleship to the humanists. Through

[33] Its heroic couplet, polished in the manner of Pope, proves a less suitable instrument than R. F.'s bland, easygoing "fourteener" (*The School of Slovenry,* 1605), to render Dedekind's assumed naïveté.

[34] See for instance *Works,* ed. R. B. McKerrow (London, 1920), I, 28-29.

[35] *The Unfortunate Traveller,* Everyman edition, p. 294.

his predominant instincts he represents the national vein, of which he gave, within a narrow range, an original and vigorous illustration.

His mind possessed the background of humor—rich, concrete, vivid notions of things as they are. He had, moreover, a faculty of comic invention, verve, mother-wit, and an ample command of the raciest words and phrases. Those resources would be handled to good purpose under the stress of a passionate, hot-blooded character that moved him to genuine anger and fitted him for the aggressive tactics of satire or controversy. But if he was a master of biting, picturesque invective, he lacked one of the psychological conditions of humor: the mental discipline that secures balance, the cool, delicate judgment without which the self-possessed manner of the humorist cannot be nicely managed or efficiently sustained. That imperfect control comes out in the desultoriness of his writings, in their audacious and almost cynical disorder. All his books are medleys, and the only really "picaresque" element in *The Unfortunate Traveller* is the freedom with which the story passes from one country and one theme to another. His realism has nothing of the steady application of the mind to the object and of the search for objective truth: it is but a determination to show his reader the worst aspects of life in a pitiless light and to spare him none of the thrills he is supposed to desire more than he may fear them. Nashe's observation is fresh and lively when dealing with the material world; his intuition, or his analysis, of motives is much more restricted. It is from the variety, the zest, and high flavor of experience that he draws his most characteristic effects.

Such a spicy relish imparted to description, satire, or vituperation is a treat somewhat akin to the enjoyment of the humorous; it will pass off into humor when the writer is clearly aware of what he is doing and keeps a sufficiently firm hold upon his own technique to let us feel that he himself is seeing through it. In not a few parts of Nashe's works he is thus a humorist along with other things. A humorist primarily he is at times, whenever impatience, wrath, scorn yield to the sense of an artist's pleasure in the mastery of his own emotion, and the tornado of scurrilous exaggerations grows transparent enough to reveal an inner sphere of half-smiling calm. *The Anatomy of Absurdity* has few of those moments; such humor as one finds there lies in the mere sauciness, or worse, the coarseness of the gibes: "It fareth nowadays with unlearned Idiots as it doth with she Asses, who bring forth all their life long."[36] But the *Pierce Penniless* is all built on the paradox of a penurious complaint that clothes itself magnificently in an idealist's denunciation of his age, while the author lets us see with a twinkle in his eye that he is not unaware of the discrepancy, but chooses to ignore it. "But all my thoughts consorted to the conclusion, that the world was uncharitable, and I ordained to be miserable."[37] To make mirth of one's distress while confessing it, to laugh at one's self with a catch in one's voice, was already the humor of the old French poet Villon.

We have here a safer and surer irony, more acceptable overstatements, a better poise altogether in the outpouring of a realistic bitterness.[38] Even the "Marprelate" pamphlets have passages of sobered invective and almost classical neatness: "*(Marprelate)* I pray you Sir, why do you call them Pruritans? *(Pas.) A pruritan.* They have an itch in their ears, that would be clawed with new points of doctrine never dreamt of; and an itch in their fingers, that would be anointed with the golden *Aemulatum* of the Church. I know they are commonly called *Puritans*, and not amiss, that title is one of the marks they bear about them! They have a mark in the head, they are self-conceited. They take themselves to be pure, when they are filthy in God's sight; They have a mark in the eye, their looks are haughty; they have a mark in the mouth, a very black tooth; they are A generation that curse their father."[39]

In the Marprelate controversy, Nashe may have stood "for

[36] *Works,* ed. R. B. McKerrow, I, 9.

[37] *Ibid.*, pp. 158-59.

[38] Nashe handles the mock-heroic manner with gusto and good success in his *Lenten Stuff* (1599), written in honor of Yarmouth and of the red herring, the source of its prosperity. That piece of consistently serious burlesque may have owed something to Sir John Harington's *Aiax* (see above, chap. ii, sect. vi), to which however in that very work Nashe alludes satirically (*Works*, IV, 393).

[39] *The Return of the renowned Cavaliero Pasquill of England*, in *Works*, ed. McKerrow, I, 73.

the past."[40] Whether actually a conservative or not, and for all his scurrility, he had in his intellectual temper an element of earnestness, derived from deep-laid, national instincts. Merry England was dying hard and kicking against the new austerity; Nashe was among those who gave that reaction a voice. Harvey called him "a Columbus of Terms"; but his torrent of abuse flowed from the raciness of the popular imagination. Harvey's moral seriousness was no less sincere, no doubt, and had a deeply English core as well. But it must be confessed that humor was all on the other side. His enemy having frequently called him an ass, Harvey "inserts a lengthy discourse upon the excellence of the ass, in which he contrives to reckon up all the asses of history, from Balaam's onwards."[41] The theme might have been treated humorously; but it needed a lighter touch.

The signs of Nashe's wide sympathy with his compatriots, with their likes and dislikes, can be seen everywhere. His pride in his own country was strong and susceptible—no exception, of course, among Elizabethan writers. Although he may have appreciated the *Grobianus*, he thought but poorly of the wit of German students.[42] He approved of plays with national subjects,[43] and of the language of the "vulgar sort in London, which is the fountain whose rivers flow round about England."[44] In his early maturity he not only declaimed against Italian vices, but gave up his former enthusiasm for the Euphuistic manner, whose only virtues, he pointed out, were borrowed from the classics.[45] His nature indeed was solidly rooted in English soil, and through his vigor and his realism he is typical of the more common temper of his age. Both in its genuineness and its imperfection, his humor has significance. He was at bottom an heir to the tradition of "flyting"[46] whom the Renaissance had intoxicated and stimulated but could not subdue to its finer spirit.

[40] *Works*, V, 67 (the editor's words).
[41] *Works*, V, 93.
[42] *The Unfortunate Traveller*, p. 298.
[43] *Works*, I, 211-15.
[44] *Ibid.*, p. 193.
[45] *Ibid.*, p. 319.
[46] Poetical invective; see Part I, chap. v.

VI. Dekker

In Thomas Dekker we have a genuine master of humor, with a sure grasp of its method, no less than of its spirit, and a range that took in not only its broad basis of observation, realism, and tolerance, but many, though not all, of the higher and subtler shades. He was very English, very "national," like Nashe, and more so than he; a herald of several developments, which have grown quite essential and conspicuous in modern England; a precursor in a direct line of Richard Steele and Charles Dickens.

His temper was genial, his mood kindly, with easily flowing social sympathies and the warmth of a generous soul; so his humor is of the cordial kind, more frequent among the English, and often regarded by them as the only authentic brand. In the *Shoemaker's Holiday* especially, he gave one of the first expressions to a frame of mind and a view of life that mixed the humorous with the humane in a cheerful, pleasant, and comforting blend. But if he made full allowance for sentiment, he was no sentimentalist; he knew how to handle irony and a sly implicit meaning; while most often negligent in his work, he could write with care, even with artistic finish. He was not an ignoramus, and although no university education appears in the slight record we have of his youth, he shows quite his time's pitch of enthusiasm for the names, figures, and memories of classical lore. The stamp of a humanism then diffuse and almost universal is upon him also. There are traces in his writings of the influence of Lucian, of Rabelais; he knew the *Grobianus*—probably in the Latin text—and translated at least part of it into English verse before adapting it to his own uses in *The Gull's Horn-Book.* When all is said, his humor is distinctly of the popular, native kind; and it owes much less to the skill of Dedekind's inverted precepts than to the suggestions of his own instincts.

In his varied work some parts, however interesting, hardly concern us. Of that number is *The Sun's Darling,* a charming masque which might seem to hold out great promise, as one of its characters is a personification of "Humour"—but only, of course, in the Elizabethan sense. Not so *The Honest Whore,* his dramatic masterpiece, with a discreet infusion of the humorous; in Candido, that worthy, long-suffering, shrewd citizen, who sees through much and takes more for granted; again, in the philosophy of that strangely moving play: a quiet mastery of the paradoxes of chance, a wistful sense of the unexpressed fun of things. *The Bellman of London* strikes one at first as quite humorless: it surveys the world of beggars and thieves, the rules, instruments, methods, and slang of stealing with dull uninspired thoroughness. But in the background a merry spirit is present and active, enjoying the broad impudence of it all; in spite of his moralizing the author feels a secret sympathy for the rogues, and the rebellious soul of Shakespeare's Autolycus breathes at times through his pages.

The most characteristic note of Dekker's humor is struck in *The Shoemaker's Holiday*, where he let himself go most freely. The question is thus raised once more of the limit up to which a humorist can actually write with perfect spontaneity. We have here no exception to the rule that humor lives in the pretense, but not in the reality, of improvisation and thoughtlessness. The mirth, the high spirits, the boisterous good-fellowship of Simon Eyre, reflected in the atmosphere of his workshop and successfully imitated by his men, cast upon us an almost physical spell; we are carried off our feet by the lively bustle and the torrent of picturesque language. But if the good humor is catching, the humor itself is a more delicate essence; it does not reside in the headlong rush, but in the reserve and the awareness that all the while maintain the central calm of Eyre's soul. The mind that speaks to us in the play has absorbed and digested the evil of the world, and choosing to see it under the right perspective of relativity, turns it into the proper seasoning of the mixed comedy of life. The rollicking farce is led and managed by an artistic intuition. Still, the quality of the humor owes much to sheer gifts, to a verve, a comic invention, a familiarity with the concrete flavor of experience. A Flemish realism gives body, color, and exuberance to a social sympathy and a laughing tenderness, the like of which was not to be found till more than two centuries later, in Dickens's *Christmas Carol*.

But Dekker's humor can be satirical and biting, though even then it is not properly wicked; how successfully, the best proof is *Satiromastix*. That retort upon Ben Jonson, called on the title page "humorous doctor" (again in the Elizabethan sense), beats him at his own game; Dekker indeed, of the two, is the humorist in the modern sense. An exquisite incongruity arises again and again from the implicit contrast between Jonson's high notion of his learned dignity and the very undignified situations in which he is placed on the stage. The weak points of his literary character, his vanities and pedantries are hit with an unerring aim; and the scene where he appears toiling at his ode, or that of Captain Tucca railing at him in most realistic style, are but average specimens of the controversies of the age. And as if Dekker had taken care to rival his enemy on his chosen ground, the style of the play, with a good deal of coarseness, reaches at times a truly classical elegance and correctness.

Merits of the same order are apparent in the humor of *The Gull's Horn-Book, The Devil Let Loose, The Wonderful Year,* and *The Bachelor's Banquet.* Dekker here is the careful writer, capable of a sustained and polished irony. The sea-change which the theme of the *Grobianus* suffers in *The Gull's Horn-Book* has been explained above.[47] The severely objective manner of Dedekind, from which he departs only to praise the worst behavior with solemn seriousness,[48] is caught to per-

[47] See section iv of the present chapter. Dekker's view of his book in its relation to the *Grobianus* is expressed in the preface "to the reader": "This tree of Gulls was planted long since, but not taking root, could never bear till now. It hath a relish of Grobianism, and tastes very strongly of it in the beginning: the reason thereof is, that, having translated many Books of that into English Verse, and not greatly liking the subject, I altered the shape, and of a Dutchman fashioned a mere Englishman. It is a Table wherein are drawn sundry Pictures; the colours are fresh; if they be well laid on, I think my workmanship well bestowed; if ill, so much the better, because I draw the pictures only of Gulls" (A. B. Grosart, ed., *The Non-dramatic Works of Thomas Dekker*, London, 1884-1886). Dekker's unfinished verse translation seems not to have been published, and not to be the same as *The School of Slovenry*, 1605.

[48] That the trick in itself was already familiar to ancient writers is pointed out by Roger Bull in his Preface to his translation of the *Grobianus*, mentioned above (*The Compleat Booby*, 1739): "Nor is this manner of writing inferior to any other, if we may believe Quintilian. '*Omnis false dicendi ratio,*' says that great orator, '*in eo est, ut aliter quam est rectum verumque dicatur; intelligitur enim quod non dicitur.*' "

fection; and through the whole treatise a scientist's attitude towards the matter of his study is strictly preserved. By the coherence of that discipline the book is important; it is an object lesson in the more material method of humor and was influential as such during the seventeenth and early eighteenth centuries. The neat turn, the deft handling of the epigrams happily set off the wealth of observation and the familiar knowledge of London with which the satire is nourished. It stands to Dekker's credit that the second part of the book, where he applies the method freely to new themes and to an original English background, should be better than the first.[49] The tone of parody, at times, and a slightly sardonic note call up the names of Lucian and More in the past, of Swift and Carlyle in the future. The logic of absurdity is pushed to a fine intensity of effects. Does not the following passage read like Swift and remind us of the famous "Meditation upon a Broomstick"?

> Grass is the hair of the earth, which, so long as it is suffered to grow, it becomes the wearer, and carries a most pleasing colour, but when the sun-burnt clown makes his mowes at it, and (like a Barber) shaves it off to the stumps, then it withers and is good for nothing, but to be thrust up and down amongst Jades. How ugly is a bald pate! It looks like a face wanting a nose; or like ground eaten bare with the arrows of Archers, whereas a head all hid in hair gives even to a most wicked face a sweet proportion, and looks like a meadow newly married to the Spring: which beauty in men the Turks envying, they no sooner lay hold on a Christian, but the first mark they set upon him, to make him know he is a slave, is to shave off all his hair close to the skull. A Mahometan cruelty therefore is it, to stuff breeches and tennis-balls with that, which, when 'tis once lost, all the hare-hunters in the world may sweat their hearts out, and yet hardly catch it again.[50]

[49] The half-conscious process in Dekker's mind can be represented logically. The starting point is the wrong scale of values, which was responsible for the selfish and coarse behavior of the "Grobian." The gullibility of the "Gull" is another false scale, based on the vanities and conventions of the city life; and the fop or "gallant," into whom the mere gull is soon made to develop, has his sense of social valuation thoroughly warped, standing in fact on the road that leads directly to Thackeray's snob.

[50] *The Gull's Horn-Book* (Temple Classics: London, 1904), chap. iii, pp. 29-30.

Other pamphlets turn that mock gravity to good use, as a further quotation may show:

The name of this strange country is Hell; in discovery of which, the quality of the Kingdom, the condition of the Prince, the estate of the People, the traffic thither (marry no transportation of goods from thence) shall be painted to the life. It is an Empire, that lies under the torrid zone. . . .[51]

In its finest shades Dekker's humor is not unworthy of being compared with Chaucer's. *The Wonderful Year* (1603), after due emphasis has been laid on the death of the queen, passes on to a relation of the plague, written with a realism equal to that of Defoe; but as a relief, the reader is next treated to stories of the highest comic flavor, told with excellent composure and skill—like the tale of the Cobbler's wife, or that of the red-nosed Innkeeper, a cross between the *Canterbury Tales* and Rabelais. "That the Hamburgers offered I know not how many dollars, for his company in an East-Indian voyage, to have stood a night in the Poop of their Admiral, only to save the charge of candles. . . ."[52] Dekker indeed had a natural gift of *finesse;* and the triumph of his humor in this more intellectual and drier vein is characteristically associated with a favorite theme of the fabliaux. *The Bachelor's Banquet* is patently imitated from the *quinze joies de mariage;* still the copy is done by the hand of a master. The work is not of an even quality; but its best chapters are delightfully sly and witty; the dire lot of the patient husband is described with lively zest, while a touch of tolerance and genial sympathy tempers here and there the hardness of French cynicism.

VII. Deloney

With Thomas Deloney the very idea of a writer who represented the lower middle class and whose culture was immune from refining and disturbing influences seems to be realized. Although he knew Latin, there is no reason to believe that he ever went to a university. He had personal

[51] *The Devil Let Loose.*
[52] *Non-Dramatic Works,* I, 138-39.

experience of the silk-weaving industry in London and at Norwich; his sympathies with the suffering multitude were expressed more freely than Dekker's, in ballads, one of which at least threatened to bring him into trouble. He was no leveler, but shared all the impatience of the citizens under regulations that impeded their economic progress and a hierarchy that did not make allowance for their expanding ambition. As would happen at that early stage, his bourgeois grievances on political and economic grounds felt at one with the social wrongs of the many; he obeyed the impulses and was stirred by the emotions of an almost democratic faith, although his vision was restricted in fact, more than he knew, by the point of view of a relatively privileged class.

When all is said, Deloney was actually in contact with the working people of his time, and his literary instincts were fashioned very largely by that contact. His novels are realistic studies in the romance of industry as it then existed, with strangely prophetic visions of the future. Although the home was still normally the seat of productive activities, he was haunted by grand vistas of large-scale workshops. And his art was guided by notions derived from popular literature. The jestbooks and collections of funny tales gave him the simplified technique of his storytelling. *Jack of Newbury*, *The Gentle Craft*, *Thomas of Reading* are just bunches of anecdotes, roughly organized round the biography of the hero, the point of which is most often at once didactic and funny. No definite influence of the picaresque model need be conjectured; the theme of an adventurous life was in the air and answered the prevailing taste of both writer and public.

It appears thus only natural that Deloney's realism should have been humorous and that his humor should be of the national, popular brand. But the case when probed reveals an unexpected difference. Deloney's manner is not only personal; in some respects it has a rather exceptional ring. His thought is clearer, his style neater and more sparing, his turn of phrase more dexterous than would normally happen with a self-taught teller of tales from the people. In spite of his social feeling and his resolute optimism, the tone of narrative and dialogue is with him matter-of-fact, a trifle hard; he reminds us at times of Chaucer's few cruel stories and of the fabliaux. Other facts than his surname, with its possible derivation, or what is known of the Huguenot immigrants who developed the silk industry in England, encourage the conjecture that he might have been of French origin.[53] The portrait of the Frenchman in *The Gentle Craft* is more indulgent than was the rule in Elizabethan literature. Whatever the roots of his personality may have been, Deloney's clever, sly mind took in the spirit and the method of indirect comedy very well; his possibly French wit was stimulated by the English atmosphere to a realization of the value of concrete raciness that was far above the normal. As if the power of cross-fertilization were once more illustrated, the resulting humor is a robust and lively hybrid, the seeds of which may be cosmopolitan, but whose temper after all is predominantly English.

Jack of Newbury makes pleasant reading. The note of merry, shrewd irony is struck from the beginning, as soon as it becomes clear to the "wild youths of the town" that handsome, well-behaved, level-headed Jack will marry his employer's widow, that "very comely ancient woman, and of reasonable wealth." Their gibes have the reserve of jokes which will not give away their point at once; the method of indirectness and understatement prevails through the whole book. And yet the likelihood of the story is in no wise impaired; a realistic manner of rendering the speech of even simple characters is quite compatible with the tone of implicit comedy, since a pregnant brevity in fun has become an instinct with uncultivated speakers in most countries. A flat explicitness and a wiser discretion are equally likely to be found in the typical products of the democratic vein, wherever the mental temper of the nation is not too heavy. That the English had a very fair share of the right intuition goes without saying, since they developed the faculty of humor through a practically independent growth. That this faculty is for them a birthright and an exclusively national privilege is a more debatable proposition.

[53] The question is discussed at some length by A. Chevalley in *Thomas Deloney: Le Roman des Métiers au temps de Shakespeare* (Paris, 1926).

There are moments when Deloney shows some lack of humor: it is when he is carried away by his bourgeois enthusiasm and pride before the prospect of an industrialized, humming, happy nation. He can then dream, with a glow, that children of five might earn an honest penny a day in the common workshop by their labor so as no longer to be dependent upon their parents. His social conscience and his power of sympathetic realization, judged by our standards, are equally at fault, and the lack of perceptive suppleness at once reacts upon the humor, which vanishes. *The Gentle Craft* is rather disappointing in the same respect and compares unfavorably with Dekker's *Shoemaker's Holiday*; but *Thomas of Reading* shows again all the liveliness of an agile mind. One may quote as an example these words of the clothiers' wives, justly incensed at their puritanic husbands:

Must we be so tied to our task, that we may not drink with our friends? Fie, fie, upon these yellow hose, will no other dye serve your turn? Have we thus long been your wives, and do you now mistrust us? Verily you eat too much salt, and that makes you grow choleric; bad livers judge all others the like, but in faith you shall not bridle us so like asses, but we will go to our friends, when we are sent for, and do you what you can.[54]

The highly flavored narrative goes on to the end, picturesque, slightly impudent, rich with observation, not without a leavening of fancy, but kept within the bounds of artistic reserve by a seeming unawareness of its aims. It has much of a Flemish picture, without the unbridled exuberance; in it French *finesse* and English realism are happily blended. It thus appears as if the popular, national vein had by that time become capable of the ease and refinement which had been the distinctive contribution of the humanists. A synthesis was possible; and it is at least a lucky coincidence that we should find the best of both traditions united in Shakespeare's humor.[55]

[54] *Works*, ed. F. O. Mann (Oxford, 1912), p. 217.

[55] It is a significant fact that the writings of the English and Scottish Reformers should frequently have gleams of what might be called humor of the indigenous, popular type. In their appeal to the consciences of the nation at large, they gave expression to a fund of instincts which they shared with the common man, and which even their zeal could not sterilize in their own minds.

As would be expected, John Knox is not exactly a case in point, although we have Carlyle's voucher that "this Knox has a vein of drollery in him. . . . He has a true eye for the Ridiculous . . . not a loud laugh; you would say, a laugh in the eyes most of all" ("The Hero as Priest," *Heroes*, IV). But Latimer's *Sermon on the Ploughers*, for instance, glows with a liveliness of racy language and imagery, and tingles with the repressed chuckling of a shrewd satirist; Stephen Gardiner keeps a vigorous hold upon the concreteness of things, and knows how to distil from them a subtle essence of humor (See P. Janelle, *Le Schisme Anglican et les lettres de Stephen Gardiner*, 1933). The palm of course belongs to Sir David Lindsay (see Part I, chap. v), whose place among the humorists of Scotland is no less secure than among her poets or the fathers of her Reformation (besides the better known *Thrie Estaitis*, see *The Answer quhilk Schir David Lyndesay maid to the King is Flyting; The Historie of . . . Squyer William Meldrum*). His quiet, sly manner is more effective than his violent outpourings. Those men were all scholars; but their humor is no offshoot from their scholarship; it wells up from their deepest and most spontaneous nature.

CHAPTER IX

SHAKESPEARE'S HUMOR: I. THE UNFOLDING OF THE INSTITUTION[1]

I. SHAKESPEARE AND HUMOR

IN SHAKESPEARE'S work the development of English humor comes to a fulness of realization unexampled before him. Aspects of the new mental attitude had been clearly, even brilliantly, illustrated by earlier English writers; but none of them had mastered the whole scope of that means of expression, with the possible exception of Chaucer, who had known best how to reconcile delicate subtlety with high-flavored realism. Even Chaucer's range, however, cannot be compared with Shakespeare's: his survey of life and character, wonderfully rich as it is, does not reach the same variety and the same depth. If from the past we turn to the future, the perspective that opens out is not very different: this or that writer will specialize, after Shakespeare, in some province or provinces of the empire of humor, and by his particular addiction to them reach original, unparalleled effects that secure for him the sovereign possession of his own field; but none will display such a broad and powerful grasp of the whole. The most decisive and most creative expansion of English humor took place long after the Elizabethan age, in the century from Addison to Charles Lamb; but there was not then, nor has there been since, any greater humorist than Shakespeare. A different conclusion was hardly conceivable, as soon as humor was studied in its proper connection with a mental background, part and parcel of which it really is: more completely than anyone else Shakespeare was lord of human life, with all its incentives to the wistful smile of the myriad-minded observer.

[1] The substance of this chapter and the next two has been largely used in the writing of my French study, *L'Humour de Shakespeare* (Paris, 1945).

To claim so much for him is equivalent to saying that in his work the two main lines of progress which we have been following through the English Renaissance meet and are united. Such a position at the point of synthesis is indeed that which the historian of humor can safely assign to Shakespeare; in him both traditions are fused and incorporated. But it would not be true to say that he represented them equally. How he came under the stimulus of previous writers and assimilated their examples is largely a mystery; no precise account of his education and culture can be given, as the data prove of course radically insufficient; only some contacts may be marked down or securely inferred between the Stratford boy or the London playwright and the books, the teachers, the disciplines through which the lessons of literary humor would reach him. That he was reached and felt the magnetic power is beyond doubt; failing new evidence, this general fact only should be taken into account.

How this works out in practice might be summed up briefly as follows. Whatever the actual course of his studies may have been, the more important models of both traditions lay open to him. We can be positive that he was not ignorant of the classics and the greater humanists. It is certain that knowing at least some Latin, he lived in circles where a warm, if perhaps not erudite, enthusiasm for the memories of antiquity was common; out of the texts, the translations, imitations, allusions, an atmosphere had been created, which he breathed eagerly, rich with a thousand hints that a quick, assimilative mind would improve. That he read anything of Lucian's work it does not seem possible to affirm;[2] but Plautus he himself adapted, and Terence was a universal possession among his fellow-dramatists. With Erasmus's *Praise of Folly*, one of the most widely known masterpieces of the European Renaissance, he must have been

[2] According to B. Rascoe, Shakespeare's "*Timon of Athens* is derived from Lucian's *Timon, or the Misanthrope*, and his plays are studded with tag-lines and phrases which were either lifted bodily from Lucian's text . . . or had already passed from Lucian, in translation, into the phrasal currency of the time" (*Prometheans, Ancient and Modern*, London and New York, 1933, pp. 120-21). Prof. T. M. Parrott is more guarded in his claim: "Some hints were caught also" (for *Timon of Athens*) "from Lucian's dialogue, . . . which Shakespeare may have read in translation" (*William Shakespeare*, New York and Chicago, 1934, p. 165). It seems safer not to go beyond this.

acquainted. One cannot resist an inference that he came across the *Grobianus*, at least in his later career, and through the 1605 rendering. Cervantes as well could be to him at best only a late discovery. A few allusions to Rabelais, some plain and important reminiscences of Montaigne, the atmosphere of French wit in at least one of his plays are sure proof that the Gallic verve and *finesse* were not outside his ken. The Italian example lay within his reach through Hoby's *Courtier* and Sir John Harington's translation of the *Orlando Furioso*. It is, on the other hand, safe to presume that he got some inkling of the works of his greater English predecessors; an acquaintance with Chaucer can be established; it is very probable that he knew More's *Utopia*, John Heywood's Interludes, and had somehow felt the stimulating shock of Skelton's racy vigor; while it is certain that he was familiar with Sidney's *Arcadia* and, among his contemporaries, with the humorous vein in Nashe, Dekker, and Deloney, for instance.

A slight body of tangible evidence and a larger one of reasonable conjecture would thus tend to make him the actual or likely heir of the schooling which books could give in the more refined as well as the broader manner of indirect, inverted pleasantry. But whatever he may have owed to books, he owed infinitely more to nature. To literary patterns, in this aspect of his work as in others, no essential, vital line of derivation can be traced; everything, on the contrary, points to the predominant force of instinct. Shakespeare's humor imbibed the lesson of intellectual suppleness from books through a process which must remain obscure; the measure of its debt to previous writers cannot be assessed; but its growth was certainly more a matter of intuition than of art, and that intuition was the flower of cravings for expression which were inborn in him and through which he stands as the supreme representative of the original English genius. So, while the influence of the humanist tradition is like a leaven whose action can be felt everywhere in his plays, Shakespeare is more fully and centrally the product of the national, popular spirit: his dependence upon the latter was not a question of reading, of conscious imitation; he absorbed it through every pore, in it he moved and had his being, and he grew along with it.

To that extent only can one speak of a synthesis. No actual combination of that kind, of course, was effected purposely from the outside. Shakespeare's development was not wilful and half artificial, like Goethe's. To all appearances it was spontaneous, as it was most rapid. A mind gifted with a marvelous prescience went through stages in the realization of its secret being, none of which seems to have been determined in advance, while all do none the less fall into line as the moments of an onward progress.

Shakespeare's apprenticeship to humor was part of his self-discovery. Within a few years he conquered its whole range, just as he was gradually making his own the world of drama. The humorist, like the dramatist, advanced by no means according to plan, but with experimental and tentative steps. In the unfolding of this more particular intuition and the development of his humor degrees can be marked out, this or that play be selected to illustrate this or that manner or shade. But there is no regularity in the details of the process; it is like the pushing up of twigs and leaves in all directions by a growing plant under the law of its own vitality and the influence of the light.

So we cannot say that Shakespeare passed from one of the two main aspects of humor to the other, although it is possible to state that on the whole he worked from a more humanist to a more national vein. Altogether, the humanist influence is especially visible at the beginning; and the greatest humorous creations are done rather on the plane of the national tradition, which he sums up, glorifies, and enriches at the same time.

In a way, then, the word "synthesis" is not misleading. Shakespeare's sway soon extended equally over the most subtle and the most racy verve of comic invention. When his growth was complete, he himself *was* the synthesis. Indeed, the matter was not one of contiguous domains being brought under one rule. The fusion, silently effected, was intimate and thorough. The essences of the two main modes of humor mixed in one rich and quintessential principle, which is its very soul; a plastic and supple genius, which can, and does, instil subtlety into the broadest farce, and the strong flavor of raciness into the most brilliant display of intellectual irony. Then, and then only, was the animating spirit of English humor, which had already been fully alive in Chaucer, finally exalted to its creative strength. The development that followed through centuries of thought and literature gave it wider and increasingly varied expressions, but did not alter its original quality. Shakespeare's range in humor remained unsurpassed by any English writer. He did not concentrate on any key or keys, like Sterne and Lamb for instance, but had them all at his command.

A connected issue might be briefly raised here. Humor is the very flower of an intellectual personality; at its highest, it expresses all the mental powers of a man. So manifold and deep are its interrelations with our tendencies and faculties that it is part of our inmost selves. Shakespeare's humor is exclusively his own; in the scenes where it is characteristic and dominant no collaboration can be thought of. On some occasions it might thus be regarded as one, and not the least reliable, among the inner tests of authenticity. But readers may not agree as to what constitutes the most characteristic quality of Shakespeare's humor; and the values upon the accurate perception of which the working of the test hangs not being objective enough, little can be expected from its application. In practice, one would have to fall back on the results of a broader test, that of the poet's intellectual development as a whole; a genuine criterion no doubt, but one from which too much has perhaps been demanded.

As all such problems are difficult and involved, we shall abstain from rushing in where angels fear to tread and avoid discussing them altogether. The usually accepted canon of Shakespeare's work will give its basis to this study. It is a fact besides that in the plays where the authenticity of some part or parts has been questioned, the humorous sections, broadly speaking, and at any rate all the best humor, are certainly genuine and almost universally held as such. So the necessity will not arise to have recourse to the test; and we shall be amply rewarded if we can in any measure contribute to strengthen the sense of a binding association between Shakespeare's humor and the very core of his individual genius.

One more preliminary remark should be made. The three chapters given to the study of Shakespeare deal with the three groups of plays which make up the whole of his dramatic work. The guiding principle in the distinction of those groups has been Shakespeare's humor itself, its matter, and its manner. Naturally enough, as his humor is bound up with the growth of his creative mind, the three parts answer to the most plainly marked and usually accepted divisions in the development of his work. To that extent—and in so far as the series of the plays falls of itself into broad periods—the order of the present study is chronological. But as a margin of uncertainty persists about the succession of the plays within a given period, the point will hardly be pressed. Inside each group the plays will be examined not strictly and systematically in their chronological sequence, but according to their affinities in regard to our subject; and the fact of growth and the presumption of gathering experience will be called in now and then, but with caution, where the data of the case safely permit.

II. The Temptation: "Love's Labour's Lost"

The unfolding of Shakespeare's intuition shows us at first various attempts to realize the possibilities of humor on the basis of lighter, rather superficial satire, or of farce.[3] This is but a different way of repeating the trite assertion that his earliest comedy will draw its effects from relatively inferior sources. These, such as they are, offer humor some opportunities; but they are far from giving it full scope. One can easily see, moreover, that Shakespeare's instinct is already developing away from those cheap devices, or at any rate feeling its way to others. If they are not exactly a conscious experiment, those attempts make up, as was said above, a stage in the process of self-discovery.

[3] The plays covered by this chapter are, in Sir E. K. Chambers's tentative order: 1590-1591, *2 Henry VI*, *3 Henry VI*; 1591-1592, *1 Henry VI*; 1592-1593, *Richard III*, *The Comedy of Errors*; 1593-1594, *Titus Andronicus*, *The Taming of the Shrew*; 1594-1595, *The Two Gentlemen of Verona*, *Love's Labour's Lost*, *Romeo and Juliet*; 1595-1596, *Richard II*, *A Midsummer Night's Dream*.

From its traditional place as one of the very earliest of the comedies, *Love's Labour's Lost* has been shifted to a somewhat later position on the list. Still, it offers the best starting-point for a study of Shakespeare's humor which, taking chronology into account, does not feel strictly bound to it.

The theme of *Love's Labour's Lost* is affectation in general—more particularly that of overingenious thought and farfetched expression. The manner runs riot here with a brilliance unsurpassed in any literature; almost all the characters seem to be infected with it; the ladies sparkle no less than the men; indeed they often eclipse them: and even the critical reader is swept off his balance at times by the contagious enthusiasm of irresponsible wit. Still, the author's purpose does not leave us in doubt; what he is after, we may reasonably surmise, is an object-lesson in complacent, self-destructive excess.

The satire is not bitter but gentle; it looks at times as if it were in sympathy with its object. The unblushing display of verbal bravura has a stimulating, an intoxicating, power from which the liveliness of the play is mainly derived. To the pleasurable excitement thus produced, a shade of amusement will be superadded without a clash. The obvious exaggeration of high-flown language, the overrefinement of exquisite comparisons—in short, the superfluous mental energy lavished upon simple things that might have been simply put—are a departure from the normal, a kind of paradox; as such they invite reference to a standard of use and wont, in their contrast with which the germ of a comic impression lies. The dazzling feats of verbal ingenuity with which *Love's Labour's Lost* is rife might be said to make up by themselves a sort of comedy. But of humor, properly so called, which demands implicitness, there cannot be so far any question. Such witty exercises are nothing if not explicit; they aim clearly at an object—that of being fine—which is plain, even if what is uttered partakes more or less of the nature of riddles. No inner sense of reserve and restraint is discoverable there. The criticism of that affectation is not, in itself, humorous either. To make an affected manner ridiculous by contrasting it with common simplicity is quite a legitimate method of comedy; but it lacks the background without which no humor, in the proper meaning of the word, can arise. An opening for the latter appears, on the contrary, as soon as the affectation is revealed as a pretense under the disguise of which the mind preserves its balance and lucidity. The animation and the amusement roused by a fantastically artificial manner partake thenceforth of the nature of play; they fall to their proper places in a silent scale of values based on normal perceptions; and the spirit of relativity, thus set loose, instils a soul of humor into the whole process, whether the main stress is laid on self-satisfied posturing or on the irony that lives at its core and mocks at it.

The rich exuberance of thought and word in *Love's Labour's Lost* can be classified under the general name of Italianism, which covers a much wider field than what should be rightly assigned to the Euphuistic manner. Euphuism in the stricter sense, as a possible constituent of humor, has already been examined;[4] and the relation thus adumbrated may be extended to the whole of Italianism. Another aspect, the conceit, will be discussed in a further part of this work, when the poets of the age, and especially Donne, are dealt with. In both cases the energy spent to lift language above the flatness of plain statement is found to preclude the possibility of the writer's being a humorist in so far as he takes himself and his fine display quite seriously; it is fully reconcilable with humor, on the contrary, and will even serve and nourish it, as soon as he evinces a consciousness of the artificiality and the limits of his own effort.

Now the presence of such a consciousness can be felt in all the play; it hovers lightly over it like a mocking spirit; it has its being chiefly in one mind, that of the author; and the humorist of *Love's Labour's Lost* is primarily Shakespeare himself. He it is whose tacit sense of sober reasonableness sets up the implicit standard by which the rashness and the finicality of the young lords are seen in their proper light. He it is, no less certainly, whose teeming fancy has called up that wonderful show of coruscating language, and in the fireworks of his own invention he has no doubt taken pleasure. This

[4] Chap. vii, sect. iv.

essential duality is the substance of his humor, which lives here, as it so often does, in the power to laugh at oneself. But how do we know that he laughs at what he enjoys? If that standard is implicit, and that sense tacit, how are they conveyed to us? Through a process of suggestion intuitively perceived, and for which it is difficult to account without altering it beyond recognition. It is mainly a matter of a subconscious inference; we gather our impression from a complex of data, most of them evanescent and subtle, the main one being the complacency with which extravagance is given its head, as if it were not felt to be extravagance, while the author's sense of values, in other respects, keeps shrewd and fine. The induction is confirmed, on the other hand, by the sober intervals, where golden truth is put in the simplest language.

There is thus created in the spectator or reader some sense of an irradiating presence, from which a genial irony, the soul of humor, is diffused throughout the play. But a more concrete stimulus brings that rather elusive impression to a head: an actual character, the most prominent indeed, that of Berowne. Those words of simple wisdom are spoken mainly by him; around him the intellectual significance of the play crystallizes; on several occasions, to all appearances, he stands as the author's mouthpiece. He is gradually revealed to us as a genuine humorist, probably the first of that kind in the development of Shakespeare's comedy.

At the first sight he is just like his gay compeers; one of them in all respects; though the most witty, the most brilliant; always on the alert, with tongue ever ready, supernaturally alive, as his skirmishes with Rosaline dazzlingly testify; a charmer among charmers.

> . . . a merrier man,
> Within the limit of becoming mirth,
> I never spent an hour's talk withal.
> His eye begets occasion for his wit;
> For every object that the one doth catch,
> The other turns to a mirth-moving jest.[5]

But this past master of the arts and graces of dialogue has

[5] II, i, 70-75.

method and a core of reason in his madness. While his companions are only the gaudy flies of an artificial world, his feet are firmly planted on the ground. He has not lost contact with human nature. From the first he pricks the bubble that looks so inviting; in the success of the young king's fine scheme he won't believe; it will be wrecked, he urges, on this or that rock. He is young, however, and lets himself be persuaded; down goes his signature to the common bond. A tempting adventure, after all, were it only for the fun and excitement of talking away the very plan to which one has just subscribed! Still, Berowne is no mere talker. In the midst of all his light-headed prancing and hairsplitting, sober lines ring out suddenly with strange power and awake deep echoes of thought:

> Study is like the heaven's glorious sun
> That will not be deep-searched with saucy looks:
> Small have continual plodders ever won,
> Save base authority from others' books.
> These earthly godfathers of heaven's lights,
> That give a name to every fixed star,
> Have no more profit of their shining nights
> Than those that walk, and wot not what they are.
> Too much to know is to know nought but fame;
> And every godfather can give a name.[6]

When the young lords' utopia tumbles down about their ears, under no more deadly fire than the glances from ladies' eyes, Berowne is ready at once to take stock of an event which he had foreseen, to point out the error, and draw the moral. That this part should fall to his share is no wonder; his is the wisdom of humor. Able as he is to think on two different planes—and in so thinking, an image of his creator the writer—he carries duality about with him. From the first his speech had overtones. While the wits said one empty thing, and meant another just as empty, his jokes managed to convey serious hints; he was characteristically brief and pregnant: his jests had the compression, the power of resilience, which belongs only to true humor:

[6] I, i, 89-98.

Maria: That last is Berowne, the merry mad-cap lord.
Not a word with him but a jest.
Boyet: And every jest but a word.[7]

He knows how to laugh at himself. How could he miss the lesson of complexity and humility? It is brought home to him. He too has fallen in love, written tender, foolish letters. With what sparkling verve he scoffs at his own defeat![8] While his friends are melting in amorous grief, ingenious sighs, and self-conscious tears, Berowne's asides make up an ironical comment upon the common fate. As by right, he gives the play its real conclusion:

> It is religion to be thus forsworn;
> For charity itself fulfils the law;
> And who can sever love from charity?[9]

Love's Labour's Lost thus appears to us, from our special angle, in a light which perhaps is not misleading, and does in fact agree well enough with the current interpretation of that early attempt. The young Shakespeare, sowing his wild oats, takes a leaf from the book of the foppery then in fashion. At once he outshines all the luminaries of Italianism and the most approved examples of courtly stylishness. Nothing can be more witty, more affected, more brilliant; and if brilliance and verbal wit are the tests of perfection, the masterpiece of Elizabethan comedy is here and nowhere else. But even while he displays the unparalleled agility of his mind, Shakespeare disdainfully throws away the bauble which, he knows, is but tinsel. Having at the first trial reached a climax in a range of values with which his instinct is dissatisfied, he will in future grant it only the easygoing favor of some relaxed moments. As a whole, his inspiration will grow away from it. Again and again his satire will be pointed at the hollow amusement of vacant brains, even if the toy is gloriously painted and a joy to the eye. We seem to hear the very accent of his voice in the lines where Berowne bids goodby to the lures of affected speech:

[7] II, i, 227-28.
[8] III, i.
[9] IV, iii, 382-84.

Taffeta phrases, silken terms precise,
Three-piled hyperboles, spruce affection,
Figures pedantical; these summer flies
Have blown me full of maggot ostentation.
I do forswear them. . . .[10]

The intoxication had already appeared in his work under various guise; it will crop up again here and there. But nowhere will it be displayed with the writer's unqualified concurrence; and his amused irony will always peep out on that imaginary countenance we make up, from the features of the mind with which we hold spiritual converse in a book. Is this to say that nothing will henceforth serve Shakespeare's turn except downright simplicity? Will his meaning always be expressed

In russet yeas, and honest-kersey noes?[11]

On these lines, so vigorously laid down with the sure intuition of genius, Shakespeare's manner will assuredly develop. But simplicity need not be poverty of thought; the grandest emotions, the sharpest thrusts at ideas that lie too deep for tears will be rendered by him, at times with elliptic energy, in broken phrases like flashes, yet in words that, being inevitable, are the most obvious. Still, that wealth of significance will also imply some indirectness of language. More will be meant than is said; each line will reverberate in our minds and grow upon us; and among those virtualities of expression the allusiveness and pregnancy of humor will naturally find its place. Have we not in these words of Rosaline's, speaking to Berowne, the very picture of that active reaction of the listener's mind, which the humorist expects and upon the expectation of which he works:

A jest's prosperity lies in the ear
Of him that hears it, never in the tongue
Of him that makes it.[12]

The superiority of implicit to explicit comedy, of humor over

[10] V, ii, 452-56.
[11] *Ibid.*, l. 459.
[12] V, ii, 936-38.

farce could not be more clearly claimed or more tellingly formulated.

The special attention we have chosen to give, from the angle of our theme, to *Love's Labour's Lost* has perhaps been justified. Whatever place may be assigned to the play in the chronological ordering of the earliest comedies, it embodies an intellectual decision of the utmost significance. It enables one to say that mere verbal wit was for a time a master temptation to the young Shakespeare, and that his humor found itself, literally, in a renunciation to mere verbal wit. This renunciation was tantamount to a complete reversal of artistic policy; and it opened the way for a progress that led to great humor, as it led to greater art. Indeed the light, merry fancy of *Love's Labour's Lost* is weighted at the core with the thoughtful amusement of the humorist; and it is from the very orgy of graceful word-play—a riot of his making—that Shakespeare withdraws into the inwardness of his own spirit. His reflective mind turns rather to the laughter that is rich with meditative echoes, and to the mirth that possesses an aftertaste of melancholy. The winding up of the delightfully irresponsible comedy is sobered with a glimpse of the real world, and its all too genuine problems and pains; an ironical doom sends the wits to actual retirement for a twelve-month, and Berowne to the hospitals, where his mirth will cheer the patients.

This does not exhaust the significance to us of *Love's Labour's Lost.* The play would show as well that the young Shakespeare could, if he had chosen, have stood in the field of humor as the representative before all of the humanist influence. The properly humorous element—that which derives from the sense of relativity in values—is here mostly intellectual and critical; it is in line with the tradition of Erasmus and with Lyly. The preference which Shakespeare was already evincing, when stock is taken of his early comedy as a whole, for the realistic, the concrete, and the national inspiration in humor, is thus the more remarkable.

This other aspect of humor is not far to seek, however, even in *Love's Labour's Lost.* Costard the clown is now a clumsy dunce, a butt for cheap laughter, now—and this is more to the point—a sly rogue, just clever enough to speculate on his thick-pated appearance; half a Puritan withal, solemn after his backsliding; and even he will dabble in big words, to match the prevailing affectation. Of affectation again, and more signally, Don Armado the Spaniard and Holofernes the schoolmaster are of course the egregious examples and victims; one a "fantastical" long-winded beau, as stiff in his sentences as in the joints of his gaunt body, the other a pedant of the pedants, his mind stuffed with the dead jargon of the schools; a worthy man after all, if only he could look straight at the world and not through his preposterous figments. Both are passive slaves to cut-and-dried whims, habits, or notions; with both life has become mechanical. They make us laugh and feel glad that we are free; they stimulate in us the craving for supple thought, the desire to see the other side and what truth looks like when tempered with relativity. Outstanding specimens as they are of the humorless character, they fulfil their function in tickling and awaking in us the sense of humor.

The glorified Italianism of *Love's Labour's Lost* had its conventions and an intrinsic monotony that made it inevitably pall upon the taste. In the *Comedy of Errors* the old classical theme of mistaken identity is intensified but not enriched by its duplication. However efficiently the idea may be worked out, it is at best a poor species of the comic. The source of the fun here is again a convention—a suspension of disbelief, to use Coleridge's phrase once more, which cannot be thorough in anybody's mind. Not only must the twin masters be

> The one so like the other,
> As could not be distinguished but by names,[13]

but their servants also must be twins, and no less alike. When once such a postulate has been swallowed, we find ourselves out of life and out of the real world. By violating elementary likelihood the writer has brought the most funny situations within his easy reach, but at such cheap price that there will be no depth or vitality in his fun. From such a germ it seems at first that hardly more than farce could grow.

[13] I, i, 51-52.

But just as in the former play the humor arose indirectly from the affectation, which was not maintained in its integrity but seen through, the convention here is handled in a humorous way because it does not appeal wholeheartedly to our acceptance. It is quite willing that no one should take it very seriously. We can almost see the playwright's tongue in his cheek. One intimation of this confessed unreality, among others, is that the characters are more or less aware of it. Their reactions when faced with the painful or ridiculous consequences to themselves of an absurd imbroglio are not quite those of flesh-and-blood people under the shrewd or humiliating blows of fortune; they grow most amusing when most persecuted by fate. The paradox, no doubt, is very cleverly managed, and each participant in the general make-believe preserves his idiosyncrasies too well not to remain individual and convincing. But it is plain, at the same time, that everybody is out to make the huge joke a success. We are the more inclined to think so, as the playwright, who after all pulls the wires, displays such genuine knowledge of human nature, moves his puppets with so much unfeigned liveliness, keeping the interplay of temperaments and the animation of dialogue at such high pitch. How superior he is to his own subject! How fine a master of psychological truth and of that close adherence to life which we cease noticing in his works until we open those of any other writer! A pleasant, though not deep, comedy of character is thus founded on a basis which our instinct knows to be unsafe, but which no one minds as the author does not really try to pass it off upon us under false pretenses. Even the rollicking scenes of the play, kept as they are within relatively sober limits, are steeped in that spirit of discreet irony, of duality and mental freedom which invests them with the quality of genuine humor.

On the whole the humanist influence may be said to predominate again in the *Comedy of Errors*. But the source is Plautus, whose comic genius was nothing if not popular; and Shakespeare needed no encouragement to make the most of the opportunities which the theme offered in that respect. The two servants are caught at times by the infection of a truly

British verve, and their language—which metrically approaches doggerel—has a most national flavor.[14]

III. Fools and Clowns, Unconscious and Half-conscious

From the first Shakespeare's comedy developed with an almost unerring aim towards an inspiration drawn from the most genuine sources, those of nature and truth. Implied in this gravitation of his art was a similar preference, gradually revealed, in the field of humor, for realism; an intuitive and safe perception again, as the realistic attitude is in such deep-laid affinity with the humorous.

Among the stock characters with which realistic comedy had been dealing were those of the fool and the clown. They would, in the spirit of their tradition, serve the turn of farce much better than that of humor. It was their accredited part to crack the cheapest or the coarsest jokes and rouse the most explicit and unsophisticated laughter. Shakespeare's use of the fool and the clown is one of the outstanding problems connected with his creative activity as a dramatist. So wide is the research that it much exceeds the scope of the present study. All that can be attempted here is to sum up its general conclusions from the particular point of view of a special inquiry.[15]

Putting it very simply, one may say that Shakespeare's departures in this respect were twofold. To begin with, he made the clown an occasion for genuine humor by turning him into a realistic illustration of picturesque thickheadedness. Although rather obvious, and often attempted before, this was no easy thing to do well. It takes acute observation and an expert handling of character to draw a dullness that is lifelike and that however is not dull. The portrait must be so suggestive as to stimulate thought, at the same time as it causes the mechanical laugh, born of the sight of mere failure in clumsy efforts to answer the calls of life. Only such many-sided pictures can rouse in us a complex perception and make us think on several planes at once. The next step, one which Shakespeare took tentatively even at the beginning of his career,

[14] III, i.

[15] See, of course, B. Swain, *Fools and Follies during the Middle Ages and the Renaissance* (New York, 1932).

was to raise the clown from the quality of a mere jester or of a butt to that of a true humorist. Due stress will have to be laid further upon his unique achievements in that line.

The best illustration of the first method would be Bottom and his friends *(A Midsummer Night's Dream)*. One can embrace their beings in a single epithet: they are fools. But when that has been said, nothing has been said. The comedy which they unconsciously create for us is humorous because it is a rich feast in which our sense of psychological truth and our susceptibility to intellectual irony are ceaselessly roused and rewarded. Nothing can be more lifelike than the characters themselves, with the individual traits and the little oddities of each; and few things are more highly charged with a pungent flavor of philosophical relativity than their honest, solemn blundering through their ill-assorted tasks. The fun is multiplied in every way, as all possible kinds of naïveté, unfitness, and paradox feed the stream of delightful absurdity; and the point of these whole scenes is sharpened by the ironical circumstance that they make up a play within a play, the extremely raw idea of dramatic illusion on which they are based being shown in a piquant analogy and contrast with the more acceptable conventions of the actual drama spread out before us. More than anything else, Bottom's magnificent self-satisfaction is provocative; it raises him to the quality of a type—that of the imperviousness to humor that makes us tingle with humorous joy. The ass's head with which he is eventually crowned sits very well upon the dullard; but with the Titania episode he is exalted to an even more refined degree of symbolism and of humor, not yet relevant to our purpose.

Although he revolves in a totally different atmosphere and stands poles apart from him, the Sir John Fastolfe of *1 Henry VI* is aesthetically akin to Bottom. He is the flesh in its naïve nakedness, without any stirring of the spirit. His brief appearance is one of unrelieved grotesqueness. The open way in which his cowardice is confessed, indeed flaunted:

> All the Talbots in the world, to save my life. . . .[16]

[16] *1 Henry VI*, III, ii, 108.

is the touch of cynicism, which makes the legendary and, as it were, stereotyped character alive. The scene, indeed the greater part of the play, may not be Shakespeare's; still, doubtful as it is, the first sketch of what was to become his own Falstaff has some interest; it helps us to realize the subtle psychological process through which, from such a humorless germ, a miracle of humor could grow, the moment slavery to the flesh received its possible compensation—intellectual freedom.

But Shakespeare's instinct seems very early to have felt that fools were much more satisfactory in every way if they were conscious, even dimly and by glimpses, of their foolishness. The duality consubstantial with humor is thenceforth, and at one stroke, carried into their very selves; the spectator has no longer to actualize their humorous potentiality out of his own mind; he finds the work ready done in them and can concentrate on the enjoyment of the suggestions they afford. In fact, as human nature will readily show, that amphibious condition is very often the truth of the matter. Complete hidebound dunces are not many; more frequent everywhere, and chiefly among rustics, are the semi-dunces partly alive to the true state of things, including themselves. The flavor of rusticity in all lands is largely made up of that mixture of naïveté, ignorance, and sly, half-shrewd awareness. To endow the clowns with the saving grace of some mental perception, however fitful, was thus good realism; it was conducive as well to the creation of incipient humorists, who were no longer mere cases in point but to some extent as well self-radiating centers of humor. Once a start had been made, greater things would rapidly follow.

The early plays offer us several characters of the half-conscious type, both butts of humor, occasions for it, and in their own way to some extent, creators of it; a shifting, uncertain condition, highly favorable to shades of doubtful, mystifying humor. Costard *(Love's Labour's Lost)* is probably, as has been seen, a member of the fraternity. Launce *(The Two Gentlemen of Verona)* is a more pronounced example.

Speed, his compeer in the play, shows no sign of the grace; his wit revels in cheap quibblings, puns, and every kind of verbal trick. Launce is a match for him at that game, nay beats him; and thence Speed's sourish charge—one he has singularly little right to press:

> Well, your old vice still, mistake the word. . . .[17]

But through Launce's brazen-faced word-play, as behind a mask, we catch glimpses of the secret countenance of the humorist. His rusticity seems to strike every one. He is called "peasant" and "foolish lout." But is he really stupid? What is the part of genuine naïveté in his silliest pranks, and what that of a pawky shrewdness? We wonder; and the distinct flavor of his character lies just in our wondering. Tentatively, we might say that Launce is half a fool, but knows that he is, and so has enough inner light to play the fool; by no means a contradictory case and one which exactly meets the requirements of elementary humor. The conviction grows upon us when we hear Launce's irresistible monologue that the rogue down under the crust of his thick-headedness is enjoying the Rabelaisian fun quite knowingly.[18]

Crab, his dog—a joy to the groundlings—is at bottom, on a level of our consciousness that we dimly feel but do not reach, a symbol of the animal in man; Launce, a man not much above the animal, can lovingly change places with his dog; the ease with which the change is effected brings out the nearness; but does it not bring out the distance as well? Launce here knows what he is about and uses strategy to save his dog a beating; is he not using strategy as well to make us laugh, by his pretended innocence of impropriety? "I am the dog;—no, the dog is himself, and I am the dog;—Oh, the dog is me, and I am myself. . . ."[19] How strangely do those quibbling words echo our secret thoughts! When the rascal offers Silvia his own cur in his master's name, is it sheer silliness, or sheer impudence, or both? How greatly does a doubt serve the ends of humor, when humor lies in the oscillation of thought be-

[17] III, i, 285-86.

[18] IV, iv. Let our excuse for not quoting this very amusing passage in full be that—like most of the best humor in Shakespeare—it is so well known.

[19] II, iii.

tween two alternatives and in the impossibility of turning the probable, that relative value, into that absolute, certainty!

Juliet's nurse *(Romeo and Juliet)* is of Launce's kindred, with perhaps a lesser allowance of light. She is too impulsive and indulges the gift of the gab; he was more wary in his verve. It takes a generous estimate to make a humorist of her; but it would be niggardly to refuse her any transient spark. Her picturesque personality can be viewed from two rather different angles: either as a good soul, talkative and fussy, or as a lively gossip with a gift of racy phrasing. Of the latter there is some hope. In the fun of which she is the center, automatism and blindness, no doubt, have a large share; but no less surely a good deal of it is to be traced to sheer native drollery and alertness. Not that she is a complex being: those various features are fused in the organic unity of a supremely convincing character. That she is not all rashness and headlong garrulousness, but keeps a cool head with some ironical sense of things, flashes out at times, as when she remarks upon Juliet's answer to her mother's question:

> An honour! were not I thine only nurse,
> I would say thou hadst suck'd wisdom from thy teat. . . .[20]

IV. Ironical Humor

To the more intellectual aspects of humor and to the influence of the humanist tradition some conspicuous examples of irony, in the plays of that early period, must be referred. However definitely the distinction may be kept up between the ironical and the humorous, there prevails between them such a deep-laid analogy of intention and manner that it would be pedantic and futile to insist upon a separate treatment of the two themes. To all practical purposes irony is a parallel method to humor, with a somewhat different atmosphere. It takes its rise in the same inner duality of perception and meaning; and the two psychological and aesthetic attitudes shade off into each other.

The character of Gloucester *(Richard III)* is a magnificent study of dual awareness and expression. At the center of that

[20] I, iii, 67-68.

fearful vortex of desires, ambition, and hatred there lives, not only the energy of repression that successfully hides murderous thoughts and the policy of cunning, but a power of detached, almost disinterested reflection; a clear self-realization that is apparent from the beginning of the play, and the evidence of which almost offends at times our sense of psychological truth. Thus clearly conscious of his inner being, Richard shapes and directs every one of his gestures or his words in a full and precise manner which has been compared with that of a professional actor. It is indeed a sinister game that he is playing; and his grim pleasure in his tactics again and again points his speech with dark hints or double meanings. This trick he himself describes:

> I moralize two meanings in one word.[21]

The dramatic irony thus created is not only diffused over the career of the hero and everything that pertains to it, but it concentrates here and there in utterances which fulfil all the requirements of humor: the enjoyment of a comic contrast, at the same time suggested and disguised under a pretense of unconcern. The total effect here is too sharp and dry to meet the preferences of readers who insist that without geniality there is no humor; but others will not demur at affixing the label upon the lines in which Richard so quietly chuckles over his triumph:

> I do mistake my person all this while;
> Upon my life, she finds, althought I cannot,
> Myself to be a marvellous proper man. . . .
> Shine out, fair sun, till I have bought a glass,
> Till I may see my shadow as I pass.[22]

Or again, when he puts his private construction upon Rivers's pious commonplace:

> *Rivers:* A virtuous and a Christian-like conclusion,
> To pray for them that have done scathe to us.
> *Gloucester:* So do I ever. (Aside): being well advised:
> For had I cursed now, I had cursed myself.[23]

[21] III, i, 83.
[22] I, ii, 253-55, 263-64.
[23] I, iii, 316-19.

That spirit of cynical derision spreads over his accomplices; it breathes through the Second Murderer's speech about his conscience (I, iv, 135-44). It passes on to situations; no example could be more striking than the manner in which an imminent fate adds a dark lining for us to Hastings' words, and his convulsive horror at the sudden sight of the pit of destruction yawning before him (III, iv). But as the play gathers impetus to its inevitable end, the growing sense of doom absorbs every other impression, and the dramatic irony itself is sublimated into the terror and the pity.

From Gloucester it is a far cry to Puck *(A Midsummer Night's Dream)*. Robin Goodfellow's kindly, not ungentle, mischievousness is flavored with a very different irony, more nearly akin to humor. His practical jokes are the least interesting aspect of it. Much more germane to our purpose is the soul of quick perception that lives in him and makes him the very symbol of the ironical duality, the sense of contrasted planes from which the humorous meaning of the play develops. Puck's roguish tricks bring out the relativity of all things human, not excluding the enthusiasms of the heart; they liberate the spirit of disillusioned serenity that broods over the errors of the enchanted night and over the desperate single-mindedness of the bewitched lovers. The humor of the play, as in *Love's Labour's Lost,* is a lambent light that bathes every object, without showing up any too sharply or cruelly; the author's imagined smile, like a spiritual presence in the background of our vision, is the focus of that indulgent, amused wistfulness. The episode in which Lysander and Demetrius seek each other through the mist which Puck has raised, hacking murderously at empty space, it farcical to the eyes of the flesh, but to the mind a scene for the eternal laughter of the gods.[24] A symbol lives there, if anywhere in literature. Has Shakespeare thought it out and mentally willed it? We do not know and cannot tell; as probably as not, there was in him no definite intellectual perception of that abstract significance. But the imaginative complex in which such a perception would first lie involved was active at some level of his consciousness;

[24] III, ii.

it contained a germ that needs must grow with the growth of modern man; and that is about as near as one can get to what one may call the actual philosophy of Shakespeare. Again, is not the "tragical mirth" whose paradoxical influence, through the "play within the play," presides over the close of the comedy, the very formula of the jarring associations in which humor has its being? The "concord of this discord," which Theseus is seeking, stands as the emblem to us, not unfairly, of the humorous reconciliation and synthesis. Is Puck aware of the meaning which we read into his part? Indeed he seems to be; the topsy-turviness which sets at naught man's stiff clumsy arrangements is to him a favorite joy:

> And those things do best please me
> That befall preposterously.[25]

The reason is that he has no respect for the antics of men, as he intimates in words which herald the lesson of *The Tempest* but still lack the softer note of a more mature wisdom:

> Lord, what fools these mortals be![26]

Irony and a vivid sense of relativity are Mercutio's weapons in youth's battles of wit and words *(Romeo and Juliet)*. His opposition to Romeo is too obvious not to impress us with a major and intentional contrast. Over against the ardor of imaginative passion, the cool critical intellect stands personified and points derisively at the secret stirrings of the flesh which give a most material aspect to would-be Platonic emotions. Romeo's hot dream is blindly led by the senses; it obeys the promptings of desire; the fabric of chimerical fancy-bred love he has set up for his Rosaline is a sentimental illusion; his slavery to obscure forces stamps him with the character of a mechanically driven being, which is to the philosopher the very type of the comic. Flashing the light of his satire again and again upon that humiliating dependence, Mercutio exposes it through pitiless hints, and so creates the implicit comedy whose name is humor. He creates it like a master, with the deadly accuracy of analytical wit. He can relax, bandy remarks with

[25] III, ii, 120-21.
[26] III, ii, 115.

the nurse, nonplus her most amusingly; he is as whimsical as he is brilliant; that deadly analyst of the romantic illusion flaunts the gay feathers of a free, sprightly, sparkling verve; he revels in all the pranks of Italianism; and here once more the besetting sin of verbal affectation in wit combats is indulged, enjoyed, found wanting. While those fireworks flare up repeatedly, shot by almost every character so that even Juliet's voice has at times a falsetto ring and Romeo brings down upon himself the Friar's gentle rebuke:

> Be plain, my son, and homely in thy drift[27]

yet on the whole the play as it proceeds reverts to a more sober tenor; as if Shakespeare's undisputed presence, which we cannot help missing now and then, finally asserted itself to the ascendancy of a saner scale of values. Altogether, it is not the "Italianate" cavalier in Mercutio that we are asked to admire; and Romeo's candid description of his friend is significant: "A gentleman, nurse, that loves to hear himself talk, and will speak more in a minute than he will stand to in a month"; being, indeed, a man "that God hath made himself to mar" (II, iv). Romeo's serious, moralizing judgment here assigns Shakespeare's own limit to our appreciation of a reckless character; but that is not the poet's final word about Mercutio. As he falls, a victim to the sacred selfishness of love—Romeo's impulsive gesture, prompted by the thought of Juliet, is the cause of the fatal wound—the fierce intensity of his spirit raises him to the height of his more thoughtful self, and he dies with the haughty smile of some Bandelairian hero upon his lips, a fearless devotee of truth at any price, whose humor was sharpened with the keen edge of realism.

Realism and the relativity of things human again unite in the mood of the brief episode of the musicians who "put up their pipes" and exchange light-hearted banter before going, at the sudden news of Juliet's death (IV, v). This has the inexplicable grip upon us of the most dramatic, as well as the most philosophical, humor; an anticlimax, it is fraught with implicit pathos; all the catastrophes of fate are evoked through

[27] II, iii, 55.

the magic of symbolism by the shallow words of unconcerned menials; in the familiarity of their harmless jokes we catch a glimpse of the daily life that will go on as ever, and the contrasts of our condition are summed up in the naïve irrelevance of the scene to the tragic blow that has just fallen. Irony and humor here at their highest pitch unite in a rich essence, a foretaste of the most original effects in the masterpieces of the greater period.

V. The Popular Vein

Those various experiments were repaying, but not all to the same degree. Among the veins struck there was one more consonant than the others with Shakespeare's deepest instinct; and from that early period his genius seems to draw more fondly from it. Some notes are heard at once in which the decisive ring of his humor can be caught. The unfolding intuition finds its most fertile field in psychological realism, a range of effects often associated with popular raciness.

The discovery is only one aspect of the self-realization of Shakespeare's original powers. Striking his roots unerringly into the truth of human nature, he was reaching the stores of vitality from which his greatness would be fed. His supreme tragedy no less than his comedy grew on that common nourishment. In the darkest drama humor will play its part to restore the balance and eke out the picture of life.

From our special point of view it was Shakespeare's achievement to turn to artistic use the native shrewdness and the reticence of the live Englishman; his instinctive gift of setting off the funny, the queer, or the lively harvest of experience, with the well-advised, efficient discretion of understatement. Humor is here really part of the English heritage, being a policy of wise self-repression in the quiet enjoyment of inevitable contrasts, and so bound up with the idiosyncrasies of the national character.[28]

Even at this early stage the instances would be many, if accidental tones, passing themes, and episodic figures were mar-

[28] A sketch of those idiosyncrasies—and especially of the instinctive control over one's impulses and feelings, as the means of a self-command which is the psychological condition of humor—has been given in Part I, chap. i, sect. i, and Part II, chap. vi, sect. iii.

shaled in full. Some substantial examples have already been adduced. It will suffice to bring up two more. The main body of the evidence on that score belongs to the next part of this survey.

That the major instinct was present from the very first is shown, if Sir E. K. Chambers's ordering of the plays can be trusted, by the presence in one of Shakespeare's earliest attempts, *2 Henry VI*, of scenes upon which the features just described are clearly stamped.

The Jack Cade episode has been universally pronounced genuine, however doubtful the authorship of the rest of the play. What is most remarkable is the sureness with which the humorous possibilities of the subject are seized and Edward Hall's suggestions improved. Although some political bias can be surmised—the playwright's satire dwelling on the stupid side of the peasant rebel leader with a gusto that seems unfeigned—we have here the magnificent objectivity and almost the serenity of genius. The key of the irony remains subdued, in a quiet unawareness of paradox; and full justice is done to the delicious absurdity of the situation. The character of Jack Cade, all compact of shrewd instincts thwarted by blind impulses, half a humorist and half a maniac, with his spiteful, blundering, rough sense of justice, and the direct vigor of his language, bears the seal of great art. But the very best Shakespeare makes only a fitful appearance through its development, by the side of what would be his second best or can hardly be his at all; and the end of the act, while leaving Cade his naturalness, adds nothing to his humor (Act IV).

It is again among doubtful shadows that Shakespeare and humor appear together in *The Taming of the Shrew*. Whatever the precise relation of the play may be to its direct predecessor *The Taming of a Shrew*, and whatever share in *The Shrew* may be assigned to another hand, some outstanding facts allow of safe conclusions. The humorous here is once more the flower of a rich observant sense of life and of a concrete invention in perfect command of itself. The sturdy scenes of the Petruchio-Katharina plot have a comic force, and, as it were, a height of impudence curbed to the drastic will of nature, which only Shakespeare will display. No more exuberant farce could well be kept within the strict limits of characters; and the liveliness is all instinct with a subtle feeling of relativity. This inner spirit of freedom it is, and nothing else, that relieves the summary brutality of the moral. There the line is securely drawn between the master and, say, Nashe. That same soul of philosophical reflection gives the broad fun of the Induction an aroma of wistful thought. Sly, the drunkard, no doubt figured already in *A Shrew;* instead of vanishing at the end of the first act, he sat there through the play, and some of his remarks were so piquantly enjoyable that no one but Shakespeare, it has been asserted on fair grounds, could have written them. But the opening of *The Shrew,* such as it is, shows the firm, unmistakable stamp of the master's personality. The old realism is all there—the tradition of popular mirth; and Sly might be just one more clown. Even the country atmosphere, redolent as it is of a Warwickshire setting, might find parallels in the comedy of the time. The incomparable thing is the thoughtful echoes that the tinker's adventure is made to stir in us by touching ever so gently, and as it were unconsciously, some of the most delicate chords of our minds. Here is a nobleman's idle whim, and here is the very type of the relativity with which our naïve faith in absolute values is checked on all sides. How grossly and amusingly does Sly's genuine being assert itself, in the fictitious world where he has awaked! But should the dream last, where would the center of the delusion finally shift? A similar aura of significance surrounds the body of plain fun in some of Sancho Panza's experiences; but *Don Quixote* is later than *The Shrew,* and the theme, besides, is a commonplace of all literatures.

By the time we have now reached—about the years 1595-1596, the probable dates of *Richard II,* that beautiful humorless tragedy, and of *A Midsummer Night's Dream*—practically the whole range of the humorous had been explored, and Shakespeare's preferences were no longer in doubt. Although he could be more brilliant than all his rivals in word-play and wit, his instinct led him rather to the implicitness of realistic comedy and to humor. In that vast field he would at will either turn the absurdities of men and things to humorous purposes by painting them with a liveliness which a wise reserve enhanced, or by uniting the gift of humor wih the cognate one of psychological truth, create characters that were themselves humorists and radiated out the magic which they pretended that they did not feel. This was the supreme consummation; and in that way was humor carried fully and finally on to the dramatic plane of art.

CHAPTER X

SHAKESPEARE'S HUMOR: II. THE GREAT HUMOROUS CREATIONS

THE PERIODS of Shakespeare's growth shade off into each other. Only when substantial groups of plays are considered can the distinction be kept at all clear. Well before the year 1596, about which we have tentatively placed the end of the first stage, the signs were not lacking that the poet had mastered the full significance of humor: and not only had he secured possession of it, but he had known how to endow with the precious essence fictitious characters that became self-radiating centers of it. Still, with his greatest comedies Shakespeare reached from 1596 to 1600 the highest degree of his power in the field of humorous creation. So truly and completely did he then embody the wistful spirit of amused relativity that all his invention was colored with it to a degree not found before or after; he made a gift of it to many of the children of his mind, and some of the most attractive or picturesque personalities he shaped forth are built round that mental impulse; in it they find their inner principle of unity; they belong to the international company of the prominent representatives and the very symbols of humor.[1]

I. The Butts of Humor

It is a less conspicuous order of beings, however, with whom we have to deal first. Before the humorists, the butts of humor must be studied—the figures that fulfil the author's end by rousing in us the intended reaction and make us share

[1] The plays discussed in this chapter are *King John*, *The Merchant of Venice* (1596-1597); *1* and *2 Henry IV* (1597-1598); *Much Ado About Nothing*, *Henry V* (1598-1599); *Julius Caesar*, *As You Like It*, *Twelfth Night* (1599-1600); *The Merry Wives of Windsor* (1600-1601). We are again following E. K. Chambers's tentative order.

in the repaying sight of unsuspecting absurdity. The characters who might be brought together under the loose description of "clowns" or "louts" are in this second period decidedly more interesting than in the first, just as they are more numerous. They have a bolder outline and stand on their own feet, the products of a creative imagination now certain of itself; as a general rule, no justification can be found for them in history or in a pre-existing plot. The sureness of the touch that gives them their highly individual features in a few strokes is unparalleled throughout English drama; and while they possess an abundant wealth of oddities, they preserve somehow the grace of truth to nature, a persuasive inevitability that belongs only to them. Invention here is guided by a marvelous intuition of life. The method of the artist is not idealization but a super-realism that, adhering closely to common experience, finally transcends it along its very lines.

Those characters are all studies in "humors," according to the sense of that word which had been current for some time and which Ben Jonson's famous comedies (*Every Man in His Humour*, 1598; *Every Man out of His Humour*, 1599) were even then making popular. The relation between Shakespeare's practice and the theory upon which his learned friend was hammering with characteristic energy and pedantry is a problem in itself and will be examined at a later stage in this inquiry. But it may be asserted at once that during this period of his development the greater playwright was in contact with the lesser's doctrine, and whether he turned it to genuine use or chiefly saw through and parodied it, his humor more or less consciously did feed on "humors." Still, when all is said, the outstanding fact is the complete autonomy of his art; and with the subtle essence that is the very soul of a humorous purpose he displays complete familiarity, which Ben Jonson's learning somehow never achieved.

It has been often pointed out that in *Henry IV* and *Henry V*, as compared with *Richard III* and *Richard II*, Shakespeare reverted to the type of the "chronicle play," thus gaining more freedom when the occasion arose to mix historical themes with comic elements—an instinctive decision that may be accounted for by the growth of his original powers. In the later plays two groups of amusing figures, soldiers and officers, are sketched with admirable gusto, standing in humorous contrast to the dignified leaders of policy and war.

Bardolph, Nym, and Pistol rub shoulders most of the time, quarreling or pouring out effusions of drunken friendship; their frequent association with Falstaff, or with those picturesque characters, Mistress Quickly and Doll Tear-Sheet, in rollicking scenes of quite Flemish realism, links them up inseparably. The "three swashers," as their disgruntled Boy calls them,[2] are truly variations on a single type; but how wonderfully individualized! The prominent member of the trio is "ancient" Pistol, with his magnificent rant and classical bombast. That the lilt of his high-sounding line should be a mocking allusion to the manner of *Tamburlaine* is an irresistible inference, which a direct echo from Marlowe's words would confirm ("And hollow pampered jades of Asia"[3]). Corporal Nym's language and ways are different. The Boy gives us a clue to his reserve: "he hath heard that men of few words are the best men";[4] and so the sly rogue hides his cowardice under a cloak of sententiousness. His phrasing indeed revolves in a narrow circle; but one aspect of his repetitive trick is of singular interest: "That's the humour of it," brought in again and again with egregious irrelevance, is not only a comic tag; it points to the contemporary vogue of the phrase, and, very probably, satirizes Ben Jonson's excessive infatuation with the word. It is significant that Shakespeare, even when apparently taking a leaf out of Jonson's book, and offering us genuine "humors" with marked oddities, should nonetheless, as it were, claim his freedom, and reveal how cheap he felt the method to be by making the method itself, and its watchword, an oddity. The three swashers show never the least glimmer of anything like the sense of their own relativity; but the blissful assurance of their beings is just what provokes humor in us. We feel all through that the poet who has conceived them and

[2] *Henry V*, III, ii, 29.
[3] 2 *Henry IV*, II, iv, 178. Cf. *Tamburlaine*, Part II, iv, 1-2.
[4] *Henry V*, III, ii, 37-38.

endowed them with their rich, plausible quaintness is silently sharing with us our joy in the wonderful diversity of creatures.

Of higher standing and better manners are the captains who step into the foreground when Bardolph and Nym have been hanged and join Pistol in enlivening the stage, while the heroic plot of *Henry V* winds itself out. With two of them, James the Scotsman and Macmorris the Irishman, the main source of the comic—the peculiarities of national speech—is rather trite, though hallowed by all dramatic traditions: not so with Fluellen the Welshman; although his consonants are funny to an English ear, his appeal to our sense of comedy is of a different order; a military faddist, his brag is all of the "disciplines of the war." His harping upon technique and constant reference to the strategy of the ancients have an exquisite flavor of pedantry; so distinct that one again wonders whether Shakespeare was not secretly having a fling, in that character, at Ben Jonson's obsession with rules and learned precedents. What more natural, if his mind did revolve on his friend and rival's stiff principles and labored practice, while he was himself bringing to the aesthetics of "humors" the vitalizing gift of his genius? But Fluellen stands on his own feet, brimming with individual truth, one of the most delightful examples of whimsical character; and the summit of lifelike absurdity is reached in the famous comparison between Macedon and Monmouth. "There is a river in Macedon; and there is also moreover a river at Monmouth: it is called Wye at Monmouth; but it is out of my brains what is the name of the other river; but 'tis all one, 'tis alike as my fingers is to my fingers, and there is salmons in both." Does not this indeed clinch the matter, and is not Henry decidedly a perfect parallel to "Alexander the pig?"[5] Humor here has all the limitless range of its elusive, subtle spirit; while the easy smile which its paradox calls up is still on our lips, shade after shade of thoughtful irony gleams and vanishes in the glow of our amusement; behind the enthusiast who is working a comparison to death, the dim image of human logic, weaving the cobwebs of its childish inferences, has flashed across our mental vision.

[5] *Henry V*, IV, vii, 14 and 27-33.

Shallow, Silence,[6] Dogberry, Verges,[7] and sundry minor figures, such as Francis the Tapster,[8] make up another set. In the case of Shallow, conjecture has been once more busy, tracing Shakespeare's satirical gusto to personal motives, so that the satisfaction of paying off an old score would mix with the disinterested joy of the humorist. This is quite immaterial to our purpose; the value of Shallow's character lies far beyond the possibility of his historical existence; his truth is that of a great artistic creation, more lifelike than the living; and as to humor, which no doubt demands a free mind, its presence is compatible with the airing of a private grudge; the pleasure of revenge, if philosophically indulged, is no paralyzing bondage to the soul. It is a fond illusion, we shall have to remark again and again, that humor must ever be kindly. And yet this would be, in support of our view, no case in point. Whatever grievance Shakespeare may have nursed, his dealing with the Gloucestershire justice is indulgent rather than bitter. Shallow is a liar, we hear from Falstaff, who ought to know about lies; but his tales of his wild youth in London may be more or less fibs, the fond reminiscences of the garrulous old man keep their charm as psychological touches, and we do not bother about their accuracy. The honesty of the self-important magistrate is elastic; he can wink at much and is no stickler for the spirit, any more than for the letter, of the law. Still, the portrait is alive with a magnetism in which artistic sympathy at least has a place. The scenes in Shallow's house or garden, with the amusing farce of the "King's press" thrown in, breathe a pleasant atmosphere of provincial homeliness and fragrant rusticity. The genius of merry England has been here at work, and true humor has humanized the satire with which it was associated. That the whole episode is instinct with a delightful quality of humor no one will deny who listens to Shallow's servant, Davy, begging him to stand sponsor for a friend:

I grant your worship, that he is a knave, sir; but yet, God forbid, sir, but a knave should have some countenance at his friend's request. An honest man, sir, is able to speak for himself, when a

[6] *2 Henry IV.*
[7] *Much Ado.*
[8] *1 Henry IV.*

knave is not. I have served your worship truly, sir, this eight years; and if I cannot once or twice in a quarter bear out a knave against an honest man, I have but a very little credit with your worship. . . .[9]

Master Shallow sees the point at once: "Go to; I say he shall have no wrong."[10] Not a Daniel, certainly; a thin, weakish man, with a doting way of repeating his words; but in him the frailties of human nature are so welded with the stuff of average, acceptable life, have so fully received the form and pressure of this everyday world, that our dislike is lost in the sense of kinship, and the figure of Shallow, tingling as it is with humorous realism, ranks among Shakespeare's very best.

Shallow, like several other characters from *2 Henry IV*, reappears in *The Merry Wives;* not to his advantage, though perhaps he loses less than Falstaff. He is now seen in a more satirical light, looks more solemn and self-important, with a new touch of Pharisaism; and it does seem as if the distinct emergence of the "deer" theme gave an edge to Shakespeare's memory of the Thomas Lucy episode. As a provocation to humor, his cousin Slender decidedly takes the wind out of his sails.

What shall we say to Dogberry? He is a joy forever, though not an occasion for the purest and subtlest humor. The sources of comedy with him do not lie very deep, and the oddities that tickle us soon grow somewhat mechanical. In the functioning of the worthy fellow's mind, automatism of course will play a prominent part; his blunders with things and words almost infallibly follow the grooves of geometrical inversion; and malapropism (before the letter)—is the law of his mind as of his tongue. But in his puppet-like slavery to the imp of stupidity that possesses him, he conforms after all to the grand principle of laughter, even if the laugh is no less superficial than its cause. Shakespeare's creative genius has turned the puppet into a flesh-and-blood character, solid and convincing. No such officer ever gave their cue to watchmen; still, three centuries have hailed in Dogberry the quintessence of official

[9] *2 Henry IV*, V, i, 47-55.
[10] *Ibid.*, l. 58.

foolery. And here again the very spirit of humor breathes through the lifelike realism of the portrait; the playwright's unruffled acquiescence in a miracle of innocent, vainglorious silliness places the whole episode above epigram or satire; he is still holding the mirror to nature, although the image is no doubt slightly magnified; and his sense of the relativity of his own method imparts to quiet exaggeration a virtue not unlike that of understatement, and practically equivalent to it.

Our last examples—although one might adduce many more secondary characters of less significance—will be the *Twelfth Night* pair of Sir Andrew Aguecheek, and Malvolio; and the *Merry Wives* group, among whom Slender easily bears the palm. Sir Andrew has some pretension to being witty. But, as he regretfully remarks, "I am a great eater of beef, and I believe that does harm to my wit."[11] Indeed, the only laughable thing about his fun is his attempt at being funny. The glaring contrast between his vulgarity and the fashionable refinement which he apes is handled with discretion, although the comedy now and then grows rather broad. He is, all told, a prodigy of naïve stupidity, with a fondness for repeating, parrot-like, the words of that superior person, his friend Sir Toby.

Malvolio raises more problems. As a butt he is plain, magnificent, unrelieved; a solemn bore, morose, and sourish to boot. Is he a Puritan? Appearances, and texts, favor the conclusion so much that the negative seems hardly tenable; but what he is before all is the prince of conceited fellows—a man "best persuaded of himself."[12] His misadventures appeal forcibly, of course, to our sense of the ludicrous; but the humor which centers about his ungainly person is neither very delicate nor quite genuine. The whole character is just a little forced, as the part of the plot that concerns him passes the bounds of probability. Well could Shakespeare confess as much when he makes Fabian say: "If this were played upon a stage now I could condemn it as an improbable fiction."[13] The more serious flaw is that gullibility and vanity such as Malvolio's cease to be

[11] *Twelfth Night,* I, iii, 89-91.
[12] II, iii, 162-63.
[13] III, iv, 139-40.

amusing; they reach the point of disease. The idea of a half-crazy character occurs to us early in the play, and the mock charge of lunacy put forth against him hardly makes us laugh: on a deeper plane we feel it is only too true. The scene in which the supposed lunatic protests that he is sane, and the clown cleverly improves the opportunity, today is painful to the more thin-skinned among us; having to prove their sanity is a pet nightmare with many, and we do not like to be reminded how the insane were then treated. Indeed the fun here leaves a doubtful taste in the mouth; Shakespeare's tragic period is near and casts its shadow before. Malvolio, in his heavy grotesque way, is a victim to self-consciousness, a very distant relative to Brutus or Hamlet. As a corrective to that drying up of the fresh sources of psychological comedy, the element of farce is rather profusely thrown in. Malvolio's cross-garters and yellow stockings, the dueling episode, the drunkenness of Sir Toby are essential to the popularity of the play; the tradition of the stage is to emphasize them to the full; they are good honest fun, and it would be pedantic to turn up one's nose at them; but the mirth which they rouse has no background, and Shakespeare the humorist in *Twelfth Night* is to be judged on the evidence of another character, that of the clown.[14]

The quality of an afterthought, and of a theme not entirely free in its inception, is stamped plainly upon *The Merry Wives*. Several of the butts in the play appear not for the first time: Shallow is from *2 Henry IV*, Pistol, Nym, and Bardolph from *2 Henry IV* and *Henry V*. One might almost add Falstaff to the list, as the fat knight, whose nimble wit made such a brilliant show in *Henry IV*, falls now, surprisingly enough, a sluggish victim to the simplest snares, and is, in some respects at least, quite destitute of humor.[15] Of those who reappear in their true and pristine light, none wins more glory by adding anything to the picturesqueness of his absurdity; even Shallow is somewhat under a cloud, as was said above: the appearance of a new simpleton, Slender, throws him into the shade.

[14] See below, sect. iv.
[15] See below, sect. v.

Of Ford, the jealous husband, with the senseless moves to which his unreasonable suspicions drive him; of Dr. Caius, the Frenchman, and Sir Hugh Evans, the Welshman, with their national peculiarities of behavior or speech, much need not be said; they belong to the stock in trade of comedy; they are swayed by the mechanical force of passion or habit, and so laughable, but human still; and the artist who has drawn their features has not dealt savagely with them; the satirical humor of Shakespeare, here once more, is in fact quite compatible with gentleness. There is a touch of hardness, on the contrary, in the verve and zest with which Slender is delineated. He is a wonderful study in stupid, clumsy rusticity, with a slight suggestion of sneaky puritanism, not unlike the parallel trait in Malvolio; we are reminded as well (in the *Merry Wives*) of Shallow and Rugby, the servant to Dr. Caius. It looks indeed as if Shakespeare, while taking obvious pains to make his play morally unexceptionable and even edifying, had borne a grudge just then to the professed sticklers for virtue. Slender's awkward shyness and thick blunt brutality, his silly pride in the grandeur of his cousin Shallow, his blundering courtship of Ann Page, and his "malapropisms"—a frequent trick, decidedly, with Shakespeare's characters in that period—may seem rather broad, almost farcical; but the optics of the part is after all that of the most approved comedy; and Molière's Thomas Diafoirus will love by rule, and kiss at his father's injunction, very much in the spirit of Slender.

One more word may be said of a few doubtful cases. In these plays, again, there are some characters who, being before all involuntary purveyors of humor, still have glimpses of the light and can laugh freely at others, or even—what chiefly matters—at themselves. They testify, once more, to the genuineness of Shakespeare's psychological realism; whatever the schemes may be through which we attempt to classify the moral world, he always baffles us with hybrids, contradictory creatures that overlap all categories; the reason being, of course, that he never thought of categories, but only of individuals. Who shall say that Sir Toby Belch[16] is not on a different plane from that

[16] *Twelfth Night.*

of Sir Andrew Aguecheek? A pretentious and a ridiculous figure himself, almost a grotesque with his coarse manners and drunken jollity, he is keenly aware of his friend's foibles; he pokes fun at him, plays practical jokes on him, and spurs him into his worst follies. Through his love of drinking and his buoyant spirits he has sometimes been regarded as a distant cousin to Falstaff. With Malvolio he assumes the part of a tormentor, and all through the dueling scene takes a devilish pleasure in frightening Viola out of her wits. In his mischievousness there will at times peep out something not unlike the grosser spirit of humor.[17] And to him it belongs to make the immortal "cakes and ale" retort,[18] voicing, at the moment, the poet's own sense of humorous relativity.

There are as well composite beings—groups swayed by common impulses, but instinct with the shrewdness of sensible men, whose hold on reality has not been permanently weakened. The citizens of Angiers[19] have the bourgeois mind; they bow to accomplished facts, and will fling their caps for the conqueror as soon as the fortune of war has spoken. Standing on their strong walls, they preserve all the forms of respect in their parleyings with the princes whose contention they watch coolly and critically; but an undertone of irony gives a sting to their words, and the situation has humorous elements, which they obviously perceive and enjoy. The chief humorist here, however, is Shakespeare himself; the parallelism of the entrances of the two heralds, with their conflicting and equally official proclamations, is good comedy, sober and subdued, in which the facts speak for themselves. Again, the Roman rabble *(Julius Caesar)* is a famous study in the psychology of crowds; its headlong impulses turn it finally into a big, blind, many-headed monster; but it is kept within the bounds of genuine realism; it feels the love of human flesh and blood for a racy joke, and the soul of popular clownery lives in the "second citizen" of Act I, i.

[17] III, iv, for instance.
[18] II, iii, 123-25.
[19] *King John*, II, i.

II. Satirical Humor

In several plays of the period a premonitory vein of brooding, serious, or bitter reflection appears repeatedly, linking up with the somber moral studies of the tragic phase. Irony, dramatic or philosophical, is the natural weapon of a saddened or restless mind in its clash with a baffling world. Ironical shades of humor are a feature of *Julius Caesar;* and in the morning freshness of *As You Like It* the sullen wit of Jaques mixes more severe notes with the fancy and the fun.

It is a commonplace that *Julius Caesar*, the drama of human will desperately at odds with fate, is in its atmosphere of thickening gloom a first sketch of *Hamlet*. The fruitless warnings and intimations of destiny to the spirit of man, helplessly carried forward by the tide of ambition, as with Caesar, or blinded by the pride of stoic virtue, as with Brutus, create a sense of tragic futility, sharpened at times to supreme irony. The confusions and errors of the final battlefield are the crowning symbol of those baffled aims. It is fit that in such a setting the only humor that can live should be grim, bitter, or saturnine. Casca's blunt manner and the "tardy form" he now "puts on," are interpreted by Cassius in that light:

> This rudeness is a sauce to his good wit,
> Which gives men stomach to digest his words
> With better appetite. . . .[20]

An acute analysis of the subconscious strategy of character, in which a half-insincerity, very close to the common trick of irony and humor, is penetratingly hit, this flash of psychological insight is to be compared with Falstaff's words, to which we shall again refer: "a jest with a sad brow. . . ."[21] Casca's narrative of the scene where Caesar was offered the crown is spiced with a rough realism somewhat like sourish humor: "Three or four wenches, where I stood, cried 'Alas, good soul!'—and forgave him with all their hearts: But there's no heed to be taken of them; if Caesar had stabbed their mothers they would have done no less. . . ."[22]

[20] I, ii, 304-6.
[21] *2 Henry IV*, V, i, 91-94.
[22] I, ii, 275-79.

The irony of Brutus is different; thoughtful and sad, rather than biting, it can even be soft with the tenderness of a gentle soul. Its scope is wide, from his not unkind raillery of Cassius in the great scene of Act IV,[23] to the tragic bitterness of his last moments:

> slaying is the word,
> It is a deed in fashion.[24]

He appeals to our sense of the ironical paradoxes of life when, after declaring, as a philosopher, against suicide, he next kills himself;[25] or when it falls to him—the man of principle, strong in book lore, rich with the treasure of vicarious experience, fully warned as to the complexities of things, but lacking Cassius's intuition of actual facts—to formulate the theory of quick decision:

> There is a tide in the affairs of men,
> Which, taken at the flood, leads on to fortune:
> Omitted, all the voyage of their life
> Is bound in shallows and in miseries. . . .[26]

Sound doctrine indeed, if he could only have acted upon it!

As You Like It is pitched in the key of that playfulness, that light irresponsible upsetting of values, which agrees so well with the spirit of the most characteristic English humor. The very title loosens the bonds of rationality and the hard laws of this material world at one single touch; the gate is opened into what will be Alice's Wonderland, or Peter Pan's gardens. Who can take seriously the winding up of the plot and the Duke's conversion? The same note is struck in the names of two contemporary plays, *Twelfth Night or What You Will* and *Much Ado About Nothing;* it had been anticipated, with a more lyrical ring, in *A Midsummer Night's Dream;* and the heyday of Shakespeare's humor is thus heralded and brought to a close by comedies, the themes of which openly testify to the intimate association between the humorous and the fanciful.

[23] IV, iii, 107-23, for instance.
[24] V, v, 4-5.
[25] V, i and v.
[26] IV, iii, 218-21.

But the fancy here is weighted with the heavy harvest of experience. Wistfulness again and again lays its reflective glow on the rosy world of youth, love, and mirth. Touchstone the clown is the quintessence of thoughtful humor. Jaques, like Brutus, is a premonitory sketch of Hamlet; more recognizable, as he is more clearly irresolute, unhinged by moodiness, solitary in an inner sphere of his own. . . .

Is Jaques a humorist? He is undoubtedly, in the Elizabethan sense. He calls his melancholy "a most humorous sadness";[27] and indeed many ingredients of temperament go to its making: it is, a critic has said, a mixture of moroseness, misanthropy, eccentricity, irony, and sarcasm.[28] Of those elements, modern humor can claim the last two; and when all is said, in today's sense as well, Jaques is a humorist; though a cynical, sardonic one, of the Swiftian type.[29] He knows how to convey the pith of his bitter philosophy in words, few and pregnant, loaded with a rich implicitness; he concocts acrid fun quickly out of the absurdities of life. But his humor revolves within narrow limits. From the tares, sown in his youth, which he is now reaping, and from his travels in many lands, he has gathered a disillusioned sadness that awakes sympathetic echoes in our sophisticated hearts; and our romantic fibers can but thrill at the electric touch of his pity for animals.[30] But when seen in Shakespeare's light, he appears no doubt as a soured man, a malcontent, with an allusion possibly to Marston; a

[27] *As You Like It,* IV, i, 19-20.

[28] Emile Legouis.

[29] This is as good an opportunity as any to explain that we take *humor* to be the broad category and word, covering all intentional indirectness in the presentment of the comic; and irony, whose field is wide enough, to be more restricted however, a kingdom within the empire of humor. Aesthetically speaking, the method of one is just the same as that of the other: they both reverse the natural correspondence between thought and speech, saying one thing and meaning another; only the inversion works differently; as Bergson puts it in his subtle analysis of laughter, humor describes what is, and feigns to believe it is just what should be; irony describes what should be, and feigns to believe it is just what is. So the inner mood of humor is generally instinct with a kind of tolerance, whilst that of irony is colored with at least a tinge of aggressiveness. The humorist normally is resigned, the ironist more or less embittered. But the test is not safe; the two attitudes shade off into each other and must not in practice be sharply separated; the prudent course is to go by the truly essential analogy that makes them alike, rather than by the different tones of feeling through which they can most often be distinguished.

[30] II, i, 21-66.

faddist, whom Orlando's nimble tongue puts out of countenance and drives off; a comic character after all, in his slavery to a peevishness exuded by his blood and nerves; as such, he does not know the suppleness, the freedom of the genuine humorist; he is brilliant, will throw off striking similes, philosophical conceits ("All the world's a stage," etc.[31]); but he has not found in humor the best it can give, the possession of one's own soul.

III. Intellectual Humor

The main roots of English humor are in the instincts of the people. Throughout its development as part of dramatic literature, popular types and characters illustrate its native quality, while wits, courtiers, noblemen, and refined ladies rather stand for the other contribution to that growth, the cosmopolitan graces of culture. Just as Shakespeare's work shows the two lines of progress merging into one, his greatest humorous creations owe something to both. It looks as if he had had some intuitive sense of that dual origin. The princes and leaders who display a gift of humor are shown in close touch with the homely national mind; one might instance to some extent Prince Hal—although his talent in *1 Henry IV* is rather irony, and his "conversion," at all events, puts an end to such trifling—but chiefly Hotspur and Falconbridge. Falstaff, a knight of gentle birth and coarse habits, bears a natural affinity to the rabble. Portia, a lady of rank and wealth, has a delightfully free, unassuming manner to all. Conversely, it is interesting to note that Touchstone, a fool, "has been a courtier,"[32] and that he mentions Ovid's exile among the Goths.[33] Feste, his compeer in *Twelfth Night,* quotes Latin, knows the pagan gods, has a mind stored with classical memories. Still, a survey of Shakespeare's plays would tend to establish the impression that the influx of vitality in humor was more on one side; that its full body, its flavor and range were inseparable from a direct experience of the rough realities of life. The cleverest cavaliers, the wittiest women, a Rosalind, a Benedick,

[31] *As You Like It,* II, vii, 139-66.
[32] *As You Like It,* II, vii, 36.
[33] III, iii, 7-8.

a Beatrice, even a Portia, charming humorists as they are, seem as far as our theme is concerned, in comparison with Feste or Falstaff, a little thin.

The two veins, although they draw nearer to each other, and in some characters are completely fused, keep distinct enough to be examined apart. It is convenient to begin with the representatives of intellectual humor.

In the plays of the first period Shakespeare had worked out his attitude towards the great temptation that at the time beset all gifted minds: Italianism, conceits, and the spurious brilliance of language.[34] But it was not with impunity that he possessed more power to shine in that field than any of his contemporaries, although he had as well more judgment to see through the lure of the talent, assess it at its real worth, and spurn it. The second period shows us a good deal of apparent backsliding; the manner crops up again and again, though it is never entirely condoned. There is always something that gives it an air of irresponsible, whimsical self-indulgence; and on occasion the faddists themselves will criticize the fad. Those relapses are immaterial to our purpose. It will suffice to dwell on some outstanding characters who can lay claim to both wit and humor.

As You Like It gives prominence to a bevy of bright young people with quick minds and ready tongues; they are of all conditions, from shepherds to dukes' daughters. Among them Rosalind bears the palm as the merriest, the most sprightly, and yet the most sensible. Though loving, she does not sentimentalize: "The poor world is almost six thousand year old, and in all this time there was not any man died in his own person, *vide licet*, in a love cause";[35] and her sparkling epigrams keep within the bounds of verbal discretion. What she offers us is an amusing verve, a piquant liveliness, rather than rhetoric, conceits, puns, and all the display of Italianism. Behind the graces of her manner her mind is at work and takes at once the measure of a situation or a character. She makes the best of her disguise and handles its comic aspects with

[34] See above, chap. iv, sect. ii.
[35] IV, i, 93-96.

finesse, reserve, and almost always decency. So the comedy which has its source in her shows the virtue of implicitness and has a humorous value. Her remarks reveal a keen power of observation, the feeling of relativity, and the habit of laughing at herself; whence such pregnant sayings as: "Do you not know I am a woman? When I think, I must speak"; or: "Time travels in divers paces with divers persons."[36] There is all the inimitable freshness of humor in her: "Pray you, no more of this; 'tis like the howling of Irish wolves against the moon,"[37] a jest that breaks the spell of the tender exchange of vows all round between the lovers, as it threatened to grow oversweet; and that unerring instinct is not only feminine intuition but a delicate intellectual tact. Thus equipped, she can aptly remember Pythagoras, and wave away in a laugh the embarrassment of Orlando's "Tedious homily of love";[38] she can prove a match for Touchstone, and beat him at his own game;[39] she can even pierce to the core of Jaques's soured moroseness.[40] It must be confessed, however, that Rosalind proves at times sadly disappointing; for example, her rebuke of Phoebe[41] is curiously harsh, almost coarse; a more grievous sin to us, it is entirely destitute of humor; and such accidents are but too many in a play of singular inequality, where the signs of doubtful authorship again and again meet the eye, and which, in spite of a charm all its own, cannot be ranked among Shakespeare's genuine masterpieces.

The case is different with *Much Ado.* The vigor of the play is better sustained, and the most authentic Shakespearean note rings almost throughout. Just like the Dogberry group,[42] Benedick and Beatrice are original creations. They are both brilliantly humorous characters; but they do not possess all the supple self-command and the freedom of the humorist. To some extent they are "humorous," in the Jonsonian sense, with a crooked bent that warps the poise of their minds. Beatrice cannot resist the shrewish impulses of her biting tongue; Benedick has in his composition something of the lady-killer and

[36] III, ii, 263-64 and 326-27.
[37] V, ii, 118-19.
[38] III, ii, 163-64.
[39] III, ii, 101-30.
[40] IV, i, 1-37.
[41] III, v, 35-63.
[42] See above, sect. i.

woman-hater. Those foibles are weak points in their mental armory, through which they lie open to the whims of fate. They have a lesson to learn, and in a way the secondary plot that develops around them is the story of their schooling. The outcome of their mutual obsession—in which an instinctive sympathy and an inevitable opposition have equal shares, as they are too much alike not to clash violently—is ironical enough: with all their acumen and clear-sightedness they are worked upon from the outside, like children, and friends must cheat them into the happiness they were unwilling to grasp. It takes the prompting of flattered pride and sentimental gratitude to start the decisive growth of their love. The whole process is a wonderful study in realistic psychology; but the exquisite humor with which the episode is permeated is not Beatrice's or Benedick's; it is Shakespeare's.

In other respects they are themselves, fully and consciously, the sources of the intellectual amusement they provide. If they fail to show all the equipment of the humorist, they are admirably fitted for a game which resembles the word-play of *Love's Labour's Lost,* but is not quite like it, and which, to speak strictly, belongs to them: it is not only a matter of eclipsing an adversary with quick repartee and stinging phrases; it goes deeper, cuts below the skin, and involves a genuine perception of character. The sharp banter and the teasing which are associated with them suppose a measure of moral insight: it is no wonder that Beatrice and Benedick should first sense the innocence of cruelly slandered Hero. Some of Benedick's cynical remarks, thrown out in the haste of wit-combats, are singularly pregnant: "Well, everyone can master a grief, but he that has it,"[43] repeated in Leonato's: "For there was never yet philosopher that could endure the tooth-ache patiently."[44] Beatrice is half a shrew, but knows it and cherishes no illusion as to the weight her word should carry: "I was born to speak all mirth, and no matter." At her birth, "There was a star danced, and under that was I born"; and so her heart, "poor fool, . . . keeps on the windy side of care."[45] In spite of her

[43] III, ii, 28-29.
[44] V, i, 35-36.
[45] II, i, 326-27, 343-44, and 348-49.

vixenish romping, she has a fine tact; when Don Pedro in jest proposes to her, how skilful her retort is![46] Benedick is probably Shakespeare's mouthpiece when he so neatly satirizes the affected mode of speech, to which he himself might often plead guilty: "He [Claudio] was wont to speak plain, and to the purpose, like an honest man and a soldier; and now he is turned orthography; his words are a very fantastical banquet, just so many strange dishes."[47] And again, to Beatrice: "Thou hast frighted the word out of his right sense, so forcible is thy wit."[48] Indeed, that famous pair, standing as they do for dazzling verbal cleverness, surrounded by a group which shares more or less in their talent—Hero, Ursula, Margaret, Claudio all shine, separately and jointly—represent, when all is said, the sterility of purely mocking wit and the futility of the mere gift of the gab. Affectation must yield to the simple motions of the heart. From endless arguing and fencing, they find their way to unashamed love and to more natural humor—joint aspects, as we presume, of one and the same discovery.

The plot of the *Merchant of Venice* develops through its dramatic climax to its serene close in an atmosphere of merry-making, to which all the young Venetians contribute their share; and Jessica the beautiful Jewess soon joins the gay frolic. The comedy that winds up so sweetly on the moonlit lawns of Belmont has its soul in Portia—a soul of delightful sprightliness sobered with serious reason; and she impersonates the peculiar brand of humor—light, fanciful, but acute and realistic—that gives its original flavor to the whole play. To Portia one may easily be unfair; a few blemishes can be found on the surface of her exceptionally attractive character; and some men will not with a good grace forgive her the proofs she gives of her superiority, even though she so modestly tones it down and bows to her lord and master. Stress is laid on the firmness in her moral nature, on her religious principle; it is no lip-service she pays to the duty of mutual charity, as of mercy: "In truth, I know it is a sin to be a mocker."[49] But how can one check one's tongue, when words so aptly hit off

[46] II, i, 330-54.
[47] II, iii, 19-23.
[48] V, ii, 54-55.
[49] I, ii, 61-62.

the weak points of disagreeable suitors, and draw such a lively sketch of each?[50] Here we have satire, epigram. Indeed, Portia must be pronounced, on two or three occasions, guilty of teasing; and in the ring episode, at the end, perhaps she abuses the advantage her cleverness gives her over her husband. Though beautifully brought off, the tormenting joke has nothing to do with genuine humor.[51]

This we shall find rather in the latter part of the play. The first acts show us the woman, breathlessly waiting for the sphinx of her future to speak. Even then she can be mistress of herself enough to enjoy much quiet fun, and discreetly to season her speech with it. When suddenly called upon to act and dare, she rises to the occasion, and her judgment and courage come to the fore. At the same time, as if the full maturity of her mind were bound up with the process, her humorous gift blooms out and expands. How charmingly quaint and delicately mocking is her picture of herself and Nerissa as "bragging Jacks" in boy's clothes![52] Young, merry, loving, she harbors few illusions, and forestalls experience; she knows how fragile married happiness must be unless built on a permanent union of thought and feeling. Though brilliant and borne along by the tide of self-confidence and success, she proves never rash, overweening, or vain; she is keenly alive to the uncertainty, the relativity of things: "Nothing is good, I see, without respect. . . ."[53] That fine precocious wisdom, carried lightly, without a shadow of pedantry, allows her to face all chances with just a perceptible smile flickering on her lips: indeed life is amusing, although so hard to bear: "My little body is aweary of this great world";[54] but doing good is a pleasant return for stupidity and mischief: "So shines a good deed in a naughty world."[55] Shylock is outwitted by Portia's clever handling of legal quibbles; his downfall, soothing to our rough sense of justice, awakes echoes of philosophical humor; and her playfulness harmonizes with the irony of a fate that baffles man's blind insistence on the letter of the law. The spirit triumphs, whatever stratagem may be necessary to bring about its victory.

[50] *Ibid.*, 42-108.
[51] V, i, 166-255.
[52] III, iv, 60-78.
[53] V, i, 99.
[54] I, ii, 1-2.
[55] V, i, 91.

Now, the name of that spirit is freedom—the freedom of the humorist, symbolized by Portia's mastery of herself and of circumstances.

Although she does not fight shy of a pun, her humor is practically independent of words, which are to her a means and no more. It is significant that Shakespeare in this play should again, while occasionally sacrificing to the fashion of the time, express his decided objection to it. Lorenzo is here the poet's mouthpiece. He remarks about Launcelot, who has been "wit-snapping" to an excess: "How every fool can play upon the word! I think the best grace of wit will shortly turn into silence, and discourse grow commendable only to parrots." Again: "I pray thee, understand a plain man in his plain meaning"; and once more: "The fool hath planted in his memory An army of good words; and I do know A many fools that stand in better place, Garnished like him, that for a tricksy word Defy the matter."[56] So the verbal wit founded upon the sudden, dry clash ("snapping") between sound and meaning is condemned, inevitably to the advantage of the gradual, discreet, indirect manner of humor; a manner that assumes the aspect of simplicity ("plain meaning"), and adheres closely to "the matter"—the realities of the subject.

IV. The Popular and National Vein

The other group consists of characters whose humor, whatever their refinement and their culture may be, is nourished mainly by its roots in the instincts of the people. They belong to all the ranks of life, from the most humble to the highest; although, as might be expected, their condition more often would keep them in touch with the mixed doings of the everyday world.

A good many are mere sketches, or play but secondary parts; still, the vigor with which they are drawn secures for them a distinct place in our remembrance. They all have original features, and the vividness of individual faces in collective portraits of Dutch corporations. But as humorists they hardly require separate study; their manner is roughly the same: a fresh, lively realism, colored with professional expe-

[56] III, v, 46-50, 62-63, 71-75.

rience, and apparently unaware of its spicy flavor; to which should be added a habit of making the most of the opportunities for mutual banter, which more often than not their mode of life generously affords. What varies from one to the other is the degree, and as it were the particular shade, of the sly, half-feigned candor with which their picturesque personalities express themselves. To that number belong for instance Mrs. Quickly, the hostess of the Boar Head Tavern, Eastcheap (in *1* and *2 Henry IV*), associated with the naturalistic figure of Doll Tear-Sheet in word-combats of the most high-flavored kind, who reappears in the *Merry Wives* as the sobered servant to Dr. Caius; the two Carriers, whose lifelike talk with Gadshill provides an amusing episode in *1 Henry IV;*[57] the Host of the Garter Inn, and Mr. Page, both worthy of enjoying the practical jokes through which the two "merry wives" win just glory; and Gratiano, a somewhat light-headed chatterbox, but no fool indeed, whose verve and jollity give him a prominent place among the gay young Venetians of *The Merchant.* There is more point than may appear on the surface in his ironical answer to Bassanio's rather priggish entreaty that he should behave himself in the presence of Portia: the mocking sketch is, once more, that of a religious hypocrite, with some features of the Puritan:

> If I do not put on a sober habit,
> Talk with respect, and swear but now and then,
> Wear prayer-books in my pocket, look demurely;
> Nay more, while grace is saying, hood mine eyes
> Thus with my hat, and sigh, and say amen;
> Use all the observance of civility,
> Like one well studied in a sad ostent
> To please his grandam—never trust me more.[58]

Launcelot Gobbo[59] deserves somewhat fuller treatment. Although Lorenzo takes him to task for his "wit-snapping," his manner is usually free from that affectation; the effects upon which he relies are broad, but carried off so coolly that as a humorist of the rougher, more elementary kind, he fears few

[57] II, i, 1-51.
[58] II, ii, 199-206.
[59] *The Merchant of Venice.*

comparisons. He is a regular "clown," out to bring the house down with rollicking farce, and to all except the squeamish his verve is irresistible. His monologue[60] is a most amusing variation upon the theme of the divided mind, dear to classical tragedy. It is cynical realism that wins, of course. All the psychological conditions of humor are present, and the name can be used here without demur. The rogue next teases his father in a most unmannerly way, to make sincere amends just in time. He will thus in everything get dangerously near the limit of stupidity or caddishness, but not go beyond; there is a spice of mystification in his fun. His jokes all along—and we shall not except the reading of his palm[61]—certainly lack refinement; but they serve their end very well; who will turn up his nose at them?

Drawn on a larger scale, the figures of Prince Hal, Hotspur, and Falconbridge are more fully delineated. Wielding authority, these characters give themselves scope, and so the freedom essential to humor appears with them in another light; instead of looking roguish and pawky, it would rather seem mocking and ironical. Their self-command in pleasantry is, so to say, just a part of their superiority to circumstances.

An ironical ring is plainly the ground note in Prince Hal's humor. Outwardly he is a boon companion to Falstaff and Poins, lets himself go, and enjoys his riotous time without remorse. Mirth, a devil-may-care manner, are among the trio by common consent the best of the game, and they crack even more jokes than they steal purses. So Falstaff addresses the young prince as "sweet wag," or "mad wag"; and he speaks of "thy quips and thy quiddities."[62] But it is not long before the superficial similarity reveals the deep-laid difference; the Prince is cooler, more deliberate, and keeps himself better in hand; his witty sayings have a sardonic undertone; many are somehow meant at his friend, or have a knack of glancing off against him; awkward allusions to a prison or the gallows will crop up. As Hal is the leading spirit—Falstaff complains that he has been corrupted by his friend: "Thou hast done much

[60] II, ii.
[61] II, ii, 166-75.
[62] *1 Henry IV*, I, ii, 17-18 and 50.

harm upon me, Hal"[63]—he is the more practiced humorist, while Falstaff is the artist, clear-headed but weak of will, who transcends the rules of humor rather than following them. All that leads up to the characteristic passage where the fat knight declares he will reform: "I must give over this life, and I will give it over; . . . an I do not, I am a villain. I'll be damned for never a king's son in Christendom"; to which Hal's quiet reply comes pat: "Where shall we take a purse to-morrow, Jack?"[64] No wonder the Prince should love a practical joke and find relish in mystifying poor Francis the tapster.[65]

By then we have heard him soliloquize at the end of Act I, and we know. His "conversion" is only a matter of time; indeed, he is already converted, or never needed to be. His turning over a new leaf will mean his decided rise to national significance, to heroism; but to us it implies a grievous change: on the intellectual plane he loses his soul by saving it, and forever abdicates his sense of humor.

Hotspur raises another problem. Fiery, eager, haughty, how can he preserve the mastery of his reactions, without which there is no genuine humor? His case indeed is interesting and throws light once more upon the utter objectivity of Shakespeare's character-studies. Not only is the playwright perfectly innocent of all analytical preoccupations, but he does not even bother about what one may call normality, the approximation of an individual to the average pattern of his type. Only the unique, the distinct temper of the being he creates, or as happens here, recreates from an historical outline, concerns him at all. His drama is so convincing just because, like life itself, it is made up of exceptions. From our point of view, Hotspur is the marginal case: and so, a rare, illogical combination of features molded by the pressure of personality into an organic whole; the result is a figure whose magnetic truth forces itself upon us at once. The plot, no doubt, demands that Hotspur should somewhat lose his balance and sin against the jealous gods that punish man's pride, on the eve of his decisive encounter with Henry;[66] but apart from that error, which is

[63] I, ii, 102-3.
[64] I, ii, 107-11.
[65] II, iv.
[66] V, ii.

quite in character, he manages, although hasty and hot, to keep an acute awareness, and that sanity is reflected in the delightful poise of a gay, sensitive, observant nature, alive to the infinite complexities of things. Generous and impulsive, though not rash, he is more attractive than his rival, which can hardly be charged as an artistic fault upon Shakespeare, since Hotspur appealed almost equally to the national sympathies of the audience. The finely shaded contrast he offers with the prince and the violent contrast they severally present to Falstaff enter into the whole comedy as well as the tragedy of the play. There is humor in the opposition; and humor flashes out again and again from Hotspur's ways and words; from his description to the king of the lord, "neat and trimly dressed," who came after the fight to demand the prisoners, and said:

> That it was great pity, so it was,
> That villanous saltpetre should be digged
> Out of the bowels of the harmless earth,
> Which many a good tall fellow had destroyed
> So cowardly; and but for these vile guns
> He would himself have been a soldier. . . ;[67]

or from his excellent derision of Glendower's ridiculous ranting—one of the most properly humorous scenes in Shakespeare's "Histories,"[68] rich with a fresh realistic verve, that wells up from the sap of the land and the instincts of the people.

Philip, bastard of Falconbridge, is even more of a national hero than Hotspur, because he is less aristocratic, though of royal blood; his knowledge of his bar sinister has tempered his natural pride with the feeling of a common humanity; he voices unfailingly not only the patriotic emotions of the crowd but the jolly scorn of the strong-limbed Englishman for the petty wiles of smaller men—degenerate lords, mean citizens, cowardly knights, and plotting priests. He has a genial, blunt, broad way of speaking out the awkward truth, and scoffing at his adversary to his face; while his quiet tone in defiance and insult sets off the stinging words and popular gibes. It is even possible to hear the accent of a modern age in his subdued jeers

[67] I, iii, 59-64.
[68] III, i.

at the hollow rites of a decaying feudal order.[69] Through his "commodity" monologue we catch something of the self-criticism, the supple sense of relativity so familiar to the humorist:

> And why rail I on this commodity?
> But for because he hath not woo'd me yet;
> Not that I have the power to clutch my hand,
> When his fair angels would salute my palm;
> But for my hand, as unattempted yet,
> Like a poor beggar, raileth on the rich.
> Well, whiles I am a beggar, I will rail,
> And say—there is no sin but to be rich;
> And being rich, my virtue then shall be,
> To say—there is no vice but beggary. . . .[70]

As the play develops, the Bastard shows more of the generous ardor and the nobility of purpose that hide under his free and easy familiarity; and the striking forcefulness of his language, with the vigorous lilt of his verse, fills out his stature, making him draw nearer to the ideal he had adumbrated—the glorified image of a full-blooded, manly, self-commanding people, in whose temper the latent or active presence of humor is ever felt.

V. The Great Jesters: Touchstone, Feste

The most original creations of Shakespeare's humor, in this the greatest period of his comic powers, are the two fools, Touchstone and Feste,[71] and Falstaff, who stands in a category by himself.

Touchstone has often been looked upon as a corrective to the fanciful elements in the plot of *As You Like It.* Indeed what he voices is realistic common sense; but that realism in his person is not destitute of half romantic features, akin to those which Russian novelists have since given their philosophi-

[69] *King John,* II, i.

[70] II, i, 587-96.

[71] The development of the fool, from "half wit" to "mock-half wit," and further, is studied in B. Swain's *Fools and Follies during the Middle Ages and the Renaissance* (New York, 1932). The fool was marked out to play a prominent part in the coming of age of humor, since his progress like that of the humorist had been along the lines of the gradual realization of his powers, and of the deepening of consciousness. A fool entirely alive to his opportunities is almost the very type of humor.

cal outcasts. He has been a courtier, we are told, and known better days; his motley coat is discreetly associated with a chronic weakness of will and with the mixed experiences which both make and mar a man. Thence some bitter hints, and a cynical undertone, which naturally please melancholy Jaques and the banished Duke. Such a varied course of life will teach an observant mind how essentially relative all things are; and Touchstone has been thus prepared to work out for himself that general upsetting of fixed values which is the inmost soul of humor.

So the note he strikes has from the first a thoughtful ring. His entrance is heralded and accompanied by the lighthearted witticisms of the two girls, Rosalind and Celia; but his own repartees awake deeper echoes.[72] Is not he indeed, as his name suggests, the touchstone that proves other people's wit? The issue he raises is no less than the paradoxical inversion of those qualities, the basic ones in our intellectual universe: wisdom and folly: "The more pity that fools may not speak wisely what wise men do foolishly."[73] He next appears with the two girls in boy's clothes; around them Arden waves its friendly tops, and the innocent cheat of the disguise seems to body forth the elegiac irony that breathes through the whole scene. Subtly attuned to it is the fool's wistful humor. He feigns to amuse himself with trifles; by taking trite metaphors literally he slyly makes conspicuous the queerness of mechanical, passive, lazy ways of speaking. Convention and illusion are indeed the stuff life is made of; no other is love itself, with its "strange capers"; a madness which the fool has known and will know again while seeing through it; luckily it does not last: "as all is mortal in nature, so is all nature in love mortal in folly." But what? Do such words become a fool's cap? "Thou speak'st wiser than thou art 'ware of," Rosalind remarks; and Touchstone's answer lights up for us the pretended unconsciousness that is the gist of the humorous strategy: "Nay, I shall ne'er be 'ware of mine own wit till I break my shins against it."[74] And so the last word of experience is disillusionment, but it may as well be

[72] *As You Like It,* I, ii.
[73] I, ii, 92-93.
[74] II, iv, 55-60.

called acceptance. Not only is relativity taken for granted, but it is itself parodied, so as to conjure away the possible excess of its haunting thought. How do you like this shepherd's life? Corin asks. "Truly, shepherd, in respect of itself it is a good life; but in respect that it is a shepherd's life it is naught. . . ."[75] Satire is tempered with indulgence; the solemn snubbing of Corin is a sheer farce; syllogism is brandished and turned into an absurdity; the emptiness of a lover's jingling verses is cleverly mocked: "I'll rhyme you so eight years together; dinners, and suppers, and sleeping hours excepted. . . ."[76]

The last feature in this curiously wrought portrait is one that makes Touchstone more human by adding to him the supreme truth of self-contradiction. A philosopher and a humorist, he acts against his pessimism and his sense of humor by marrying. A marriage not of love but of convenience, which perhaps is its excuse in his eyes. The whole business is shorn of all pretences; the bridegroom's thoughts run upon horns, and his compliments to the bride are to the effect that being plain, she might be honest. But what! As he explains to Jaques, "man hath his desires; and as pigeons bill, so wedlock would be nibbling." Should the priest bungle the marriage, it would be clear gain: "not being well married, it will be a good excuse for me hereafter to leave my wife."[77] That cynicism, of course, is meant to grate on our ears; but let us look at the facts: it does not preclude gentleness in Touchstone's treatment of poor Audrey. He is half in earnest while he nonpluses, mystifies, and terrifies his rival William, the country clown, with a display of logic, rhetoric, and law words; and the broad parody is enlivened with remarks that tell: "The fool doth think he is wise, but the wise man knows himself to be a fool."[78] Finally Touchstone claims a place, with his willing bride, among "the rest of the country copulatives," whose procession Hymen will bring in. "A poor virgin, sir, an ill-favoured thing, sir, but mine own," he points out apologetically, thus touching, with some bluntness, on the profoundest root of marriage; and he treats himself to a most amusing, but most

[75] III, ii, 12-14.
[76] III, ii, 101-3.
[77] III, iii.
[78] V, i, 34-36.

methodical, skit, upon the minute regulations according to which the honor of a courtier was impugned or defended. Well can the Duke, as a conclusion, pay a tribute to the indirect strategy which makes humor so efficient: "He uses his folly like a stalking-horse, and under the presentation of that he shoots his wit."[79]

The fool in *Twelfth Night,* Feste, is a figure more boldly conceived, whose outline is purer and firmer. The spirit of humor is the animating principle of his life. It is easy to feel that in creating him Shakespeare has faced the problem squarely. An active mind will be naturally urged to philosophize by the very existence of a fool—a character that is the impersonation of unreason. Shall the fool be such in effect, or only in the estimation of the world, which is not wise—with all the consequences that must follow? The solution here is that of all satirical thinkers and of most moralists. The average condition of man being so far from a state of reason, the official spokesman of unwisdom stands a good chance of voicing just the reverse. That thesis, discreetly urged, is none the less plainly put forward. Feste is conscious of his relation to the world around him; but he knows as well that intellectual humility is the sign and the condition of healthy thinking. I am, he says, "the better for my foes, and the worse for my friends"; because the friends "praise me, and make an ass of me; now my foes tell me plainly I am an ass; so that by my foes, sir, I profit in the knowledge of myself."[80]

Indeed the superiority of the fool lies mostly in his knowing that he is one; whilst the folly of the reputed wise man consists in his believing he is no fool. So, as both will act against the qualities which are supposedly their own, the advantage is decidedly on the fool's side. The argument runs through the first scene in which Feste appears: "For what says Quinapalus? Better a witty fool, than a foolish wit."[81] Thus Feste carries about with him the modest and unassuming, but quick and lively, awareness that just because he sees things at an inverted angle, they will often appear to him in their truer

[79] V, iv, 111-13.
[80] V, i, 13-14 and 18-21.
[81] I, v, 39-40; and again III, i, 67-75.

light; and such is the inexhaustible source of the paradox which seasons his every word, giving his speech the zest of an ever fresh revelation. An altered point of view will change all values; the outlines of virtue and vice are at once blurred because they overlap; the sense of that disorder, in which a new order is implied, along with the relativity that is its immediate consequence, is the philosophical soul of humor. In Feste the development of Shakespeare's jester to the quintessential fool reaches its final stage, and a character is created whose pregnant influence subsequent literature, especially the work of Sterne, was abundantly to show.

He stands not only for the freedom of an unattached mind, but for a supple, unprejudiced perception of life as a tangled web of pleasures and pains. The humorist's reaction to experience is original because it is neither one nor the other of the conflicting verdicts which man for thousands of years has alternately, or at the same time, passed upon this world. That is why Jaques and even Touchstone *(As You Like It)* fall short of the purest humor; they have not known how to keep their inner freedom entire; they have taken sides. Feste the fool is not an optimist; the laughter he awakes is rarely merry; his repeated thrusts into the underside of things feel along complex, awkward realities; from the first a tinge of melancholy is spread over him: "Many a good hanging," he points out, "prevents a bad marriage,"[82] and marrying, he hints elsewhere, is foolish.[83] A singer and a musician, he would prefer, like the Duke, "a dying fall";[84] he likes to repeat the "old and plain" lament of a lover;[85] even his beautiful love lyric[86] is a call to joy sobered by the vision of fleeting youth; and the famous song with which he concludes the play is the strangely moving confession of a simple fellow, which holds us through the quaint sincerity of its appeal, and whose naïve refrain has become to many the aptest symbol of the drabness of days. But Feste cannot be called a pessimist either; he takes good luck—a handsome tip, for instance—as it comes, with genuine glee; a menial, he manages to steer a middle course between servility

[82] I, v, 20-21.
[83] III, i, 38-40.
[84] I, i, 4.
[85] II, iv, 52-67.
[86] II, iii, 40-45 and 48-53.

and insolence: there is, he quickly asserts, "no motley in his brain," and he makes good the proposition that his lady is the fool;[87] thanks to his wit, he has his say while keeping ever on the safe side; and his vitality is equal to all new chances. He has not lost his gusto for life. The wisdom which his folly has distilled from an unceasing study of mixed happenings is resignation, a disillusioned view of man tempered with unfeigned tolerance and indulgence; the constant sense of the duality of events, never wholly good or wholly bad, has taught him to expect little and to be grateful for every smile of fate; his irony is not unkind, and his sadness never bitter. Heart and brain alike being thus at the same time open and free, not tied to any bias, habit, or mood, he possesses the best, the most typical background of humor, and reaps its supreme reward.

It is impossible to resist an impression that however organic and independent Feste's personality may be, he is largely a mouthpiece of Shakespeare's thought, humorously and indirectly expressed. He is the poet's fearless intelligent self, his critical mind; he is a revolutionary and, like Hamlet, must live under the disguise of madness. Realism in character thus concedes something to symbolism; truth becomes significant, rather than experimental. But is not the whole play "what you will," bathed in an atmosphere of irresponsible fancy; and does not the author hint as much to us, with admirable humor, in Fabian's words: "If this were played upon a stage now, I could condemn it as an improbable fiction"?[88] Malvolio's undisguised hostility to Feste is a trait of the same symbolic order: in the poet's mind the Puritan, the man of doctrine and rule, committed to one-sidedness, must violently clash with the humorist. An unequal fight; one strikes heavy blows, denouncing his foe, refusing him a brain, brandishing death and the day of judgment; the other lightly parries and thrusts and, in a combat of words, easily wins. Feste hears with ironical dissent Malvolio's ponderous sermon to Sir Toby, and joins in the "cakes and ale" retort, with the parallel "ginger shall be hot in the mouth."[89] On human nature he takes his stand. And it

[87] I, v, 42-86.
[88] III, iv, 139-40.
[89] II, iii, 123-27.

is from human nature that he derives his assurance of retribution: "pleasure will be paid, one time or another."[90] Of his religion, indeed, excessive respect for the clergy is no part: "would I were the first that ever dissembled in such a gown," he remarks, when dressed as a priest.[91]

So his humor is an ever-ready, infinitely varied response to the calls of circumstance; a response supple as well as subtle, hinting at the obscure side of truth, at the hidden ironies of life, with a discretion, a brevity, an apparent innocence of all intention, that fit in naturally with his humility as a social character and with the professed infirmity of his judgment, but that, in fact, sharpen each arrow of thought. That suppleness, that pliancy he praises in the Duke, whose mind is "a very opal," and who finding "his intent everywhere," will make "a good voyage of nothing."[92] Feste's answers are not always indirect, involved; when the quality of the subject is plain, he may be content with epigrammatic terseness: such his pointed description of a drunken man.[93] He will even quibble and pun to amuse himself, or in a mood of parody; like many of Shakespeare's characters, he censures word-play, the hobby of the age, but at times succumbs to it. "A sentence is but a cheveril glove to a good wit; how quickly the wrong side may be turned outward!"[94] He is not above mischievousness either: when Malvolio must be punished, he acts as tormentor, how shrewdly! But the genuine humorist cannot be pitiless, and he is first to relent: "I will fetch you light, and paper, and ink. . . ."[95]

When all is said, his most salient feature is the extraordinary density and pregnancy of his retorts; the compressed mental energy that charges his words with so much fresh, piquant, illuminating satire of the world, or of himself. We think here, not of Russian novelists, but of Pirandello. Feste's humor is very definitely a matter of intellectual power; and that is why he lays such stress on the feebleness of his brain. That kind of modesty is both sincere and part of his humorous game; it serves his turn. His insight is penetrating; he knows

[90] II, iv, 72-73.
[91] IV, ii, 6-7.
[92] II, iv, 76-80.
[93] I, v, 138-41.
[94] III, i, 12-15.
[95] IV, ii, 126-27.

at once that Cesario is a woman and that her errand is of love. He is well read, cracks humanist jokes, attacks pedantry with its own weapon; his mind is stored with the current Renaissance learning. But the main source of his verve is the intensity of his observation, the keenness of the vision that takes in the stuff of life and character, both what is apparent and what lies below the surface. Even the flights of his invention arise from the ground of facts. He has harvested and garnered a wide field of experience; and having full control over himself, he makes use of the treasure in a discreet manner that will not give him away. So clearly has Shakespeare realized the whole process that he puts in Viola's mouth lines of outstanding importance:

> This fellow's wise enough to play the fool;
> And, to do that well, craves a kind of wit:
> He must observe their mood on whom he jests,
> The quality of persons, and the time;
> And, like the haggard, check at every feather
> That comes before his eye. This is a practice
> As full of labour as a wise man's art:
> For folly that he wisely shows, is fit:
> But wise men, folly-fallen, quite taint their wit.[96]

[96] III, i, 67-75. A number of hints are thrown out in the Shakespearean plays as to the fool's tactics of indirectness, which to us are part of the strategy of humor. Celia's words on seeing Touchstone: "[Nature] hath sent this natural for our whetstone: for always the dulness of the fools is the whetstone of the wits" (*As You Like It*, I, ii), are only so to say a distant approximation of the truth, as the fool's dulness is feigned, and he is much more than a springing-board for others' pleasantry. His covert way of conveying his jokes acts on responsive minds like a stimulus, and in that positive sense he can be said to be a "whetstone." Falstaff is nearer the mark when he points out: "I am . . . the cause that wit is in other men" (*2 Henry IV*, I, ii, 10-11). Feeling the stimulus of the fool's irony, even its victims cannot help laughing at his slyness; as Jaques puts it: "I must have liberty withal, as large a charter as the wind, To blow on whom I please: for so fools have: And they that are most galled with my folly, They most must laugh" (*As You Like It*, II, vii, 47-51). But the closest descriptions of the fool's method are given by the Duke: "He uses his folly like a stalking-horse," V, iv, quoted above; and in these words of Viola's. Altogether there are very few points in the whole range of Shakespeare's art on which so much light is directly shed by the playwright himself; perhaps because few make such demands upon the audience. One more, and not the least significant, proof of Shakespeare's clear realization of the essential manner of genuine humor can be found in Hamlet's advice to the players (*Hamlet*, III, ii; see below, chap. xi).

And yet, the last word belongs to common humanity. At the end, before the other players have all withdrawn, during the short moment when the convention of the stage is only half vanished, the mask suddenly falls off, and there for a moment stands the man, still a humorist, still laughing at himself, but no longer quite willing to repress the melancholy, even the self-pity, that well up from the sorry tale of his past—the past of Everyman. After the light-hearted years of childhood, there have been the evil doings of a stormy youth; then an ill-advised marriage and conjugal brawls, with ignominious defeats; the usual refuge, drinking bouts with boon companions, and their aftermath; and a crowning touch, the sense of the depth of ages, the sadness of a world feeling old in the eternal effort of living. Meanwhile, the duties of everyday have gone their monotonous round, under skies ever rainy. All that passes off as flashes of remembrance, just revealing enough to make us descry the repressed world within. But the reaction is brief, and the fool, before his short song is over, ceases to let himself go; resignation, acceptance, doing one's bit, being funny, come into their own once more, with a twinkle in the disciplined but quick-glancing eye of humor.

VI. The Supreme Achievement: Falstaff

There is little mere buffoonery in Feste's part; there is a great deal in Sir John Falstaff's.[97] Still, the latter is, all told, Shakespeare's most significant creation in the field of humor. He owes it to the sheer exuberance of his features, and the fulness of the characterization. In one way, he is just a glorified example of a Jonsonian "humor"; in another, he sums up and pushes to its conclusion the development which has been here followed.

The duality, properly so called, is not in Shakespeare's hero; it is in Shakespeare himself. The character that he had selected and animated to play a given part in his drama assumed in the making not only an importance but a meaning that went far beyond; and Shakespeare's less conscious creative purpose—his subconscious purpose, if we must use the phrase—made his

[97] The text of this section, except a few additions and omissions, was first published in the *Johns Hopkins Alumni Magazine*, XXIII, Nov. 1, 1934.

bragging coward grow into something much more rare, interesting, and original.

Of that originality, the very essence is humor in the modern sense. Under the wide connotation of that word, we shall find in their subtle interplay elements which are, so to say, on the level of their own age, belonging exclusively to it; and others, which point the way to the further progress of thought.

The general aim of this survey makes it imperative that the latter elements should be stressed. The many problems that arise about the inception and growth of Falstaff's part—its historical origin, his relation to Oldcastle, the sources of the various accretions that went to the expanding of the character, etc., cannot be here touched upon. Our purpose must be to analyze the psychological process through which, from that unpromising germ, there developed a figure that ranks with the highest expressions of modern humor. We take it thus for granted that the eternal meaning of Falstaff is a real object and worthy of our attentive scrutiny, even if scholars should be concerned to point out that to speak of such a meaning is an illusion, because Shakespeare's contemporaries, and for aught we know, Shakespeare himself, must have taken a more limited view of the matter. This may be conceded, without cutting at the root of our inquiry. It leaves us *our* Falstaff—a perfectly legitimate growth, the character that our modern mind has fashioned out of the Elizabethan figure, and one that is in no wise arbitrary, since it actualizes suggestions which Shakespeare's genius did create, and of which he cannot himself have been entirely unaware; though they are to be found, no doubt, on a plane of his imaginative life which his clearer self-consciousness did not probably reach. In that sense, our Falstaff is the real Falstaff—to us; and in every sense that matters he has not ceased to be Shakespeare's Falstaff.[98]

The Falstaff of tradition, the bragging and lying soldier, is mostly a farcical figure that will raise in us broad laughter and will himself, being jocular, make jokes of the same quality. Good fun that; and it would be silly to despise it, since Shake-

[98] The line here taken is thus in agreement with that which A. C. Bradley (*Oxford Lectures on Poetry*, London, 1920) and H. B. Charlton (*Falstaff*, Manchester, 1935), have followed.

speare and Molière did not at all look down upon it. But if Shakespeare's Falstaff were nothing else, we could hardly speak of Falstaff's humor, in the proper sense. The super-Falstaff, the glorious creature that somehow grows upon the first—a growth that takes place, we must not forget, in the creative mind of Shakespeare—is, on the contrary, the greatest example of humor in English literature, from the earliest days to the end of the eighteenth century.

Let us turn to the two parts of *King Henry IV*. Falstaff is first shown to us as rather his simpler self; then he develops into the super-Falstaff; after that, the two sides of the character are presented together, with a predominance now of the former, now of the latter. The more elementary Falstaff is in the foreground again at the end of *2 Henry IV;* and he has the *Merry Wives of Windsor* almost entirely to himself. That succession, no doubt, is far from answering any deliberate purpose on the part of Shakespeare. Still, we may take stock of the fact that the richer expansion of Falstaff's character has a tendency to occur, neither at the beginning nor at the end, but in the middle sections of each part of *Henry IV*, and especially of the first part. The reason is obvious: the setting of a plot under way and its winding up being the occasions in which the freedom of the playwright's mind is most restricted by technical cares, the moments of greatest ease, those in which Shakespeare would let himself go, are those in which Falstaff is allowed to assume his fullest originality. That in the inception and treatment of the *Merry Wives* Shakespeare's initiative was particularly limited is affirmed by tradition, and very generally accepted as a fact.

It would be superfluous to study at length the pranks of Sir John, when he is chiefly his own bulky, drinking, uproarious, quibbling, sensuous, cowardly self. About the drollery of that sort of thing we all agree, and not much hairsplitting is necessary. He is then a traditional type; but he is that, we must confess, with a boldness of outline, a height of coloring, a gusto, and a bravura which are all Shakespeare's own. Still, there is nothing very subtle, at first sight, about the comedy he gives us. He figures primarily as a butt, a grotesque; he rouses laughter by the monstrous size of his body, the frankness of his animal appetites and all that appertains thereto; he tickles our fancy, as well, by his gift of the gab, his punning, his impudence, his verbal inventiveness, his wit. So, of the fun which gathers about him, the larger part is not of his own making; and even the part for which he is responsible is almost exclusively of the plain, direct kind. There is little humor in all that; although there is assuredly some. Shakespeare, indeed, was too good a playwright not to fuse his two Falstaffs somehow into one, or rather, not to make them to some extent shade off into each other. But Falstaff is here, in every sense of the word, a very funny person, not a humorist. In the first scene where he appears at all,[99] so free, spontaneous, and aboveboard is his gaiety that it is Prince Henry, not he, whose cool self-command and detachment in pleasantry would better fit in with our notion of humor.

And yet, we feel all along in that scene and in the next where Falstaff appears,[100] that his jollity is not simply what it looks on the surface; it sounds with an undertone, which, from the moment we are aware of it, becomes more and more audible. The impression is borne in upon us that the fat knight is perfectly conscious of himself and plays with his whole personality, physical and moral, as he plays upon words. Such a triumphant exhibition of his own foibles is a comedy that the rogue is giving himself, and so to say a part which he performs as for a wager. He knows that the part sits well upon him—being, indeed, in a way, the projection, the glorification of his own nature—and into the playing of that part, the essence of which seems to be pure irresponsibility, he throws a cool-headed feeling of artistry. There is archness, for instance, and a subtle understanding of stage effect in his putting up a pretense that he wishes to reform: "Before I knew thee, Hal, I knew nothing; and now am I, if a man should speak truly, little better than one of the wicked. I must give over this life, and I will give it over; by the Lord, an I do not, I am a villain!"[101] He says that with his tongue in his cheek; and so we have at least a flavor of the humorous; one thing is said, and another meant.

[99] I, ii. [100] II, ii.

[101] *I Henry IV*, I, ii, 104-8.

In that inference we proceed on a principle of analogy and probability. The nimbleness of wit, the readiness of tongue, the mental agility of which Falstaff shows himself past master do not possibly go, in our experience, along with the naïve unconsciousness, the dull sluggishness of inner sense, the blindness to one half, and that the better half, of mental life, which his acts and speech would imply, if he did not see any further than his speech. Now, his nature must be more or less of a piece; and so the bluntness of perception which Sir John parades again and again can be but a mask which he puts on, and enjoys putting on. At this stage we are already far from the stock figure of the bragging soldier; out of the clown which he received Shakespeare has made a complex being, with a wealth of individual peculiarities, a talent for farce, a gift of more subtle comedy, and gleams of genuine humor. But before long his creation assumes the full stretch of its originality.

With the fourth scene of Act II Falstaff rises to new heights of paradoxical extravagance, of poetical impudence, and of humor. The thickness of his body, his heavy casing of flesh, make the brilliance and the rapidity of his invention more wonderful. The farcical comedy which he had been playing for the pleasure of his companions and for his own, widens and deepens into a mockery of the whole of life, a sort of topsy-turvy parody of it in which satire, criticism, and a general upsetting of values run riot. The physical figure of the fat knight remains unchanged; but his mental self puts on a character of authority, a prestige of power and freedom; he is no longer the slave of his senses and of his heavy fleshliness; he is a free spirit, rejoicing in the independence born of complete detachment. Giving an ironical, defiant twist to the decent, the normal, and the rational truth of things, he is the creator of a world—the world of humor, the inmost principle of which is relativity.

Those are large claims, and it would be well to justify them at once. To do so is no easy task; the superior level upon which Falstaff's pleasantry gives itself scope can hardly be described in a quotation or two; it must be gathered from his whole self-expression, with its fertility and range, and chiefly from his success in playing with life.

We have, first, the poetry of lying. There are many ways of telling an untruth. Falstaff's manner is free from all utilitarian motive; he cannot, he does not, expect that anyone will believe him. The logic of his invention runs away with him; and in a fine frenzy of dramatization, the law of which is purely aesthetic, he builds up his mountains of lies to ever more towering heights; he adds to the pile with a total neglect of verisimilitude, which his cleverness, if he were bent upon avoiding detection, would certainly have allowed him to escape. We have here a clear case of the lyricism of exaggeration—an enthusiasm which lets itself go for its own sake, while the sense of actual truth, in a corner of the mind, keeps cool and clear. Just as Daudet's hero remains all through the telling of his fibs a level-headed realist, so Falstaff entangles himself helplessly in the relation of his glorious fight with the robbers, and the moment the game is up and the whole fabric crumbles down about his ears, adjusts himself to the bewildering change with extraordinary agility:

> By the Lord, I knew ye as well as he that made ye. Why, hear you, my masters; was it for me to kill the heir-apparent? Should I turn upon the true prince? Why, thou knowest I am as valiant as Hercules: but beware instinct; the lion will not touch the true prince. Instinct is a great matter; I was now a coward on instinct. I shall think the better of myself and thee during my life; I for a valiant lion, and thou for a true prince.[102]

How could he have hoped to take in anybody? His lies, as the Prince tells him, are "gross as a mountain, open, palpable."[103] His impudence, he must clearly realize, may be superb, but it is not effective. Running full tilt against the very suspicions one feared to arouse, and brazening it all off with a careless gesture, if it were a policy, would be no good one. The pure, the philosophical joy of transcendental audacity breathes in such cheeky words as these, when it is a Falstaff who speaks them: "There live not three good men unhanged in England;

[102] II, iv, 294-303.
[103] *Ibid.*, 250-51.

and one of them is fat and grows old"; or in his pathetic rejoinder to the Prince: "What, art thou mad? art thou mad? is not the truth the truth?"[104] That complete upsetting of the values of veracity, done with a thoroughness that actual life will hardly bear, can only be a game played for sheer pleasure; and it implies a clear intelligence of the relativity of things, a mood of free experimenting in the interversion of the real and the fictitious; it supposes a duality of mental planes and an indirect mode of expression, the actual intent offering itself in disguise—that is to say, the very conditions of humor.

But that manner, as it were, is generalized; and the latter part of the scene gives us an incomparable display of the transvaluation of all values. Two or three different backgrounds of meaning are confusedly perceived behind each of Falstaff's speeches, imparting a rich implicitness of significance to what he says; so that joking and earnestness, earnestness and joking keep shading off into each other, rousing in us a sense of their close interrelation and of the illusion of all clear-cut categories. Falstaff plays into the hands of his companions, who are laughing at his figure; he emphasizes the grotesqueness of his own person by calling up the slim image of the youth he was; he exaggerates that slimness and makes it funny in its turn; the new fun enhances the old and yet kills it, since one excess loses its absolute value, grows only relative by being set in opposition to another excess; and more deeply still, there arises from the discreet tone of self-pity with which the rogue has conjured up his younger image a subtle humanization of his comic character, a softening of his moral figure, which blunts the edge of our pitiless laughter and scorn. The note of kindred humanity which, not for the first time, is heard here amid the loud dry laughter mellows the humor of Falstaff into the rich complete thing it is.

The Prince: How long is't ago, Jack, since thou sawest thine own knee?

Falstaff: My own knee! when I was about thy years, Hal, I was not an eagle's talon in the waist; I could have crept into any

[104] *Ibid.*, 143-45 and 254-55.

alderman's thumb-ring: a plague of sighing and grief! it blows a man up like a bladder.[105]

The climax of dramatic irony and the most suggestive humor are reached soon after in the mock dialogue where Falstaff, impersonating first the king then the Prince, puts in a plea for himself with roguish indirectness. This is not only the most brilliant demonstration of his mental resourcefulness; the fun has depth because the clever handling of another person's point of view is a lesson in the relativity of our judgment; because, at the same time, the praise of Falstaff, which Falstaff himself makes the king supposedly deliver, is piquantly unexpected upon those lips; because that praise, meanwhile, takes on a very different coloring when we realize that it comes from the very person who is being praised; because the impudence of the fiction being seen through, the validity of the plea is crushingly, ridiculously impaired, no one being a disinterested judge of himself; because the rogue's audacity, finally, turns out successful after all, and his argument recovers the validity it had lost when we reflect that under the cloak of comedy Falstaff is seriously pleading for himself, and his earnestness is more than justified from the human angle: he is getting old, the Prince is moving away from him, and that is a friendship he cannot afford to lose. His call to pity under the disguise of farce and fun is plainer still at the end, when it is into the mouth of the Prince that Falstaff puts his exquisitely clever and soberly moving appeal to the indulgence of the young man, whose heart he feels is more and more hardening against him:

But to say I know more harm in him than in myself, were to say more than I know. That he is old, the more the pity, his white hairs do witness it. . . . If sack and sugar be a fault, God help the wicked! if to be old and merry be a sin, then many an old host that I know is damned; if to be fat is to be hated, then Pharaoh's lean kine are to be loved. Ho, my good lord: banish Peto, banish Bardolph, banish Poins; but for sweet Jack Falstaff, kind Jack Falstaff, true Jack Falstaff, valiant Jack Falstaff, and therefore more valiant, being, as he is, old Jack Falstaff, banish not him thy

[105] II, iv, 360-66.

Harry's company, banish not him thy Harry's company: banish plump Jack, and banish all the world.[106]

We have here a subtle handling of the finer and implicit shades that enter into the composition of humor; what is said, and what is understood are both involved in infinitely complex relations; the dialogue reverberates through our minds in long echoes of amusement, thought, and feeling. The essence of that playing with the hard and fast notions and judgments of normal life, through which they are brought into paradoxical, suggestive connections with one another, is the veriest spirit of philosophical humor.

To transpose actual issues and problems into intellectual terms which one may combine at will is to secure freedom from the urgency of life in contemplative detachment; and Shakespeare's Falstaff, the slave of his body and of his senses, finds supreme liberty in humor; he is freer than the Prince, whose personality stiffens by degrees into the strictness of utilitarian virtue. This aspect of the subject has been perceived and expressed so clearly by a critic that his words remain unshaken; they establish a relation independent of space and time: "The bliss of freedom gained in humour is the essence of Falstaff. . . . He is the enemy of everything that would interfere with his ease, and therefore of anything serious. . . . For these things impose limits and obligations, and make us the subjects of old father antic the law . . . they are to him absurd; and to reduce a thing *ad absurdum* is to reduce it to nothing and to walk about free and rejoicing."[107] That life and conduct are terribly serious and cannot long put up with such freedom goes without saying; Falstaff discovers it to his cost. The pharisaic king is to him the instrument of "father antic the law." But modern humor here assumes its full meaning as a self-sufficient spirit, like those of art, poetry, and truth; not amenable to conduct because it rises above the values of life, and able to claim independence provided it takes the implied risks.

The greater Falstaff is still very much himself in the third scene of Act III, where he plays so wistfully with the fantastic

[106] II, iv, 511-14 and 516-27.

[107] A. C. Bradley, "The Rejection of Falstaff," *Oxford Lectures on Poetry* (London, 1909), pp. 262-63.

theme of his own conversion, and fires off at the impudent Bardolph such a devastating volley of splendid imaginative abuse; where again, after that "flyting," and the high-flavored dialogue with the hostess, he throws out one of those revealing sallies in which the essence of a character is conveyed: "Thou knowest in the state of innocency Adam fell; and what should poor Jack Falstaff do in the days of villany? Thou seest I have more flesh than another man, and therefore more frailty." And as the Prince, somewhat haughtily, remarks: "I am good friends with my father and may do anything," out comes the admirable rejoinder: "Rob me the exchequer the first thing thou doest."[108] We have here truly in full the paradox and the fascination of irresponsibility; a transcending of the plane of good and evil to which Shakespeare does not deliberately commit himself, but the humorous and poetical appeal of which the artist in him thoroughly enjoyed.

After that a decline is perceptible. Falstaff as a recruiting officer is very good fun,[109] but the psychological interest is waning. It revives in the cynical monologue upon honor,[110] where the humor lies in the cold matter-of-fact testing of ideal and conventional values by the crude, unashamed standard of practical utility. The implied contrast of this attitude with the evasion of the issue, which is almost universal in the discussion of the problem, is handled here with a beautiful unconsciousness of there being a contrast at all. The same might be said of the end of V, iii, in which Falstaff's doings and words set up an exquisite, though an implicit, parody and denial of the high-flown chivalry and rant which are giving themselves scope all about him. We have here to the very life the humor of Sancho, by the side of his Don Quixote—at a time, needless to say, when Cervantes had not yet written. Falstaff's behavior and his language in V, iv, are no less eloquent of the strong racy common sense that is the humble attribute of realistic cowardice:

S'blood! 'twas time to counterfeit, or that hot termagant Scot had paid me scot and lot too. Counterfeit? I lie, I am no

[108] III, iii, 185-89, 203-6.
[109] IV, ii, 1-52.
[110] V, i, 127-44.

counterfeit: to die is to be a counterfeit, for he is but the counterfeit of a man who hath not the life of a man; but to counterfeit dying, when a man thereby liveth, is to be no counterfeit, but the true and perfect image of life indeed. The better part of valour is discretion; in the which better part I have saved my life.[111]

One seems to gather, from Falstaff's last words in the play, that Shakespeare felt his knight must be toned down; he descends from the glorious "amorality" of humor, to hints of a conversion—this time in a manner that might well be earnest: "I'll purge, and leave sack, and live cleanly, as a nobleman should do."[112] We are here leaving the purely artistic sphere, and definitely passing on to the ethical one.

The character, indeed, could not be left for long at its full intensity; imperious necessities forbade. The plot must follow its prescribed course, the play develop to the consummations that Shakespeare's dramatic instinct, his sense of the spectators' needs, his patriotic and moral theme demanded. Falstaff must remain a butt, a thoroughly ridiculous, though a glorified, type of the braggart, the coward, and the dishonest soldier; he must raise the scornful laugh of the audience against him, even more than he calls up at will their indulgent smile by his lyrical impudence and his superhuman readiness of wit. The groundlings must fully take in and digest the lesson of the national hero, the shrewd, strong, scheming, nobly ambitious Prince, shaking off the follies of his youth and the greyhaired companion of his mad pranks. It all means that the humor of Falstaff is to lose most of the subtle, creative originality, which had lifted him, for a moment, to a level of conscious intellectual superiority over the vulgar circumstances of his life, over the pragmatism and cool cunning of the heir to the throne, and chiefly, above his own lamentable fleshly miseries. A comedy of the usual type, in which farcical elements more and more largely enter, tends to extinguish the flashes of philosophical self-mockery. That descent to a lower plane, that tainting of the spiritual sources by the springs of coarse merriment, are discernible in most of the second part of *King Henry IV*.

[111] V, iv, 113-22.
[112] V, iv, 167-70.

That play still offers us, though, gleams of fine humor, as in I, ii, where Falstaff displays his wonderful power to bend ideas and words, with apparent unconsciousness, to all the quibbles and double meanings that they can possibly suggest; his manner expressing a set resolve to take life as a play, while he utters the freshest as well as the most vulgar fun. Again, in III, ii, he rises to the full height of his cynical wit, while examining his new recruits. Significant, as well, are some of his remarks: "I am not only witty in myself, but the cause that wit is in other men";[113] we can read there Shakespeare's realization of the double value of Falstaff's character, as both a conscious creator, and an object, of comedy; and the proof that Falstaff is aware of his humorous method, which consists precisely in giving others causes for laughter, with which he seems himself to be quite unconcerned. That consciousness of the inmost trick of humor comes out even more clearly in these remarkable words: "I will devise matter enough out of this Shallow to keep Prince Harry in continual laughter. . . . O, it is much that a lie with a slight oath and a jest with a sad brow will do with a fellow that never had the ache in his shoulders!"[114] *A jest with a sad brow!* ("Sad," of course, in its Elizabethan sense of "serious.") It is fit, after all, that Shakespeare should have shown intimations of the gradual self-discovery of humor, which was to occupy a full century; and that he should have lent his clearest glimpse of the characteristic attitude of the humorist to one who is himself a brilliant representative of humor in being.[115]

But at the same time, the old man who shows such insight into the character of Shallow, for instance, loses all his penetration whenever his Prince is concerned. Shakespeare seems

[113] *2 Henry IV*, I, ii, 10-11.

[114] V, i, 87-88 and 91-94.

[115] "We may gather from this," says Clarke (quoted by Rolfe, notes to *2 Henry IV*, p. 197), "that Falstaff enhanced the effect of some of his jokes by staid utterance and a quiet dry manner; but others, be sure, he accompanied by a broad roar; and *all* with a twinkle of his eye that spoke volumes in archness and roguish meaning." We entirely agree to the twinkle; as for the "broad roar," in the absence of all stage directions, we see no reason why we should regard it as more frequent than the "staid utterance." The former would suit the farce and the mere fun, the latter would be the fit accompaniment to the humor. Here again, we have the two Falstaffs in one.

to have taken pains to prepare us for the blindness with which Falstaff meets his fate more than halfway, and brings down upon himself the new king's devastating rebuke, by stressing the signs in him of physical decay and of a softness, so to say, that would imply some loss of his former mental agility.[116] An almost naïve good nature, a silly trust in the power of long-standing friendship are features of Falstaff's character at the end. His reaction when the news of the old king's death is brought him is all of exuberant good-fellowship and bounty to his friends. And so he, the former master of intellectual subtlety, rushes madly into the ironical anticlimax of his disappointment and disgrace. He must be no more now to the spectators, than a clown who has outlived his welcome, and a conspicuous example of the cheapness of stale fun; the ridiculous butt, in him, has displaced the supreme humorist; and with absolute disregard, apparently, of the possible clash, in that final instance, between conflicting sides of the character he had created, Shakespeare goes on his way unperturbed.

How far he could go we know from the *Merry Wives of Windsor.* There it is not enough to say that Falstaff is no longer his former self; he is a direct negation and contradiction of it. "To picture the real Falstaff befooled like the Falstaff of the *Merry Wives* is like imagining Iago the gull of Roderigo, or Becky Sharpe, the dupe of Amelia Osborne."[117] And the impossibility cuts even deeper than to the intellectual being of the character: by falling again and again into the same trap, by succumbing passively to the same witless impulses of greed, vanity, and lechery, the Falstaff of the *Merry Wives* is a type of the automatism induced by moral weakness in mere mortal man, that is to say, the very antithesis of the freedom which his superior self would display in supple reactions to events. The prince of humorists has dwindled into a clumsy purblind fool. So much for the character generally and the situation. In the details the author or authors of the play have taken care to gild the new Falstaff with some reflection from the glow of his former self. Gleams of moral liberty in rising above cir-

[116] That note, of course, is struck again and still more clearly in the relation of Falstaff's death (*King Henry V*, II, iii, 5-46).

[117] A. C. Bradley, *op. cit.*, p. 248.

cumstances, and playing with one's self—outbursts of that lively, obvious exaggeration which is an art and mockery of one's own artificial social pride—still somewhat link up the Falstaff of the *Merry Wives* with that of *Henry IV*. But he is now only the ghost of his former being: the play has very little of that quintessential spirit of humor through which Shakespeare was supreme. We have come down to the level of broad common fun.

Of those gleams the final scene (V, v) shows not a few, as if the playwright had felt it necessary that in his ridiculous disaster Falstaff should preserve at the last something of his elasticity and his readiness, in order to leave with the audience an image of himself they might somehow reconcile with his traditional figure.

It does seem bold, and perhaps futile, where Shakespeare is concerned, to put forward a psychological interpretation, except on points of detail. All fairly wide problems have been subjected to the scrutiny of so many acute minds that it takes a stout heart to propose at all a new view. But the view here explained is not by any means new. It is a commonplace to stress the margin of divergence that may and often does, with Shakespeare, interpose between what a character should be simply to fulfil its part in the plot to perfection, and what a sense of free development, and as it were the enthusiasm of individuality, have made it. Among the most obvious cases in point one thinks at once of Shylock and Hamlet. Falstaff and the Prince of Denmark belong to different worlds; but in both cases the deeper genius of Shakespeare ran away with his own dramatic creation, to the wonderful enrichment of his art as a picture of human life, and somewhat to the loss of his plot in coherence, as of his dramatic intent in clearness. Such, at least, remains the view of many, even after the stress has been shifted by the critics of the historical school.

In the present instance the conjecture is the more tempting, as Shakespeare must have been guided in his creation by an especially pure instinct of psychological truth. He could the less have expressed to himself what he meant by turning his Falstaff into a representative of essential humor, as essential humor was still very far from being recognized, analyzed, and named. The notion of a peculiar mode of pleasantry, with a range of its own, characterized by a certain complexity of mental attitude, was still going through the obscure slow stages of its growth towards the final elucidation that was to be reached some hundred years later.

One cannot help fancying that Shakespeare, here as so often, was guided only by his sheer intuition of life, by his sense of moral interrelations. His Falstaff is not only a legendary character, with more or less historical features; he is a human person, the result of the intuitive realization without which the heroes of novels or dramas have no life. And one can imagine pretty well how Falstaff was realized—how his self was grasped as a whole, in the interplay of its physical and moral elements. We have all come across potential Falstaffs—very stout men with agile minds, whose tongues were the glibber for the heaviness of their bodies. We have noticed how they made their physical disgrace into a trump, and laughed first at themselves so as to forestall the laughter of others. They would be bound more narrowly than most to the infirmities of the flesh—usually, huge appetites dwelt in their bulky frames; but as if a compensatory instinct were at work, they had found an escape in a mental detachment, a faculty of looking round all subjects, a free, if not a cynical habit of mind. Jollity was not only their natural mode of being—one which perhaps had been partly a cause, through self-indulgence, to their fatness; it was as well an effect of it, a mood upon which they had fallen back under the guidance of that instinct, which makes most people grow the attitude and even the character that suits their exterior personalities best. They would give themselves, and others, no quarter in pleasantry, expecting none. All their refinement of feeling and ardor of imagination, being refused the ordinary outlet of poetry and aestheticism, that accorded but ill with their physical appearance, would discover equivalent channels in an inventiveness, a verbal brilliance and felicity that astonished and awed down the disrespect of the uncharitable. Being inclined to make fun of their own selves, and possessing the mental nimbleness that could see at the same time both sides of a subject, they would be at least incipient humorists; their jocularity would tend to the paradoxical presentment of fun, that enlivens it and sharpens its edge, and the name of which is humor.

Whatever Sir John Oldcastle and the "miles gloriosus" of tradition may have done for Shakespeare, they are not the origin of what is most interesting in Falstaff. Shakespeare's intuition worked directly from life and built round those suggestions which he gathered out of experience. His Falstaff is the glorified type of a category of human character, a type no actual and full justification for which may have existed but whose truth is none the less profound and immediately accepted by us. He is very probably not a picture but a composite portrait, a masterpiece of individualization, and of no one is it truer to say that there is logic in his madness: that logic which demands that even the freaks of Nature, if they are living, should be organically related wholes. The figures in Chaucer's *Prologue* are formed in that very way; the accent falls on the significant feature, but the other traits are such as to make that feature perfectly natural, almost inevitable in its close connection with them.

Shakespeare's supreme discovery of humor in Falstaff is thus guided by his insight into the life and actuality of character. What helped him besides was his sense of relativity—a sense which was in him dramatic, but also, potentially at least, philosophical. The result was a ten-act drama in which the open purpose of the writer is thwarted, almost as much as it is helped, by one of the main characters. It is no use pointing out that those plays were primarily made for the stage, and that the complexities of Falstaff appear mostly to the reader, who is thus the victim of an irrelevant illusion. The heroes of Shakespeare belong to us, for all intellectual purposes; we are within our rights in subjecting them to tests he may not have foreseen: by so doing, it is his own subconscious self that we test and probe. Indeed the two parts of *Henry IV* are lopsided, in our sophisticated and overinquisitive view, because Shakespeare's Prince Henry is to us a calculating politician, and Falstaff, the butt, the cynical braggart and coward, is a pioneer of the freedom of the modern spirit. But of course

Shakespeare did not care, at bottom, for dramatic consistency in the abstract; he enjoyed the freedom of the artist; we are faithful to his best intent in drawing to light what was implicit, probably even to himself.

Whether more or less is granted to the "disintegrators," the unexpected and so to say the abnormal development of Falstaff must have taken place in one single mind. Definite and clear-cut artistic issues can be worked out in collaboration; but subconscious growths, if the result is not simply chaotic, are individual processes, except in the field of purely emotional or instinctive reactions, such as are the subjects of mass psychology. The leading spirit among the dramatists who may have had a share in the turning out of the Falstaff plays, the mysterious Shakespeare himself, should be responsible—and is, by all the tests of genius and language—for all the superior Falstaff; a direct link is thus established between his shadowy personality and those parts of the play. The best of Falstaff—in our modern estimation—belongs to him alone.

One more point must be stressed. Falstaff is a landmark in the progress of Shakespeare's humor, as Shakespeare's is in the development of English humor. There had not been yet in the literature of England anything like the degree of subtlety he displays in self-mockery. That full realization of what humor is had never been reached before; not even by Chaucer, who comes nearest to it; not by Sir Thomas More, by John Heywood, by Sir Philip Sidney, nor by Shakespeare himself in his earlier plays. Although the notion was to remain entangled yet for a century, the thing itself, for the first time, is there, completely grown, with all its intellectual implications. Shakespeare here is on a par with Cervantes. His fat knight, who in fact is spiritual brother not to Don Quixote but to Sancho, opens the way to the numerous family that are heirs in some respect or other, and whether consciously or not, to the immortal pair. With that posterity, it may seem that the rogue has but little claim to rub shoulders; but now is the time to remember Mrs. Quickly's significant words: "I have known thee these twenty-nine years, come peascod-time; but an honester and truer-hearted man,—well, fare thee well."[118]

[118] 2 *Henry IV*, II, iv, 412-15.

CHAPTER XI

SHAKESPEARE'S HUMOR: III. HUMOR IN CONFLICT AND SERENITY[1]

I. HUMOR IN TRAGEDY

THAT WITH *Hamlet* there begins in the atmosphere of Shakespeare's work a period of conflict, leading up eventually to one of serenity, may be regarded as an accepted generalization. A darkening of the tone, indeed, is perceptible after 1600. Seven plays[2]—*Hamlet, Troilus and Cressida, All's Well, Measure for Measure, Othello, King Lear, Macbeth*—offer some similarity of spirit; and although their aims are different, four being tragedies and three comedies, such epithets as "dark" and "bitter" have been equally attached to them. It is a fact as well that after some six or seven years the cloud seems gradually to lift; and finally we have tragicomedies of an almost smiling temper.

It is tempting to infer, from those symptoms and a few others, that Shakespeare's inner life at the time underwent corresponding phases. Many critics, following the lead of Dowden, have agreed that the poet must then have known predominant moods, first of depression and anguish, next of resignation; he must have been swayed by a sense of baffling wrong before he found rest in an acceptance that opened the way to sober peace.

Upon the validity of the inference, it would be presuming to commit ourselves here. But this at least may be said, that

[1] The plays studied in this chapter are: *Hamlet*, 1600-1601; *Troilus and Cressida*, 1601-1602; *All's Well that Ends Well*, 1602-1603; *Measure for Measure, Othello*, 1604-1605; *King Lear, Macbeth*, 1605-1606; *Antony and Cleopatra*, 1606-1607; *Coriolanus, Timon of Athens*, 1607-1608; *Pericles*, 1608-1609; *Cymbeline*, 1609-1610; *The Winter's Tale*, 1610-1611; *The Tempest*, 1611-1612; *Henry VIII*, 1612-1613.

[2] Eight, if *Timon of Athens*, possibly later than *Macbeth* by one year, is regarded as part of the same group.

the conclusions to be drawn from a special study of Shakespeare's humor do not in any way clash with that view. Of course, to begin with, as soon as the general atmosphere becomes more somber, and a tragic inspiration gains ascendency, making itself felt even in the comedies, humor, without vanishing, recedes more or less into the background. In a truly comic play it is part of the natural purpose of the whole and easily fuses with the action; whenever the self-revelation of the characters, the incidents, or the dialogue tend to rouse it in us, it merges in the predominant effect which the playwright is seeking to create. When original humorists are shown us on the stage, absorbing life on their own account and giving it a humorous turn, their reaction is after all consonant with the aim of laughter, even if their amusement is tinged with the serious hues of reflection; their attitude chimes in readily with that of the spectator; and we expect them instinctively to be more or less the author's mouthpieces.

In a tragic play the humorous, while nowise excluded, can be only a side issue. It mainly fulfils the part of a relief and eases the strain; but as a means to that end it is less efficient than plainer, more direct kinds of the comic, which tell at once and produce a stronger contrast; it turns us inward upon ourselves, makes us chew the cud at a moment when the relaxation of sheer physical laughter is needed. Moreover, humorists among the characters must be, as such, no part of the action itself; for inevitable detachment is their lot, and they look on things from the outside. In so far as they come forward and assert themselves, they interrupt or delay the progress of the plot. They are thus liable to be pushed into corners and to play, at best, the role of some incidental chorus, unless it happens that the tragedy is hinged on the very unfitness of a contemplative nature for action; and then we have an exceptional masterpiece, *Hamlet*. Conversely, the tragicomedies of Shakespeare's final phase, in their relaxed mood, show us a freer emergence of humorous themes, developed independently on their own merits.

But the quality of the humorous, no less than its quantity, varies with the general atmosphere; and this again is natural enough, since humor is an attitude of the whole mind and mirrors the deep-laid incidents in the moral life of the writer. To all appearances the meditative brooding upon life, which nourishes Shakespeare's essential humor, is tinged with bitterness during the years of the dark tragedies; it is enlivened with a glow of mild sympathy during the final time of the tragi-comedies. So the playwright's own attitude to life must not be left any longer out of account. A dramatist's philosophical reaction can be passed over when, as is usually the case, it does not appear in the foreground; and broadly speaking, such was the case with Shakespeare during his early and middle career. But if that reaction seems to manifest a bias, it has to be recognized and considered.

It has thus proved possible to plan out this chapter on a basis which, while strictly chronological, is psychological at the same time. The presumed order of the plays is followed, except that *Timon of Athens,* assigned to 1606-1607, would clash, if that dating were final, with the temper of the humor in the two contemporary tragedies: *Antony and Cleopatra,* 1606-1607; *Coriolanus,* 1607-1608. As an intellectual symptom *Timon* belongs to a slightly earlier moment, and is the last of the "bitter" comedies, with which one may study it.

In this period as a whole, although characters are still found on which the main stamp is that of humor, there are none of that kind as important as Feste or Falstaff. It thus becomes less material to group together the butts of humor, and the humorists, according to their kinds. So the plays themselves will be here examined separately, in their probable sequence.

II. Sardonic Humor

Hamlet

Humor in Hamlet[3] subtly and constantly calls up the grim features of the Swiftian manner. Shakespeare's hero strangely adumbrates the man of genius who certainly did not feign madness, but perhaps had madness lurking in the depths of his being.

[3] This section, with some changes, reproduces a lecture printed in the *Rice Institute Pamphlet* for July, 1937.

The relation between Hamlet's character and humor is an intimate and deep-laid one. Some rather plain facts must be stressed. The tragic predicament in which he finds himself forces upon him a policy of dissimulation. He must repress his feelings, hide his thoughts; and thus he is led to express nothing but under a veil, to use hints, riddles, puzzling and mystifying words. His mental life develops on a double plane; and the duality of his consciousness is so persistent that it becomes as it were normal. His mind, however, is vigorous and penetrating; it reaches at one stroke profound intuitive conclusions, sees through the affectations and hypocrisies of others. His judgments upon life and people are too shrewd not to destroy the glamor of illusion; and the dark mystery of crime in which he finds himself desperately involved brings him into contact with the lowest depths of guilt in men. All that, as well, he must hide, except in his musings, his monologues, or his talks with his safe friend, Horatio; but for those occasions, his watchfulness and caution raise a barrier to the free utterance of his personal feelings and plans or of his views about the world that surrounds him.

He is able to bear such a strain. Of a quick, agile mind, ingenious and eloquent, he is past master in the art of ceaselessly raising a fabric of verbal phantasmagoria; and he knows all the vanity of "words, words, words" the better for his native proficiency in the craft of handling them. Not that his motive is a desire to deceive for the sake of deceiving; what Hamlet wants to communicate is not a spun-out figment of his brain; in all his sincere or affected wildness, he never crosses the line beyond which actual lying would begin; his is a proud, fastidious soul that will not stoop to the mean, self-interested comedy of fear, to the low devices of cheating. What he is after is ambiguity; a manner, on the face of it, fit to bear a normal construction; vague and enigmatical enough, on the other hand, to make his least intelligent hearers obscurely uneasy and rouse in the sharpest a disquieting sense of a conscious evasion. It is part and parcel of his strategy to create uncertainty, especially at critical moments, in the minds of his natural adversaries; and he finds in such mystification and bravado a thrill, which owes something to the emotion of danger, for Hamlet is brave, he even shows temerity; he tastes as well in those moments the secret pleasure of not really disguising his thought; indeed, it is not the least significant aspect of the drama that such a sensitively truthful and candid man should be bound to a policy of equivocation and reticence. His subtlety thus enables him to sustain for a long time the paradox of that twofold mental life, and from his daring as well as from his intellectual alertness he gathers an ironical, bitter pleasure, the quality of which is hardly distinguishable from that of humor—its constituent elements being the same—and which seems to anticipate the humorous manner of Swift.

The presence of a hidden meaning, in almost all that Hamlet says, imparts to each and every word a kind of virtual expansiveness. The mental stimulus which we derive from such a method of expression hardly ever rouses actual laughter, neither does Hamlet himself laugh—one fancies him, at most, chuckling inwardly; but the fact that we do not laugh, and rarely smile, is no proof that we are outside the proper field of humorous perception; it must be confessed, however, that no variety of humor can compare with this in concentration; no one possesses a greater force of repressed energy; and by liberating itself in our minds, it sets going a series of endless echoes—in the present instance, of meditative, intellectual ones; while the absence of all physical relief, of all discharge and fulfilment through laughter, holds us fast in a sense of violence and coercion, of harshness and bitterness. That is no healthy humor; but the seal of the abnormal, even of the morbid, or of the tragic, is plainly stamped upon the whole play.

Let us try and catch that original quality of Hamlet's humor in being, as the plot progresses, under some of its aspects; they will appear to us in a series of particularly revealing moments.

Hamlet the humorist literally plays with Polonius. The old man indeed is tempting game; an easy prey, but so repaying that it may well appeal to a fastidious palate. Their natures are parted by a gulf. Whatever can be seen on the surface of things with clear-sighted, one might say with shrewd, eyes Polonius sees, and nothing else. Whatever human eyes can perceive beyond the surface Hamlet perceives; and his sight takes in the surface as well, but chooses not to dwell upon it; he registers it as a matter of course, and from it he derives only the pretexts of his humor, its starting-points, one of the planes upon which it plays. Polonius thinks very highly of himself: is he not an experienced counselor of state, cautious and wise in the estimation of the world? His is a normal, average, tame wisdom, correct enough within its narrow limits, but shut in all round by invisible barriers, unable even to suspect, much less to cope with, the secret dramas of life and the unfathomable problems with which we are all beset. He is sententious and would be Machiavellian; but he is only naïve; in his inferences he regards himself as secure, whilst he is a prey to the passive working of a judgment which has lost all elasticity. A humorous flavor, since there is implicit comedy, dwells for us in that character of a worthy man whom dotage threatens on every side and who insists upon laying very obvious snares to catch his betters. Of course he will claim to be fully aware of the risks of error—what should experience be good for else?—and triumphantly immune from them. The dramatic irony which all along arises from his hidebound cleverness, from his mental associations swayed by merely verbal analogies has already in itself the tang of pungent humor.

But the potential humor springs into actual, abundant life when Hamlet, strained, intense, alive to his finger tips, comes across the respectable counselor, who has taken it upon himself, for the sake of the king, his master, to pluck out the heart of the young man's mystery.

Polonius: How does my good lord Hamlet?
Hamlet: Well, God-a-mercy.
Polonius: Do you know me, my lord?
Hamlet: Excellent well; you are a fishmonger.
Polonius: Not I, my lord.
Hamlet: Then I would you were so honest a man.
Polonius: Honest, my lord!
Hamlet: Ay, sir; to be honest as this world goes, is to be one man picked out of ten thousand.
Polonius: That's very true, my lord.[4]

[4] II, ii, 171-80.

One need not any further quote so familiar a text. Hamlet here, as elsewhere, plays a bewildering game; but in the display of his irresponsibility the shafts of implicit satire take effect more surely. As Polonius puts it, there is method in his madness. Is it not worth our while to note that "madness with a method" would be an acceptable, although an outside and wide definition of humor? And when Polonius goes on to remark that Hamlet's answers are "pregnant,"[5] does he not show himself alive to that suggestive power, which is the characteristic of humorous presentment?

Indeed the virtuality, the expansive force of Hamlet's words, in his most casual retorts, are exceptional even with Shakespeare. The play as a whole is the drama of reflection. Let us instance that short passage of words between the prince, Rosencrantz, and Guildenstern, which begins:

Hamlet: What news?
Rosencrantz: None, my lord, but that the world's grown honest.
Hamlet: Then is Doomsday near, but your news is not true. . . ."[6]

To the repressed power of resilient thought in compressed expression there is joined the constant sense of a relativity in all things; and what should be born from the union but the very soul of humor? "There's nothing either good or bad," Hamlet says, "but thinking makes it so."[7] Those words are an illuminating flash of light upon the play; they sum up the essential experience of a soul that ceaselessly broods over the universal illusion of life. That essence is bitter; it is flavored with skepticism, with pessimism. Let it impregnate, indeed prompt, the sly exercise of reticence, the understatements of irony, and it will find its natural outlet in the covert significance of humor. Since everything is relative, why should there not be a dissociation, in language, between thought and words? Why should not a serious meaning, the vital discovery of illusion, clothe itself with apparent lightheartedness, and the smile of the philosopher lurk behind the naïve gravity of the clown?

A converse proof of the importance, the quasi-permanence, that the inverted method of presentment assumes in the play is

[5] II, ii, 207-8 and 212.
[6] II, ii, 240-44.
[7] II, ii, 256-57.

that on the few occasions when the repression relaxes—for example when Hamlet is speaking to himself, with nothing indirect about his manner—a sense of flatness will creep upon the reader. The monologues of the play are not its most interesting moments: Shakespeare's art there is plain, honest, still vigorous, but distinctly on a lower level. The writer's intuition would not fail to teach him, of course, that some sort of alleviation to constant pressure was indispensable. But even the famous soliloquy of Act III ("To be or not to be")[8] owes its fascination to the direct simplicity with which the most poignant theme in man's individual experience is handled. This transcends art, this is genius. Still, to the reader spoilt by the prodigious wealth of virtual significance which the ironical scenes lavishly offer, there is almost an anticlimax in the transition from humor to genius.

One may interpret Hamlet's attitude and words in the first interview with the players[9] as showing an undercurrent of irony. Other constructions, of course, have been put upon the passage; but in view of Hamlet's usual manner a fair case, at least, can be made out for the impression that he must have his tongue more or less in his cheek when he finds in an obviously ranting piece the virtue of "modesty" and praises it for "an honest method, as wholesome as sweet." One alternative is to launch upon the dangerous waters of textual conjecture and to hint that un-Shakespearean elements can be detected in the play. That, one may probably say with a measure of safety; but the giants of criticism are still at odds about the how much and the where.

When Hamlet meets the players again, the advice he gives them is certainly straightforward; and what does it amount to? That actors are to preserve the values of discretion, and not to "overstep the modesty of nature"; they must leave the audience the pleasure of meeting them halfway. The clowns, in particular, must not overdo their effects; they arc to speak no more than is set down for them, nor must they lose caste in the manner of those "that will themselves laugh, to set on

[8] III, i, 56-88.
[9] II, ii, 465-66.

some quantity of barren spectators to laugh too."[10] The stress is laid here indubitably upon the reticence, the reserve of genuine art and, by the same token, of humor, since there is no humor without some restraint. The rule that the comic characters are not themselves to laugh does hit unerringly the central trick in the strategy of humorists. Taken in connection with Falstaff's remarkable phrase: "A jest with a sad brow,"[11] this passage throws full light on the very clear realization which Shakespeare had worked out, before any other English writer, of the characteristic manner of humor.

The further progress of that scene,[12] with the "play within the play," shows us Hamlet, once more, in company with his mother and the king; and his few answers to them, brief and steely, are loaded with a dreadful intensity of implicit meaning, with a threatening, murderous irony, probably the extreme form of what humor can be when divested of the gentleness with which it is most often humanized.

Is Hamlet always master of himself? Not by any means. His fierce exulting triumph, when the king can bear the strain of remorse no longer and hastily walks away, breaks through his guard; as does indignation in his scathing words to his mother.[13] This, again, is true to nature: not only must the mask of indirectness be at times laid down—for instance, in the relaxed moments of communion with one's self, in the monologues—unrestrained feeling. Irony here gives place to bitterness. It might be tempting to explain in a similar fashion Hamlet's extraordinary outbursts of brutal, insulting grossness to Ophelia.[14] But the more probable interpretation is that while the degree of his rudeness may be miscalculated under the stress of his bitter passion, still his behavior is largely a matter of desperate policy; he wants to kill his affection and hits upon the savage plan of desecrating it in his own eyes. What concerns us is that on all those occasions as the indirect method of expression is dropped there is a perceptible falling

[10] III, ii, 21-22 and 43-45.
[11] *2 Henry IV*, V, i, 92; see above chap. v, sect. v.
[12] III, ii.
[13] III, iv, 40-101.
[14] III, i.

off in the character from its usual pitch of concentration and self-command.

More than ever filled with a grim humor of ominous, threatening significance are Hamlet's answers to Rosencrantz, Guildenstern, and the king himself, at the beginning of Act IV.[15] He now is no longer in doubt; and the edge of his scorn is sharpened by his certainty. No wider background of implications can be conveyed by words on the stage; and the minds of the spectators must be singularly quick if in the rapid succession of those flashes the mental fields illuminated are to be caught up and explored. It is impossible not to remember, when reading the play at leisure, that its length much exceeds the average duration of an Elizabethan performance and that Shakespeare, here at least, must have written whole speeches with the assurance that he was writing for himself—or possibly for the library—not for the stage.

The end of Act III and part of Act IV are inferior in concentration and power of phrasing. It seems plain that the poet is working upon the pattern of a previous play, however free his recasting may be; and that he is raising an ordinary "revenge tragedy" to heights which it had not been planned to reach. At all such moments, again, the quality of the art is perceptibly lowered; facts, naked explicit facts that must be shown or told, are breaking the spell of a purely implicit play, which tends to be enacted only in our imaginations.

Lastly, the fifth act and the scene in the churchyard offer us the quintessential spirit of the play—a tragic, philosophical soul of humor. Supremely rich, supremely moving suggestions reverberate through our minds in silent echoes from the theme, the situation, the spoken words. In that wealth of implicit significance the properly comic element is very small, and such as there is appears only at intervals. Humor here lives exclusively in intellectual emotions; its quality is almost entirely serious.

The poignant episode of the churchyard is of an extraordinary simplicity in its boldness.[16] Never before had a writer

[15] IV, ii, and iii.
[16] V, i.

dared to put upon the stage the attendant images of physical death with that unflinching directness. The whole thing is obvious, elementary—and bears the stamp of genius. The tone is more than ever that of Swiftian irony. Puns, verbal quibblings enter into the atmosphere of sinister suggestion. Their very presence points to an irresponsibility of the mind, which we interpret instinctively as a sign of an inner strain, so violent that it must find relief at any cost.

One of the points where the strong undercurrent of grim humor most plainly breaks out, and where the groundlings are distinctly appealed to, is the jocular passage of words about England: in that country Hamlet's madness must have passed quite unnoticed, since everybody is more or less mad there.[17]

The moment when Yorick's skull is dug out with its empty sockets and gaping mouth is loaded, of course, with symbolic meaning.[18] An association is thus created between two sets of images: a tragic, a funereal background suddenly appears behind the very type of human pleasantry, in its most specialized and professional form: the jester. Yorick's skull laughs now with a different grin; and death himself stares through the vacant sockets of the silenced fool. It is no wonder that Sterne, the most complete humorist of the eighteenth century, should have selected for his literary personality the name of Yorick and thus have linked up his finished, absolute humor, with that symbol of the grim contrast which the thought of destruction forces upon the mirth of man.

After that we still have Hamlet's humor at a relaxed pitch, almost lively enough to make us laugh in the scene with Osric,[19] where he plays in masterly fashion with that servile courtier's meanness. He mocks Osric's farfetched, artificial manner and caps his conceits with a more dazzling display. Shakespeare's object is plain: he wishes to satirize, once more, such cheap tricks of verbal jugglery, the besetting sin of the time; and whilst proving himself second to none in the art, he shows up the sheer vanity of it.

[17] V, i, 162-70.
[18] *Ibid.*, 189-221.
[19] V, ii, 81-190.

But the shadow which approaching events cast before is drawing near, and every one of the spectators shares in Hamlet's awareness of it. He meets his fate with open eyes. When he falls, after finding strength in a quick, desperate rush to fulfil the duty of justice that had wrought so strangely upon his life, his last words call up again that sense of the unexpressed, if not the inexpressible, which is the center of his personality, as it is that of humor: a significance is finally liberated that will grow and expand forever; and how could any comment be of further purpose, when this has been uttered: "The rest is silence"?[20]

Since in the most thoughtful, and one of the most tragic, of Shakespeare's dramas—in the tragedy of reflection—humor of a kind can be found, entering so intimately into the very texture of the principal character and through that character, of the play, shall we not be justified in saying that humor is, to a greater degree perhaps than has been generally conceded, essential to, and co-extensive with, Shakespeare's mind? Its presence and diffuseness in *Hamlet* should no longer remain a paradox, as soon as we take stock of the fact that the tragic mood, tempered and modified by searching thought, provides just the duality and the contrast which are the main constituents of humor. The comedy here is so entirely a matter of reflection that the resulting humor hardly ever materializes into a smile-provoking energy; it hovers, like a refined and a sardonic essence, over the drama as a whole; the tragic Muse, watching it, will show on her lip just the slightest twitch of irony within the quieter curves of pity and sadness. But that spiritual portrait of the greatest dramatic genius, which each of us does create and call up from the fascination of the play, from the experience of a moved, a wondering, and an enslaved spirit, will not fail to wear, in the wistful contemplation that transcends laughter and tears, the gleam of a pensive amusement that sublimates and includes them both.

III. The Bitter Comedies

Troilus and Cressida

There is a good deal of humor in this play, and it is all of the dry, ironical kind. The subject and the treatment would

[20] V, ii, 369.

hardly allow of anything else. Not only is romantic love flouted and a satirical image drawn, with subtlety and vigor, of the fickleness of woman; but the grand setting of the *Iliad* is here bathed in an atmosphere of familiar realism that often creates a sense of parody. The modern mind, inevitably sophisticated, can hardly emulate the genuine simplicity of Homer; and even the straightforward directness of Elizabethan England here fails in the attempt. The glamor of legend, story, and poem, the associations of ages are too strong and appeal too much to the imagination; we feel, rightly or wrongly, that the writer's purpose is at bottom disrespectful, as soon as the heroes are placed in the light of common day. Whether or not he was aware of the consequences, Shakespeare made his Greeks and Trojans lose caste, even if he endowed them with the wonderful vitality of his own genius. In spite of the very different inspiration, we are reminded at times of the artificial epics of the classical age, when poets, while bowing to the prestige of ancient themes, would subconsciously liberate their repressed boredom by throwing in a spice of burlesque.

The burlesque here is laid on with no sparing hand. Homer suggested Thersites, and Shakespeare was not slow in improving the opportunity. His deeper mood seems to have been one of anger against hollow values, sentimental fictions and the naïve idealisms of the heart. He injected into the railings of Thersites the animus of a mind still rankling from unforgettable experiences. There is little in the scurrilous stream that is properly humorous; the satire and the insults are mostly coarse and open. But at the back of it all, a sense of the glaring contrast between the dignity of the epic world and the vulgarity through which it is being dragged keeps alive in us; that impression remains implicit and gives the farcical comedy an aftertaste of humor. Thersites moreover grows beyond the part of the cur, barking at the heels of warriors and princes; he rises to the stature of a cynic philosopher or some foresketch of Goethe's Mephistopheles; he is an impersonation of critical, ironical intelligence. In his careless audacity he shows something of Falstaff's freedom. It is even possible at times to hear in his words the poet's undisguised censure of lawless love and sensuality.

Pandarus, by his side, looks singularly tame; an easygoing fellow, lax in his principles no doubt, but almost a good soul. He errs rather on the naïve than on the shrewd side, and in his low, shallow cynicism lays himself open, again and again, to our ironical amusement. To the name of humorist he has himself very little claim, except that his moral insensibility has now and then a queer look of being at least half-aware; and it is difficult to say whether his leering eye does not occasionally wink at us.

The humorist in the play, if we leave out Ulysses's sly sententiousness, would be no other than Cressida. That the jilt is witty goes without saying; but her personality is varied and subtly shaded; she has charm and brilliance, as well as a ready tongue; her fencing and parrying with Pandarus[21] implies a sharp penetration of character, intellectual independence, a hard knowledge or divination of life, and a power of condensed, indirect expression.

All told, the notable humor of the play is a diffused essence, soaking through most of the unequal and at times frankly dull five acts. That the spiritless hand of a collaborator was at work in those intervals is more than likely; and a name even forces itself upon the reader. Where the lift and the lilt of Shakespeare's manner are unmistakable, that flavor of disillusioned, mocking irony can be breathed almost uninterruptedly. Titillation of a kind for our sense of the ridiculous, the grotesque, or the absurd, is to be found there, but very little refreshing laughter. One might discover a premonition, or a hint, in those words of Troilus at the beginning:

> Lest Hector or my father should perceive me,
> I have (as when the sun doth light a storm)
> Buried this sigh in wrinkle of a smile:
> But sorrow that is couch'd in seeming gladness
> Is like that mirth fate turns to sudden sadness.[22]

[21] I, ii.
[22] I, i, 36-40.

All's Well That Ends Well

All's Well is an even more unequal play, with a corrupt text, inferior parts, few passages of the first order, a good many, however, which are unmistakably Shakespeare's. The subject is not pleasant, and the reader's finer susceptibilities are more than once shocked. It seems altogether a kind of adumbration of the bolder and more vigorous *Measure for Measure.* Humor is not lacking, without being abundant, or very good. What there is should be distinctly labeled bitter or pessimistic.

Two characters are mainly responsible for it: Parolles and the Clown, Lavache. The former, like Thersites, but in a more marked way, derives from the Falstaffian type; he emulates the fat knight in his cowardice, his lechery, the zest of his unblushing lies; he is found out and shamed, as happens to Falstaff in *The Merry Wives;* but he keeps on a sadly lower level of wit and humor. Still, he rises once or twice to a height of invention and impudence that makes him not altogether unworthy of the comparison.[23] Again, his equivocating and quibbling, at the end, is more than clever; it is spiced with a cynicism which we may not relish, but which, under the circumstances, becomes almost philosophical.[24]

The Clown is an egregious failure most of the time, with that something strangely forced and creaking, in thought and language, which causes the reader to wonder whether Shakespeare could really write in such a key. But he has much better moments, as for instance IV, v; his bandying of repartee with Lafeu, in that scene, shows at least readiness of tongue and a gift of phrasing. His significance goes further; he stands as the very symbol of a play which is, like himself, "unhappy."[25] It is no romantic flight of conjecture to trace this epithet to the author's awareness that his fool, the professional mouthpiece of mirth and incentive to laughter, was at bottom moved, like himself, by a reflective and saturnine disposition; a mood in which earnest thoughts of conduct and visions of the beyond interweave with a realistic and satirical view of life. Although the Puritans come in for their usual share of damag-

[23] IV, iii, for instance.
[24] V, iii, 236-73.
[25] Lafeu's description of him, IV, v, 67.

ing hints, who can read any other than a religious, and indeed a puritanic meaning in the allusion to the devil, who "sure, is the prince of the world"; and in the allegory that sounds so unexpectedly like John Bunyan: "I am for the house with the narrow gate, which I take to be too little for pomp to enter: some that humble themselves may; but the many will be too chill and tender, and they'll be for the flowery way, that leads to the broad gate and the great fire"?[26] Here as in *Twelfth Night* the fool is after all a man, and that man a sad one. Part of the humor resides in the surprise thus sprung upon us; and the effect is piquant; but it is not exactly amusing.

Measure for Measure

Humor, in this admirable but uneven play, is charged with significance. The plot revolves round the opposition of reality to appearances, with a special thrust at the hollowness of a moral austerity that will rot within. The cheat of Puritan pretense is associated with the flaw in human justice, as soon as the written law is not tempered by equity. Angelo's hypocrisy and his cruelty are bound up together; "measure for measure," or an eye for an eye, far from being the conclusion of the drama, is transcended by the spirit of wise mercy. The sticklers for rules are given the lie by events, or by their own impulses. Isabel, whose chastity is not free from a self-righteous hardness, reveals an inner core of puritanic materialism and preaches the gospel of the substance of guilt being in the act:

> Thoughts are no subjects,
> Intents but merely thoughts.[27]

In her heart she does not actually forgive her brother, and pleads but coldly for his life. So she has to take in the lesson of experience, which ripens her fine but somewhat narrow character. There is a laxer fiber but more tenderness in Mariana, who loves Angelo with all his crimes and finds such moving words to save him in the hour of his crushing downfall. The Duke, a shrewd inquirer into social health, an anxious searcher

[26] IV, v, 54-59.
[27] *Measure for Measure*, V, i, 458-59.

of consciences, presides over everything under a disguise, as providential as Prospero in his island; he represents man's straining after a higher spirit against the letter that kills; still observing, still learning, and no less aware of his own faults than of others' sins. Thus based on a desperate reaching out for finer issues, the tragic comedy is subtly attuned to the intellectual sense of illusions dispelled, which is at the core of humor; and as the disillusion here is but partly softened by the lucky presence of an all-seeing Duke, so that the play, in spite of its happy ending, leaves us wiser and sadder, the humor is steeped in a pervasive flavor of pungent pessimism.

Such is its deeper and truer aspect. Most of it is reducible to dramatic irony, an irony that lingers in our remembrance and is more than usually pregnant. But there are as well properly humorous personages, scenes, and episodes. The best vein is once more that of a popular realism, in which the vigor of Shakespeare's invention is felt at once, and which, whenever questions of authorship arise, creates for us the safest token of the master's actual presence.

It may be a humbling thought that Pompey, the bawd, is the most genuine humorist in the play. Of course he is not refined; but he has verve, readiness, and that fund of first-hand observation without which mere would-be wits are thin and inefficient. At his better moments—as in IV, ii—he is not unworthy of standing for the poetry of absurdity, with a something that leaves a sting behind and reveals a hidden reason in the absurd. Abhorson the hangman has his feet likewise on the solid ground of his occupation and its "mystery"; his jokes smack of a professional originality. By the side of those two, Elbow the constable is only a farcical character, a puny brother to Dogberry, with some of the latter's genius for fussy silliness; and Lucio, the irrepressible "fantastic," as the playbill calls him, proves a wag who can be funny, by repeating Falstaff's trick of irresponsibility and cheek; but he overdoes it signally, and will be impudent at the wrong time to the wrong person, so that the laugh is finally turned full against him. Laugh we must, however, and it is Lucio who preserves a comic atmosphere during the tense last act; indeed, through his persistent efforts he adds a good deal to the amusing ingredients in a rather grim irony.

In spite of all, grimness remains the characteristic note of the play; the idea or the image of death lurks everywhere and constantly faces us. The prison scene with Claudio condemned to die, and Barnardine who first does not care to live, then unaccountably will not hear of laying his head on the block, has much of the somber power of the churchyard episode in *Hamlet;* Pompey, a much less dignified person, answering to the gravedigger. Words pass that flash across the humor of every day, reaching the ultimate contrasts of man's fate, known or surmised.

Timon of Athens

This is the acme of sardonic humor. So fierce is the bitter mood here that the expression often loses even the pretense of humorous indirectness; invective and derision take the place of satire and mockery. Is that mood exactly Shakespeare's? It would be rash to assert it, as the play obviously is the work of more than one hand. Even the persuasive vigor of the passages where the master's personality is clearly stamped upon thought, language, and verse might be, in principle, accounted for through dramatic sympathy. But a careful reader will not resist an impression that, whatever may be the actual history of the present text, it bears mainly the imprint of one powerful mind, who had gathered from experience the counts of a formidable indictment against man. Those grievances were part of his knowledge of life; they were part of himself. Other elements, no less experimental, could at other times check those influences, make themselves equally felt, and diversify the picture; here, for some reason beyond the fortuitous choice of a subject or the rehandling of an older play, a freer course was given to indignation, and a rankling story of accumulated pessimism poured out. The writer who had thus fully expressed emotions normally kept under a curb would feel the healthier for the purgation. *Timon*, like *Lear*—the plot of which offers some general similarities to it—probably belongs to the vicarious confessions through which the unknown Shakespeare worked his way to serenity.[28]

Still, the passion of hatred and scorn does not always run freely; and where moral checks are lacking, artistic restraint will persist. The dramatist's control of his theme reintroduces at times the necessary indirectness. The outcome is a scathing irony, very much in the Swiftian style. This is the outstanding feature of humor in the play.

Before the crisis which is the turning point of the plot, Timon is almost a "humor" in the Jonsonian sense, an unbalanced character, nursing the enthusiastic hobby of a princely, tireless generosity. He fancies that his friends, if the necessity should arise, would rush to his assistance at the first call; and that naïve illusion, while it reveals a noble heart, puts him in a somewhat laughable posture; to that extent he is an occasion for humorous amusement. The subject brings in a series of lively episodes, and the realism of the first scenes has some of the high flavor which we associate for instance with *Volpone*. Dramatic irony next becomes dominant, as the unexpected, which we knew all along to be the inevitable, decidedly happens, and the friends sneak or bully themselves off under a finely graded range of evasions. This is all very fair comedy, implicit enough, and efficient. The crisis then supervenes. Before Timon gives way to the frenzy of his anger, he can still display some self-possession in the "practical humor" of the banquet-scene,[29] where the well-managed stages leading to the climax introduce a sort of rough, grim fun. But the rest is almost all sheer fury, acrid brooding, and rank abuse; with the exception of some few moments when hatred, under the pressure of concentration, turns to a biting savageness, which can only be matched in the work of Swift. The analogy is the more

[28] A. C. Bradley "would place it [*Timon*] between *King Lear* and *Macbeth*, and partly again on metrical grounds" (Edmund Chambers and Charles Williams, *Short Life of Shakespeare*, Oxford, 1933, pp. 120-121). These critics prefer to place *Timon* in 1606-1607, and point out that "mental disturbance may come in waves." This is true; but as the grounds upon which the dating is done are not incontrovertible, we have presumed, as explained above, to study *Timon* along with the bitter comedies, the last of which *(Measure for Measure)* may antedate it by two or three years.

[29] III, vi.

striking, as the two writers seem equally to labor under the obsession of the animality of man, and to ruminate the fascinated disgust of the flesh. One of those triumphs of sarcasm is Timon's pretendedly relenting answer to the Athenian Senators, who humbly beg for his support against Alcibiades:

> I have a tree, which grows here in my close,
> That my own use invites me to cut down,
> And shortly must I fell it: Tell my friends,
> Tell Athens, in the sequence of degree,
> From high to low throughout, that whoso please
> To stop affliction, let him take his haste,
> Come hither, ere my tree hath felt the axe,
> And hang himself. . . .[30]

Meanwhile Apemantus, the "churlish" philosopher, has been railing impartially at the flatterers and the flattered and devastating fictions and lies with his sharp dry chuckle. He now points out that disillusioned Timon, who should laugh at everything, is only rushing from gullibility to senseless frenzy. Apemantus had wielded from the start the weapon of derision, which Timon takes up in despair; and all along he handles it with more deadly effect because he keeps his self-command; he is thus by far the better humorist. The foul-mouthed cynic has indeed the gift of the gab, and when it comes to the bandying of abuse, makes notable hits. His final clash with Timon is a clever device; it finishes off the portrait of the maddened man and throws a suggestive light on the nature of his unreason.

The fool, lastly, must not be passed over. He fools it quite decently in the few words allotted to him, and the implied meaning that gives his quips a lining of interest elicits a compliment from Varro's servant: "Thou are not altogether a fool"; to which the answer comes pat: "Nor thou altogether a wise man: as much foolery as I have, so much wit thou lackest."[31] The painter should not be forgotten either: his speech on promise and performance has point and humor:

> Promising is the very air o' the time;
> It opens the eyes of expectation:
> Performance is ever the duller for his act. . . .[32]

[30] V, ii, 210-17.
[31] II, ii, 122-25.
[32] V, i, 25-27.

Timon's end is strangely steeped in an orgy of pessimism and of self-pity that is supremely romantic. One catches there premonitions of Byron and Chateaubriand; the former writer looms forth in these words that read like a quotation from *Manfred:*

> my long sickness
> Of health and living now begins to mend,
> And nothing brings me all things. . . .[33]

The latter's bitter aloofness is prefigured in Timon's choice for his grave of a site daily washed by the salt tides.[34]

There is no spirit more alien to humor than that of romanticism.

IV. The Dark Tragedies

Othello

The quickly tightening plot and the shadow of the catastrophe steadily drawing near leave little room for humor. However, the interest is sufficiently varied, and the need for relief is hardly felt. The clown discharges the tension through jokes of the traditional kind, on the two short occasions when he appears.[35] Of professed comedy there is hardly any more.

But all through the play, diffused in the heart-gripping "pity of it,"[36] one breathes a tragic irony of a bitter kind. This is pessimistic and rather implies the triumph of evil. Noble-minded Othello only provokes it unawares; in it Iago lives and has his being. He it is who gives *Othello* its peculiar atmosphere in relation to humor.

Here again the author seems to have meaningfully stressed the theme of contrasted masks and faces. The recurrent phrase: "honest Iago" is an epitome of the false valuations upon which social life can be founded. The grotesquely unfit epithet strikes us with a sense of derision; while the whole character, one of the most finished in Shakespeare, radiates out something self-possessed, hard, and ironic. Iago is an "immoralist" of the Machiavellian type. His constant, though often veiled, denial of a moral order based on what he regards as mere illu-

[33] V, ii, 191-93
[34] V, ii, 219-24.
[35] III, i and iv.
[36] IV, i, 206-7.

sion gives his thought and speech the aggressive liveliness of a cynical interpretation of the world. Reducing life to the gross cruelty of his own instincts, he can draw with zest an image of it that looks unconventional and fresh. Those personal views he knows how to repress, as soon as prudence forbids that he should reveal himself; dissimulation is one of his major habits. But whenever he stands to lose nothing, or even expects to gain, by the contrary course, out he comes with innuendoes, more or less plain, as the occasion permits. The tenets implied are best conveyed, he feels, through a method of suggestion; they would hardly bear formulating in direct terms; they are mainly destructive; they tend to replace a solid nucleus of belief by an ill-defined doubt, a sinister suspicion, or a hostile scorn.

The hints Iago thus throws out make up in fact a doctrine of nihilism and desecration, aimed mostly at ethical values. Cool and rational as he is, secure in the absolute command of all his impulses, he can play freely with the weapon of his sharp mind, pitilessly clear-sighted, although blind to not a few intangible realities. He has thought out his attitude to life, and once states to Roderigo the grounds of what one may call a utilitarian system—coarse, blunt, and supremely matter-of-fact: "Put money in thy purse. . . ."[37] In a general way his tactics coincide, at least externally, with those of the humorist, who thinks on two different planes—one of which necessarily is, or tries to be, that of objective reality, implying a measure of disillusionment. Again, Iago's manner has the indirectness of expression which is common to irony and humor. One may characterize his part as that of a harsh and foul-minded critic of life, who prefers, for personal reasons, to insinuate his criticism; not very different from a humorist of the saturnine and sarcastic variety; a Swiftian figure, like Timon, in his preoccupation with the animal side of man; but more especially a prey to the obsession of physical love; thus marked out by fate to inoculate, foster and goad to fury Othello's passion of sensuous jealousy.

[37] I, iii, 344-69.

His attitude, like that of the humorist, implies a high degree of self-consciousness. "I am nothing, if not critical,"[38] he justly says of himself; and indeed his monologues are pieces of deliberate analysis and explanation which, contrary to Shakespeare's normal practice, border close on the classical French type of explicit psychology.[39] Lastly, he has wit—how ready, biting, and clever, we can judge from the naughty couplets he improvises when Desdemona, in a light irresponsible mood, wants to dispel her vague premonition of sadness.[40] Invention, in words as in everything, never fails him; and the instinctive skill with which he manages to sow the seed of madness in Othello's mind, as well as his responses to all the sudden demands of the dangerous game he is playing, are worthy of a profound student of the human heart. Iago almost realizes Oscar Wilde's admiring and fascinated notion of the entirely unmoral artist.

That irony keeps unabated to the end, and although Iago is to face torture and death, his punishment hardly clears the air. He will die sullen and impenitent; to him, as to Hamlet, the rest is silence.[41] The only approach to the geniality which English readers are wont to expect from humor, would be found in the lively bustle and familiarity of the first scene, where Brabantio is awakened by a noisy clamor to the painful, humiliating fact of his daughter's elopement. Again, the tragedy is relieved with a touch of genuine philosophical humor, in the almost comic contrast between Emilia's very earthly prattle and Desdemona's unblemished poetry of feeling, just before and after the "willow" song.[42]

King Lear

In this darkest tragedy, where fate is persistently unkind, and our one major feeling remains the unutterable wretchedness of the human lot, genuine humor is of course very scarce.

[38] II, i, 120.
[39] See for instance II, i, 295-321.
[40] II, i, 125-65.
[41] V, ii, 303-4.
[42] IV, iii, 34-86.

There is, once more, a great deal of "dramatic irony";[43] and from the crushing misery of events there arises so to say a contagion of madness—lunacy, real or feigned, being the only possible answer to the obstinate unreason and cruelty of things. In that distracted revolt there does live the principle of a spiritual anarchy, very much like some kinds of philosophical humor, that enters into the more profound spirit of the play.

The fool is the chief mouthpiece of the irony, but not the main example of the madness; he is past the stage of mental disorder which Lear for instance reaches through his sufferings; he has learnt acceptance, humility, the moderation of desire. In the wisdom which he conveys, not always indirectly, a bitter flavor is none the less infused. At an interval of a few years the difference here from the fools of the great comedies is striking. The quick penetration, the flashing originality are gone; there remain the common sense, now a little hard, the jests, now a little forced, and the old method of fanciful absurdity. Lear's fool is something of a moralist; he coins saws and proverbs, often in doggerel verse; he voices the realistic lore of experience, against the illusions born of pride. These he derides sarcastically, with a measure of verve and wit, and some rather cheap fun. But he has his share of the hold upon us, which the play owes to the thrilling intensity of its story. During the scenes on the heath[44] we forget the indifferent quality of his jokes; he is raised, like his diversely demented companions, to a poetical height, as an emblem of the havoc which fierce evil will work with the concord of man's faculties. In fact, Edgar, who only shams mad, outshines the fool in invention, readiness, and quaintness of fancy. That third act brings to a climax a tragedy of conflict, in which the elements join the raging passions of man; and humor here is less in the

[43] By this phrase, here as elsewhere, we mean the irony that implicitly results from the contrast between what characters do, think, or feel mistakenly, and what the spectator knows to be the truth or the actual fact, with the more or less inevitable consequences, the laws of life being what they are. That sense, the first precise example of which in England is hardly more than a century old (Thelwall, 1833, according to *N.E.D.*), answers of course to a fundamental idea of Greek tragedy, and is now a common notion in English criticism. What we are anxious to point out is that the wider and different meaning of "irony" as a category of aesthetics, in its relation to "humor," remains unimpaired.

[44] III, i, ii, and iv.

words than in the situations; a humor mostly of episodes and inarticulate feeling, the despairing confusion of a reckless topsy-turvy world.

We need not dwell on the comic relief of brief moments. But a whole scene, that on or near "Shakespeare's cliff,"[45] mingles efficiently the pathetic and the humorous. The incident of Gloucester's fall, as he believes, from the dizzy top, is saved from grotesqueness by its intense realism; and the vein of irony that lurks in it all links up with a latent spirit of relativity, the gist of humor. The second part of the scene, with Lear, is pitched in the same key. The king's words are especially pregnant with the half-conscious wisdom of the mad, and their bearing on things and people endows them with overtones of implicit, ironical satire. The trend of the whole is an attack on the orthodox fabric of society, and the suggestion of a more humane order based on love. That there should be, as Edgar remarks, such "reason in madness,"[46] is of course a convention of humorous significance. Still, the predominant strain all through is that of dramatic irony—the contrast between speeches and acts, appearance and reality—forcibly stressed from the beginning; the powerless sense of all that is done amiss, of all the folly and crime that will have to be paid for; a sense in which there is no amusement and certainly no lightheartedness; the philosophy of a grim play, powerful, uneven, often superbly Shakespearean, strangely unlike Shakespeare at other times, with a sort of dull subservience, on the latter occasions, to a prescribed scheme, and with a curiously stiff or archaic language in some prosy parts.

Macbeth

In *Macbeth* we have a play of a denser, more solid texture than *Lear*, though not quite free from dubious elements, and with a persistently tragic atmosphere; humor in it gathers round only a few episodes or themes.

Of the latter, the most obvious is that of the witches. Like all powers of evil, they revel in a general upsetting of values.

[45] IV, vi.
[46] IV, vi, 179.

"Fair is foul, and foul is fair."[47] As a result, there is nothing fixed, and all is relative—a mental uncertainty eminently favorable to humor, and one which humorists are usually led to postulate. So the mere inversion creates an affinity to comedy; and in fact the weird sisters, grim as they are, chuckle over their doings with a kind of sinister amusement. The feats they call up remind one of some painting by Breughel or Bosch. The humor of their tricks is not only in the mischievousness, but in a sort of intellectual irony; their victims are deluded, mystified, as much as they are tormented; they believe, for instance, they act freely, while they obey the promptings of malevolent beings. This vein of practical joking, in fairies and wizards, is a well-known trait of the popular imagination; its origins are deep in the past, and Shakespeare's witches, though different from Middleton's[48] in being more fearful, thus link up with his Puck and his Ariel;[49] one might even discern a trace of the same tendency in some of his ghosts.[50]

Another aspect of the game played by supernatural agents is to show mortals glimpses of their fate, which they fail to interpret properly, out of naïveté or blindness. The images presented to Macbeth are a veiled intimation of his future, so combined as to hide, as much as to reveal, what is to be; and the assurances which he is given against fatal possibilities are managed in such a way as to bear a double meaning—a classical feature of ancient oracles. Out of the contrast between the outer and the inner sense of the forecast there arises an ironical lesson which is one of the major motives of Greek drama. Like the morbid dreams of his own perverted conscience, the predictions of the witches to Macbeth are thus invested, in our sight, with an irony which clings to the sisters themselves, and is, so to say, the philosophy of their whole part. The inversion and the perversion of values, in which they delight, are symbolized as well, on another plane, by the uncouth

[47] I, i, 11.

[48] *The Witch*, 1613?.

[49] See above, chap. x, sect. iv; and below, sect. vi.

[50] We can put up with Charles Lamb's assertion that "The weird sisters are serious things. Their presence cannot coexist with mirth" *(Specimens of English Dramatic Poets)*. But an atmosphere of grim humor is quite different from mirth.

ingredients of their hell-broth: around the infernal mixture there develops a peculiar kind of humor—that which arises from the odd, the queer, and the grotesque, especially when seen through an atmosphere of seriousness.

The porter's scene[51] is assuredly rich in humor. To begin with, the situation, the fellow's behavior, his unwillingness to bestir himself, his satirical or Rabelaisian talk contain in themselves many and various elements of comedy, some of them rather low. But the contrast between farce and tragedy, between the vulgar familiarity of the scene and the bloody event that has just taken place, with its tragic consequences now let loose, is of a higher order in the scale of the comic; it belongs to the field of the humorous because it remains implicit and evolves entirely in our consciousness. The humorous here, as is so often the case, while it includes a laughable element, far transcends it: that contrast is charged with dramatic significance; in one way it is a relief after the horror of the previous scene, and quickens us for new emotions; in another it prolongs the moral and philosophical echo of the episode: daily life, with its round of duties, is stepping back upon the stage, prosaic, innocuous, safe, setting off the violent disruption which crime inflicts upon normality. Lastly, our modern imagination actualizes a symbolical meaning which may have been latent in the deeper layers of the playwright's mind, and which adds a poetical grandeur to the realistic episode: it is Fate, Macbeth's doom, that is knocking at the gate. That symbol itself is in a contrast with the farcical elements of the scene, and this fact, while it would tend to blunt the edge of the pure comedy, still enriches the humor.[52]

[51] II, iii.

[52] See the discussions of the episode by Coleridge (*Notes on Shakespeare*, pp. 368 and 377), and De Quincey (*Collected Works*, XIII, "On the Knocking at the Gate in Macbeth," pp. 192-198). Coleridge's view, that the Porter's scene is "disgusting," probably "an interpolation of the actors," or was "written for the mob by some other hand, perhaps with Shakespeare's consent"; as well as his further opinion, that "there is an entire absence of comedy, nay, even of irony and philosophic contemplation, in *Macbeth*—the play being wholly and purely tragic" —shows little of his usual acumen. De Quincey's interpretation is much nearer what we should regard as the truth. He acknowledges the profound impression left by the scene, and explains it through what is really, in our view, one of its major causes: the sudden reassertion of the normal world after the momentary triumph

A few more touches may be worth mentioning. In the banquet scene the sudden appearance of Banquo's ghost, while it shakes Macbeth with a thrill of horror, awakes in him a grimly humorous perception of the unexpectedness, and almost the unfairness, of the surprise visit: what is the good of getting your enemies murdered if they will next come and take your own seat at your own table?

> The times have been,
> That, when the brains were out, the man would die,
> And there an end; but now, they rise again,
> With twenty mortal murders on their crowns,
> And push us from our stools. . . .[53]

In the scene between Lady Macduff and her son,[54] the boy's prattle has not only the piquant charm of amusing cleverness, precocious and witty; it shares in the privilege of the irresponsible, of those who, like the fools, seem to be ever adventuring beyond their depth, blurting out the heretical truth that no one is willing to see. There is a graceful play of ironical fancy in that lively passage, more vivid for the sinister setting where it takes place, and for the shadow which the coming murder is casting before.

V. The Dawning Light

Antony and Cleopatra

Whatever the cause, and whether or not the change may be traced to the writer's inner mind, it is a fact that the temper of this tragedy and of the next *(Coriolanus)* shows a marked

of a "fiendish" one: "the pulses of life are beginning to beat again; and the re-establishment of the goings-on of the world in which we live, first makes us profoundly sensible of the awful parenthesis that had suspended them." The point is shrewdly made, but with an exaggerated insistence on the ethical aspect of our impression. The horror of the murder as a deed has been absorbed and digested before the Porter's scene. What strikes us most in that episode itself is the violent, physically ominous announcement of a Power that had been forgotten, left out, that now comes back, stern, persistent, irresistible: the law of retribution, a doom heard in the symbolical knocking of a vaguely personified Fate, which is no other than that of Greek tragedy.

[53] III, iv, 78-82.

[54] IV, ii.

difference from that of the bitter dramas.[55] There is now more light, more resilience, a kind of springy youthfulness, apparent even in the lilt of the magnificent verse; and the humor is not only more abundant, but more genuine.

It is here, so to say, ingrained in the very stuff of the play. The moving tale of infatuation, love, and death winds itself out along the lines laid down by Plutarch's *Life of Antony* with its highly imaginative setting; it awakes in its actors as it proceeds rich echoes of sympathy, spite, devotion, courage, treachery, despair; and among those accompanying notes, that of humor, almost ever audible, at times dominant, gives the heroic theme the natural relief of contrast.

That note can be heard from the opening. Before and after the enamored couple have appeared on the stage, we listen to the detached, critical comments of the two observers, Demetrius and Philo; we have thus at once the duality of planes, the two points of view, and the consequent relativity upon which humor thrives. In the next scene a truly humorous zest seasons the light talk and the banter of Iras and Charmian. The genius of humor, along with that of drama, hovers over the great scene between the two lovers in the first act;[56] if anything, it is comedy, the highest comedy of character; we are busy gathering the hints out of which the obverse side of the romantic situation is to be inferred; we know that Cleopatra plays a self-interested part, and that Antony is driven by an inner fate which only he fails to perceive. An undercurrent of subdued mirth and minute ripples of humor can be felt in Cleo-

[55] It gives one pause to find one's self in disagreement, as to the general mood and temper of these two plays, with such a penetrating critic of Shakespeare as Sir Edmund Chambers (see "Antony and Cleopatra" and "Coriolanus" in *Shakespeare: A Survey*, London, 1925; especially pp. 259-60, where the author's view in this respect is summed up). But we feel it impossible to agree that the two plays, when probed, ring with quite the same bitterness as the darkest tragedies. They may both evince "the same readiness of bitter criticism, the same remorseless analysis, probing and dissecting, as with a cruel scalpel, the intimate weaknesses and basenesses of mankind" (p. 259), and still be instinct with a spirit different from that of *Lear* or *Timon*. The distinguished critic himself finds that the tragic mood in *Antony* is imbued with a "serenity" comparable to that of the *Tempest* (p. 257). This may be one of the occasions when the special test of humor could after all be applied with not entirely negligible results, and yield us a deeper and more intimate clue as to the temper of a play than even its philosophy.

[56] I, iii.

patra's dialogue with Alexas;[57] while in the next scenes with messengers (II, v and III, iii) she is too much in earnest to keep her self-control; and if her temperamental display does raise some humor, it is at her own expense. Her character, indeed, is a lifelike compound of passion, pride, coquetry, cunning, wilfulness, and girlish fun; a superb creation in which Plutarch's outline is admirably developed and improved.

> Give me mine angle—we'll to the river; there,
> My music playing far off, I will betray
> Tawny-finn'd fishes; my bended hook shall pierce
> Their slimy jaws; and, as I draw them up,
> I'll think them every one an Antony.[58]

The contrast thus worked from the first into the deepest structure of the play appears again and again; humor and poetry, for instance, mingle in the charming scene where Cleopatra wants to help Antony to put on his armor;[59] the sense of doom is present there and active, but fancy and gaiety play freely around and enliven it. No more convincing example can be given than IV, xiv, in which before Antony preparing to kill himself, Mardian pours out the lying tale of Cleopatra's supposed suicide, thus tempering genuine pathos with a strain of ironical comedy.

Shakespeare's play is pitched in the key of a mixed, allround humanity. Like Cleopatra, Antony has a sense of humor; his weakened will and sinking heroism have not destroyed the appeal of a generous nature, and his inner decay has ripened the tolerance of a mind now more open to the conflicting claims of reality. But the humorist of the play is Enobarbus. Not one of the leading characters, he keeps very near the central focus. Within talking distances of the masters of the world, he watches them, cool, moralizing, or ironic—a shrewd onlooker, whose commentary upon men and things is consistently clearsighted, with occasional spurts of bland, smooth-faced satire. He it is who all along reads the future most penetratingly. A complex and interesting character, he is marked out for the

[57] I, v.
[58] II, v, 10-15.
[59] IV, iv.

contradictions which the clearest mind will not spare a man, when duty, in the hopeless tangle of events, is chiefly a matter of feeling. Enobarbus the stout soldier, long faithful to Antony through thick and thin, betrays him at the eleventh hour, and dies finally from remorse: a most sentimental end for a humorist;[60] and one that in Shakespeare's view probably testified to Antony's extraordinary hold upon his followers.

The comedy that mixes so well with the world-shaking drama bubbles up at times in scenes and episodes where the mind of the playwright seems given over for a moment to life's little ironies. Such is the very amusing interlude on board Pompey's galley.[61] The demigods fight seasickness with generous potations; they nudge each other and tell good stories, among which Antony's farcical description of the crocodile tops everything; broad fun that, but its flavor is singularly heightened by its contrast with what comes next, Menas's whispered words into Pompey's ear. Finally there is a chorus, a tipsy dance, and the probable addition of a masque; while Octavius Caesar looks on, with his thin-lipped smile. Plutarch offered the hint; improving it, Shakespeare has delayed the action overmuch, some commentators say; but how humorously does the orgy come off! Another striking proof of the dramatist's fondness for the relief which such digressions could afford is the short episode of the peasant bringing to Cleopatra the asp in the figs.[62] The plot is then at its tensest, the climax is come; the fellow's thick-pated gossip with its lifelike raciness, its futility, its naïveté, awakes a thousand humorous echoes; it is worthy of the porter's talk in *Macbeth.* Shakespeare's comic invention never was more fresh and realistic; his intuitive sense of the infinite laughter and tears enclosed in the silent eloquence of humor never more inspired.

Coriolanus

Here again the animated tragedy moves forward at a swift pace, carrying along with it a rich diversity of human elements; and humor, inseparably bound up with realism, is one of the constituents of the broad picture. It is, as in *Antony and Cleo-*

[60] IV, ix.
[61] II, vii.
[62] V, ii.

patra, a component part of the plot, the situations, and the characters.

Dramatic irony is rife in the play. After all his services to his countrymen, Coriolanus receives for his reward the hatred of the fickle multitude. Persistently proud, bitter, inflexible, he yields to the prayers of his mother and settles his doom by the very act that puts his personality on a higher moral plane. He dies by the hands of the former enemies in whom he had found allies against his fatherland. Nations and leaders prove equally blind to fate; just as the tribunes and the citizens are congratulating one another on the happiness they owe to the banishment of Coriolanus, they hear of the imminent peril which it has drawn upon them.[63] The crowd, to the end, keep acting against their own interests, baffling the exertions of their friends, playing into the hands of their foes.

A few beings read the stars more clearly. The wisest of the Romans is Menenius, and his political insight is inseparable from his sense of humor. Both are based on an acute perception of things as they are. The humorist comes out brilliantly in the great opening scene, when he tackles the hot, rash prejudices and passions of men who smart under their wrongs and must find a scapegoat. The famous apologue[64] is an impressive piece of sophistry; it begs the question, implying as it does, between the members of the state, an actual solidarity which is only an ideal, and whose cruel imperfection is the very point at issue; but the whole episode is charged with good, quiet, implicit comedy. Menenius comes off well too in II, i, when he faces the blatant tribunes and gives them a piece of his mind. "I am known to be a humorous patrician," he says, thus using the adjective in the current meaning of odd and impulsive, but with a tinge of the love of quaint fun that was to color the word more and more. As the tribunes charge Marcius with pride and boasting, he forcibly brings the reproach home to them. His manner is frank, with an exasperating suggestion of scornful irony. His game is to pretend that he means just what he says: "What I think I utter, and spend my malice in my breath."[65] His language is picturesque and knows how to be

[63] IV, vi.
[64] I, i, 99-167.
[65] II, i, 51-52 and 58-59.

popular. He is another Enobarbus, with more pronounced features.

His gift is shared by others. Coriolanus is too hot-tempered to be a humorist. But if he lacks the self-control, he has practically all the other qualities that go to the making of the manner. A man of instinct, standing squarely on his legs, and no hero of the philosophical kind, he is a born fighter, seasoned by war, used to coming to grips with realities. Out of the rough contact of men and things, he has stored a fund of concrete experience, the more vivid for the irritability of his skin. Thence his sharp, high-flavored railing. There is originality in that vein of fresh observation, and art of a kind in the relative coolness with which the biting epithets and ironical similes are flung. This is not altogether humor, but approximates to it, as near as a "flyting" of the old school ever did.[66] The women can be quieter, and the common sense of Valeria has a shade of the humorous in its realism;[67] Volumnia baits the tribunes in a manner worthy of her son.[68]

Except the excellent fun of the servants in Aufidius's house,[69] before and after Coriolanus's interview with the Volscian chief—for that fun savors of humor, being handled with such truth and simple discretion—the most genuinely comic episodes are all in the first half of the play, down to III, ii, from which point the demands of tragedy grow almost exclusive. In the series of humorous scenes before that, one stands out and sums up the others: the canvassing in the Forum.[70] This is a rich feast to us, if we relish the latent grotesqueness of an impossibly absurd situation. The humor here is not with Coriolanus; it would rather be against him. His desperate, clumsy efforts to act up to the coaching of Menenius and behave with proper deference to the popular beast; his momentary success, in which the seeds are sown of future disaster, and all that lifelike study in the moods and paradoxes of democracy make up an enjoyable comedy, the more efficient for the unfailing tact that keeps it clear of farce. The three citizens are masterpieces of characterization, variously true to human nature; the

[66] See for instance I, i; I, v; I, ix.

[67] I, iii.

[68] IV, ii.

[69] IV, v.

[70] II, iii.

first a good fellow, the second a sound hater of privilege, the third a humorist—in his own way. Such sayings as: "if we give you anything, we hope to gain by you,"[71] are not mere jokes but flashes of illumination. The homely speech, the rough and ready sense of those men, the likelihood of their feelings throw light on the whole process of imaginative creation in such a passage. As has been often pointed out, Shakespeare sees the Roman people in terms of the London crowd of his time. The atmosphere in which he bathes the whole scene is called up from his personal memory, and the roots of his humor are more plainly than ever in the national soil, the instincts of the people.

VI. Serene Humor

Pericles, Prince of Tyre

It is agreed on all hands that Shakespeare is not responsible for the whole of this play. The first two acts, commonly ascribed to another writer, have hardly any touches of humor, except the talk of the fishermen;[72] and this, while not bad, is just the indifferent thing, done according to recipe. The author seems a moralist who fulfils his obligation to be funny. "How well this honest mirth becomes their labour!"[73] Pericles cries out, having heard the fishermen; and the manner of such praise is fatal to the thing lauded. In the part that is very probably Shakespeare's, the plot, which was not of his making, called for scenes in a brothel; and the comic element of the play must be mainly put there, since the rest was claimed by narrative and sentiment. It is a fact that the playwright did not fight shy of the predicament in which he found himself. The humor of those scenes,[74] although it may offend our delicacy, is genuine, and very good of its kind. The figures of the Bawd, the Pander, and Boult, his servant, are outlined with breadth and vigor; whatever contrast, incongruity, or absurdity might come within the possibilities of the situation and the place—not excluding the chance customers of the trade—in the exceptional circumstances created by the arrival of Marina, is turned to use by a master of comedy, with no timidity, but without any superfluous smut. The method of discretion and reserve which the

[71] II, iii, 77-78.
[72] II, i.
[73] II, i, 102.
[74] III, iii, v, vi.

nature of the subject demanded fits in to good purpose with the exigencies of humorous indirectness. Altogether a study of Shakespeare's humor would be incomplete if justice were not done to those scenes; and it may be added further that without the least pedantry or moralizing the author manages to convey a clear sense of his sincere disgust with that aspect of social evil.

Cymbeline

The eventful plot of *Pericles* is directed to a happy ending by auspicious stars. Tragicomedy, after that successful though patched up experiment, had all the field; and humor obeying the same impulse—whether spontaneous or not—assumed a coloring that was compatible with a general atmosphere of serenity.

It is not plentiful in *Cymbeline*. The unwinding of a tangled and most romantic story leaves little room for the realism of observation. Still, a humorous gleam every now and then lights up a character or an incident; and almost in no case is the tone of the passage sardonic or bitter. Cloten, the oaf, is a snob besides; his stupid vanity and his suit to Imogen, brutally urged, make him odious as well as laughable; he is a standing butt to the court; and in the veiled jokes that are repeatedly cracked about him, his person becomes the center of a kind of satirical humor. But he himself does not prove unworthy of the saving grace: he receives it through his contact with the instincts of his people. Speaking as the mouthpiece of the national British pride against the Romans, he shows sense and that quiet hold upon the funny contrasts of life, the name of which is humor. "Come, there's no more tribute to be paid; our kingdom is stronger than it was at that time; and, as I said, there is no more such Caesars: other of them may have crooked noses; but to owe such straight arms, none." And again: "If Caesar can hide the sun from us with a blanket, or put the moon in his pocket, we will pay him tribute for light; else, sir, no more tribute, pray you now."[75] Here is the butt turned humorist; not quite an unexampled, though a rare oc-

[75] III, i, 34-38 and 43-46.

currence; and he owes it to the fact that standing solidly upon his feet, he feels the inspiration of the land.

Guiderius and Arviragus—especially the former—have the high spirits of healthy youths brought up in the semi-idyllic state of nature which the author is at pains to depict; being British, and disciplined, they indulge their gaiety with that instinctive reserve which Shakespeare already gives as a characteristic feature to his national heroes. Thence the flickering of humorous scorn in Guiderius's words, when confronted by Cloten's ponderous challenge:

Cloten: Know'st me not by my clothes?
Guiderius: No, nor thy tailor, rascal,
Who is thy grandfather: he made those clothes,
Which, as it seems, make thee.[76]

Imogen is not only the living image of tender wifely faith; to her virtue and her charm she adds a gift of sprightliness that makes her a cousin to Portia and Rosalind. Her tongue is quick, and her speech can be piquant:

Hath Britain all the sun that shines? Day, night,
Are they not but in Britain? I' the world's volume
Our Britain seems as of it, but not in it;
In a great pool, a swan's nest; prythee, think
There's livers out of Britain.[77]

The gaoler who brings Posthumus the summons to die is of a waggish disposition; the fun he makes of hanging and the launching of a life into eternity belongs to a tradition largely represented in Shakespeare's work; still, it is above the commonplace, and the humorous changes the fellow rings on the idea of death bear being associated with parallel themes in *Hamlet* and *Measure for Measure.* The original note here is the relative lightness of heart that deprives the episode of all bitter sting; partly because Posthumus is wound up to a pitch of stoicism that welcomes a quick end, but chiefly because the audience expect the inrush of ecstatic happiness in reserve for him, to which all the auguries of the play have been pointing.[78]

[76] IV, ii, 81-82.
[77] II, iv, 139-43.
[78] V, iv, 152-215.

The Winter's Tale

Humor is once more one of the chief constituents of this admirable play. Not a little attention is claimed by the plot, with the surprising turn of events; still, the playwright allows the realistic observation of character and the fun of things their proper place in the picture of life. He lets himself go, in that respect, as he had done years before in the comedies and the histories of the period 1596-1601. A comparison between *The Winter's Tale* and *As You Like It* for instance is of course irrelevant, as the two plays are on quite different planes; the element of tragedy is here in the forefront, although not exclusively emphasized; and the appeal of a romantic story is even more liberally indulged. But comedy is admitted on its own merits almost as freely, and the total impression of the variegated world that remains with us, from the distribution of light and shade, is rather similar.

A happy lightness of heart is the note struck at the beginning; Queen Hermione has vivacity and wit as well as virtue and charm, and it takes Leontes's jealous temper to find fault with the graceful, sweet freedom of her ways. She keeps true to herself in misfortune, and her answer to her husband's public indictment is dignified and sober, with a touch of irony.[79] The delightful episode with which Act II opens owes the quality of implicitness and a deeper shade of humor, in its pretty, smiling fun, to the impending shadow of the crisis whose approach is felt. The talk between the boy Mamilius, the ladies in waiting, and the Queen is delicate comedy, so weighted by the truth of nature and character that realism cannot be more perfect or more quietly humorous.

With Paulina's entrance upon the stage we welcome a Jonsonian "humor," who is nonetheless a humorist. The worthy lady, a genuine creation, is true in every feature to the slightly heightened life that drama demands. A courtier's wife, she awes not only her husband, but the king's officers and the royal person; she bears down all resistance—a triumph won by transparent honesty, courage, and the power of a biting tongue. The lively force of her railing is due to a robust hold

[79] III, ii.

upon the parodoxes of an absurd situation; indignation carries her forward, but shrewd sense guides her to victory. She is the instrument of the kindly fate that soothes, and finally heals, the souls poisoned or crushed by the madness of one selfish man.[80]

The shifting of the scene to Bohemia opens the second part of the play, in which humor grows prominent, its only rival being wonder; the plot thenceforth is swayed by a silent conspiracy of events that makes for alleviation and redress. We entrust ourselves to the onward urge of things, sure of the result and doubtful only about the means. The shepherd and his son the clown are masterly studies in rustic simplicity; entirely unable to think two thoughts at a time, they are the kind that create for others rich opportunities of humorous amusement. The assertion needs hardly be made good: analysis here would be a tedious commentary upon the obvious. What matters more is the soberness, the reserve of those realistic portraits, by no means caricatures, and finely differentiated. The shepherd with his limited outlook is almost an idyllic figure, credulous but dignified, and intuitively aware of many things beyond his ken; the clown is a boor with the thickest skull, in whom speech is a doubtful, still undeveloped faculty. Their reactions in front of the surprising incidents suddenly thrown across their path make up a delightful comedy, to such as cultivate a lively perception of the relative in all things.[81]

In Autolycus the humorous spirit has a disreputable, but a singularly efficient servant. Humor is before all detached; it loosens at least potentially the bonds with which man, a moral and social being, has tied himself; a total irresponsibility is its very soul. In practice English humorists have most often fought shy of a freedom which, to their disciplined instincts, was dangerous and awkward; they have acknowledged the limits which religion and ethics set to the disruption of values upon which they were engaged. The exceptions to that rule are, of course, chiefly to be found in the periods when the

[80] II, ii and iii; III, ii; V, i and ii.
[81] III, iii.

pressure of convention was more vigorously pushed back by the craving for inquiry or experience; the eighteenth century was such a time, as Swift and Sterne abundantly testify in the field of humor; but the Renaissance had been another; and Shakespeare's Autolycus is one sign, by no means exceptional, of the boldness with which some possibilities of imaginative anarchy could then be followed out. The literature of roguery, while professing to serve a moral purpose, was often secretly an accomplice to the desire for independence; it edified its readers but owed an indefinable part of its success to the fascination of evil. Autolycus, a "rogue," is one of Shakespeare's most audacious ventures in a direction where the logic of humor pointed; even Sir John Falstaff, if his final "rejection" is taken into account, does not so glaringly fall foul of the proprieties. Autolycus is treated, moreover, with surprising indulgence at the end; he escapes scot-free, giving the clown the vaguest promise to amend his life;[82] it looks as if in the eyes of poetical justice he did not much matter—an easy-going verdict we certainly owe to the spirit of humor in him, or rather in his creator.

The humor of Autolycus is indeed that of release—from all the impediments that check the play of desire. He is not a Tamburlaine or a Don Juan; the grandeur of conflict with the law, divine or human, is absent from his career of petty larceny and fraud; he is none the less a breaker of rules, and fully aware of the fact, in spite of his unblushing impudence. Pitched in the very low key of a tramp's life, his daily sinning is a round of cheats, lies, thefts, and every fleshly excess. He walks along the byways with a huckster's pack, singing loose songs, robbing orchards, gathering sheets from the hedges, and palming off his cheap wares upon the maids at fairs and markets. Cheek, the gift of the gab, a cool invention, make him a great mystifier of simple souls.[83] The poetry of adventure and the lure of the open road raise him above sheer vulgarity; he takes genuine pleasure in the flowers and the birds of spring; on a lower plane he is a distant cousin to Touchstone

[82] V, ii, 166-67.
[83] IV, iv.

and Feste: like the former, he has known better days, "served Prince Florizel," worn "three-pile";[84] like the latter, he shows some acquaintance with humanist lore, knows that he bears a classical name, mentions Mercury;[85] like both, he has a vein of thoughtful reflection in his mirth, and his jolly praise of the free irresponsible life awakes at times wistful echoes of Feste's song, "When that I was. . . ." Still, the main source of his appeal is conscious, sly roguery. The climax is reached when he nobly refuses to accept from the charitable clown the money which is no longer in the boor's pocket, since he has picked it.[86] This is practical humor glorified; but it is only a symbol of the cynical upsetting of values which flavors with philosophical salt his every word and deed. There are many rogues in the English literature of the Renaissance; but none more convincing, more brazen, and tricky than Autolycus.

The charming love scenes between Florizel and Perdita do not charge the atmosphere with cloying sweetness; the light strain of merry, youthful humor is diffused everywhere; and the lyrical fervor of passion is gracefully tempered with sprightliness.[87] It is only in the last scene that the chords of ecstasy are too deeply struck for a smile, and the serene happiness of the conclusions keeps unmixed.[88]

The Tempest

In *The Tempest* serenity prevails more fully and at less cost; it is established almost from the first as the mood of the play—itself a serene conclusion to Shakespeare's work. Through that more even tone the contrasts or the conflicts of the human world are largely smoothed down, and humor accordingly loses some of its best opportunities. There is a plot in *The Tempest*, but it resembles such stuff as happy dreams are made of—rather the quiet winding up of a moving tale

[84] IV, ii, 13-14.

[85] *Ibid.*, 24-25.

[86] IV, iii, 78-89.

[87] IV, iv.

[88] The clown's words: "I love a ballad but even too well, if it be doleful matter merrily set down, or a very pleasant thing indeed and sung lamentably" (IV, iv, 187-90), again point to Shakespeare's clear awareness that humor is very directly concerned with a clash, a discord, between matter and manner. See Bottom's and Quince's artless words (*Midsummer Night's Dream*, I, ii).

than a tragic action woven of alarm and suspense. Before the end of the first act our knowledge of Prospero's power makes his victory a foregone conclusion, and from the middle of the third, the only uncertainty that subsists is as to the aftereffects of his triumph. By then a peaceful evening light already smiles upon the romantic prospect of the island.

But although humor is toned down like the rest, such touches of it as can be found show a good deal of diversity; they answer to the various qualities and degrees of life, which are symbolically represented in Prospero's domain, and composed into harmony by the sway of his providential wisdom.

Harsh irony and sardonic hints are not absent from the play; but they fall entirely to the share of the villains. Guilty consciences and hardened hearts, proof against the searching touch of defeat and of forgiveness, go with the aggressive ironies of Antonio and Sebastian; they display their biting wit at the very moment when murderous thoughts are striking roots in their minds. Their favorite butt is old Gonzalo, and their contrast with him is significant indeed; it reaches down to the bedrock of a psychological opposition, which it is impossible that Shakespeare should not have clearly perceived, and wished to underline. Antonio and Sebastian are clever and cynical; they seize at once upon the weak spot in everybody's armor. They will generously deal out shares in the responsibility for the common disaster to all their shipwrecked companions, only forgetting themselves; their haughty noses sniff the virgin air of the island with no pleasure, and their eyes catch nothing but rough outlines in the lovely strange landscape upon which their cursed fate has thrown them. Their plan to kill Alonso while asleep is perfectly logical, if it is once agreed that every deed is to be guided by gross self-interest. They pride themselves on seeing through empty words: What is a conscience? Antonio asks; "I feel not this deity in my bosom" (II, i, 266-67). But somehow they fail, because they are up against moral powers that escape their grasp and baffle their very perception. Prospero's wisdom is that of the reason, not of the understanding; Ariel, the symbol of the spiritual forces of Nature, deprives the two would-be

Machiavellians of the very power to do evil. With all their gibes, they are eventually turned into nerveless, shamed dastards; but no assurance is held out to us that their sinister will is amenable to remorse, and their hearts capable of a sincere change.

Gonzalo, "an honest old counsellor," has a heart open to feeling, and senses not barred to the appeal of Nature: so he nurses a naïve optimism; he has kindly promptings—sympathies which he candidly expresses, thus getting off his guard and giving himself away. To be anything but critical is dubbed silly by the sophisticated; Gonzalo moreover has some of the garrulousness of age; no more is needed to bring down upon him the ridicule of the two wits; to them he is an old dotard, and they treat him accordingly. But is he? To all appearances, Shakespeare never meant him for such. With his tendency to verbosity, he has what the others lack, plain sense. His power to take in simple things makes him a better judge of realities than they are. His view of the island, after all, proves more to the point, because it is direct and fresh. No one but he notices the strange fact that in spite of their immersion in the sea, the party have dry clothes. His willingness to feel commits him with sentiment but opens his mind; his plan for a perfect state, adapted from Montaigne, is probably to Shakespeare, at least, a fine utopia.[89] Gonzalo's goodness wins him Prospero's affectionate regard.[90] But what is more to our purpose, keeping in touch with the concrete, Gonzalo has a twinkle of humor in his old eyes. During the storm he shows neither panic nor haughty defiance, but quiet courage, and his self-control takes the form of humorous flashes.[91] When openly laughed at by Antonio and Sebastian, he gives them tit for tat with dignity and a good grace.[92] In the surprises of the last scene, he recovers first his presence of mind, and his jest.[93] Humor in his person is challenged by wit, and decidedly gets the better.

[89] II, i, 144-68.
[90] V, i, 68-71.
[91] I, i.
[92] II, i, 171-88.
[93] V, i, 216-20.

Caliban, Trinculo, and Stephano make up a trio of most pregnant significance.[94] Caliban, the "mooncalf,"[95] the picture of our animality, nakedly shows the instincts of the brute in us; the contrast between his primitiveness and our decencies is fraught with a silent eloquence, which is comedy and which is humor. He outdoes all the rustic fools; as a realistic object, no clown or lout can compete with him. The working of his sluggish mind, the play in him of desire, fear, treachery, blind, stupid hero-worship are a study in the lower stages of human consciousness; and from his every reaction and word eddies of amusement and thought go broadening out to our intellectual horizon. Grotesqueness and fun are so intricately bound up with the serious, almost disquieting lesson of his whole being that the sight of him on the stage is to all of us a joy; and the philosophers meanwhile have not yet plumbed his symbolical value to the bottom. Trinculo, the jester, and Stephano, the drunken butler, fall with him into a natural harmony. Hardly higher than Caliban in the moral scale, they are yet superior to him; being able to think on two planes at a time, they show a rough sense of elementary humor. Ironically enough, the tipsy verve of Stephano, his coarse jokes, and his liquor eclipse the feeble though professional attempts of Trinculo; to Stephano goes Caliban's admiration and his gratitude for the discovery of the bliss there is in wine. The scenes where the three are brought together give us the most thoughtless mirth and food for the sober self-examination that is the aftertaste of philosophical humor.

Ariel, the airy spirit, of course matches Caliban in symbolical value. What matters here is that the missions he fulfils on Prospero's service turn out almost all to the comic confusion of sinners and that he enjoys them as such. His mischievousness is not unlike Puck's, but his whole being shows a different temper—much more eager, quick, and spiritual. The world of music in which he lives, and his graceful songs, make him a poet among fairies. There is too much fire in his constitution for the coolness which genuine humor demands.

[94] II, ii.
[95] II, ii, 111.

To his master it belongs to show such coolness, taking a sober view of life, in a pensive, earnest mood, but with a detachment and a freedom that give his meditation some tinge of the humorous. There is irony in the course of events on Prospero's island; the enemies whose attempts he baffles are more or less like puppets in his hands; the tragedy they have enacted in the past, that which themselves and others are now plotting, come together to a final abortion; and one aspect of the disaster is a farcical anticlimax, in which Trinculo and Stephano play an even more humiliating part than Caliban.[96] For the way all things eventually shape out, Prospero is responsible; he stands as a benign demiurge, and the half smile of a wiser power at the sight of mortal follies sometimes shows upon his lips in the intervals of graver expressions, wistful or melancholy.

Of the humorist Prospero has the aversion to pure dogmatism, the sense of relativity; he knows his own nature is not proof against wrong impulses; he checks himself after nursing thoughts of revenge;[97] though somewhat impatient still, he is modest, self-critical, tolerant of much; he does not feel quite sure about the working of his charms, the efficiency of his servants.[98] The punishment he deals out to the guilty is rather indulgent than severe; by wounding their pride to the quick, it would find a way to their hearts. The most typical incident in that line is the sudden vanishing of the feast—a keen disappointment of appetite that makes the victims ridiculous, followed by a direct appeal to them for remorse and penitence. The ironical object-lesson and the lecture support each other.[99] Prospero's humor is a refined, quintessential spirit in which the complementary aspects of life are so mixed and tempered one by the other that the contrasts tend to disappear, and the outcome is a feeling equally poised between tears and laughter.[100] Serenity indeed is the word; but not an Olympian

[96] IV, i.

[97] V, i, 25-30.

[98] V, i, 2-3.

[99] III, iii.

[100] So we cannot agree to L. L. Schücking's verdict that Prospero is entirely destitute of humor (*Character Problems in Shakespeare's Plays*, London, 1922, p. 258). This difference in interpretation is largely due to the widely divergent meanings that are attached to the word *humor* and that can be traced to the very notion of the thing. Indeed Prospero never makes us laugh; but that is not the whole question.

peace. This is no Goethean impassibility: "every third thought shall be my grave."[101]

Henry VIII

It would be imprudent to base much induction upon this play, which at best is Shakespeare's only in part—the extent of his authorship, besides, being variously gauged. A humorous coloring over the incidents and characters can be found in some scenes where his hand is generally recognized—as II, iii, with the high-flavored ways and speech of the "Old Lady," a delightful creation; and V, i, in which the same Lady manages to make her short reappearance very amusing.[102]

No doubt the parts attributed to Fletcher offer us successful humor as well—for instance I, iii, where the Lord Chamberlain, Lord Sands, and Lovell treat us to a lively satire of the Frenchified fops; and V, iv, with the bustle of the crowd outside, and in the Castle Yard the realistic talk between the porter and his man; good work this, done by a gifted playwright, the same probably who about that time wrote *The Knight of the Burning Pestle.* But it seems safe to say that the passage quoted above has more vigor in the rapid sketch of an episodic character, and humor of a more concentrated kind, than Fletcher's fertile talent and wit give us in the comedies that are undoubtedly his.

[101] V, i, 311.

[102] *King Henry:* Is the queen delivered?
Say, ay; and of a boy.
Old Lady: Ay, ay, my liege;
And of a lovely boy: the God of heaven
Both now and ever bless her!—'tis a girl,
Promises boys hereafter. Sir, your queen
Desires your visitation, and to be
Acquainted with this stranger: 'tis as like you
As cherry is to cherry.
King Henry: Lovell,—
Re-enter Lovell.
Lovell: Sir?
King Henry: Give her a hundred marks. I'll to the queen.
Exit.
Old Lady: A hundred marks! by this light, I'll ha' more.
An ordinary groom is for such payment.
I will have more, or scold it out of him.
Said I for this, the girl was like to him?
I will have more, or else unsay't; and now,
While it is hot, I'll put it to the issue.
Exeunt.

VII. Shakespeare's Humor, a Retrospect

Humor in a great writer is more than a system of aesthetic means intended to produce definite effects; it is more even than a particular attitude of the whole mind. It is the mind itself seen from a special angle; it is an aspect of its thinking and of its originality. A study of Shakespeare's humor is thus in the last instance a portion, however modest, of the attempt to catch that most elusive essence, which has called for repeated efforts: his general reaction to life, his philosophy. The rashness of one more endeavor may perhaps be excused if it means only taking stock of the results reached by a series of special inquiries, and summing up, in a retrospect, the conclusions of the preceding chapters.

That survey has refreshed more than anything else our impression of Shakespeare's objectivity and impartiality. His humor is the flower of a sense of life that ignores no part, and gives none a preference. The writer's attention keeps close to facts—not in an artificial, painstaking way, but with the easy application of a mind to what is its genuine interest. A magnificent possession of the world and of men as they are is the basis Shakespeare the humorist builds upon. Realism, the starting-point and constant law of a humorous work, is not only the accepted principle of his art, but the breath of its life. Such an openness to the infinite variety of things and people excludes all bias, all theory and preconceived choice. Now humor indeed demands the freedom of an unattached mind; it lives in the relativity that is fair to all creatures. Its exigence here coincides with a condition of sound dramatic art; and although there is no binding association between the two terms, it is no wonder that Shakespeare, the greatest of dramatists, should be one of the greatest world humorists as well.

His humor thus clearly reveals the main intellectual tendency reflected in the most characteristic English philosophy: empiricism, pluralism. Nature is sufficient, and nature is manifold; any attempt to unify it under a single category is less useful, and so matters less, than the determination to explore its various aspects; finally, when all is said, such attempts do not yield a comparable reward of truth.

Shakespeare's humor therefore is the effluence of a great mind keenly aware of the infinite contradictions of life and willing to put up with things as they are while discreetly smiling at their incongruities. To smile in that view is wiser than to weep; it is wiser as well than to laugh. As has been often pointed out, Shakespeare is neither an optimist nor a pessimist; to his instinct both systems are wrong, in so far as they are systems. Pleasure and pain are universal, and inevitably bound up together. Only one thing counts, the sovereignty of facts that are all unique, and of experience which is always particular. But conduct meanwhile is necessary; some general laws of behavior are discoverable from life, and it is best to follow them; the ages have gathered a priceless body of wisdom; only fools will set it at naught. Those rules can be easily summed up: excess is wrong; there is a line of relative safety in moderation. Shakespeare's thought here is in close sympathy with that of Montaigne, who was also, to some extent, a humorist. Now humor deals with the comic; and excess is laughable, since all departures from the normal tickle our sense of the ridiculous. So humor has its function and is ethically justifiable. But it will show up excess and punish delinquents in the silent, indirect manner most agreeable to the best dramatic art; it will do it in the way most congenial to the English character—the quietest, the least obtrusive; and the apparent indifference of the method will suit the cool temper of a people that hates to show its feelings.

This does not mean that the craving for fresh experience and the inquisitive zest of the mind are not to be felt in the humor of Shakespeare. Dealing mostly with the world as it is and smiling at the vagaries of unbalanced characters, it is not, like the genius of pure comedy, the blind servant of custom. The humorist is a poet in a manner; he leads the way to the realm of the possible, which surrounds the real on all sides and into which the domain of familiar safety shades off. Falstaff is an early explorer of regions where the modern spirit of adventure has taken risks; Jaques, Feste, Prospero look at things from an angle which is not that of orthodox wisdom because they stand too much aside from the common point of view or too high above it. But the soul of freedom here is weighted with such a major sense of the predominant authority of moral nature that in its flights it chooses still to have no other permanent guide.

In its clinging to balance as in its adventurous spirit, Shakespeare's humor is outstandingly national. It owes much, of course, to humanism and to foreign influences; an indebtedness not very plainly visible, perhaps, because its results are assimilated and embodied in all his work. But it owes more to the home tradition and to the spontaneous growth of an original English attitude in pleasantry. From that instinctive store it takes its main nourishment. It is thus, broadly speaking, a synthetic product, the culture of the cosmopolitan Renaissance being happily fused with the creative force of the independent English genius. Shakespeare's pre-eminence as a humorist among the writers of his time may be interpreted in the light of that reconciliation: no other dramatist kept so close to the popular vein, while imbibing all the refinement of humanism; none had such a wide range, from the brilliant intellectual display of *Love's Labour's Lost*, or the subtle suggestion of a Feste, to the broad fun of so many characters and episodes. With his rivals, the clowneries of the traditional type were apt to become cheap and coarse, or the vagaries of an allusive wit would grow thin, artificial and farfetched. From coarseness or artificiality Shakespeare's humor is not free; but through all its central region it shows a splendid combination of "finesse" in indirect conveyance, and quiet vigor in realistic presentment. On account of that synthetic character it occupies a middle position, not deviating towards any freak of individuality, as will later be the case for instance with Swift or Sterne. It is already in line with the most distinctive achievements of English humor; a privilege which even Chaucer, although wonderfully sane, did not quite possess to the same degree, because slightly eccentric from the national type and leaning a little on one side, that of finesse.

Thought, reflection, philosophy have much to do with humor; but one thing is even more necessary: a quick eye for the natural comedy of life, a power to recreate it fictitiously from the data of experience and observation. Shakespeare's invention in the domain of humorous character and incident is not indeed inexhaustible—there are moments in his work when the verve seems to grow stale and the inspiration flags; but it is altogether extremely fertile and varied. It works ever close to nature, taking stock of the real and starting from the ground of facts even in the moments of freest fancy. As was said above, the spirit of Shakespeare's humor is not always realistic, nor is it always orthodox; it overruns the stricter limits of experience and revels in a more intense world, braced and lighted up by the magic of comedy, as it can be exalted by the genius of tragedy; still, that world is like our own in every significant feature; it is not warped or altered in anything essential. His *vis comica* is no doubt a still wider faculty than his humor, since the latter word is to be restricted to comic elements presented in a certain way; but being the greatest English writer of comedy, he is assuredly at the same time in the forefront of the humorists.

Shakespeare's humor is thus an emanation from the deepest core of his personality. But it does not always reach us as if it were the audible voice of the writer's implicit consciousness. Being an incomparable creator, the father of a prodigiously large spiritual family, not only did he let his humor play upon many of his sons and daughters, touching up for our amusement their odd, naïve, or distorted features; but he knew as well how to endow his children, even the most humble of the scapegraces among them, with his own gift. His humor is thus reflected upon us from scores of beings who, owing their existence to him, are nonetheless, to all practical purposes, highly individualized men and women. His total treasure is made up of all that wealth; all the humor in his work derives from him, whether directly, or at one remove. It is only when that plenty is inventoried and computed that some estimate can be made of his rank as a humorist.

Again, the humor of Shakespeare does not rest only, as might have been expected, upon the theory of "humors." This worked at bottom on the old principle that abnormal, crazy characters with one strongly exaggerated feature were lopsided, and so good game for comedy. The doctrine was sound; but the obsession of the twisted line unduly set bounds to the independence of the observer and the artist. Shakespeare took the theory for granted and went further. He felt his way to the modern notion of humor, which he intuitively discovered and adumbrated in more than one place. More definitely than any of his predecessors, he showed through pregnant words that he had analyzed the characteristic traits of the humorous attitude, and could describe them with accuracy. Some of Falstaff's phrases and of Hamlet's words to the players, expressions in the mouths of Touchstone, of Feste, or descriptions of their tactics, are landmarks in the history of the gradual self-realization of English humor.

So to Shakespeare the field of comedy was much wider than the gross deviations from type with which Jonson mostly dealt; and all contrasts, all the infinite laughter of life were amenable to the technique which he instinctively preferred and developed to perfection: instead of the explicitness of farce, where the writer laughs outright and demands our amused concurrence, he let things and people speak for themselves; he showed them up with superb objectivity, and the presentment is so true that we enjoy our smile the more for its being our own reaction, not the contagion of another's. The wise passiveness of the artist who holds the mirror up to nature becomes, in the field of comedy, the humorist's attitude of calm unconsciousness, and yields us the rich joy of a refined, redoubled tickling of the fancy. Thus justified, humor occupies a very large place in Shakespeare's picture of the world; it is the animating soul of the comedies, while giving most tragedies the benefit of its complementary truth and of its momentary relief.

Objective as the presentment is, we can descry some mood or other at the back of it. Although unbiased, Shakespeare's humor has nonetheless an atmosphere, a spirit. Is it savage like Swift's, or genial like that of most English writers? It shows no set tendency, and would hardly bear out the oversimplified assertion that all humorists are kindly. But it does reveal a series of stages and a changing temper of soul. It is a fact that a ready and youthful acceptance of life prevails first; that midway through his career the playwright's mind seems to be clouded over with mists of sadness, and that the humor of a whole phase is largely sardonic or bitter; lastly, that acceptance grows predominant again in the serenity of the end. A view put forth by the critics as to the characteristics of successive moments in Shakespeare's emotional development would thus be rather confirmed. Taking his work altogether, his reasonableness—the companionship with reality that prevails in his plays and grows perceptibly more mellowed in the last ones—has in his humor one of its major tests, and perhaps the most revealing of all.

Humor, in principle, always preserves some connection, near or distant, with laughter; it is a mode—a rather interior, self-contained one—of the discovery and enjoyment of the comic, and Shakespeare's comedy tingles with that condensed, repressed fun of life, the more expansive and contagious for the repression. But humor has an unlimited range, as wide as the whole stretch between the two extremes of unalloyed good and evil, happiness and misery, exultation and despair. And its most exquisite shades, its most refined suggestions, dwell in the middle zone, where the whole scale is reflected in a delicately shifting synthesis. The highest humor of Shakespeare is neither merry nor sad; it is a smiling pensiveness which takes in the full scope of man and plays one of his numberless freaks against another in an ever fresh wonderment at his infinite variety. In it the sheer exhilaration is often eclipsed, passes into concrete highflavored knowledge, thoughtful possession, quiet brooding over the contrasted world. Its inmost spirit is thus an acceptance, tolerant without being skeptical, subdued without being depressed. Its most typical representatives, Falstaff in his less fleshly pranks, Touchstone, Feste, Prospero, have seen through things and through themselves, and still keep enough mental vitality to be interested in the adventure of living; at the pageant of the world they look with unjaded eyes and a zest untainted with the melancholy that will at times exude from their words. Humor indeed here is philosophy in being; Shakespeare's humor at its best is indistinguishable from his wisdom. And his wisdom, as we have tried to sketch it above, is not essentially original; but the expressions, humorous or other, through which it is reflected and diffused are the richest that a single human genius has ever originated.

CHAPTER XII

HUMORS AND HUMOR

I. A Survey

IN SO FAR as the development of English humor is concerned, the figure of Ben Jonson looms largest among Shakespeare's contemporaries and immediate successors. The view traditionally held was that even in this respect Jonson would be the more important of the two dramatists. The present study has taken its stand on a different valuation, the grounds for which need perhaps not be again emphasized. Although Jonson's insistence on the theory of humors and his signal success in the cultivation of a comedy based upon it mark him out as the central character in the history of the word, Shakespeare's contribution to the advance of the thing itself was much more substantial. And since the progress that mattered most, the self-realization of humor as a special attitude in pleasantry, was delayed by the confusion that grew out of an ambiguous word, quite as much as, or more than, it was in the long run furthered by the very existence of that name, there is clearly good reason for putting the thing before the word.

Still, it is an outstanding fact, and not to be ignored, that Jonson did more than any other English writer to popularize the term "humor" in a sense which was not of his own creating, as it had been in use long before him, but which he stamped with the strong authority of his dogmatic mind; and it cannot be denied either that by so doing he associated himself inseparably with the psychological problem which we are investigating. So his work has a special claim to be studied in connection with that problem. On the other hand, just because the growth of modern humor, both as a notion and a name, is involved in a good deal of obscurity, it is convenient that the early stage in that growth should be considered as a whole, at some moment in the progress of this inquiry. Now there could be no more favorable opportunity for that survey than an examination of Jonson's theory and practice as a comic writer.

We are thus led to assign to this chapter a double object; it will be indeed given to a discussion of the historical relation between "humors" and "humor"—a relation in which Jonson is an obvious case in point. But after due stock has been taken of his views and his practice, enough material will have been gathered, in this as well as the preceding chapters, to support a discussion of the linguistic transition which led from the Elizabethan to the modern use of the word. This will be a preliminary and a tentative survey, in the course of which a glance will have to be cast not only over the Elizabethan period itself, but over the later Renaissance down to the Restoration. It will be left for the final chapter, when the remaining blanks have been filled and Shakespeare's rivals or successors in drama, the poets, the prose-writers, have been successively examined, to take up the problem again on a broader basis; we shall then try and reach a definite conclusion as to the modern humorist's decisive realization of his own attitude during the hundred years that followed the Restoration—a period in which English humor came fully of age.

II. The Doctrine of the "Humors" about 1600; Jonson's Two "Humors" Comedies

It does not concern us to give a detailed account of the rise and fortune of the word *humor* in its physiological sense; all that is needed here is a very brief outline of that long history down to Jonson's time. More germane to our purpose is Jonson's attitude to that notion; but even in this much more restricted field a general examination of his theory and his practice will be enough.

It is now well known that as a student of "humors" Jonson was the heir to a tradition, the origins of which are in classical medicine and which can be traced on English soil at least from the fourteenth century.[1] The medieval notion of humor that

[1] We are indebted here primarily to the full and scholarly researches of C. R. Baskervill (*English Elements in Jonson's Early Comedy*, Bulletin of the University of Texas, 1911).

came to a head between the age of Chaucer and that of Shakespeare testifies to the long predominance of the medical point of view, derived from the ancients, over the psychological one, which was a tardy growth of the European mind and began gathering strength only during the Renaissance period itself. The old doctrine that there was an organic connection between the individual features of a person's character and the special abundance of some natural fluid in his or her body remained a rooted belief of both the learned and the untaught well into the modern age. The fluids selected as "cardinal humors" were blood, phlegm, choler, and melancholy or black choler; and to the predominance of each a temperament, physical and mental, could be attached. Such was the primitive and common background of the theory. But as time passed the emphasis was shifted from the normal to the abnormal aspect of the influences and significance of humors. Temperament reveals itself through idiosyncrasies of character; and the better marked the temperament, the more pronounced these features would be. The notions of oddity and eccentricity thus became the very core of the idea the word humor conveyed; and by the latter half of the sixteenth the century, when the word was in constant use and the idea grew to be almost an obsession, the meaning that most often crops up is, as the *New English Dictionary* describes it, "a particular disposition, inclination, or liking, especially one having no apparent ground or reason; mere fancy, whim, caprice, freak, vagary."

The coming to the front of what was after all a psychological element opened a rich vein for satire and dramatic characterization; and it is no wonder that historians of literature should largely ascribe to the success of the "humors" theory the quickened sense and observation of moral traits, which led to the appearance of individual, living characters on the stage, in place of the abstract types with which the Moralities had been contented. It is possible as well to connect, partly at least, the rise of a new literary kind, the Theophrastian portrait or "character," with the same lasting influence. Attempts have been made to find an adjuvant source of that whole development of curiosity and interest in the classical notion of "decorum," which had been particularly emphasized by the Italian humanists.[2] This would link up with the idea of "humors" in two different ways: the "decorum" of a character, first, was its consistency, its keeping true to the predominance of a given feature, once drawn—and the notion here is positively contiguous to that of a person's "humor"; again, "decorum" has a tendency to broaden into a meaning which is practically equivalent to that of the whole code and rule of conduct; and the relation to "humor," though here negative, would be efficient as well, because the stress laid on the idea of a standard of manners would naturally contribute to sharpen the perception of the deviations from that standard, the vagaries of behavior. But this would hardly be more at best than a secondary aspect of the process; and the all but universal spread of the "humors" craze in late sixteenth-century literature must be attributed to a native tradition that had spontaneously grown and become an element of the national culture.

It is thus possible to look upon Jonson's "humors" comedy as the consequence of a long development in which most of his predecessors in the two adjoining fields of storytelling and playwriting from 1550 to 1600 have a claim to figure. Of special significance in that respect would be Sir Geoffrey Fenton, whose *Tragicall Discourses* (1567) translate tales of Bandello through Belleforest, and improve upon the latter by insisting on the idea and the name of humor, which with him denotes a seriously vicious bent; Thomas Wilson (*The Arte of Rhetorique,* 1553); John Lyly, who through his *Euphues* (1578-1580) uses the word definitely in the Jonsonian sense; Gabriel Harvey, whose pugnacious vigor in his attacks upon Nashe will not be content with the notion of a "humor" as a whim, but must often imply that it is an affected whim—a view in which Jonson was to follow suit, and which became common enough during the interval between the two writers; Greene; Nashe, whose use of the notion and the word is as extensive as Jonson's; Lodge, who in *Wits Miserie* (1596) strikes out no

[2] J. E. Spingarn, *Critical Essays of the Seventeenth Century,* Vol. I, 1605-1650 (Oxford, 1909), Introduction, sect. vi: "Wit and Humour."

less ambitiously than Nashe towards the plan of a general catalogue of follies or humors. As for drama, marked approaches to Jonson's practice can be detected in Lyly's comedies, Marlowe's tragedies, and more especially in Chapman, who just before Jonson's "humors" plays gave in his *Humorous Day's Mirth* a surprisingly wide and efficient treatment to the same theme. Shakespeare's use of "humor" in the comedies that antedated Jonson's calls for no special remark; it was in agreement with what had become by that time a settled and practically universal fashion of language.

All through that line of predecessors, the moralizing trend which is so characteristic of most native growths in English literature made itself felt; the study of erratic traits in character was more or less verging on satirical treatment, with a moral aim. Donne's earliest *Satires* (1593) would be of course no exception. Under those prevailing conditions, it was only natural that the didactic genius of Jonson should seize upon a theme that would serve two ends, to him equally important: give a definitive status to the dramatic use of "humors," and at the same time ridicule a fad which was a signal instance of passive thinking and parrot-like speaking. As one of the poet's mouthpieces, Asper, puts it in the Introduction to *Every Man Out of His Humor*, the object is:

> To give these ignorant, well-spoken days
> Some taste of their abuse of this word humour. . . .

A wrong use is best described in reference to the right one. It would be courting singularity not to quote here the well-known passage which defines the blessed word in the light of the medieval notion, still accepted without reserve, at least as a starting-point.

> and hence we do conclude,
> That whatsoe'er hath fluxure, and humidity,
> As wanting power to contain itself,
> Is humour. So in every human body,
> The choler, melancholy, phlegm, and blood,
> By reason that they flow continually
> In some one part, and are not continent,

> Receive the name of Humours. Now thus far
> It may, by metaphor, apply itself
> Unto the general disposition:
> As when some one peculiar quality
> Doth so possess a man, that it doth draw
> All his affects, his spirits, and his powers,
> In their confluctions, all to run one way,
> This may be truly said to be a humour.

The adverb "truly," in the last line, has its full force. Under that single word the passing from the physical to the psychological sense is implied; but the whole process is only just adumbrated; it is not in the least explained.

This, thus, is the fullest statement of the doctrine; one that was to be regarded as plain and clear, and upon which the critics, as well as the cultivated public, were to live for more than a hundred years.

But the theme, as it has been pointed out, is introduced in the guise of a denial and a protest. An absurd fashion has set in, to cover all vain eccentricities and affectations with the cloak of a word that claims for arbitrary whims the necessity and relative simplicity of a natural bent. If, as Cordatus puts it,

> the poor innocent word
> Is racked and tortured,

it is because, under a convenient label, the silliest and the most gratuitous affectations are everywhere disguising themselves:

> But that a rook, by wearing a pied feather,
> The cable hat-band, or the three-piled ruff,
> A yard of shoe-tie, or the Switzer's knot
> On his French garters, should affect a "humour"!
> O, it is more than most ridiculous!

By a circuitous route, we are thus led back to the normal purpose of the satirist, which is to lash at false values and hollow pretenses.

To such artificialities no quarter is to be given. Jonson's comic Muse "will scourge those apes." A mirror "as large as is the stage" will be held up, in which all eyes may see "the time's deformity Anatomized in every nerve, and sinew. . . ."

It is thus less easy than it may seem at first sight to describe Jonson's attitude to his "humors" with complete precision. Indeed he does not seem to have thought out the matter quite clearly. In his two plays he aims apparently at showing up and deriding an exaggerated but sincere bias of character, a kind of organic and mental fate, rooted in a person's inmost nature. But very often the bias is presented as an affected whim, and the notion of affectation looms indeed so large that it almost covers the whole field.[3] Jonson's war is now against unconscious excess, in the name of sanity and balance, and now against a kind of social vanity that corrupts the whole being for the sake of a silly gratification. Again, the "humor" of a character is now a central and prominent feature, around which and in relation to which the other traits are naturally organized; now, an unnatural and as it were a cancerous growth, which upsets the coherence of a living whole. Lastly, the difference in the point of view of the second play, as compared with the first, remains rather ambiguous to the end. With some characters, being "out" of their humors means seeing through their hobbies and being cured of them; with others it seems rather to mean playing false to the truth of their own natures and superimposing upon genuine oddness a hollow pretense and a more or less artificial craze; with others again it is very much like being out of humor, or ill-humored, altogether. As for the abuse made of the word, Jonson denounces it vigorously in the Induction to the second play, and the point fits in there with the shifting of the general emphasis towards the idea of affectation; but he himself had

[3] These lines had been written for several years, when I came across the article by H. L. Snuggs on "The Comic Humours: A New Interpretation" (*PMLA*, LXII, March, 1947). The thesis is there put forward and solidly supported that what Jonson has almost always in view are not mere temperamental oddities but "the pseudo-humours of affectation and eccentricity." As to the very frequent presence, in Jonson's "humorous" plays, of the idea—and the fact—of affectation I find myself in agreement with the writer of the article. I must only submit that the idea—and the fact—of a naturally warped temperament are diffused as well through those plays; and that Jonson has allowed the coexistence of the two notions, and his shifting from one to the other, to leave a good deal of ambiguity in his general conception of what a "humor," as food for comedy, really is. However that may be, the outstanding thing, to the following century, was not so much what he had done, as what he had said that he was doing. His general definitions and descriptions are almost all on one side.

been, and was to be, a sinner in that respect; and when all is said, his main purpose is not to kill a phrase to the right use of which he does not in the least object; with the doctrine of "humors," medically and morally considered, he is in substantial agreement; and the whole theme to him is a fair pretext for that all-round castigation of the world, which is a boon to a satirist, and to which his temper was irresistibly prone.

The humors of Captain Bobadill and Master Stephan, of Fastidious Brisk, Sordido, and Sogliardo are still amusing enough, in spite of some overemphasis and stiffness in the repetition of effects; a fund of vitality and a genuine zest for the huge fun of caricatural life have gone into the creation of those figures; whatever one may object to the explicitness of Jonson's comedy, that he possessed the *vis comica* with a remarkable breadth and vigor of touch goes without saying. Of humor, in the modern sense, he had his share on the other hand, as is apparent chiefly from the later comedies and the poems. In these two plays it is much less in evidence, and the little that there is belongs exclusively to the author; his characters—which are very far below the standard of Shakespearean truth and complexity—do not evince anything of the saving grace. Although Bobadill is another braggart, he moves in an altogether different sphere from Falstaff's.

It is in other terms that the relevance and significance of the two "humors" plays to our inquiry must be stated and measured. Through his prestige as a critic of life and manners, through his authority as a legislator of taste and literary fashions—an authority which he owed largely to his intimate knowledge of the classics—Jonson stamped himself decisively upon the history of the word *humor;* and from that history the progress of the notion towards its modern meaning is after all inseparable. Whether he did more to sponsor a prevailing mode, or on the contrary to check its excess in the name of common sense, it is difficult to say; but at all events he gave a popular notion and phrase the consecration of a direct challenge through the powerful influence of the stage. No writer did more than he to achieve the already advanced development of the word and of the concept of humor from the physical and medical to the mental plane; although the idea of organic roots to the moral bent lingered for a long time in the background, the stuff and essence of "a humor," after him, belonged primarily to the world of character.

And in that way, although Jonson never shared in the intuitive perceptions which give Shakespeare his standing as one of the earliest and most lucid pioneers of what was to become modern humor, he contributed more than any other to make it inevitable that "humor" should be the name for the yet unnamed thing. He did more than that: through his strong relish for the raciness of full-blooded eccentricities and his abundant vein of comic invention (rather plentiful than rich or subtle) he destroyed whatever impression might still linger that the physical bondage implied in the medical sense of "humor" was a tragic element, fit rather for pathos than for comedy. He made the atmosphere of the word and the notion definitely comic. The association thus confirmed and clenched between "humors" and laughter was to be pregnant, far beyond his own ken.

III. Jonson's Other Plays

It may seem a superfluity to declare, after due examination, that Ben Jonson had a sense of humor. But this privilege was not at all implied in the authorship of the "humors" plays. One may indeed point out that it is usually when his main obsession relaxes that Jonson's humorous gift has a chance. Stiffness of any kind is deadly to that gift, and the systematic purpose at the back of the two plays is as stiff as can be. Such a determined aim in literary composition has much more to do with satirical moralizing than with the free, subtle creation of indirect comic values.

In fact Jonson's general relation to modern humor can be described easily enough. His mental equipment was far from ideal in that respect; neither was it actually deficient. Among his positive qualifications, one may single out his strong grasp and unfeigned enjoyment of the full flavor of things. He had his share of the natural shrewdness which goes along with popular instincts. That the learned writer who gloried to be the heir and apostle of the ancients was yet very much a man of his age, with his feet firmly planted on the soil of Elizabethan England, should be no surprise: a classical bent in that period was something fresh and vital, rooted in the very ardor and enthusiasm of life, not a dry, bloodless, and exhausted hobby; and was there not after all a rich, indeed a rank vein of realism in the Latin satirist whom Jonson so much loved? Again, the classicism of his taste would induce in him a temper of balance and self-mastery in expression, favorable to the restrained pitch which is the usual manner of humor. Against that ideal of guarded measure he, no doubt, repeatedly sinned; yet his intuition of it was right; only his actual sense of the classical virtues was none of the finest, and the self-appointed English Horace had some slight traces in his constitution of what one must call, with all due respect, barbarian vulgarity.

The negative elements are no less obvious. From the point of view of modern humor, Jonson labored under an uncontrollable itch to moralize, an unbounded trust in the right of knowledge to display itself on all occasions, and a stubborn personal pride, not free from some vanity. Pedantry, dogmatic didacticism, and the naïveté implied in self-conceit are hard phrases to use; and Jonson had to such an extent the good qualities of his defects that one is loth to charge him with weaknesses that did enter into his frank, honest, and lovable personality. But it must be confessed that he signally lacked the supple detachment, the sense of relativity without which genuine humor cannot thrive.

It is nonetheless a repaying task to look for genuine humor in the other comedies. They are, for this purpose, of very unequal interest. There is only an approach to the humorous in Jonson's earliest attempt, *The Case Is Altered; Cynthia's Revels* (except the "Induction"), and *The Silent Woman*—where the savageness of the satire creates a rather unfavorable atmosphere—are least fruitful in that respect. *The Poetaster* proves more fertile, although literary rancor and egregious self-satisfaction have too much to do with the play. *Volpone, The Alchemist,* and *Bartholomew Fair* make up Jonson's best-founded claim to be regarded as a humorist. What the reader remembers before all is the joy of enormity and Rabelaisian realism, a vitality and a gusto in satirical derision that do not exclude a kind of burly good nature, and are often handled with enough adroitness to keep above the level of pure farce; there may even be something poetical about those episodes—the poetry of exaggeration; while the author keeps cool and quiet in the midst of his imaginative enthusiasm.

The three plays can almost equally bear witness, in many scenes—though not in all—to the presence of a rollicking verve, just colored with a reserve, a shrewd self-consciousness. That discreet background, the set purpose to avoid excess, is felt in the persistence of an implicit element: the whole effect of even broad fun is not given away loosely, but presented in the objective spirit of the greatest comedy, which leaves something unsaid for the hearer or reader to supply. That shade of economy in method tallies, as was suggested above, with the properly classical tendency in Jonson's art. The key has an extensive range; and it runs all the way from the most amusing scenes in *The Alchemist*—with the excellent drollery of the encounters between Subtle, Ananias, and Tribulation Wholesome—to the fierce intensity of the episodes, in *Volpone*, where Voltore, Corbaccio, and Corvino successively appear, as sinister variations upon the same theme. The humor here is almost Swiftian; but shall we on that account refuse it its just name?

IV. The Shifting of the Word: The Semantic Growth from the "Passive" to the "Active" Meaning

The semantic development of the word *humor* from the medieval and merely physical sense to the fully grown Jonsonian one can be followed with precision through all its stages, the records of which are plain in English literature. But it is only a preface to another and a more subtle change, through which the Jonsonian meaning, while on the one hand it persisted and remained practically unchanged, at the same time was the origin of a new derivation, whose outcome is embodied in the modern idea of humor. The latter process was roughly speaking spread over the seventeenth century and the first half of the eighteenth, although its earliest symptoms can be detected before the end of the sixteenth. These initial symptoms, however, consist less in the appearance of perceptible shades in the use of the word, than in the dawning awareness, with a few, of a mental attitude, a special manner of pleasantry—an awareness whose presence we have tried to establish, chiefly in the work of Shakespeare. The growth thus initiated continued through the seventeenth century on independent lines; but to us who know the end, it is inseparable from the more precise fortune of the term itself.

How the word was gradually drawn into the sphere of the new idea, which shaped it to its own uses by loading it with novel values, is a fascinating subject for a historian of language and thought, but a most difficult one. The development in this second stage is mostly psychological; it has to do mainly with changes which have left no direct record, and the results of which can be perceived and assessed only when they have reached their consummation. It had been our ambitious hope to examine the process in its entirety, from the time of Jonson to the middle of the eighteenth century. But the passing of time, unexpected events, and the pressure of other work have forced us to give up the fuller plan. We must be content with exploring English literature as far as the Restoration, taking stock of the progress made about that date, and giving only a tentative sketch of the further emergence of modern humor in the hundred years that came next.

Meanwhile it is convenient, and we hope not too adventurous, to take at once a bird's eye view of the mental change that must have occurred in that respect from Jonson's time to that of Temple. The following remarks, of necessity, are based partly on conjecture—or rather, work back from effects to causes, in a retrospective inference.

Some conditions in the background of the period must first be outlined. The realization of the humorous attitude as an aspect of thought, and of the modern sense of "humor" as separate from its Jonsonian one, would demand an increase in intellectual complexity and greater skill in the distinction of shades of meaning. Now it is a historical commonplace that after the end of the Elizabethan age, properly so called, its great imaginative ardor subsided into a temper that brooded more quietly upon the working of the mind itself. The reflective mood of the seventeenth century, still shot through with the eagerness and fervor of the preceding period—a spirit that comes out in the brilliancy and fancifulness of the conceit—was on the whole characterized by a gradual predominance of rational pursuits. That among the issues which forced themselves upon thought, the thrashing out of religious, political, and social problems should have a large share was only too natural in the unsettled time of the civil war and the Puritan ascendency. But when the restoration of the monarchy and the Church had, to all appearances, brought back stability to belief and government, the scientific movement, so characteristic of the later century, still stimulated and extended the trend towards a rationalist examination and interpretation of reality. That trend was not to be checked, either, when with the Augustan age England entered a phase of her modern development in which, more decisively than at any other, reason, tempered with practical instincts, became the acknowledged guide of faith, art, and life.

It is thus no wonder that what may be called the self-realization of modern humor—a psychological process—and the linguistic change which, parallel with and closely related to it, altered the meaning of a current word in order to meet the needs of that realization, should have taken place in the highly analytical age which followed the end of the Renaissance. It is typical of that evolution that, as it was drawing near its close, men of a particularly lucid type, critics of literature and manners—Sir William Temple, Addison—should have given us our leading clues and shown themselves ahead of their contemporaries in realizing a change which the common mind felt yet but dimly.

The earlier stages, which left hardly any material records—those that worked themselves out obscurely in the collective thought of the nation, could be figured out more or less diagrammatically, and at any rate tentatively, as follows. One may apply the epithets "objective" or "passive" to the Jonsonian use of "humor," as the word denotes a mode of being which is unconscious of itself, and is perceived as a fact by persons other than the one who harbors it. Conversely, it seems legitimate to call the modern sense "subjective" or "active," as everything here hangs upon the sly intention of a conscious mind; and as the perception and enjoyment of that intent by other persons actualizes a virtual energy of significance, raising it to its full value. If as much is granted, the whole process can be summed up by saying that the objective sense gradually shaded off into the subjective one.

Such a change of course would not be effected at one stroke, or even within a short time; it must be progressive, acting by slow degrees and not being realized, except by the most acute observers, until it was practically completed. There would be a very great deal of overlapping; at a given moment the use of the word would show a wide range of differences, some speakers or writers being in advance of the common usage, whilst others—and very probably far the greater number—would reveal a conservative bent, and stick to senses that were already getting more or less antiquated. Now that confusion, and that shifting of gravity—quite normal circumstances through the history of language—do show themselves in what concerns the word "humor" during the late seventeenth and the greater part of the eighteenth centuries.

The first quotation in the *New English Dictionary* where we may find an undoubted example of the modern use of the word dates back only to 1682. From the unused slips prepared for the "Early Modern English Dictionary,"[4] we gather two slightly earlier but uncertain examples—one, just possible, dated 1672; the other, more probable, 1676. The reason for that relative lateness is not far to seek: the language instinct felt fully satisfied with the consolidation of the Jonsonian sense, by the side of which the medieval one was to remain current for a very long time; a natural repugnance, mental economy, would make it more difficult to pass on from an already derived meaning to another. It is thus possible to say that Jonson's robust effort stood in the way of further progress

[4] The matter will be reverted to, and treated at greater length, in chap. xvi.

in intellectual analysis. The "humors," as was pointed out above, checked the advance of "humor," even more than they favored it. And before the language registered a second change, the necessity for it had to be generally and intuitively felt; a period must elapse during which the dim premonition and confused perception of a new meaning could grow. The three quarters of a century between Jonson's "humors" plays and the first example known to us of the word in the modern sense were that period of obscure and mostly silent preparation. Then it was that the cultivated mind of England—as indeed this extension of usage certainly took place more quickly among the groups in which analysis and mental realization were at their keenest—grew conscious of an attitude which in fact had been long rooted in the temper and the instincts of the nation, numberless illustrations of which had been given by literature and life, but which so far remained indefinite, vague, and elusive because it lacked that indispensable nucleus and support of every notion: a name.

It is not impossible to give a conjectural account of what took place in the obscurer mind of the nation, at different levels of consciousness so to say, and in a diffused and scattered way, but with the indestructible unity of a process that answered a genuine psychological need. For an "objective" meaning to turn into a "subjective" one, the quality of subjectivity has to appear in the object naturally and spontaneously, as it cannot be forced into it from the outside. Now this is exactly what happened: the person who was "a humor" in Jonson's sense would begin to realize that he or she was odd, that oddity was fun, and that fun, handled in the proper way, was a means of enjoyment for one's self and others, as well as a social advantage. The unbalanced, freakish character that had been the occasion for amusement, the source and cause of comedy to the shrewd onlooker, gradually grew into the not unwilling creator of comedy, in his own eyes as well as in those of others. The former butt and the observer coalesced as it were into one person, who consciously made comedy of a particular kind.

Special traits, indeed, were implied in the whole development from the first. The characteristic feature of the comedy of "humors" had been that it was sprung unconsciously, so that it took two persons to achieve it: one who was the involuntary occasion of it, and another who raised it to full existence by realizing its potential quality. Now experience showed that it was useful to preserve the appearance of that unconsciousness, in order to give everybody the pleasant sense of co-operating actively in the consummation of the full effect. So the tactics of apparent unawareness were preserved and even instinctively developed; the more easily, as that unawareness harmonized very well with the queerness, the "oddity" of the "humorist" in the older sense. Seen from the outside, and described in historical terms, the new "humorist" was thus a person who looked oddly, preposterously unaware of the fun he was creating for the enjoyment of others and—silently but certainly—for his own.

But is it safe to suppose that Jonson's "humor"—the man with a crooked mind and a hopeless mental bias—might ever conquer that essential passivity of his, that slavery to impulses he could no more value, and even perceive critically, than he could control them? The answer is that psychological reality is never whole and simple. Just like the "mutations" in the field of biology, we have to reckon here with a range of varying degrees and shades. In fact, Shakespeare's plays, for instance, have offered us a number of perfectly convincing characters, who were neither quite unconscious nor quite conscious of themselves as possible sources of amusement—the class of which Launce *(The Two Gentlemen)* and Juliet's nurse *(Romeo)* are types; clowns or dunces who were half-aware of the fun they initiated, "humors" who guessed just enough what they were to handle their stupidity with some cleverness, to "play the fools" and evince a glimmering sense of their comic virtuality. Once that ray of grace had shone out into the thick-pated butt of satire, there was no limit to his progress, as actual life shows us again and again. Have not the best observers of the most elementary, primitive mind illustrated the endless number of shades, reaching more than half way to a lively sense, that will diversify and alleviate the dullness of nature? That would be the beginning of the process, the germ of the whole development, through which the "humor" by degrees turned into what we call the "humorist." It is those intermediate beings and those partial revelations, repeated thousands of times and spread over generations, that were the substance of the psychological growth in the nation at large, and the real basis of the linguistic change.

Moreover, when all is said on a plane of general, if not abstract, consideration, allowance should be made as well for the part played by instinctive, intuitive discovery. This is no longer a question of an awakening that takes place in the consciousness of a few, but of the revealing experience that those awakened minds themselves are to many others—to those that watch them, and are by them in their turn initiated. There is a power of contagion in the example and practice of humor, especially if the atmosphere of the social "milieu" is favorable. So we are led here to the main tendencies and persistent features of English psychology. The spontaneous affinity of the national character with modern humor is a fact which of course must not be overstated—as British critics have sometimes done when they have claimed for their race an exclusive privilege of the humorous gift—but it must not be minimized either. That temperament pre-existed in the nation; we have observed traces of its diffused presence from the earliest centuries of English literature; it had been feeling its way to expression, and in the works of some eminent writers—above all Chaucer and Shakespeare—it had reached a very high measure of development, short only of the decisive consciousness of itself. As time passed and the average level of mental complexity rose, the groping search of the latent faculty for a recognition that would be crowned by a definite name went on in the mass of the people, and chiefly among the most cultivated circles. That search would avail itself of more or less obvious possibilities, seize upon the notions and words that seemed promising and offered to meet it half way. That the Jonsonian "humor" proved to be the most encouraging hint available, and the best peg, so to say, upon which modern humor could hang the final stage in its quest for individuality, remains an outstanding fact.

Too much should not thus be made of the circumstance that just because Jonson's "humors" were funny and aroused other people's laughter they sidetracked the whole problem for a pretty long time and caused a confusion of ideas that proved stubborn; or that they seemed to point to an essential unself-consciousness in the modern humorist, whilst a consciousness of his sly intent is the very soul of his being. All things considered, there was no paradox at the heart of the central episode in the history of English humor; the psychological progress was natural, and the linguistic derivation legitimate.

V. Parallel Developments in Italy and France; Their Limited Scope

A conclusive proof that they were so is to be found in the parallel development that, outside the frontiers of Great Britain, associated in very similar ways the same medieval and medical idea and the identical Latin root with the theme of an original mode of pleasantry. To an observer from some other planet, it might have looked for a time as if the modern notion of humor were to find itself decidedly and to evolve its name in Italy or in France before it did so in England.

Italy had the advantage of its earlier cultural growth and of its more precocious addiction to literary criticism and aesthetic analysis. The Italian *umorismo,* colored by special shades of meaning, and not at all identical with modern English humor, was still nearer the real thing than the Jonsonian "humor"; it flourished in the sixteenth and the seventeenth centuries, long before humor as an independent mental attitude finally emerged on English soil. The point, of course, is not to be pressed too far. From its early stages Italian literature had shown a marked proneness to the many modes of satire, to the mock heroic, and the burlesque; that manner was particularly successful in the fifteenth, sixteenth, and seventeenth centuries; and it is not necessary to quote more than the names of Pulci, Ariosto, Berni, and Tassoni; writers whose diffused influence in England entered for something into the growth of mocking, ironical satire, and through that irony, of humorous literature. But when the Academy of *Umoristi* was founded in 1602, much more than the spirit of parody or implicit raillery, the animating soul of the company was—as appears in the later choice of Marini for its leader—the cult of the brilliant refinement and artificiality of the *concetti*. The genuine analogies to that movement are to be looked for, not in the concrete and realistic vein of English humor, but in the whole series of the attempts at a fashionable, "precious" refinement in thought and style, from Euphuism to the "conceits" of the metaphysical poets. So the kinship between the words, with an undeniable background of some similarity, should not be mistaken for an index to anything like actual sameness. Still, the element of originality and quaintness implied in Italian umorismo was the germ of a possible growth that would have brought it nearer to the final form of English "humor"; and although such was not to be the case, it is a fact that with a very different set of overtones, under other names (*beffa*, *arguzia*, etc.), national varieties of humor have played a prominent part in the history of modern Italian literature. But it was only in the eighteenth century that *umore* was revived, under the influence of England, and perhaps through France, in a meaning which had been almost completely lost, and which now became definitely parallel to the new sense of English "humor."[5]

In France, whilst the fortune of humor itself—an unrecognized and unnamed vein—had been hardly less sustained than in Italy, the critics eventually borrowed from the English, in order to name it, a word which they did not at first salute as their own. This took place in the eighteenth century; but some time before it happened—more precisely, in the earlier half of the seventeenth century—their language did offer some signs of turning the native form *humeur* to uses which, if they had been pushed further, might have led to a development parallel with that of the English term. This is a long story, the main stages of which it will be sufficient to recall. It is pretty well known that Voltaire in 1761 vivaciously protested to the Abbé d'Olivet that there was nothing original in the

[5] F. Baldensperger, quoting B. Croce, in *Etudes d'Histoire Littéraire* (Paris, 1907), p. 192.

use the English made of the French word *humeur*, which, he pointed out, they spelt "humour" and pronounced "yumour," as the very same meaning was to be found, for instance, "dans plusieurs comédies de Corneille." Génin in his *Récréations philologiques*, almost a century later,[6] again took up Voltaire's plea, and quoted more examples from seventeenth century authors; and no less a scholar than J. E. Spingarn practically made Génin's thesis his own, though he did not agree with the assertion that even as late as 1765 Diderot, in his *Salons*, was still using "humeur" in that special sense.[7] According to Spingarn, that special sense of "humeur" "apparently lost currency in France about the middle of the [seventeenth] century"; but he is positive that "it was in France . . . that the term was first extended, from its secondary sense of singularity of character, to its third (and in England its final) sense of the keen perception or the unconscious expression of the odd and incongruous."

We may pass over the startling use of the adjective "unconscious" in the words just quoted; what the writer means is very probably that when a person says or does "odd and incongruous" things unconsciously, the listener may make humor out of the experience by his "keen perception" of the oddness and incongruity; a leveling down of the subjective (and only genuine) with the objective (and superannuated) aspects of humor under one name, which the history we have been following explains only too well, but which is regrettable in the twentieth century, as it tends to perpetuate a traditional confusion of ideas.[8] As to the historical argument, we must demur to the validity of Génin's and Spingarn's thesis. The passages Génin quotes do bear out the conclusion that "humor" on occasion could mean a fund of personal tendencies and impulses, which would make a person unwilling to conform to type, and might bring him or her to come out with sallies of good humor, what Génin calls "*la belle humeur, l'humeur vive et leste, et fertile en bons mots.*" This is altogether a background of

[6] Paris, 1856, I, 213.

[7] *Critical Essays of the Seventeenth Century*, vol. I, Introduction, vi, lviii-lxiii.

[8] Another conjecture would be that by "unconscious expression" Spingarn meant "apparently unconscious expression."

meaning rather similar to that of the Jonsonian "humor"; but of the essential element in the modern idea of humor—the peculiar twist of expression in its relation to thought, the "*transposition humoristique*"—there is absolutely no trace in the passages one may quote from Corneille, Molière, or Scarron. What probably happened was that Voltaire, and Génin after him, were unduly swayed by the fact that a semantic development, already complete by 1765, had deprived the word *humeur* in French of its "ambivalent" connotation and brought it, when used by itself, to mean ill humor, a sourish disposition. In contrast with that restricted sense, the early seventeenth-century use of the word had been wider and freer; it preserved much of the idea of self-centered spontaneity and something of the expectation of good humor. That is all one can prudently infer from those texts. After 1650 or 1660, the classical spirit was hard at work in France, pruning, clarifying, and classifying the language; it started the restriction of sense which gradually gave *humeur* a pejorative shade of meaning, and cut short every possibility the word might have had, in the French instinct, of undergoing the same creative evolution as *humour* in England.

So, we may accept of Spingarn's assertion that "at the end of the XVIth century all the nations of Europe were alike in possessing the term 'humor' in its primal medical sense as one of the four cardinal or constituent elements of the make-up of man; . . . and by a natural extension of the sense the word was used throughout Europe for disposition or temperament in general." Having in mind especially the examples of Italy and France, we may even grant that the development which the English language associated with itself so signally from the latter half of the seventeenth century was not exactly unique. It was sufficiently rooted in permanent and so to say international data of human nature and social life to show itself, at least under incipient forms, in several other countries. But when so much has been said, the outstanding fact remains that in no nation was the third and momentous extension of meaning which brought the medieval term to its full modern sense so decisive and consequential as in England. Slow as the change was, and crossed by the persistence of older meanings, it succeeded finally in altering completely the use of the word; it created a category in criticism, gave a new concept in aesthetics a distinct existence, and was the focus of a contagion which spread over countries and literatures near and far. The world learnt to speak of "humor," not of "umore" or "humeur"; and French people had an impression, when they used the word, that not only did it imply an English background, but that it was itself thoroughly English.

It is thus permissible to take Sir William Temple to task, as we shall have to do, for first putting forward a claim to the exclusive possession of the word *humor*, and of the thing itself, in favor of England and the English. The claim was to become traditional, and the cue was followed down to the nineteenth century by critics who might have known better. But Temple is on more solid ground when he traces the brilliant fortune of word and thing in England—he does not explicitly speak of a new meaning, and has in mind the Jonsonian sense, with a strong tincture of the modern one—to something ingrained in the nature of Englishmen, and to the conditions, physical, political, and social, that ruled their lives.

The decision of fate that placed the home and nursery of European humor on English soil has its justification in the English temperament itself, in the number of odd characters, and the vigor and quiet assurance of their oddities—among which the essential one, from our point of view, was the power of saying queer, paradoxical, and funny things, quite seriously. Owing to those circumstances, the gradual self-realization of English humor was spread over a wide surface, found its basis in a multitude of individual cases, and grew to be a feature of the national mind itself. Pregnant are Temple's words, and they throw light on the whole subject: "We have more humour, because every man follows his own, and takes a pleasure, perhaps a pride, to show it." The matter is thus clearly and fitly summed up; in fact, the pleasure and the pride of being odd do imply the consciousness of one's oddity and of its value; and Temple was here very close to an intuition of the final emergence. Symbolically speaking, the initial stage in the process of growth was that Jonson's "humors" found pleasure and pride in playing off their vagaries upon the world; a change which would make the craze much more innocuous, and turn a mental or moral abnormality, almost a disease, into a source of innocent amusement for all; a change, again, which would endow those originals with a sense of quiet, wistful relativity and double-mindedness that was much more than a trick: it was the germ of a new soul.

This chiefly psychological and partly a priori view of the contribution which the seventeenth century made to our problem will be, we hope, confirmed and established, as well as more fully developed, in our last chapter.

CHAPTER XIII

HUMOR IN ELIZABETHAN DRAMA

I. The Order Followed

IN RESPECT OF humor, Shakespeare and Jonson stand apart from the main body of Elizabethan dramatists; the former because he had more of the thing than all the others; the latter because he played a signal part in the history of the word. Leaving out Jonson, we have now to survey the wide field of Shakespeare's contemporaries and successors. His immediate predecessors on the stage have already been dealt with.[1]

The order followed in this chapter will be roughly chronological and based not exclusively on a writer's date of birth, but on the whole span of his life. Of course there cannot be anything strict about it, as the biographical data concerning several of those dramatists are, at least partly, involved in obscurity. A place is to be assigned to each from the relative position in time of the chief body of his work. Such an order is best suited to the point of view of the present study—that of a collective development, individual traits and local incidents being merged in a general growth.

It must at once be confessed, however, that the possible significance of that ordering is very limited. No revealing inference about the psychological development of humor—its gradual realization of itself—can be hoped for from the examination of a group of writers who belong, when all is said, to one and the same age of literature; an age, besides, which possessed such intrinsic strength of characteristics and molded

[1] As we confessed above (in a note at the end of chap. vii, sect. v), a measure of arbitrariness is hardly avoidable in the order of our survey. Dekker for instance, who was studied in chap. viii before Shakespeare, cannot be called one of the latter's predecessors, but was fully his contemporary. The reason is that through his inspiration he belongs decidedly to the "popular vein."

men's lives and minds so powerfully. The facts at first sight do not encourage the expectation that the dramatists who wrote just before the closing of the theaters would necessarily have a clearer notion of humor, as an aesthetic category, than those who lived one generation earlier. From Shakespeare and Jonson to Shirley, the ups and downs of humor cannot be organized into a regular curve, and each writer's relation to the subject is mainly a matter of individual temperament. Whether any other conclusion can be drawn from this part of the survey is a question that will arise at the end of the chapter.

II. Chapman

We may be excused if we feel some misgiving when we begin to look for humor in Chapman's work. The massive and vigorous figure of Shakespeare's "rival poet" looms large indeed in our mental view of the Renaissance; but to such an inquiry as ours it holds out scant promise of a reward. The personality of the man and the features of the writer are pitched in a very different key from that of humor. While the humorist takes his stand on seeing at once both sides of a subject, Chapman has given us decisive proof that he was determined, when faced with some of the most essential problems, to see but one. About moral values he was radically in earnest; and aesthetic values to him had been forever ordered by the achievements of Greek and Latin writers. A moralizing and a dogmatic humanist, though no Puritan, he wielded his pen with an energy that was not free from stiffness; and the poet who tacked on to Marlowe's *Hero and Leander* just that second part, signally lacked—at least in some respects—the sense of humor. The main body of his work for the stage lies in tragedy, not comedy. Indeed he promises little; and he seems to have none of the supple liveliness, of the double mind that humor demands.

And yet our pessimism is given the lie; we find much more than we expected. We are made to realize, once again, that there is no safe a priori inference from such complex data as those of character and mind; and we bow to the wealth of tendencies in those rich Elizabethan personalities. Chapman is a case in point to support the argument that as the vein of humor in English thought and literature went deepening and broadening out, so that it assumed the importance of a national characteristic, humor appeared more and more severed from its early association with light-headed pleasantry. The wistful amusement of the serious-minded: that was to become the main source of the most creative and original development in a manner and tone of feeling and speaking that emerged decidedly during the seventeenth and early eighteenth centuries; indeed humor—as it had done in Cervantes, in Shakespeare—was growing to be not only a special mode of joking, but a way of thinking and an orientation of the whole mind.

A look into Chapman's *Homer* might have given us better hopes. Apparent in his translation is a vein of unaffected simplicity and raciness which betokens a mind in contact with the realities of life and true to its instinctive perceptions; to such a writer the saving grace of humor may be allowed, as his erudition and his literary beliefs do not stand between him and the concrete world.

Chapman's comedies are in fact a far from negligible part of his work. *A Humorous Day's Mirth* has the special claim of having preceded Jonson's "humors" plays, and more than sketched out the same theme. As could be expected, the "humors" themselves—which are, quite in the Jonson manner, the whims and automatic responses to life of more or less cranky persons—are to our taste the least humorous part of the comedy. But there is a genuine verve and comic life in many characters and scenes; and although the treatment is often clumsy, or even coarse, an element of slyness and indirectness in the presentment of fun, that discretion and reserve which are the salt of humor, redeem the play from the atmosphere of mere farce. Good-natured mirth will well up again and again from an invention which very unexpectedly reveals fresh, lively features; and the youthful spirit in which not a few incidents are steeped has some of the impudent coolness in the handling of extravagance which belongs to a distinct vein of modern literature. Even the gift of humorous dialogue and rejoinder is not missing; much will be forgiven the playwright who could make his pattern Puritan lady, Florilla, rise to the occasion so beautifully, when she tells her foolish husband with the grand air: "For as men should ever love their wives, so should they ever trust them; for what love is there where there is no trust?" And being reminded that with her fine principles she has steered clear of adultery by the breadth of a hair, she has a pat answer: "Cursed be he that maketh debate 'twixt man and wife."

The text of *All Fools* (1605), imitated from Terence, is headed by a dedicatory sonnet, in which Chapman strikes a strangely sad note:

> Being mark'd with age . . .
> And drown'd in dark death-ushering melancholy.

And yet the same writer, in the Prologue, objects to the bitter "spleens" and the satires that have, he says, with the consent of the public, driven away the more spontaneous forms of comedy, "merely comical and harmless jests." The preference just expressed, in itself, would tend to imply a dislike to indirect joking and the method of humor. But that the sad man who thus preached good-natured mirth had in that very duality of spirit the root of the matter, no one will deny who gives the play a fair trial. There is from the first an ironic vein of pleasantry, for instance, in the dialogue of the two fathers (Act I), with subdued, discreet effects; and the same quality of repressed, allusive fun, diffused through many of the following scenes, keeps them sweet to our most fastidious taste. Gostanzo the old miser remains as a figure far short of the dramatic vividness of Jonson's Volpone; but his portrait is more finely shaded. Is not this defense of ready adaptability in speech—and thought—worthy of Molière?

> Beasts utter but one sound; but men have change
> Of speech and reason, even by nature given them,
> Now to say one thing, and another now,
> As best may serve their profitable ends.

The mixture of broad comedy with a gentle amusement, which tickles our sense of the ludicrous rather than makes us laugh —a gentleness which it would not be fair to trace only to Terence—is kept up till the end. Gostanzo can make us smile in his final discomfiture, by his solemn remark: "Young men think old men are fools; but old men know young men are fools," in which the self-satisfied, obstinate infatuation of age is so cleverly hit off; and Valerio's oration in "praise and honour of the most fashionable and authentical HORN," is a most successful piece of brazen, grotesque absurdity.

It is perhaps sufficient to say that *The Gentleman Usher* (1606) reminds us at times of *Love's Labour's Lost, Midsummer Night's Dream*, or *Twelfth Night*, and that the comparison, dimly stirring in our minds, is not disastrous to Chapman's comedy. Here again, the spirit of humor is spread through most of the play; but if it be permitted to quote from a not very familiar text, Pogio's speech in honor of brooms and those that wield them (Act II) is worthy of recalling Swift's "Meditation upon a Broomstick":

> And more truth to deliver,
> Grim Hercules swept a stable with a river. . . .
> Philosophy, that passion sweeps from thought,
> Is the soul's broom, and by all brave wits sought. . . .
> . . . Now if philosophers but broom-men are,
> Each broom-man then is a philosopher.
> And so we come (gracing your gracious graces)
> To sweep care's cobwebs from your cleanly faces.

Indeed only Chapman of all the brilliant dramatists of the time could be the "rival poet": he had at his command powers—a vigor of invention, a verve, a sustained force of thought and expression, a natural, spontaneous felicity and ease in dialogue, an unsought elegance—which at times are comparable to Shakespeare's, although on a lower plane; and that quality comes out chiefly in his comedies. His tragedies, with high merits, leave more to be desired; and in the tragic manner it is another name, that of Beaumont, which we think of putting immediately below Shakespeare's. This does not mean that the serious parts of *The Gentleman Usher* do not deserve our admiration; in fact Strozza's speech: "Oh, what a treasure is a virtuous wife," is justly famous; and the modern reader enjoys with a feeling of surprise the nobleness and quiet pathos of the end of Act IV, in which Chapman's deeper mood of austere, devout, and almost mystic idealism gives itself vent finely, with bold sincerity.

The genuine gaiety and sprightliness which, governed by a sure instinct of artistic self-possession, raise the fun of those plays to the plane of humor permeate as well a comedy of rather inferior merit, *Monsieur d'Olive;* even there, the farce shows an admixture of serious raillery; and the vain, bragging, irresponsible hero has that touch of self-mockery in his impudence, that twinkle in his eye which make incipient humorists of not a few Shakespearean fools.

Of *Eastward Ho* it is difficult to speak here, since Chapman's part in the play must be inferred only with due caution. On the whole, the comedy, so generally cried up, falls a little short in its humor of *All Fools* and *The Gentleman Usher;* the buoyant, easy verve of Chapman's individual work is somewhat burdened here with a bitter, coarse realism in which one is tempted to discover Marston's hand, and a heavy handling of repetitive tricks which seems to spell Jonson's presence. Naturally the chief interest of the play lies in the picture of middle or lower-middle class London life; the significance of such a frank apology for the City, honest trade, and the "natural gentleness," cannot be too much emphasized. Now, as that adherence to local truth is steeped in a spirit of good-humored, sympathetic bantering, not unlike Dekker's, a whiff of genuine humor mixes again and again with its atmosphere. Indeed one would like to fancy Chapman's inspiration more particularly in the concluding scenes, where the sly mixture of love and raillery reaches a subtle, rich quality, and calls up to the modern reader's mind the range of humor which Dickens, Barrie, and Kenneth Grahame, for example, have more especially made their own. The conversion of the sinners is meant to be serious and edifying; but there is a gleam in everybody's eyes—of those who repent, and of those who draw the moral; the sentimental note is quite purposely overdone; and the element of exaggeration, of unreality in realism, creates a perceptible effect of self-mockery and humorous fancifulness. No doubt, the tone is more often that of mere farce; but such farce as the end of the third and the beginning of the fourth acts, with the gushing expression of the "Virginian" dream and Sir Petronel's adventure on the "French" shore of the Isle of Dogs, disarms criticism, and sweeps us along in an amusement, to the quality of which it would be pedantic to take exception. When all is said, this highly moralizing play stands at the source of a literary vein which was to run conspicuously through the works of Bunyan, Defoe, Lillo, Richardson, and Dickens—humor being, among heirs, the privilege of the last.

Of humor, the tragedies are not destitute. Let one example suffice: the bragging and the ranting of Byron, in the second part of the historical drama that bears his name, do not carry him quite off his feet; from the heart of his fury and despair there flashes out again and again a spark of fierce, scathing irony at the canting servants of power, and at the grim ceremony in which he is to play the central part.

III. Middleton

Middleton's relation to humor is comparatively simple and easy to define. The two epithets, realistic and cynical, most often applied to his attitude, give us a clue to the vein of temperament which nourishes and explains his successful handling of the humorous manner. He knew well, thoroughly felt, and enjoyed the flavor of things and people as they were; especially, of course, in the low and disreputable circles of London life. So far the background of his comedies is largely similar to that of Dekker's; the difference lies in Middleton's cooler reaction to the unedifying facts he will display, and in a less sentimental view of the fate of his characters. Not that his relative aloofness goes as far as absolute indifference to ethics; a moralizing instinct is in some measure at work through his plays; and free as he is in his pictures and innuendoes, he manages to make dramatic justice most often coincide with the wishes of the conscience. But his purpose undoubtedly is to give us opportunities of relishing the zest of things, rather than to rebuild the world in accordance with the heart's desire. That atmosphere of subdued cynicism harmonizes very well with the detachment which is a major trait of humor.

Whilst broad farce is most often present, or at least hovering not very far off, a good many episodes and scenes do deserve a better name.

At the same time, Middleton's cleverness in the management of a plot, the fertility of his invention, his grasp of character, and the lively ease of his dialogue contribute to heighten the literary merit of his plays; a sense of naturalness in situation and incident, the likelihood of what happens, the truth of psychological development again and again take the comedy, as it were, from the hands of the writer and tend to identify it with a chapter in genuine experience. The trend towards farce and the occasional freaks of obvious exaggeration qualify this feature of his manner without effacing it. Now whatever carries a play from the plane of an artificiality inherent in the stage on to that of possible actuality favors the growth of that subtle impression of independence, inevitability, and self-sufficiency which characterizes the higher and humorous forms of the comic.

As could be expected, most examples of this effect are to be found in the comedies. Such an early work as *A Trick to Catch the Old One* already shows us several aspects of Middleton's cool mastery in the treatment of comic themes. Not at the highest level, of course, should be placed the last scene of Act III, though it is admirable of its kind: we watch Dampit, a drunkard, being put to bed by his servant Audrey; and nothing can be more lifelike than the glimmer of sense that lives at the heart of his intoxication, arguing and insisting and making a desperate attempt to preserve his dignity. The humors of drunkenness are eternal and a little cheap; but the coarseness of the passage is redeemed by raciness and by a touch of the manner of Rabelais; indeed, as with Rabelais, a kind of lighthearted innocence is diffused through all the gross realism. The same gifts are displayed with no less vigor, but on a more properly psychological plane, in the third scene of Act IV, between Witwood and the creditors who have had him arrested; the fun here is quiet and has the slightly bitter aftertaste which seems inseparable from the higher forms of comedy. The vein of *A Chaste Maid in Cheapside* is more abundant and flows with even more ease; still, a fine sense of discretion, a close approximation to nature and truth keep the effects above the vulgarity of mere farce. The scene of the christening (Act III), with the talk of the gossips, their forecasts, the coming of the comfits, and the all too earthly behavior of the Puritan ladies, is a most enjoyable picture of contemporary manners, in no way inferior to Jonson's *Bartholomew Fair;* indeed Middleton's characters are, if anything, more finely shaded and freer from the suspicion of caricature.

Another difference from Jonson's painstaking descriptions is that the author here handles the brush more lightly and naturally. His realism is often poised in a delicate balance between tameness and brutality, through which the instinct of a born writer and artist is revealed. The same manner prevails for instance in the third act of *The Roaring Girl* and its very amusing scenes, which we are strongly tempted to attribute to Middleton, whilst Dekker's name seems to be written large over most of the last two acts. It is again in the third act of *A Mad World, My Masters* that the comedy which revolves round the successful character of Sir Bounteous Progress reaches its highest level of frank burlesque, and yet sober and careful efficiency.

It is no surprise that the humor which shows itself so plainly as a virtue of Middleton's comic invention should find, or make, room for itself in the tragedies. Too much stress should not be laid here on that great play, *The Changeling,* in which other merits of grim pathos, high poetry, and the deeper grasp of character shine so brilliantly; but in the parts commonly attributed to Middleton, realistic episodes (such as Lollio's and Pedro's dialogue, I, ii) now and then happily relieve the tension. *Women Beware Women* gives the comic element such ample room that the play, but for its unhappy ending, might be called a tragicomedy. Middleton's verve never let itself go to better purpose than in the scene (II, ii) between Livia and the widow, which Lamb and Swinburne have praised so warmly. Indeed the figure of Livia, the "good neighbour," is worthy of being compared with Chaucer's Wife of Bath; and as Lamb puts it, the high quality of that wonderfully close realism lies in its absolute likeness to life; the perfect effacement of the author, of his personality and point of view, behind the pattern of the real, which he follows so accurately, pitches the fun of those passages in a key of supreme objectivity, which is that of supreme humor. But in a less amusing scene, where the realism is more plainly instinct with an ominous sense of tragedy, Bianca's behavior to her husband (III, i) is handled with a sureness of psychological intuition which stamps upon the dialogue the masterly truth to nature that is Shakespeare's unique gift, though not his exclusive privilege. Of course Middleton here is indebted to Shakespeare, and not Shakespeare to Middleton.

IV. Webster

It may well seem a paradox to mention Webster and humor in the same breath. The association should be altogether rejected, if an element of sympathy and geniality, as the current English opinion has it, is an indispensable constituent of humor. But enough has already been said as to our grounds for not subscribing to that view. The concentrated bitterness and cruelty of Webster's tragic world implies the brooding of a clear-sighted mind upon such aspects of life as those which the decadent spirit of the Renaissance had endowed with temporary prominence, especially in Italy. Their pathos is powerfully but soberly emphasized, whilst their pity, which is left in a latent state, oozes from the whole subject as a subtle, repressed essence. Such a mood has one essential kinship at least with humor: it relies on the implicit eloquence of things not said but suggested. In the grim resolve which is the soul of Webster's imaginative realism there lives the germ of a scathing dramatic irony and of a sardonic humor, which one may compare either to that of *Hamlet* or to the Swiftian manner.

Of comic relief, properly so called, there is little of course in drama of this kind. A fertile invention in the field of laughter demands a modicum of acceptance, an intuitive feeling of life, if not a decided sympathy with it; and this is the partial truth involved in the traditional English notion of humor. What we find in *The White Devil* is not properly amusing; it is a subdued irony that mixes most often with the tragic atmosphere of the play. It crystallizes at times into a few words, as when Vittoria at bay addresses one of her murderers: "Thou hast too good a face to be a hangman. . . ."

The Duchess of Malfi, which reveals a firmer and a surer hand, has a superior density of style, and its concentration of meaning is more powerful. In a significant passage at the beginning (I, i) Webster shows himself aware of the policy of repression and reserve in laughter, as an aspect of moral and social fastidiousness; although the remarks he puts in the mouths of Ferdinand and Castruccio cannot fairly be twisted to cover the tactics of the humorist. Very characteristic of the temper of the play is the single scene in which the proper spirit of comedy can be said to be given its chance: the episode of the madmen (IV, ii). The amusement of the spectator or reader, even here, is at best the half-smile that the antics and coarse jokes of the "fourth madman" will call up; and it is impossible to drive away an impression that the grim and weird spirit of major scenes in *Hamlet* or *Lear* was present and active here at the back of Webster's mind.

V. Tourneur

Of Tourneur, in this connection, there is very little to say. With an intensity of tragic pathos traditionally compared to Webster's, he has a narrower range, and his concentration on his main purpose leaves even less room for relaxation. The occasional treatment of comic themes in *The Atheist's Tragedy* (one may instance the fifth scene of Act II, and the character of Snuffe, the Puritan) shows something of discretion and reserve. In *The Revenger's Tragedy* the fuller display of Tourneur's power brings out better that density of ironical suggestion, as it does the other traits of his talent. Vendice the "Avenger" has the pregnant brevity of speech which a self-contained, brooding temper and the secrecy of a long-deferred scheme will naturally breed. Whatever flashes of humor one may find in that powerful play should be labeled with the epithet "sardonic." Not a high rank in the scale of humorous effects must surely be claimed for this bit of dialogue; but would it not be unfair to exclude it altogether?

Vendice: Shall we kill him now he's drunk?
Lussurioso: Ay, best of all.
Vendice: Why, then he will never live to be sober.
Lussurioso: No matter, let him reel to hell.
Vendice: But being so full of liquor, I fear he will put out all the fire.

VI. Marston

Marston's temper is different from that of Webster; it is none the less pitched in a not very distant key, and its relation to humor can be described in somewhat similar words. Here again the prevailing mood has but slight affinity with the genial effusion of gentle banter; but it is naturally akin to a strong, concentrated, bitter sense of ironical contrasts. The concentration and the bitterness sharpen the expression of that sense by adding to it a realization of its probable or certain futility. To a sophisticated mind well aware of the obstinacy of the world, to throw out more than hints in the field of satire is a proof of naïveté; moral judgments, so trite and so perfunctory, should at least be refreshed by being made indirect and implicit. Thus the clipped, elliptic manner of understatements or incomplete statements, is rooted in the pessimism itself. From no other root springs the approximation to humor which crops up here and there in the works of a playwright whose urge to write has so little to do with the joy of creation. Marston's violence, his forcible denunciation of Machiavellian treachery and of lust are an index to the uneasy state of his divided soul, clearly aware of the destructiveness of evil and no less conscious of its presence in its own instincts. What a sincere, though veiled, self-confession his "Malheureux" is!

That is the deeper impulse. But Marston can live and think, at times, luckily, on a more superficial plane; then it is that his mood relaxes enough to let comedy have its chance, while the concentration is still there and stamps the expression with something of the reserve of humor. The verve that develops in that way will invent for itself characters of some substance who like Shakespeare's half-dunces are the butts of our amusement and yet tip us the wink at the same time. *The Dutch Courtesan* shows us several of those humorous figures;

and as good an instance as any is Mrs. Faugh, the procuress. "I must confess, we all eat of the forbidden fruit, and for mine own part, though I am one of the family of love, and, as they say, a bawd that covers the multitude of sins, yet I trust I am none of the wicked that eat fish o' Fridays" (I, ii). The irrepressible Cockledemoy plays his pranks to some purpose as well, although his pleasant invention is none of the most subtle; and of special interest to us is the passage in which the chance association of two words seems to point to a half-conscious growth gradually bringing the ideas together: "I have an odd jest to trim Master Mulligrub, for a wager; a jest, boy; a humour" (II, ii). In Ben Jonson's use indeed, a "humour" has the quality of making us laugh; but the jest is only in us.

To that vein in Marston's work must be referred the liveliness of *Eastward Ho,* the play to which he contributed with Chapman and Jonson; still, since we have given Chapman the credit for the best humor in it, we cannot claim it for Marston. Earlier than the *Dutch Courtesan* by one year, *The Malcontent* remains the chief prop of Marston's reputation as a dramatist. The Induction by Webster is only a fair example of the latter's cynical wit. The idea of the "malcontent" is not in itself conducive to comedy; there lives in it the soul of that serious, almost tragic rebellion against the ways of the world, which found so many successive expressions through the seventeenth century and after. No doubt, like Shakespeare's Jaques, Malevole is a "humor" in the Elizabethan sense, but Marston's inner preference has managed to tone down this aspect of his character, the emphasis being decidedly laid upon the serious side. Malevole's ranting (for instance in IV, i) is only mildly funny. We can hardly be much tempted to laugh at a man whose main failing is one with which we are almost all at least secretly familiar, and over which romantic literature for a century and a half has been casting a pathetic glamor. "The elements struggle within him; his own soul is at variance within herself," Pietro says; and this does not strike us as ridiculous; to many, as to Pietro himself, it is rather appealing. We have thus to fall back, for the humor of the play, on the pretty frequent flashes that are struck out in passing from the externals of the characters and the plots. Passarello, the jester, is not a very convincing imitation of Shakespeare's fools; but in the quaint grumbling of Bilioso, in Maquerelle's cynical wit, in such momentary displays as the image of the well and the two buckets (III, iii), or the dialogue of Pietro and the Page (III, iv) a fancy is at work that takes a somewhat grim pleasure in playing off the little ironies of life one against the other. That is about the utmost one can say of Marston's humor; it is certainly not missing, but no plentifully rising fountainhead.

VII. Beaumont and Fletcher

Although the personalities of the two writers are very different, and in some ways strongly contrasted, their respective shares in their joint works are not distinguishable with such safety that it may be possible to examine them separately. Still, the idea of their individual tempers is to be kept in the foreground through a study of their humor.

That Beaumont's mind is the more vigorous, self-possessed, and so to say virile of the two is generally acknowledged. There was that in his reflective turn which would agree better with the reserve and the indirectness of humorous presentment. The plays or rather scenes upon which his personal manner is most certainly stamped, as the greater part of *Philaster*, show a tenor of sustained force and beauty which have often been compared to Shakespeare's touch. A Shakespearean note indeed is to be heard as well in his humor. Few of the Renaissance writers have possessed—though, no doubt, with only a glimmering of intellectual consciousness—the creative instinct of humor so unequivocally, and put it to practice so unerringly, as Beaumont did.

A few examples may be adduced. The short passage of words in which Pharamond, Prince of Spain, pays his cynical addresses to the Lady Galatea and catches a Tartar (*Philaster*, II, ii) compresses a world of meaning into most courtly language; the ease, the unruffled surface of the speech, covering the brutality and the ironical scorn, agree beautifully with the implicitness and the understatements of humor. Dion's quiet, pregnant replies to the angry expostulations of the king (*ibid.*, IV, ii) are no less valid a case in point. The sketch of a "country fellow" (IV, iii), flavored with the essence of rusticity and slyness, is worthy of Shakespeare. The episode of the City rising and of the valiant deeds of the shopkeepers (V, iv) is already steeped in that spirit of not unkind parody, which was a very few years afterwards to permeate the central theme of the *Knight of the Burning Pestle.* The latter play owes it special significance to the undoubted fact that the impact of *Don Quixote* (1605), already felt in England, though the translation was to come out only in 1612, reverberates here not only in the subject itself but in the tone and manner of the comedy. The posthumous prologue to the 1635 edition, whoever wrote it, lays stress unerringly on the mixture of sense and wit, amusement and seriousness which gives the humor of the play its gentleness, as it inspired the grave reflective banter of Cervantes's novel: "Our intent was at this time to move inward delight, not outward lightness; and to breed (if it might be) soft smiling, not loud laughing; knowing it, to the wise, to be a great pleasure to hear counsel mixed with wit, as to the foolish, to have sport mingled with rudeness." But too much should not be made of that historical link between Spain and England, in the development of modern humor: to all practical purposes, the English humorists had not been in need of the lesson of Cervantes; they may have been indebted to him for a stimulus, but certainly not for a revelation. Of at least equal importance is a purely national reaction, that of an increasingly sobered and disillusioned age against the glow of the Elizabethan heyday, of common sense against the ranting of Kyd and Marlowe, and of the courtiers' wit against such glorifying of the middle classes as Heywood's *Four Prentices of London.*

The very idea of clothing the enthusiasm of knightly prowess in the homely garb of the grocer's trade is of course a rich source of humorous fun; it results in a number of comic contrasts which are made plain enough, but not heavily or cruelly underlined, as the satire remains light and breathes a spirit of amused sympathy. The method of presentment thus keeps true to an essential discretion, within the bounds of restraint—and of humor. Some scenes not only recall Dekker but point to the vein which Steele was to make particularly his own a century later. While the tone is undoubtedly aristocratic, we have none here of the savageness with which Restoration comedy was to satirize the naïve self-importance of the citizens. When all is said, this is, in spite of some weakness and cheap reiteration, one of the most thoroughly humorous plays in the period; chapter and verse for the assertion would be very easily given; and if one example must be selected, it may as well be the second scene of the last act, where Ralph parades his company of soldiers, and Hammerton and Greengoose pass muster.

Various opinions will be held of Fletcher's humor, according as one gives this word a more ample or a narrow range of meaning. In the strictest sense, he has less of the gift than Beaumont; his temper was more effusive and light; concentration and self-repression are not his forte.[2] But if the notion of humor is at all relaxed—and no doubt it can be to some extent without destroying the principle of its identity—a humorous flavor is to be enjoyed very frequently indeed in the long series of Fletcher's comedies. He had a ready fund of sprightliness and wit, a faculty of comic invention, a swift, supple style, and handled dialogue cleverly. While he causes his reader no mental strain and writes fluent prose or verse, he can command the sly indirectness, the implications that make one pause and relish the hint better the second time.

The range of his racy episodes is very wide. Like Shakespeare in *Love's Labour's Lost*, he went to France more than once to have the benefit of a liveliness of temper and speech that suited his own manner. Mirabel, in *The Wild Goose Chase*, is a "humor" who realizes the fact just enough to let us guess that he turns it to good account; we may grant him the name of humorist. A scene quite typical of Fletcher's light humor, from the same play, is that in which the two "airy" girls, Rosalura and Lillia Blanca, take to task their tutor, Lugier, because he has not taught them the proper way to allure husbands (III, i). Verve is the word here, but a

[2] Dryden, who grants Fletcher much wit, denies that he had humor in the Jonsonian sense of the word, as we gather from the contrast in which his work is set with that of Jonson (Preface to "An Evening's Love," *Essays*, ed. W. P. Ker, Oxford, 1900, Vol. I).

verve that lets itself go with wariness. The next conversation between the girls and Mirabel reminds a French reader of the bouts between Mascarille and Molière's "Précieuses"—a later work of course; and Belleur's desperate panic at the onslaughts of marriageable ladies (V, ii) has the humor of overstatement. Husbands are finally caught, and a Shakespearean grace, with a vein of looseness in talk that the Forest of Arden never knew, presides over the happy winding up. La-Writ, in the *Little French Lawyer*, keeps on the mystifying verge between sheer crankiness and humor; humor predominates at first, as in the excellent dueling scenes (III, i and ii), but the play soon degenerates, and in the last (Massinger's?) acts his crestfallen part is quite humorless. One more instance, from the *Spanish Curate*, may not be amiss: Diego, the sexton, complains to Lopez, the curate, of the stubborn health of the parishioners:

> They are so hard-hearted here too,
> They will not die; there's nothing got by burials. . . .

And the gay play goes merrily along, giving us a good deal of humor, but—if the truth must be told—not of the highest brand certainly.

To some extent *The Humorous Lieutenant* deserves our special attention through its title. The adjective here is used of a character that amuses us because of its paradoxical originality, but at the same time is shrewd enough to be more or less conscious of it; the Elizabethan sense of "humor" and the modern one seem to be caught in the transitional stage that was leading from one to the other. Such lines as the following point to a sly perception of contrasts, and to the instinctive art of setting them off by means of objective expression:

> Such frisking, and such flaunting with their feathers,
> And such careering with their mistress' favours!
> And here must he be pricking out for honour,
> And there got he a knock, and down goes pil-garlick,
> Commends his soul to his she-saint, and *exit*.
> Another spurs in there, cries, "Make room, villains!
> I am a lord!" scarce spoken, but, with reverence,
> A rascal takes him o'er the face, and fells him:
> There lies the lord, the Lord be with him! (II, ii)

But here once more, our hopes are toned down as the play proceeds. The Lieutenant, a grandson of Falstaff, with some of the humor of Sancho Panza in his constitution, falls far below that illustrious line of descent and reverts to the Jonsonian type; the last episodes show him in the light of a half-crazy fellow, a prey to mechanical impulses.

In *Rule a Wife and Have a Wife,* the fat and bragging usurer Cacafogo, who is made an ass of by the Lady Margarita, bears only a distant relation to Falstaff and is anyhow quite destitute of humor. But the servant Leon, who answers Juan de Castro's questioning with a mixture of silliness and slyness (I, v), is one more of those "half-humorists" we have tried to describe. And Juan puts it in a very significant way:

> This fellow has some doubts in's talk, that strike me;
> He cannot be all fool.

VIII. Thomas Heywood

There is nothing sardonic about Heywood. He stands with Dekker among the representatives of those deep-laid, permanent traits and feelings through which the "merry England" of Elizabeth's time links up with the world of Steele in the reign of Ann, and that of Dickens in Victoria's. Heywood's point of view is somewhat different from Dekker's; he is rather a spokesman of the higher middle class, with no narrow partisanship, a breadth of sympathy, and a genuine sense of the claims of the people. None of the contemporary dramatists was more thoroughly English or more national. That is why we are not surprised, after all, to find that such a serious, earnest, moralizing writer has a vein of humor in his constitution. His temper would not seem to mark him out for the gift of comic invention; but he has the tricks of the playwright at his fingers' ends—with over two hundred plays to his credit, he could hardly be short of practice—and knows how to bring in the bit of fun, the joke, or the innuendo that will please the groundlings. For the loose hint he shows a partiality that might strike us as undignified, did we not know how far the taste of the time demanded that a moralist should be no precisian, and a deeply religious dramatist no Puritan. What matters more is that he did possess the saving grace of humor and gave it vent in his own way. Could anything else be expected of a writer who made it a labor of love to turn Lucian's *Dialogues* into English verse? This is one more of those contacts, through which the influence of Lucian appears as a thread of importance in the weaving of the web and woof of modern English humor.

The pathos and the sustained earnestness of *A Woman Killed with Kindness* preclude the very possibility of comic relief, although the servant, Nicholas, makes some weak attempts to raise a laugh or a smile; the greatness of that truly Richardsonian play—with a more humane, a less tense and fanatical spirit than that of Richardson—is not in need of such relaxation. *The English Traveller*, with a fine and truly moving close, takes us down to the more mixed tone of Heywood's normal manner. Here we have a clown: Roger, servant to Old Wincott, who tries to draw people out in the style of Touchstone or Feste; and the attempt is a distinct failure; it was ill-advised, on the part of Heywood, to take a leaf out of Shakespeare's book. More successful is Clem the Vintner (*The Fair Maid of the West*), who has a fund of racy talk and homely impudence, and does enliven not a few episodes of that romantic play. Indeed Heywood's real vein of humor is one which contributes to make him so typical an augury of the future. He is not averse to rollicking farce, and some of his scenes are among the broadest in the comedy of the time; but he can command as well laughter of a somewhat more refined kind; and this is a diffused gaiety, a light-heartedness which rings with a pleasant sound, a genuine and unaffected geniality. In that not unkind amusement at the little oddities of life, good humor is constantly shading off into gentle humor. The tone and the manner are unmistakable: we have here one of the first emergences of a vein that was to appear again and again, all through the following centuries, from Richard Steele to our days.

The best examples of that cheerfulness which does not entirely let itself go, but keeps itself in hand and has a background of intention and reflection, would not be found in that broad farce, *The Wise Woman of Hogsdon,* though the realism of the tavern scene (I, i) is fresh, lively, and truly amusing; or even in *The Rape of Lucrece,* although the jesting, singing, and irrepressible Valerius is only the center of a Lucian-like spirit of merriment that suffuses the whole play and makes it rather like a schoolboys' parody of the classics—a theme, again, that was to know a brilliant fortune in the early eighteenth century, testifying both to the popularity of heroic figures and to the disrespectful familiarity bred of long acquaintance; but it would be found in that charming play, *The Fair Maid of the West,* where Heywood stands as a forerunner of many aspects of English middle class literature. It embodies some of the obstinate preferences of the average reader, in its sentiment, its noble picture of faithful love, the image it draws of the adventures and the exploits of the sea; more particularly, from our point of view, the last two acts give us a kind of pantomime or fairy tale, where the wonders and strange ways of exotic lands serve as a frame for the happy conclusion of a touching tale, while the author allows us to guess that he takes nothing quite seriously, and the puppets he shows us are at once edifying, amusing, and unreal. That obvious complicity between the writer and the public, in a cooperation of make-believe and delighted tolerance, is just one of the characteristics of humor on the stage.

IX. Massinger

Conflicting views have been held, by equally competent critics, as to the presence or absence of humor in Massinger's plays. The difference of opinion may be partly accounted for by the shifting nature of the very notion of humor; but there are other causes to it, rooted in the mind and temper of the playwright himself. It is a fact, on the one hand, that Massinger was not endowed by nature with a gift of comedy. He is a serious, staid, not unduly optimistic observer of life, and the latent or open presence of a moral or religious purpose is felt throughout his work. The lasting impression a reader derives from his personality is made up before all of the intense and moving pathos which raises several parts of his *Maid of Honour* to the high nobleness of Corneille. At the same time, he knew that comic relief was desirable, and attempted to create it. The attempt is most often disappointing; and even when it may be said to meet with a measure of success, what we have is a plain, unvarnished bid for drollery that belongs to the order of farce or comedy of the direct type. Justice Greedy, with his voracious, impatient appetite, in that overpraised play, *A New Way to Pay Old Debts,* is a case in point; as is that egregious oaf, Sylli *(The Maid of Honour),* whom one may find annoying, but certainly not amusing. Calandrino and Petzonella *(The Great Duke of Florence)* may do their best—or worst—to make us laugh: if the ghost of a smile plays on our lips, it will be with a distinct sense that we must be tolerant to an author who has given us charming scenes. Indeed the words which Massinger puts in Calandrino's mouth sound very much like an open confession of failure:

> Why the whole race
> Of such as can act naturally fools' parts
> Are quite worn out, and they that do survive
> Do only zany us. . . . (V, iii)

Still, the rule holds good, even in Massinger's case, that none of the successful dramatists of the age was entirely destitute of humor. And once more, grace is granted to a writer when he is not painfully, of set purpose, and against the grain, asking for it. The slight but genuine flavor that we taste in not a few scenes of Massinger's work is a spontaneous effluence of his shrewd knowledge of life; not unaware of itself, indeed, as there cannot be any quite unconscious humor; but blossoming out of a natural wistfulness, lightly tinged with sad irony. This manner one finds, for instance, in *The Maid of Honour,* and more particularly the third act; in *The City Madam,* with the pranks of Lady Frugal's daughters (II, ii); the scenes in Secret's house (III); the display of Luke's fortune and greatness (IV, i), or his retrospective survey of the Frugal family's rise to wealth (IV, iv). A realistic intent is the soul of those episodes, and so the humor which enlivens them is not merry;

but there Massinger's seriousness is instinct with that tickled sense of the relativity of things which can aptly soften the moralist's stern purpose.

X. Ford

No one will expect to find much humor in the plays of John Ford. Still, the ingredient is not quite missing from the strong, tense stuff of his tragedies. The main feature of his manner is concentration; his thoughtful, stubborn analysis of character reveals a self-possessed, attentive, and brooding mind; and so his temper might have fitted him to be at least a saturnine humorist. But humor demands a realization, a possession of the world which, even though it be joyless, still should take in the form and color of things; whilst Ford's glance is focused passionately, almost bitterly, on the inner man. As his imagination is not nourished by the diversity of creatures, it does not properly feed the faculty of comic invention. The vein of humor in him is sterilized by a stiffness of outlook which impoverishes his verve; his reflection and reserve are deprived of their natural outcome.

Like Massinger, he went out of his way to secure some sort of comic relief, with equally poor results. Borgetto, the "dolt" *('Tis Pity)*, and all that appertains to him, are sadly deficient in the lifelikeness and incomparable flavor of a Slender. Farce of a mediocre kind has its share of *Perkin Warbeck*. The Prologue to *The Broken Heart* warns us not to expect "apish laughter," or "some lame jeer at place or person"; and thus all endeavor to bring in comic themes is in principle given up; but the best humorists have thriven on a renunciation of explicit fun, and Ford's serious, tragic purpose did not necessarily rule humor out. In fact, he did not abstain, in that very play, from appealing to a sense of subdued amusement: the end of the second scene of Act I, with the banter exchanged between the two maids of honor and the courtiers turned soldiers, might be with only a little indulgence dignified by the name of humor; as may be, with more readiness on our part, the fragment of the first scene of Act II, where Grausis, Penthea's "overseer," airs her whims and vagaries, somewhat reminiscent of Juliet's nurse. In the same way, *'Tis Pity* has at least a faintly humorous passage, the dialogue between Putana and Annabella (I, ii), which obviously takes a hint from Shakespeare's *Troilus and Cressida*, but after all turns it to acceptable use. In those few gleams of a light that is generally deficient, what saves the attempt from total failure is a modicum of realistic zest and genuine observation which vitalizes the irony of a melancholy mind.

XI. Shirley

The talent of Shirley, facile, elegant, and cynical, is under no compression or repression of any sort. The comic elements spread through his plays are mostly quite explicit, and even farcical; but that obvious fact does not settle the question of his humor. Over and above his open bids for laughter, he has a true vein of sprightliness, a paradoxical invention, a sense of absurdity, quaintness, and contrast, and is at times well inspired enough to give vent to those promptings with the salutary virtue of discretion. The result is a number of passages in which the implicitness and the reserve of the fun create a distinctly humorous flavor. The impression is sufficiently plain for Gosse to have used the phrase "conscious humor" of an episode in *The Grateful Servant*;[3] a judgment with which we shall easily agree, with this qualification only, that humor, as a literary effect, is always "conscious." Other examples would easily be found in *The Witty Fair One*, with the scene between Sir Nicholas Treedle and his tutor (II, i); or, again, that between Penelope and Fowler, who coolly moralizes upon his supposed decease, with a rather serious background to the irony (V, iii). The animated and picturesque episodes in the Park (*Hyde Park*, especially IV, i), with the fresh, exciting novelty of the various doings there, are told and shown in a spirit of sober amusement, tempered with the unperturbed mood of an objective chronicler.

But it is in *The Lady of Pleasure* that the best tenor of subdued pleasantry is displayed, with the light, and not unkind, satire of all the affectations imported from France; several scenes strike the reader as an early sketch of Molière's

[3] Edmund Gosse, ed., *The Works of James Shirley*, Mermaid Series (London, 1888), p. vii.

Précieuses Ridicules, with something of the quiet mastery of the ridiculous which sets the stamp of the best humor on so much of the French playwright's work. On the contrary, *The Humorous Courtier* is a sad anticlimax from any hopes its title might awake. It is difficult to fancy a more humorless character than that of Oncolo, the "woman hater." Although the play is probably late enough,[4] the words *humor* and *humorist* are used throughout in a way that betokens not the slightest change of meaning from the time of Jonson.

XII. Conclusion

It seems possible to draw one guarded conclusion from the preceding survey.

No wonder must be felt at the fact that all those playwrights should have more or less felt the instinctive need of easing off the tension of tragedy with the admixture of comic relief; the national preference for mixed drama had by that time settled into a well-established tradition. But what is more remarkable is that the comic elements themselves, whether in tragedy or in comedy, should practically always reveal the presence, over and above explicit farce, of the indirect, subdued treatment of contrasts, to which the name of humor must be properly restricted.

Several among those writers would not strike us, from the general habit of their personalities, as likely humorists. It does not seem obvious or probable that they would, of themselves, have developed a sense of the value of the method, or anyhow, tried their hands at it. In more than one case, the presence of self-possessed, restrained pleasantry in their works comes as a surprise.

It does not much signify that such a manner of pleasantry should not be here the outcome of a method, but of an instinct. Instinct is normally contagious, but for the contagion to spread, it must first have appeared spontaneously in some mind or minds; and the existing conditions of the others have to be favorable. So we are brought back to the essential point: the general tone of the English temper, and the bent of the national character, at that time, did favor the diffusion of the

[4] But no later than 1640, when it was printed.

instinctive manner of humor. The idiosyncrasies of the English people, which had just finally settled into their modern shape, made the growth of a humorous attitude, as a typical feature, a possible, one should even say, a probable, development in the individual.

Many historical and more or less external influences, of course, can be called in to account for the efficacy of an inner inducement that may have contributed to the trend. The prestige of some types at least of classical comedy, of Terence especially, may have had to be referred to again and again in the previous chapters of this inquiry. And within the limits of English literature itself, we have substantial evidence of the spell that their predecessors, especially Shakespeare, had cast upon the writers of the new generation.

But it seems possible to say that this very action of the home models should not be exclusively, or mainly, regarded as a literary matter. What is in question is deeper than that. All through that age—the later Renaissance—the mental point of view of humor was consolidating, so to say, as part of the normal equipment of English dramatists. A habit, a tone were being thus created, that anticipated a clear realization of the humorous method. Whilst the evolution of the word was still in its early stages, the inclination to the manner was striking roots that tended to make it a widespread, almost a general, if not an obligatory, possession of most writers; especially of those who, dealing with life, would be called upon to make man's reaction to the variegated scene of living their chief artistic material.

That a Chapman, a Webster, a Thomas Heywood, a Ford should in the most precise meaning of the word have their flashes of humor is a symptom of the hold which the mental habits connected with that intellectual attitude were gaining at that time upon the average English temper.[5] That hold was not to relax, through the changing fortunes of literary periods, down to our day. It was growing into a permanent trait of the national mind.

[5] Less significant, though not entirely negligible, is the fact that the plays of the witty poet, Thomas Randolph (especially *Aristippus*) turn realism to humorous purposes through a trick of forceful exaggeration not unlike Jonson's.

CHAPTER XIV

POETRY AND THE CONCEIT

I. A Survey

IT IS ONLY in a restricted field of poetry that one can reasonably look for humor. The lyrical inspiration, with its ardor and glowing single-mindedness, is essentially alien to the duality of intent which is a necessary feature of the humorist. Now the spirit of the Renaissance had wrought up the poetic mind to a higher pitch, and lyricism then finally grew to be the very heart and staple of singing. It is thus to be expected that only in the nonlyrical provinces of poetry, such as satire or verse parody, can humor normally have a share.

Drama, including the parts of comedy written in verse, has already been examined.

The satirical mood in Hall and Donne, and in Ben Jonson's poems, will yield us a plentiful store of humorous material. Parody will supply its modicum, with Drayton. The outstanding poet of the age, Spenser, should not be left out of set purpose, as he has gleams of satire and even of parody. In the next generation, and stopping short of Marvell and Butler, Herrick's jollity, the piquancy and wit of Suckling, the epigrammatic force of Cleveland are often so close to humor that a dividing line can hardly be drawn. As Donne's and Cleveland's names plainly show, the "metaphysicals" themselves are not to be excluded. Germane to humor, at times, is that straining of the power of invention after farfetched effects, which in the absence of a better name, is covered by the word "conceit."[1]

So long as the poet who is addicted to that manner takes him-

[1] The conceit is studied here exclusively in its aesthetic connection with humor. Such humorless poets as the religious metaphysicals—Herbert, Lord Herbert of Cherbury, Vaughan, Crashaw, Traherne—who abound in conceits, do not come within our field. The devout seriousness of their purpose precludes the possibility of a half-conscious element of intentional grotesqueness in their manner.

self quite seriously, he keeps on a plane of thinking and writing that is just the opposite of humor. Indeed one may point out that often enough a writer of that class gives us ample ground to conclude that when he indites, the glory of the fun of things is to him extinct. But it is no unfounded guess that the human mind being after all generally endowed with a measure of sanity, the conceits of late Renaissance poetry are not always free from an admixture of a subdued perception of their own queerness. It is of course a difficult matter to sift out such cases from the common run of the feats of mental ingenuity that want to be brilliant and nothing else; and the inference will rarely be quite safe. But taking the whole mass of Elizabethan and Jacobean poetry at a glance, we may affirm that in not a few pieces the maker of conceits has a divided mind, one side of which is delighted with the fertility of his wit, while the other is more or less dimly aware of the grotesqueness of his achievement. One can hardly doubt that this obscure intimation is at times clearer, so that the poet does realize the presence in his work of a virtually comic element. On some occasions it can even be guessed that this second way of enjoying his own cleverness grows predominant, and that to all practical purposes he writes so to say with his tongue in his cheek. The sum and body of those instances in the literature of the time would testify to the presence, in an indefinite number of cases, of a frame of mind which is of pregnant interest to our inquiry: a duality of purpose, accompanied with some perception of the laughable, and cloaked by the uniform appearance of seriousness—that is, exactly the characteristics of humor. Whether that incipient sense remains only virtual, or actualizes itself fully in the writer's, not to speak of the reader's, consciousness, is not quite material to our research. Taking things in the lump, some of the ingenuity displayed in the elaboration of conceits is suffused with a mixed mood that is not averse, as it might well seem at first sight, to the growth of humor, but rather conducive to it; and the great humorists of the classical age may have owed more than one would surmise to the ingenuity and mental alertness of the metaphysical school.[2]

[2] We find a distinct confirmation of this view in R. L. Sharp's study, *From Donne to Dryden, The Revolt Against Metaphysical Poetry* (Chapel Hill, N. C.,

II. Spenser

It would obviously be a paradox to find a humorist in Spenser. The energy of the spiritual zeal with which he raised his poetic monument in homage to exalted values, the good and chiefly the beautiful, shows him a fervent votary of single-mindedness; in the disturbing conflicts and contrasts of things he would not find his main theme, or a sufficiently inspiring motive. Still, too much has perhaps been said, or implied, about his imperviousness to humor. The body of his work offers evidence that of those contrasts he was quite plainly aware; that he could, from a realization of them, derive the many-sided amusement that sets the seal of fulness on a man's view of life; that he could as well, in passing, convey to the reader that slight titillation of the sense of fun, and even make it one of his conscious ends. The fact that he would have nothing to do with some prominent aspects of Ariosto's spirit in the conception and treatment of the *Faerie Queene* sets his greatest achievement in a key alien to humor; and we should leave it at that, whatever flickers of irony one may detect in more than one episode. But *The Shepheardes Calender*, *Muiopotmos*, and *Mother Hubbard's Tale* are definitely to us cases in point. Our excuse for dwelling at some length on mere shades is that not only does the argument tend to redeem a great poet from the charge of a somewhat stiff concentration on dogmatic purposes; but at the same time, by bringing him, in spite of his strongly ethical bent, within the range of a common humanity and of the national character, which was then solidifying, it would support the general impression that a sense of humor was fast becoming a normal, almost an indispensable trait of the typical Englishman.

A slightly humorous flavor is diffused through the *Shepheardes Calender*. It is not in vain that the memory of Chaucer is repeatedly called up in the eclogues; the spiritual presence of "Tityrus," whose "mery tales" would soothe the pains of lovelorn shepherds, or help them to while away the

1940): "As the century wore on, their [the metaphysicals'] excesses became more extravagant, conspicuous, and grotesque" (p. 41); and "In their use of perverse diction the metaphysicals were, doubtless, often playful . . ." (p. 46).

long hours afield, strikes a definite keynote; and "E. K." underlines the hint quite plainly: "That by Tityrus is meant Chaucer, hath bene already sufficiently sayde, and by thys more playne appeareth, that he sayth, he tolde merye tales. Such as be hys Canterburie Tales" (*June*, 81-88, and note). And yet the subjects of all the eclogues are either serious or of an elegiac order. But even the sad themes are treated in a light, gracefully artistic manner, which blunts the edge of grief and wraps seriousness in the pleasant veils of fancy. This is not the dull, flat convention of so many pastorals; but a delicately unreal atmosphere, in which the hardships of a shepherd's life are toned down by gentle idealization. There arises from the first a sort of tacit understanding between the poet and the reader; and the latter, if he is to taste the pleasure that is meant for him, is warned by subtle hints that he must not take anything too seriously. The plane on which those pieces develop is one of discreet fiction. Now an essential aspect of the make-believe is that contrasts, which are obvious all through, should be intuitively felt but not expressed. There is a contrast for instance between the naïveté of the shepherds—do they not think that "the hills bene nigher heuen," and does not "E.K." call our attention to it: "Note the shepheards simplenesse" (*July*, 89) —and on the other hand, the rustic shrewdness that prompts and points, among other bouts of bantering, that of Cuddie and Thenot *(February)*. There is a contrast as well between the artlessness of the life depicted and the exquisite artistry of those homely characters in their words and their improvised rhymes, between the archaism of the language and the realistic background of contemporary facts. The sense of that manifold diversity, glossed over by the smooth and careful tenor of the style, keeps all along stirring within our consciousness; it is the source of a rich enjoyment in which a vein of quiet amusement is to be traced; and the subtle, subdued comedy that mixes with the poetry, with the delightful scenery of the moods of the year, has all the characteristics of humor.

The vein of indirect, implicit pleasantry appears in a few passages more plainly. While the portraits of the individual shepherds are mere sketches, a feature is here and there deftly characterized. Over against pining, woebegone Perigot, roguish Willye, in *August*, is a budding humorist. Too much, perhaps, should not be made of his sly remark: "Never knewe I lovers sheepe in good plight" (20); but his "undersong" to Perigot's plaint (53-124) is distinctly a series of anticlimaxes; the passage as a whole is instinct with unmistakable humor. Contrast here again is the key word; the sentimental and the cynical views of life are set side by side in an antithesis to which the tripping gait of the couplet brings a skeptical overtone; and each tearful line of the melancholy shepherd meets with the quick, pat rejoinder of his jolly friend, more vivacious and pointed for its shorter measure, and for the ironical "hey ho" which often starts it. The intention comes to a head at the end:

> *Per.* And you, that sawe it, simple shepe,
> *Wil.* hey ho the fayre flocke,
> *Per.* For priefe thereof, my death shall weepe,
> *Wil.* and mone *with many a mocke* (117-120; italics ours).

That *Muiopotmos* is a burlesque—or rather, more properly, a mock-heroic poem—will be generally conceded. But the particular province of the comic to which it is assigned hardly matters. What counts is the method used in order to create the impression of comedy which permeates the graceful allegory. That method is finely discreet and reserved; all the effects are kept within the range of implicitness; and so it does not seem unfair to use the word "humor" in connection with it. A major contrast, a defiance of the natural proportion of things, obtains all through; the prestige of classical memories is cast upon a Lilliputian anecdote; a systematic overstatement magnifies the fluttering pleasures and the tragic death of a butterfly, finally caught in a spider's web, to the height of epic dignity. Mythological and learned comparisons are so to say the points of emergence of the trick, where one can most safely put one's finger upon it. The plate which shines upon poor Clarion's breast must be compared with the shield of Achilles; the "hairy hide" he throws about his shoulders is like the Naemean Lion's skin. His fate is hailed by an outburst of lamentation which might befit the catastrophe of a great historical tragedy:

> Who now shall give unto my heavie eyes
> A well of teares, that all may overflow?
> Or where shall I finde lamentable cryes,
> And mournfull tunes enough my griefe to show?
> Helpe thou Tragick Muse. . . . (409-413)

Whether or not the poem should be interpreted as a disguised attack against Burghley is an irrelevant issue here. Ernest de Selincourt, while denying the inference, nonetheless calls *Muiopotmos* a "delicious jeu d'esprit."[3] The phrase is certainly apt; but the play of fancy which rouses the reader's delight, besides being witty, has humor.

Mother Hubbard's Tale is an apologue in the manner of Chaucer. The political background of the poem, and the extent to which Burghley is aimed at, need not detain us. Moreover, the humor is so patent that a long argument would be superfluous. To the predominant spirit of Chaucer, there is added a stimulus from the "Renard" cycle through Caxton's translation. The pleasantry at times has the lambent quality of Chaucer's bland equanimity. The scale of moral values is quietly upset or ignored, and the most dignified light, for instance, thrown over the ancient profession of begging. The ironical intent grows more plain, and the hints more scathing, when Anjou, the Ape, is personally concerned:

> Be you the Souldier, for you likest are
> For manly semblance, and small skill in warre. (199-200)

But Spenser's moralizing bent and his instinctive prudence almost at once tone down the irony:

> Shame light on him, that through so false illusion
> Doth turne the name of Souldiers to abusion, . . . (219-20)

We thus realize how exaggerated it would be to mention Spenser's humor in the same breath with Chaucer's. The author of the *Faerie Queene* is very far from the almost complete detachment which gives Chaucer such a rare position

[3] Ernest de Selincourt, ed., Introduction to Spenser's *Poetical Works*.

of spiritual independence in the history of English literature. The humorous passages in *Mother Hubbard's Tale* are interrupted by stretches of direct, purposive narrative; the satirical aim is continuous, the slyness only intermittent. So strong is the predominance of the mood of satire that some of the flashes aimed at the clergy and the court are almost bitter enough to destroy the pretense of humorous fiction. Altogether, the poet labors under an indignation and a resentment which do not leave humor its full chance. Among other breaks, the long piece in which the ideal of an honest Courtier is painted (717-792) sets the tone in a key of downright teaching. Still, when all deductions are made, the poem definitely settles the question of Spenser's ability to turn humorist at will. The faculty was not lacking in him; but he was more gifted and more sincerely eager in very different strains. The significant fact remains that the saving grace has paid to him more than one visit.

III. Donne

On account of the early date of Donne's satires he should come next in the chronological order.

A study of Donne reveals at once that his relation to humor is positive and important. The attitude is deeply rooted in his mental and moral temper. It stands with him both as an effect and a cause of the search for intensity which is his dominant characteristic. Humor here is by no means a relaxation, as it may be said to be in the practice of some writers; and it has even less to do with the genial sympathy which some critics will regard as one of its constant elements.

Although Donne's humor is most often satirical and indeed sardonic, his *Satires* are not its main repository. Their usual method is one of scornful and violent denunciation, with preposterous overstatements. There is plainly a central calm at the core of the anger, and the obvious exaggeration is the source of an implicit grotesqueness. One may speak here of the writer's tongue being in his cheek: such execrations, so much out of scale with their object, are an outlet for a picturesque, high-flavored verve, which enjoys its own display; and moral indignation is a very secondary element in the rich mixture of wit and fancy. The "fondling motley humorist" of Satire I, who would have been called a fop one century later, and to us would be a snob, is of course entirely innocent of any humorous intent; but the writer's mood, while describing his antics, approaches very nearly what we now call humor. There is none of the apparent objectivity which is the ordinary trick of the manner; but there is another and a roughly equivalent method in the transparent affectation of a serious realism. Meanwhile the quick turns, ready invective, and quaint comparisons of these poems stimulate our interest and keep it alive. At bottom, all this shows very little of a genuine attempt at castigating vices or drawing a lifelike picture of manners; the satirical theme is a pretext for an orgy of amusing conceits. The state of repression under which Donne writes, and which it serves his turn to pretend confessing, is sketched by the poet himself in the first lines of Satire III:

> Kinde pitty chokes my spleene; brave scorn forbids
> Those teares to issue which swell my eye-lids;
> I must not laugh, nor weepe sinnes, and be wise,
> Can railing then cure these worne maladies?

With an emotional tone that can be different, but remains at times similar, the *Elegies* use very much the same tactics. Love is not a privileged theme; all subjects are thrown together, and the satirical mood, at times, is predominant. Here the realism, genuine or affected, while still dwelling fondly on the variegated, absurd scene of Vanity Fair, more definitely enters the inner world of mind and soul. This moral realism is of unique originality. Its purpose might be described as a bitter, violent refusal to play up to our conventional, sentimental expectations, and conform to the orthodox view of love, of family feeling, social respect, etc. The values set implicitly above everything are those of sincerity and truth; and the outcome of the daring, pitiless search through the darkness within is a variety of Christian pessimism, working out to an implication of the only absolute, in faith and God. The humorous trick lies in the pretended unconsciousness of the shattering force, the destructive candor, the insolence, the impertinence of those expostulations, dissections, ironies, and apologues, in which a number of the various shades of love are cynically shown up—and where the cynicism sometimes, far from quenching the ardor of passion, sets its hidden but felt presence in stronger relief. Sheer indecency crops up often enough as one of the aspects of the desperation, the fierce desire for truth at any price, or as an opportunity for an untapped vein of audacious conceits.

The spirit of defiant, sardonic humor thinly diffused through those poems can at times be more palpably caught. Such is the unperturbed marshaling of evidence in proof of the great and solemn right of man's inconstancy; a survey of precedents, analogies, and testimonies that savors indeed of the scientist's objective enumeration—a very frequent way with the humorist (III, "Change"). Such is the impudent, witty, crude realism in the portraits of his mistress's family—from her father to the porter at the street door (IV, "The Perfume"), all leading up to that most unexpected, ridiculous catastrophe, the lover found out by her perfume. Through "The Bracelet" (XI), the fun lies in the minuteness of the data which set that trivial anecdote of lost and found articles in the light of an important historical event, a light still enhanced by the dignity of verse. The fresh, surprising, picturesque imagination which gives itself vent through that, and almost all the other "Elegies," creates an element of piquancy, quaintness, and drollery that the poet's unruffled manner keeps within the key of perfect seriousness. Such brilliancy of humorous illustration will be equaled only by Sterne or Lamb, in their verbal feats as full-grown humorists.

The *Songs and Sonnets* bring their contribution as well; and here, even more markedly than in the *Satires* and *Elegies*, the humor that generally hovers in the background finds a center and a focus in the conceits.

Something has been said already about the possible connection between the conceits and humor. Those of Donne are in this respect among the most pregnant. A few examples may be adduced. The second stanza of "The Canonization" runs thus:

Alas, alas, who's injur'd by my love?
    What merchant ships have my sighs drown'd?
Who saies my teares have overflow'd his ground?
    When did my colds a forward spring remove?
        When did the heats which my veines fill
        Adde one more to the plaguie Bill?
Soldiers finde warres, and Lawyers finde out still
        Litigious men, which quarrels move,
        Though she and I do love.

The reader's mental energy is not all spent in admiring how ingenious, how new, how appropriate while absurd the comparisons are, and in sifting out the actual points of analogy or contact from among the discords and absurdities. There is a joy as well in the very preposterousness of the illustrations with which the poet has chosen to bear out his point of what one might call, referring to the etymological sense of the word, the innocence of his love. We watch Donne's antics breathlessly but with the pleasurable excitement which displays of dazzling cleverness and wit will raise. Nothing is surer than that the poet shares in those impressions and himself enjoys a fertility of fancy pushed to that height of audacious extravagance. At the same time, his amusement is severely repressed, hidden behind the grave countenance which his theme, the assumption of a passionate attachment, and the mask of a rational, logical argument are binding him to; and that seriousness of manner is a condition of our own enjoyment. Those are the very characteristics of a humor which is conscious in the poet's mind, and liberates itself in ours. Conceits developed to that pitch, of unlimited flights away from common sense, abound in Donne's poems.

Of course the element whose presence we are here singling out is not found really in an isolated state; it merges within a general suggestion. Extravagant comparisons are instinctively sought by the writer to serve other ends than that of implicit humor; they contribute as well to the central feeling of intensity which is, as we have already pointed out, Donne's main object; they add to the diffused atmosphere of passionate ardor, even in cynical mockery, and to the impression of a lyrical fervor which radiates out, in spite of all, from the tenor of those ironical and realistic effusions. Still, the very existence of a lyricism made up of such constituents is a paradox in itself, and tends to stamp the whole performance as more or less akin to a poetical mystification; so that the humorous flavor, after all, is essential in its composite aroma.

One variety of that species is what we might call the "conceit of impertinence"—the comic effect produced by breath-taking frankness and cynical candor in matters where reticence of thought and expression was expected as of right; the "conceit of indecency," we said above, being closely related to the kind. Well-known examples of impertinence are "Community" and "The Flea"; or "The Curse," with its final fling:

> For if it be a shee
> Nature beforehand hath out-cursed mee.

The common feature of all those effects is overstatement, a major trick of which understatement is only an inverted kind. The systematic exaggeration builds up a fictitious scale of values, which Donne consistently pretends to be the right, normal one; this superimposes seriousness on absurdity, and is the method of his humor.

IV. Joseph Hall

It is not necessary to dwell at any length on the *Virgidemiarum*. That it shows humor is generally acknowledged. The roots of the manner are plainly in Hall's temperament; the shrewd, pointed hints he is fond of throwing out, with a dense brevity of form that sharpens the shaft, would not have been handled repeatedly with such success unless the writer had a natural gift for epigrammatic expression. So we find here one more instance of that reserve and telling discretion in phrasing which, used in the field of pleasantry, is the mental background of humor. The fact, confirmed by cumulative evidence, that the number of the writers who show that instinctive bent, when dealing with the comic, is very notably on the increase about 1600, should support an inference as to the development of humor to the importance and prominence of a national trait, which it has been our purpose to follow.

At the same time Joseph Hall is very clearly a disciple of Juvenal, Persius, and Horace. His manner owes something to each of them, and the humorous element in his work should be distinctly classed under the label of "the humanist influence." Regular English satire of the traditional type in its incipient stage was largely shaped by the classics. So, to the terseness of his Latin masters Hall adds not a little of the purity of their diction. The "humor of conceits" is not to be found here, as the writer keeps away from any indulgence in quips and pranks of fancy. Very conspicuous, on the contrary, is realism as a means of humor, stressing aspects of life whose shocking injustice, rankness, or indecency opens an easy way for the exercise of the indifference and objectivity which is the affectation of the humorist. A concrete imagination combined with a pithy, concise wording very frequently produces a humorous flavor, which now and then concentrates in vigorous, almost cynical flings. Many examples could be given; the following, a well-known text, is the Sixth Satire of Book II:

> A gentle Squire would gladly entertaine
> Into his house some trencher-chapelaine;
> Some willing man that might instruct his sons,
> And that would stand to good conditions.
> First, that he lie upon the truckle-bed,
> Whiles his young maister lieth o'er his head.
> Second, that he do, on no default,
> Ever presume to sit above the salt.
> Third, that he never change his trencher twise.
> Fourth, that he use all common courtesies;
> Sit bare at meales, and one halfe rise and wait.
> Last, that he never his yong maister beat,
> But he must aske his mother to define
> How manie jerkes she would his breech should line.
> All these observ'd, he could contented bee,
> To give five markes and winter liverie.

Those rhyming couplets, with their even, balanced flow, are not only classical in their spirit; their very rhythm points to the future and the verse of Dryden's age.

V. Ben Jonson's Poems

Ben Jonson of course is no less of a classicist than Hall; and the humorous bent is quite as deeply rooted in his robust, rich personality. It comes often to the surface in his poems: *Epigrams, The Forest,* 1616; *Underwoods* (posthumous), 1640; and it is no paradox to say that Ben the humorist, to our modern view, is to be found quite as much in these, as in the more explicit "humors" plays.

Most of the satirical epigrams, especially the short ones, have a humorous quality through their dense, terse implicitness. One might instance that "To Alchemists":

> If all you boast of your great art be true,
> Sure, willing poverty lives most in you.

Practically in all, the development of the thought and form is as balanced as it is vigorous, managed with a sense of proportion and order which, along with the regular measure of the rhymed couplets, shows a natural affinity to the classical ideal of form; and the lines work up to a successful final trait. The impression of a force that holds itself in hand and deals out its effects with severe economy creates as it were a presumption, an expectancy of humor, generally fulfilled. A place apart is to be assigned to "On the Famous Voyage," a fearfully realistic rhapsody of more than Rabelaisian verve, where the fun, if any, lies in the dignified manner of treating such a theme.

But it is in *Underwoods* that we find most of the humor. As examples, we shall mention pieces IX and X of "A Celebration of Charis," with the ironical anticlimax; the racy realism of "An Epistle to a Friend, to Persuade Him to the Wars"; the final fling of "An Epigram on William Lord Burghleigh"; parts of "An Execration upon Vulcan; A Speech, according to Horace"; "The Poet to the Painter, an Answer"; and "The Rules of the Tavern Academy." Humor it is of a sort, and none of the best, no doubt; but the flavor is there; and Jonson must be ranked among the poets who, sparely favored with the lyrical gift, draw pleasing effects of lively interest from a compensating vein of shrewd observation.

VI. Drayton

With *Nymphidia, or the Court of Fairies* (1627) we have a distinct appeal to the spirit of parody and a confessed imitation of Chaucer's "Sir Thopas," in whose meter the poem is written. Effects of ironical anticlimax are produced almost inevitably by the shorter fourth and eighth lines. Precedents are claimed as well in Rabelais and *Don Quixote*. The light, graceful theme carries us onward with ease and has a gentle, faint flavor of humor in the association of epic dignity with such trifling incidents. That mock-heroic tone is deftly sustained all through, keeping up a sufficient measure of unruffled seriousness to invest it with a quality of reserve. But most of the charm which the airy fancy undoubtedly possesses is born of another intention, close and parallel to the former though distinct from it: the fresh, picturesque description of the world of fairies; and the analogy here is not with Chaucer but with *A Midsummer Night's Dream*. A "humble bee, their minstrel," plays the "hautboy" to the dancing fairies. To give the name of Pigwiggin to the goblin whom Mab favors with her doting love is broad enough, but we can indulgently smile at it. All that is very English and wells up from a national, a deep vein of inspiration which, although put here to fastidious uses, is popular in character. The panic spread by the coming of Oberon to avenge his offended honor and the hurried flight of the dancing fairies, for instance, are realistically described:

> When, like an uproar in a town,
> Before them everything went down;
> Some tore a ruff, and some a gown,
>   'Gainst one another justling;
> They flew about like chaff i' the wind;
> For haste some left their masks behind;
> Some could not stay their gloves to find;
>   There never was such bustling.

As Oberon and Pigwiggin are going to fight to the death, Proserpine lets out a mist from a bag, and the two infuriated heroes lose sight of each other. The precedent of Demetrius and Lysander in *Midsummer Night's Dream* (III, ii) is obvious, but the mocking effect none the less efficient: no image could more ironically symbolize the gratuitous, brainless futility of heroism according to superannuated medieval standards; Don Quixote tilting at his windmills is just a case in point; Drayton's humor, modest as it is, links up here with Shakespeare and Cervantes. On the other hand, it has seeds and promises which point forward not only to *Hudibras* but to *Peter Pan.*

VII. Suckling, Herrick

Sir John Suckling was one of the wittiest of the Cavalier poets; and the acknowledgment that he had wit is commonly eked out today by the classical tag: "and humor"—a coupling of words which did not yet obtain in his own time, but was to become almost inevitable half a century later. Indeed his brilliancy in repartee and his talent for giving the right turn to the neatest epigrams are sobered and raised in value by a reserve and self-control which qualified him to be a humorist. Did not his brother state after his death that he was a man of "grave deportment"?[4] His letters show proof of the same easy, thoughtful sprightliness. The cast of seriousness which is thus, in a growing number of individual examples, being superimposed on the more exuberant, irrepressible temper of the Renaissance courtier, is a token of that solidification, so to say, of the average English character, to which the spreading of the properly Puritan influence beyond the limits of the lower classes certainly did contribute. The mental tone thus created, which answered the permanent mood of the British people—a mood that is easily discerned, from the Middle Ages, even at the heart of "merry England"—was to remain practically unchanged, in spite of some superficial or momentary eclipses, till the end of the nineteenth century; and it is no chance coincidence that the coming of age of humor, as a national trait, should have taken place at the same time. The wider development was reflected in the more special one, which gave it one of its most characteristic aspects. Humor is thus in actual historical fact one of the most distinctive flowers of the ripening English character.

[4] *Poems and Plays,* ed. W. C. Hazlitt (London, 1892), p. xiv.

Suckling had elegance and polish; and he could poke fun slyly and gracefully not only at others but at himself—one of the sure marks of the true humorist—as *A Session of the Poets* testifies. The fun is not always of the most refined kind; but the courtly Muse of the period shied at few things. Still, could there be more gentle or better banter than this quatrain:

> The first that broke silence was good old Ben,
> Prepared before with canary wine,
> And he told them plainly he deserved the bays,
> For his were called works, where others were but plays.

To wit is added here genuine humor. Looking for the reason, one must fall back upon a "simplicity" (the epithet is Wordsworth's), a virtue that is very different from the mere brilliancy of witty sarcasm and adheres to that concrete reality, that truth of things, the fruit of which is naturalness.

Suckling could mix some gleams of humor in his otherwise indifferent comedy of *Brumoralt*, as that justly famous line testifies:

> The prince of Darkness is a Gentleman (III, second song).

But his masterpiece from our point of view, and altogether, is the "Ballad upon a Wedding," which really captures something of the spirit of what a popular epithalamium would be. The whole piece has raciness, a happily naïve, rustic manner, and is at the same time charmingly roguish. The lines about "her feet beneath her petticoat" are in everybody's memory; but is not this of the bride's cheeks, for instance, just as good?

> For streaks of red were mingled there,
> Such as are on a Catherine pear
> (The side that's next the sun)!

The perfection of these lines is made up of their easy, unforced success in the combination of two elements that are rarely compatible: the realistic, matter-of-fact imagination of a peasant, and a courtier's refined sense of fitness. The former supplies the concreteness that humor demands; the latter, by its pretended abdication, provides the inverted turn, the "transposed" expression that is the essential trick of the humorist.

Jolly Herrick, with his frank love of pleasure, his liveliness, and charming lyrical gift, had to maintain some sort of keeping between the pagan freedom of his *Hesperides* (1648) and the professional piety which made perfunctory amends in the *Noble Numbers.* So there is some check, at least in the expression, upon the good parson's enthusiasm for sack, roses, daffodils, and his mistresses; and the frequent presence of that curb upon his otherwise spontaneous vein may have strengthened the natural bent of his temper to an implicit, half-hidden roguery. Herrick's humor is decidedly of the Chaucerian, more normal kind; it links up with good humor; it will often shade off into mere slyness, a way of throwing out hints and innuendoes. The raciness and realism which are so congenial to humor were not far to seek; they would crop up naturally from the features and the atmosphere of Devonshire life in the fourth and fifth decades of the seventeenth century. At times the humorous aroma that one breathes through many of those pieces assumes a stronger degree of concentration; not a few of the most typical examples would be found among the epigrams; and it must be confessed that if Herrick's humor has nothing sardonic, it can be bitingly satirical. As instances of the latter category, one may quote "Another," "To Criticks," "Upon Blanch," "Upon Bunce," "Upon Pink"; and for the former and more easygoing type, the "Farewell to Sack," "Welcome to Sack," parts of "Corinna's Going a Maying."

The significance of Herrick's humor is that it shows us the manner being integrated with a mode of poetry that had been generally alien to it—the lyrical; lyricism, here, truth to say, being an individual brand made up of familiarity and realistic verve. No less interesting is the admixture of humor with love poetry, shorn of all its conventional trappings. So its further naturalization in literature is made possible by a reaction of the truth of instinct and impulse against the old tradition of "amour courtois" and the more recent fashion of "metaphysical" conceits.

VIII. Cleveland

In John Cleveland the same reaction is very plainly discernible, but it assumes a different form, of the highest interest to us. In the words of the scholar who edited his poems, he was "the last and most characteristic poet of the metaphysical school."[5] It is our point that with him the half-hidden and hardly conscious reaction of the metaphysicals themselves against the absurdity of their practice—a reaction, the outcome of which was a perceptible vein of exaggeration and parody—comes to its natural end: a fully conscious use of the conceit to serve a humorous purpose. Berdan's parallel assertion that Cleveland was "the most popular poet of his time," although its terms may be slightly exaggerated, conveys an accurate sense of his widely representative character, and thus emphasizes his value as the token of a mental change which entered into the final growth of English humor.

What contemporaries said of his manner is significant; they stress the compression of his style, "his fancy . . . summing whole books into a Metaphor, and whole Metaphors into an Epithite" (David Lloyd); the particularly marked violence he did to language, "wresting and torturing a word into another meaning" (Dryden); and they regard him as having pushed to an extreme the common method of the metaphysicals: "so great a Man hath Cleaveland been in the Estimation of the generality, in regard that his Conceits were out of the common road, and Wittily far-fetch't" (Edward Phillips).[6] The last judgment is the most suggestive. We are not to read into it that Phillips felt the presence of an ironical intent in the writer's display: "wittily" probably means only cleverly, ingeniously; but the critics agree in thinking that Cleveland did out-conceit the makers of conceits.

Now, what created only an impression of double brilliance and reinforced audacity in his use of words and phrasing strikes us today more clearly and revealingly. An intuitive perception as sure as any literary impression may be gives out to us the secret of that cool, dense, calculated, breath-taking absurdity. The exercise of his "wit" is to the poet himself a composite pleasure in which pride at his own cleverness is only one element, the other being a secret, silent enjoyment of the comic

[5] J. N. Berdan, *The Poems of John Cleveland* (New Haven, 1911), Introduction.

[6] *Ibid.*, pp. 54-55.

exaggeration he chooses to indulge. It is impossible to read for instance "To the State of Love," without finding in it the metaphysical method run mad.

> Is not the universe straight-laced
> When I can clasp it in the waist?
> My amorous folds about thee hurled,
> With Drake I girdle in the world;
> I hoop the firmament, and make
> This, my embrace, the zodiac.
> How could thy centre take my sense
> When admiration doth commence
> At the extreme circumference?

The same conclusions are forced upon us again and again—by "To Julia to Expedite Her Promise"; "The Hecatomb to His Mistress":

> As your philosophers to every sense
> Marry its object, yet with some dispense,
> And grant them a polygamy with all,
> And these their common sensibles they call,
> So it is with her who, stinted unto none,
> Unites all sense in each action.
> The same beam heats and lights; to see her well
> Is both to hear and see and taste and smell.
> For, can you want a palate in your eyes
> When each of hers contains the beauteous prize,
> Venus's apple? Can your eyes want nose
> Seeing each cheek buds forth a fragrant rose?
> Or can your sight be deaf to such a quick
> And well-tuned face, such moving rhetoric? . . .

Or again, by "The Antiplatonic," "Upon Phillis Walking in a Morning before Sun Rising," etc. The burlesque aim of the conceits is quite obvious in "Mark Antony" and "The Author's Mock Song to Mark Antony." Even the political poems, proverbially stinging in their satire, are full of verve and of humor; as are for example the "Dialogue between Two Zealots," and "The Rebel Scot"—a piece that rankled long north of the Tweed, and not without good reason.

> Before a Scot can properly be curst,
> I must like Hocus swallow daggers first.
> Come, keen iambics, with your badger's feet
> And badger-like bite until your teeth do meet. . . .

In his frequent use of scientific similes to serve an end of parody, Cleveland recalls Marvell, whose poems at times run, independently, on similar lines. But the main historical interest of Cleveland's personality appears through his certain connection with Samuel Butler. In *Hudibras*, after a very short interval, the course of modern English poetry was to begin in good earnest, with humor as one of its main constituents.

IX. Conclusion

Cleveland is thus of special importance as an index to a mental change which was to make humor, in some respects, the heir of the conceit. After the Restoration the new taste in poetry gradually banned and drove out the forced, far-fetched comparisons in which the readers of the preceding age delighted. But the refinement of taste, commonly attributed to John Dryden and the new school—to Dryden who, let it not be forgotten, wrote his earliest lines in the worst spirit of the "conceited" fashion—was not exclusively their work; a share in the responsibility for it is to be laid on Samuel Butler, Cleveland's friend and disciple; *Hudibras* made conceits decidedly ridiculous by riding the hobby purposely to death, turning it into an instrument of burlesque, as it made the social aspects of Puritanism laughable. It was all part of the great victory of sense and rational moods, which heralded the beginning of another era in literature and thought.

While acknowledging the part played in the process by such poets as Cleveland and Butler, it must not be forgotten that from the first, from the time of John Donne, indeed from that of John Lyly, the conceit had been pregnant with the excess that killed it; and of that excess the writers who cultivated it were hardly ever completely unaware, although their awareness most often was repressed into the dim regions of their consciousness. The mania of the conceit-mongers was a suicidal one and contained the germ of its own destruction.

Now the relation of the conceit to humor, while predominantly negative, was positive as well. In appearance it turned its back doggedly upon humor; but the seeds of humor were laid in its innermost being because the human mind cannot long put up with obvious unbalance, and the cure for absurdity will be laughter—or rather, more efficiently, a smile. The final stage in the life of the conceit was reached when simply through a silent change in the poet's inner intent, and a slight alteration, perhaps, in the turn of his wording, the very means that were to create admiration for his imaginative inventiveness roused it for his sense of humor.[7]

[7] It need hardly be said that, especially when poetry is concerned, the progress that this chapter has been studying is that of literary humor. Meanwhile, however, the development as a whole had its roots in the national character itself, which was assuming its final features in the exalted and highly conscious days of Elizabethan greatness, and this has been hinted again and again in the course of our study. But popular humor has left very few records; it has mostly to be inferred from the sure traces of its existence implied in indirect documents, in all the texts and facts that go to the building of the image of the average Englishman. Literature, properly so called, remains one of the best of those documents; some of the evidence that bears on the social life of the period might yield a modicum of information. A psychological history of the British people, as distinct from a history of ideas in Britain, would be a fascinating task, but involved in so many difficulties that no one has yet attempted it. The historian of civilization, still, has more or less touched the fringe of the subject. A survey of the controversial literature between 1600 and 1660 would bring a far from negligible contribution, in spite of the fact that the hardening of religious conflicts and the outbreak of the Civil War raised the key of most pamphlets to a pitch little favorable to humor. As for the popular songs and ballads, the difficult problems of chronology involved in the history of almost all of them make it unpractical to localize any in this relatively short period of the early seventeenth century (except "The Dragon of Wantley"). So nothing should be added here to what has been said above of the subject (Part I, chap. v, sect. iv; and Part II, chap. viii: The Popular Vein, sect. ii). It can only be asserted that with the passing of time, as the political, warlike, and romantic themes of the earlier ballads tend to recede into the background, those of social and realistic interest are rather on the increase.

CHAPTER XV

PROSE

THE GLIMMERS of humor one may detect in Bacon's *Essays* are too few and far between to deserve study. This chapter will be devoted to a discussion of only three writers of unequal merit: Coryate, Burton, and Browne.

The remark has often been made that the first half of the seventeenth century, as it was the age of the "metaphysicals," was that of the eccentrics. In fact, the writers just mentioned all come under the latter category.

Like the mania for conceits but more decidedly, literary eccentricity overlaps humor and shades off into it. The eccentric is so to say a potential humorist, one who having the gift, has reached only an incomplete awareness of its possible exploitation.

I. Coryate

Thomas Coryate, as he comes first in date, is far and away the queerest figure of the three. His life and his personality are the full revelation of an original temperament, which imperfectly developed its self-expression through literature. One fancies him, with his comically shaped head, playing the butt at the court of James I, putting up with jokes and a handling that were at times pretty rough, but somehow saving his face and regaining some shreds of dignity through the defensive or offensive tactics of his wit. There is something of Falstaff in him, and of Shakespeare's clowns. He reminds one of the half-dunces who manage to say arresting things, and seem at times to tip us the wink like a sly one that shams folly. His theatrical gestures on occasion, the inordinate number of commendatory poems, most of them ironical or mock-heroic, which he succeeded in getting for his book, the hanging up in Odcombe church of the shoes in which he had walked back from

Venice, the very title of his work: *Coryat's Crudities, Hastily Gobbled up in Five Moneths Travells in France, Savoy, Italy, Rhetia commonly called the Grisons country*, etc.—look as if he enjoyed playing practical jokes under the cloak of grave behavior. His book makes more sense than one might expect after that. But all in it is not delighted or dull naïveté and wonder; a twinkle of genuine humor flashes again and again in Coryate's eye, as he looks at the vast strange world. His tongue is in his cheek through the famous relation of his call on the Venetian courtesan, all for the sake of a social and moral inquiry. He had the humorist's genuine power of realistic perception; his remarks upon France are interesting. And so we are inclined to take at face value his enthusiastic declaration:

> Of all the pleasures in the World travel is (in my opinion) the sweetest and most delightful. For what can be more pleasant than to see passing variety of beautiful Cities, Kings and Princes' Courts, gorgeous Palaces, impregnable castles and fortresses, Towers piercing in a manner up to the Clouds, fertile territories replenished with a very Cornucopia of all manner of Commodities as it were with the horn of Amalthea, tending both to pleasure and profit, that the heart of man can wish for. . . .

Through the oddity of his work, and chiefly of his personality, Coryate may be called a "humorist" in the Elizabethan sense. At the same time, he has some incipient features of one in the modern sense. This is indeed the special interest of the eccentrics: they illustrate the transition from the former meaning to the later, and contribute to give weight and substance to what might seem otherwise a rather abstract derivation.

Of the two elements, the older remains predominant in Coryate; the proportion is reversed in Browne; Burton's stage is intermediate, and he shows us a complex mixture of naturally queer idiosyncrasies, with a self-possessed strategy of deliberate quaintness. He ranks highest, as a humorist, among the prose-writers of his age.

II. Burton

Burton's book is eccentric mostly in details and arrangements, upon which one can put one's finger. The justly celebrated frontispiece to the original edition is an epitome of that aspect. The author's portrait as "Democritus Junior" presides over a set of naïvely amusing allegorical figures, including that of "Democritus Abderites"; and even viewed on the background of an age when such illustrations were common, the care and minute complexity of those images startle us. Whatever shares may be assigned respectively to Burton's invention and to the printer's zeal, an author who chose to come out before the world in that external garb made profession, as it were, of following up the intricacies of his thought to a very unusual point of imaginative realism; he did not mind if by that he could catch a reader's attention, creating an impression of queerish originality. After all, his confessed purpose was to amuse, as it was to instruct. Again, in the process of instruction he put extraordinary reliance on method and order. The several "Synopses," with the incredible variety of their sections and subsections, rouse so overwhelming a sense of the vastness of the theme that the work looms indeed as what it is, the sum total of the then extant knowledge of man—body and soul. And it is, to say the least, no commonplace attempt to compass such a topic from the special angle of an ailing sensibility, and of melancholy. Lastly, Burton's use and abuse of learned quotations is more than pedantry; it is other than pedantry; it is the functioning of a mind that thinks in Latin more naturally than in English; it is thus mental duality, or automatism; a feature of thought here abnormally grown and almost pathological.

But of eccentricity, properly so called, there was very little in Burton's life. The home-keeping, quiet, book-reading parson and scholar was, if not exactly true to type, at least exceptional only in his prodigious erudition; the contemporaries lay stress on his companionable character and even the merry turn of his conversation. The monster melancholy that, as he put it in the inscription intended for his tomb, "gave him life, and death," raged all within and devoured him silently.

That it did devour him, at least in metaphor, we cannot doubt. Nothing is more impressive than the deep seriousness of his purpose. About the prevalence of the disease and the havoc that it plays he is in dead earnest. Through his book the course of man on the earth appears as a long defense against an arch enemy; a battle that, while it hardly knows dramatic climaxes and does not seem to threaten life and limb, is a never-ending fight, and often a losing one. The publication of Burton's book (1621) in fact coincides with the period when "merry England" was beginning to fade away, and the splenetic Englishman, already introduced by Froissart in the fourteenth century, became decidedly prominent.

And yet, *The Anatomy of Melancholy* is a thoroughly humorous treatise. That is the reason of its outstanding significance in the prospect of our inquiry. There had been already—as in *The Praise of Folly*, the *Utopia*, *Don Quixote*, or parts of Shakespeare's plays—supreme examples of the complete fusion of seriousness and humor, in which the two elements are inseparable, indeed hardly distinguishable from each other; the background of seriousness giving humor its proper depth of content and richness of flavor, as the presence of humor lent to the gravity of a writer's thought sharper relief, a more poignant edge, and a fuller human appeal. But there had been in England nothing like this huge synthesis of medicine, ethics, and what will later be psychology, the work of a man's whole existence, containing his total view of the world, something similar to Montaigne's *Essays*, which Burton knew well and often quoted. With him English humor reaches the final stage of its development; it has grown to be an independent attitude of the whole mind, permitting and offering scope to the use of all its powers; asking nothing of farce and common pleasantry, from which it had become at last plainly differentiated. The thing—a mode of thinking, speaking, and writing—that a number of the sharper observers began to realize had a separate existence, and was thus growing, so to say, more and more conscious of itself, would not be long now in coining its own name, or—a more convenient and likely method when instinct has its way—turning an old word to novel use.

Burton's humor is usually a light essence that pervades his work, though one chiefly breathes it in the long introduction

(Democritus to the reader). Occasionally it will flash out more vividly. Of the two modes, the former remains the more characteristic and also the more enjoyable. But as the latter can be briefly dismissed, we shall deal with it first.

Burton is willing to confess that he intends to be amusing: did not Democritus make it his philosophy to laugh? "Gain sense from precept, laughter from out whim" (Democritus Junior to his Book); "whim" here is an open oddity that does not try to hide itself behind a mask of unawareness. This more patent pleasantry, though kept within due bounds by a general discretion of manner, borders upon explicit fun. Such is the passage where we hear of the unfortunate man who "thought he had some of Aristophanes' frogs in his belly, still crying Brecc, ckex, coax, oop, oop, and for that cause studied physic seven years, and travelled over most part of Europe to ease himself."[1] Such again are the endless enumerations of ill-assorted things and words—a Rabelaisian trick that Sterne was to learn to good purpose. "And for those other faults of barbarism, Doric dialect, extemporanean style, tautologies, apish imitation, a rhapsody of rags gathered together from several dung-hills, excrements of authors, toys and fopperies confusedly tumbled out, without art, invention, judgment, wit, learning, harsh, raw, rude, fantastical, absurd, insolent, indiscreet, ill-composed, indigested, vain, scurrile, idle, dull and dry. . . ."[2] Or we come across brazen, breath-taking statements: "The Jesuits profess both" [priesthood and physic]; "at this time, divers of them *permissu superiorum* [are] chirurgeons, panders, bawds, and midwives."[3]

That blunt method is much more frequently toned down to a finer shade of whimsicality, absurdity, grotesqueness; and then we have the exquisite flavor that permeates the huge mass of the book, keeping it an inexhaustible mine of thoughtful enjoyment and silent half-smiles. Here humor is not a passing activity, but a permanent attitude of the writer's mind; it is that mind itself, in its set habit and functioning. Burton has reached such a point of view as that of Lucian, whom he quotes

[1] Robert Burton, *The Anatomy of Melancholy* (London, 1845), p. 5.
[2] *Ibid.*, p. 8.
[3] *Ibid.*, p. 14.

constantly, of whose works "in 4 Tomes," from his own shelves, his will makes a special donation; this being one of the sure and significant contacts between the humanist vein of English humor and the ancient writer who was its most signal forerunner. The main element in a humorous view of life, the sense of universal relativity, impregnates Burton's book through and through; it welcomes the reader at the very entrance into the vast structure, in the guise of that "Author's Abstract of Melancholy" which probably suggested to Milton his contrasted presentment of the *Allegro* and *Penseroso*. "Naught so sweet as melancholy," "naught so sad as melancholy," such are the alternate burdens of succeeding stanzas; and the full confession of a divided mood follows us through the whole disquisition, like an ironical undertone to its endlessly repeated or implied lament.

The presence of that saving grace which qualifies all dogmatism, of that "alibi" that keeps the mind always on some other plane as well, instead of a mountain of pedantic learning, makes the book a fresh thing, alive with intellectual stir. The huge disquisition is aware of its relativity, conscious of the thousand oddities that must arise from such a deliberate survey of the structure, habit, digestion, working, and behavior, normal or abnormal, of our bodies and our souls. Out-of-the-way observations, strange and paradoxical prescriptions, awkward remarks, realistic details crop up everywhere; and the grave, gentle, earnest, ponderous physician and moralist in one, who could crush us under the weight of his innumerable authorities and texts, has a reassuring and friendly glimmer in his eye. The whole is decidedly not a joke, it serves a genuine purpose of medicine, hygiene, ethics, proper living, proper dying; but a subtle intimation is all along created and maintained in our subconscious sense that somehow we are parties together to the development of a solemn though lively scheme, which may bring us mental health, save us from the cave of despair, but from which we are free meanwhile to gather a mild relief of sober merriment. Of all the weapons that are brandished against melancholy, that strategy is the single one that is never mentioned; but we know intuitively that it is the most efficient, and that the monster will lose its strength if we get used to looking at it with the invincible freedom that is born of a wistfully amused spirit.

Of a sly atmosphere everywhere diffused, it is difficult to give proper instances. Perhaps this quiet promise, without a flicker, is as good as any: "If this my discourse be over medicinal, or savour too much of humanity," Burton tells his reader, "I promise thee that I will hereafter make thee amends in some treatise of divinity."[4] Or this: "and as that great captain Zisca would have a drum made of his skin when he was dead, because he thought the very noise of it would put his enemies to flight, I doubt not but that these following lines, when they shall be recited, or hereafter read, will drive away melancholy (though I be gone). . . ."[5] Or again, the episode in which, while Hippocrates was sadly pointing out that his duties, neighbors, friends, "frailties and mortalities," robbed him of his time, Democritus "profusely laughed (his friends and the people standing by, weeping in the meantime, and lamenting his madness)."[6] What a perfect and pregnant, a Shakespearean, symbol of our variegated scene, the conflicting human emotions, and their common arbitrariness! But to tear such fragments from the living tissue of the text is hardly fair. One is thrown back upon general statements. As sometimes with Montaigne, but in a much more pronounced way; as ever with Sterne, but in a much more guarded, dignified, and decent manner, Burton allows a background of silent amusement, self-criticism, irony, and secret complexity to peep out; the endless contradictions and absurdities of human experience are the constant theme of a survey which, on the face of it, keeps dealing with a number of serious topics. The innumerable texts quoted, we feel sure, are part of the humorist's armory and serve his turn. They shift—or pretend to shift—the responsibility for a method of profusion, for often queer or grotesque statements, on to the approved habits of scholarship and the accumulated wisdoms of the ages.

In the *Anatomy of Melancholy* English humor has come into its final stature and complete heritage. It is fully grown,

[4] *Ibid.*, p. 15. [5] *Ibid.*, p. 16.
[6] *Ibid.*, p. 22.

and the diverging lines of its future development can be discerned. Germs of Addison, Sterne, Lamb, Dickens, Lewis Carroll are embedded in the unwieldy mass. And it is of major importance to us that the independence and self-sufficiency of humor, its freedom from the broad laugh with which it had been long mixed up, should be asserted, placed beyond doubt by its association with what was, on the face of it, the enemy and the opposite of mirth: melancholy.

III. Browne

Sir Thomas Browne is, in the field of our inquiry, less important and significant than Burton. While some analogies of manner may appear between them, the temper of Browne's mind is decidedly different. More of a poet, more deeply religious and devout, even avowing a fondness for superstition, he is less free intellectually than his predecessor; his thought is captivated by the spell of images and the incantation of rhythm; is does not play with the same suppleness round the contrasts and contradictions of things.

Still, he has his touch of eccentricity. Like his beliefs, his interests tend to wander away from the common grooves. The man who wrote *Hydriotaphia, Vulgar Errors,* and *The Garden of Cyrus* relished the byways and odd corners of knowledge; his life shows us a collector of antiquities and rare specimens, a virtuoso in the domain of the natural sciences, with a persistent taste for the supernatural. As to humor, Leslie Stephen went too far in finding it at the core of his work; but Olivier Leroy's pronouncement is a shade too negative about the little that is to be found.[7] He is assuredly wrong, again, in asserting that Browne's mind is thoroughly abstract; it evinces on the contrary, most often, a sense of the variety, picturesqueness, and flavor of the concrete, which qualifies him the better to be a humorist. On the other hand, the same critic is amply justified when he warns us that Browne's humor is of the lightest, most evanescent kind; indeed one can easily be mistaken as to its presence, and caution is indispensable. All things considered, it is less unfounded to say that *Religio Medici* (1643) has no humor than to suspect gleams in some passages where

[7] *Le Chevalier Thomas Browne,* (Paris, 1931), part II, chap. iv.

an ironical or a skeptical thinker would very probably have felt the temptation, and yielded to it. The purpose of the whole book is overwhelmingly serious.

In the other writings the author's earnestness being far less fervent, humorous intents can unmistakably be detected. Let one instance suffice: the scientific account of an experiment made with a toad and seven spiders, shut up together in a box, in order to see which of the two traditional foes would bite first and whose venom would kill faster; of how the spiders and the toad made very good friends for some time; and then the toad never bit, but swallowed the spiders one by one with much deliberation.[8]

This is broad enough, but not bad of its kind in its unruffled objectivity. Like Burton's, Browne's humor is most often only quaintness, a quaintness that is apparently just conscious enough to call up a vision of one cheek in the dignified author's face suspiciously more bulging than the other. But the vision is flitting, and readers may wonder and ponder. The epistle dedicatory of *Hydriotaphia* to Thomas Le Gros wishes the newly discovered urns "might have the effect of theatrical vessels and great Hippodrome urns in Rome, to resound the acclamations and honour due unto you." This is so farfetched that we can call it a conceit; but indeed the imagination of Browne, a prose poet, dwells frequently on the undefined borderline of the empire of conceits, and the spirit of the metaphysicals is never far to seek in his work. The solemn eloquence and organ tones of the beautiful last chapter of *Urn Burial* lights up at times with a flash of wistful amusement: "Mummy is become merchandise; Mizraism cures wounds, and Pharaoh is sold for balsams." Both this treatise and *Pseudodoxia* would yield a long list of such illustrations. The disputed points in natural lore, or in the interpretation of Scripture, with which Browne loves to deal, can hardly to a normally constituted person be thrashed out in complete seriousness; the contrast between the manner of the argument and the absurd, trivial, or ticklish nature of the subject seems to preclude the possibility of an unperturbed whole-minded-

[8] *Vulgar Errors*, III, xxvii.

ness which would look very much like naïveté. Will a diamond placed under a pillow betray an unfaithful wife? Would sleeping on the fourth book of the *Iliad* cure a quartan? Might not more beasts be taught to speak, since Eve was addressed by the serpent? In such cases, we are to resist immediate inferences, as Browne's was no ordinary mind. We are to forget, as well, that he had read Rabelais and quotes him, when a loose hint does seem to lurk in the background; of all such he is probably innocent. But if we sum up our impression from our perusal, there remains in the hollow of our hand a little of the concentrated essence of humor, enough to diffuse the pleasant, well-known aroma through many pages of a writer who might have otherwise so easily fallen a victim to an excessive dose of his own sincere earnestness.

And thus Browne is one more positive item in that story of the spreading of an intellectual attitude, which we have been following from the time of *Beowulf*, with an ever more substantial body of evidence. The quality has not been persistently on the upward grade. Chaucer, at one stroke, had reached a degree of *finesse* in humor which it took several centuries to equal or surpass. But the quantity, at a given moment, has been almost constantly on the increase. By the middle of the seventeenth century, the odds are that an English writer of note will show some humor; the negative cases make up a minority. The era of generalized humor, of its coming of age so to say, has been reached when the parallel growths of the national character, and of that single trait, are involved in such a consummation.

CHAPTER XVI

THE CRITICAL REALIZATION: A PROSPECT

I. The Generalization of Humor

THE RESTORATION period was certainly in some respects a deep-reaching break through the continuity of the English people's social and intellectual development. Many strands of the past were apparently disrupted; the atmosphere that prevailed during the reigns of Charles II and James II was aggressively different from that of the Protectorate; and although the new change in 1688 was much more easy and smooth than that in 1660, the nation did not settle down into the grooves of its modern government and life without a perceptible shifting. Still, the more profound forces, both economic and spiritual, that had been at work in the England of the "Civil War" reappeared after the Revolution in their essential continuity. The wild reaction of the Restoration in politics, manners, and thought then assumed its true perspective as a transitional stage. The higher middle classes, which for a century had been gaining ground towards social ascendancy, now quietly assumed the reality, if not the external marks, of power. The Parliamentary system in its fully evolved form was more thoroughly connected with their ideals and interests than with those of any other class. The fibers of seriousness and responsibility had been braced and strengthened by the religious controversy and the Puritan influence. During the age of William and of Ann the marks of a clearer sense of duty, of deliberate citizenship, a revealing symptom of which is to be found for instance in the *Spectator*, were set upon society; and an acceptance of the issues of life as reducible to a conflict between good and evil was embedded in the very conscience of the people.

Genuine humor, which has more to do with seriousness than with mirth, lost less than it gained through such changes, one aspect of which was the more pronounced decline of "merry England." The spreading of the humorous attitude and gift to a larger number of individuals, and the progress of the manner among the recognized pioneers of literature, which had been symptoms during the earlier half of the seventeenth century, continued through the period that followed; their uninterrupted development reached its final stage from 1660 to 1800. Then it was as well that humor grew completely conscious of its own originality and method; a slower process, which it is the object of this concluding chapter to survey.

The exceptions are by no means to be ignored. Above the literature of the mid-seventeenth century rises the great personality of Milton—a humorless man and writer,[1] exclusively devoted to truth, beauty, and single-mindedness. The divided mind without which there is no humor cannot be found, either, in the religious poets of the semimystic type, the two Herberts, Vaughan, Crashaw, Traherne: their conceits do not lend themselves to any suspicion of double meaning. Just after the Restoration, if more proof is needed that the diffusion of the humorous attitude is only very relative, leaving out the unregenerate who are still an important minority, a representative figure, that of Samuel Pepys, comes opportunely to teach us modesty in our generalizations: he it was who could not discover any fun in *Hudibras*.

On the other hand, evidence is conclusive that of those who wrote for pleasure or for gain—leaving out almost all the scientists, philosophers, preachers, lawyers, politicians, and such writers generally as had some axe to grind—an increasing number were naturally adapted to the manner of indirect pleasantry. On the eve of the Restoration the last of the metaphysicals, Cleveland, turned most of his conceits into a kind of parody. Overlapping from the Commonwealth to the new age, Andrew Marvell is a particularly convincing example, so solidly and widely typical of the deeper, the more national

[1] Milton's "two humorous epitaphs on Hobson" (*D.N.B.*, under Hobson [Thomas]), are no sufficient qualification to this statement.

strains of his time; still quaint and fanciful in his images, but endowed with a fund of virile, robust English humor. Of Samuel Butler it is dangerous to assert too much; he is abnormally clever, intellectual, and his ironies are the nearest approach to those of Swift. We must not forget that Dr. Johnson thought there was so much wit in *Hudibras* that it eclipsed the humor. It would be more fair to say that there is a very great deal of both; as they shade off into each other, a sort of compromise is effected between them, and they borrow a tinge of each other. Butler's humor is of the dry, sardonic kind, as is that of Swift. In respect to our inquiry, he is a sign of the integration of humor with the rational age that is beginning. Of cordial or kindly humor he certainly has none to offer.

No less thoroughly English and national than Marvell, John Dryden is the greatest Restoration writer; and in his many-sided nature a rich realization of the concrete has a large place; his satires especially abound in the most genuine kind of humor. The reopening of the theaters, after a twenty-year interruption, found French influence strong both in heroic tragedy and the comedy of manners. Among the features which distinguish the latter from its French parallels, it is impossible not to notice a more vivid realism, a spirit of rough, often brutal satire, and a more highly flavored presence of the concrete.

There is a pointed, concentrated shade of humor in the plays of Etherege, as well as in his letters; a bitter humor as well as wit in the savageness of Wycherley, and repression has much to do with the verve of a playwright who hates more than he enjoys the world he depicts. With Shadwell the cult of Ben Jonson's "humors" is paramount; the painstaking, often effective description of odd figures and social backgrounds is realistic enough to awake humorous impressions in the modern sense. The brilliant, refined cynicism of Congreve is perhaps, of those individual styles, the least national, the least colored with humor properly so called; but Vanbrugh's Flemish touch restores the balance by stressing again a more robust image of life. In Farquhar's plays the humor is more gentle, the satire tempered with a sympathetic interest in domestic manners, and the way is opened for the de Coverley papers, with which kindly, delicately shaded humor comes into its own.

It was Addison's and Steele's privilege to put upon modern English humor the stamp of an originality that was to remain henceforward, in its consciousness of itself as in the opinion of foreign critics, one of its most characteristic traits; they shaped the final instrument for the display of a half-smiling amusement in the keen sense of oddities and whims that keeps genial while imperfectly concealing an undercurrent of not unkind raillery. This is the manner which through Fielding, through Goldsmith, Jane Austen, Lamb, Dickens, to mention only some masters, and all the way to Barrie and Kenneth Grahame, will raise the humorous strain in modern English literature to its rich, precious, and varied eminence. Somewhat apart from that central development, the vein of Arbuthnot and Swift and Samuel Butler the younger stands on one side, as does on the other side the half-sentimental, half-cynical refinement of the most subtle possibilities of humor in the work of Sterne. For two centuries and a half there has not been an age of English letters—not even that of the heyday of romanticism—through which the humorist did not play his prominent part in the expression of the national genius.

II. The Growth of Its Self-Consciousness

Those are pretty obvious and safe generalities. But much more complex and difficult is the problem—a practically untouched one yet in English or foreign criticism—of tracing with any degree of probability the growth of the self-consciousness of humor; the gradual realization, by the writers themselves and by their readers, of the original manner for which a name was being evolved through the semantic transformation of an old word.

In a general way, one may take stock of the fact that this aspect of the development lagged far behind the other. Almost a majority of English writers had been humorists for a long time before they knew precisely that they were. This does not mean that they had been humorists unconsciously: if the word is taken in the literal sense, there never was any humor, but that was conscious of itself—of the intent that is its essential spirit. The "unconscious humorist" of current and unguarded literary criticism is simply the odd person whose sight stirs humor in us; he is only the butt, the object lesson. But all the way down from Chaucer and pre-Chaucerian gleams to the early eighteenth century, humor was conscious of being pleasantry of a kind; it did not distinguish itself clearly from other modes of pleasantry; it did not know that it was a very special, very significant manner of joking. Among the glimmers of self-consciousness which we have been able to discover in the course of this inquiry, the most remarkable so far, as we have more than once pointed out, are found in Shakespeare's work.

Two main reasons may be assigned for this long delay. One is the undoubted fact that literary and aesthetic criticism in England awoke later than in Italy and France; that the English genius, which is so gifted for intuitive and concrete perception in the field of the inner consciousness, proved much less prone to the peculiar twisting of the mind upon itself, which the intellectualization and the analysis of artistic creation demand. The investigation and the rationalization of humor were never, from an international point of view, a special asset of the people who produced the most brilliant galaxy of humorists.

The other reason is that the massive, commanding personality of Ben Jonson buttressed up, for a whole century and more, the theory of "humors," itself a modified form of the medieval and purely medical view. The very imperfect infusion of some psychological element into the notion of temperament, regarded as a product of the predominance of a given fluid in the body, caused a misleading sense of security in the possession of a complex, many-sided truth, and blocked the way to fresh, free inquiries upon the matter; the Jonsonian idea of "a humor," that is to say, an eccentric person under the control of his or her physiological temper, long prevented all normal awakening of the mind to the intimation that from that stage, in its turn, quite a new development had been taking place.

Meanwhile an original mode of pleasantry, which resembled Jonson's "humor" in the oddity, the paradox of its strategy of indifference and seriousness, and turned the whims of the "humorous" person into a rich opportunity for realistic, quiet fun, was more and more enjoyed, sought after, practiced by an increasing number of speakers and writers; as compared with "wit," and in contradistinction from it, this was a more sedate, more reflective, more guarded method to bring out the contrasts of things; it was one that better suited the dispositions of the English, in allowing them to preserve an unmoved appearance and not to yield to the emotion they were trying to call up. The native claims of self-control, of concreteness, and to some extent at least that of neighborly kindliness (since an indirect way of suggesting laughter and inflicting satire will blunt the satirical edge and render the criticism impersonal and objective)—all those claims of the spontaneous English mind and character did find in that repressed, unruffled manner of being witty a mode of wit that answered them more fully and easily; the cravings of the national instinct were thus much better satisfied.

But the energy that would have been necessary for a clear realization of a process already effected was diverted into other channels. A confusion had been created in which writers and critics remained helplessly entangled. Jonson's authority stood in the way of all new effort; his theory seemed sufficient; it was clear, and the facts of literature apparently bore it out: was not the minute description of oddities, more or less connected with physical temper, the staple of comedy and satire? So the confusion was allowed to persist; it prevailed to the end of the seventeenth century, and later; down to the beginning of the nineteenth, the oversimple and superannuated "humors" psychology will reappear, side by side with the most brilliant flashes of the new intimation. And in spite of these, the problem of modern humor—what it is, and how it links up with its past stages and its name—remained one of the most stubborn, proverbial tangles of criticism, instinctively avoided by critics with a sense of humor.

Still, some landmarks in that semantic development allow us to follow it through its main stages. The present work had had, at the start, the ambition of investigating that history in detail. The unforeseen events of World War II have delayed its completion and brought the author to cut down his former plan to more modest lines; instead of a full relation, it now winds up with a bird's-eye view of what took place in the decisive period of that progress, from 1660 to 1750 or 1800.

The starting point is plain enough. Before 1660 no single use of the word *humor* is to be found in which the modern sense can be safely read. All through the Renaissance period, while masterpieces of genuine humor were not wanting—as for instance in More's *Utopia,* in the creation of Shakespeare's Falstaff, Touchstone, and Feste, in Burton's *Anatomy of Melancholy*—we meet only with dim anticipations of the consciousness of the new manner and rarer inklings of the new meaning that was being worked out in the word. "Humor," "humorous," and "humorist" are used persistently in the older sense; the originality of the person who made humor by calling attention in an implicit way to the potential fun of odd characters and contrasts is still merged in a confused mass with that of the persons who prompted that initiative because they "were" humors; and no one seems to realize the specially important part played by the "humor" who more or less grew humorous, as we should say, through a growing discovery of the significance of his own oddity. Shakespeare's outstanding flashes of divination have been duly stressed; they thrust out towards the thing, much more than towards the word.

From 1660 on, the stages of the development can be tentatively marked out. What follows is based mainly on the quotations in the *New English Dictionary* and on the unused slips collected for that work, as well as for the *Early Modern English Dictionary,* down to the year 1770. Those materials have been made available to us through the obliging courtesy of Dr. Onions.

Attention must be called again to the fact that the period of thought and literature which began in 1660 is characterized by the coming to the front of properly intellectual tendencies.

The age of Dryden, and chiefly that of Pope, set a new price on the virtues of lucidity and order. The spirit of the neo-classic school, with the French influences which it absorbed and integrated, was naturally attuned to a more vigorous inquiry into the interrelation of mental activities; the scale of values that it evolved and respected created a premium for the classification of moral and aesthetic problems; art became rational; satire—based on the assertion of canons—was the most flourishing kind of literature; and modern criticism took its rise. Dryden and Pope, the two leaders of poetry, were keen critics as well as original writers. In such an atmosphere it was natural that the slow and tardy progress of the self-consciousness of humor should be quickened; and nothing is more explicable than that the crucial years in that process should have been those from 1670 to 1750.

Shadwell comes in first in our chronological list. In other respects he took his cue stubbornly from his master Jonson, as these lines testify:

> A Humour is the Biass of the Mind,
> By which with Violence 'tis one Way inclin'd;
> It makes our Actions lean on one Side still,
> And in all changes that way bends our Will;[2]

but he shows us at work the incipient habit of mentioning wit and humor in the same breath: these words are repeatedly associated in the Preface to his comedy, *The Humorists* (1670). The play and its title are purely Jonsonian; but the fact of considering humor, implicitly, as an activity of the mind, a mode of pleasantry, since it is compared to wit, was full of significance and pregnant with future developments.

It is possible that a glimmering of the new sense may be found in Buckingham's *Rehearsal* (1672), where a part of a play, not a person or a situation, is referred to in these words: "Do you understand the true humour of it?"[3] The passage seems to echo Nym's famous tag in *Henry IV;* but "humor" here is more plainly detached from the individual and the

[2] Quoted by A. Nicoll, *A History of Restoration Drama* (Cambridge, 1928), p. 192.

[3] Arber's reprint, 1868, p. 35.

temperamental basis which used to go along with it, as the very core of its meaning.

Durfey's *Madam Fickle* (1676) has this bit of dialogue:

Zech: and then for humour.
Tob: Ay, ay, I warrant thee Boy! If I can get a little Wit into this Tale of mine, let me alone for humour.[4]

This is decisive as to the glib association of "wit" and "humor" —two comparable modes of pleasantry.

It is very tempting to read in the following quotation from W. Robertson's *Phraseologia Generalis* (1681) a germ of the essential distinction between the passive and the active senses of the word humor:

Humour or meaning; sensus
A Humour or fancy
Humour or disposition; Indoles
A humour or trick.[5]

We read in Banks, *Vertue Betrayed* (1682):[6]

Acquaint this Noble Lord, and all here present,
If e'r you saw in all my Nights, or Days,
Or in my looser Hours of Mirth or Humour,
The smallest sign of that most horrid Guilt
That I'm condemn'd for?

The association with "mirth" is revealing.

We now come to the first quotation given by *N.E.D.* of "humor" in our specifically modern sense (under 7. a); in the translation of Glanius's *Voyage to Bengala* (1682, p. 142): "The Cup was so closed, that 'twas a difficult matter for us to open it, and therefore the General gave it us on purpose, to divert himself with the humour of it." This is convincing enough; but what is in question is only the "practical humor" of a joke. Moreover it is interesting to find, from the unused slips, that the same translation has the word as well in the old sense: "Whether his vision were real, or a pure effect of his melancholy humour, yet several persons lookt upon it as a bad omen" (p. 2).

[4] Ed. of 1677, p. 9 (I, i).
[5] Ed. of 1693, p. 768.
[6] Act V, p. 70.

In J. Lacy's *Sir Hercules Buffoon* (1684), we have: "I was told you were in a gay humour last night, good company, and very witty" (I, i); and: "I loved thee dearly before, but this jocose humour of thine makes me admire thee" (II, ii). This is not so significant as the preceding text; but we may gather from the two quotations that by that time the word *humor* would naturally call up an idea of pleasantry; the association with "gay" and "jocose" follows a natural affinity of things.

Still, that the older notion was dying very hard and clung to minds that might have known better is usefully brought home to us by the following definition, from Samuel Butler's *Genuine Remains* (Butler died in 1680): "Humour is but a crookedness of the mind, a disproportioned swelling of the brain, that draws the nourishment from the other parts, to stuff an ugly and deformed crup-shoulder."[7]

III. Dryden, Sir William Temple

Spread out all over the last forty years of the seventeenth century, the critical works of John Dryden—whose relation to humor as an original writer has already been briefly discussed—are a rich mine for the study of the word itself and its development. Dryden's use of it shows abundantly that his sense of its value is in a state of transition. The *Essay of Dramatic Poesy* (1668) has most often "humors" in the traditional meaning, with frequent references to Jonson. But a dim intuition of another value, that attached not to the tribe of odd characters but to the mental activity that exploited them, seems to be at work, appearing here and there; the word is then in the singular, and as a generic name it covers a whole field, capturing the very essence of the manner which handled "humors" to good profit. As an instance, one may quote this remark: "In the rest of Corneille's comedies you have little humour," where the stress does apparently fall on a deficiency in the art of the playwright. Using the word in the singular was of course no new thing; for a century almost it had meant the quality of oddity or the presence of it in general; but here

[7] Ed. of 1789, II, 325; a crump or crooked shoulder *(N.E.D.)*.

the context suggests a different sense.[8] It looks as if abstraction had been again at work, but on the aesthetic aspect of the facts, no more on the temperamental accidents; as if its result denoted, not a common characteristic of odd situations—as was the case with Nym's "That's the humour of it"—but the trick of dealing with them; not a passive bent of character, but an active faculty of the mind. Little does it matter, if one duly weighs those signs of an awaking intuition, that Dryden should still define "humor" as a general notion, in the pregnant page which he devotes to the subject, like an orthodox follower of Jonson: "humour is the ridiculous extravagance of conversation" [social behaviour, intercourse] "wherein one man differs from all others. . . . By humour is meant some extravagant habit, passion, or affection, particular (as I said before) to some one person, by the oddness of which he is immediately distinguished from the rest of men; which being lively and naturally represented, most frequently begets that malicious pleasure in the audience which is testified by Laughter. . . ." His practice points nonetheless to the existence in his mind of a perception, still diffuse and indefinite, from which the fully grown concept was to emerge.

We reach next a text of outstanding importance: Sir William Temple's *Essay of Poetry* (written 1690, published in the *Miscellanea*, Vol. II, 1692). In the background of this well-known treatise the past and the future are both active; but Temple's clear, sensible, judicious mind shows even more proof of his openness to the new, than of his lazy acceptance of the old. He does not definitely give up Jonson's view; to him, as to practically all critics at the time, humor remains indissolubly connected with temperament, in the physical sense; to the English climate with its constant changes, and to

[8] Another significant sentence would be: "We cannot so speedily recollect ourselves after a scene of great passion and concernment, as to pass to another of mirth and humour." This, after all, is of a piece with the coming into common use, at the time, of the phrase "wit and humour." The word is frequently employed in that marginal sense through the first pages of Dryden's preface to *An Evening's Love,* side by side with the traditional one. It may not be amiss here to remark that in Soame and Dryden's translation of Boileau's *Art Poètique* (1680-1683), we find "humorous" with its modern sense, the first example of which in *N.E.D.* is dated 1705: "In short, to finish this our humorous tale"; the French text runs: "Enfin, pour abréger un si plaisant prodige" (IV, 879). The value of "plaisant" here is quite plain.

the rich living which the fertile soil permits he traces the widespread frequence in the English character of a racy originality, for which he claims that the nation is especially, almost uniquely gifted. The freedom of government and of manners has something to do as well with this privilege: "we have more humour, because every man follows his own, and takes a pleasure, perhaps a pride, to shew it." The fickleness of the climate is paralleled by that of the inner man: "We are not only more unlike one another than any nation I know, but we are more unlike ourselves too at several times." So far we keep on traditional ground. But the notion of that inborn originality passes on by degrees from the organic to the intellectual and aesthetic planes. What matters, finally, is that such a wealth of odd characters should offer such ample opportunities to the satirist.

Temple's essay is the first text in which the existence of a peculiar literary manner, answering to the name of humor, is implicitly and explicitly registered. The question is no longer one of spontaneous, more or less unconscious oddities, but of the deft exploitation of those traits. The center of meaning shifts now to that exploitation. Humor is on a par with comedy; it distinguishes itself from it only through its more marked fondness for the individual and concrete: "humour is but a picture of particular life, as comedy is of general." No nation outside England can show anything like it; the very word is "peculiar to our language too, and hard to be expressed in any other." Drama has been the choice medium of its development: "Shakespear was the first that opened this vein upon our stage, which has run so freely and so pleasantly ever since. . . ." It is very remarkable that Temple should single out Shakespeare for special admiration in this domain, where a whole century had been giving the palm to Jonson—a sure sign that what he has mainly in view is the creative faculty, and no longer the mere imitation of the "comedy of humors." Indeed one may safely conjecture that the heavy stuff which Jonson doggedly forced upon his audience under the cloak of his doctrine is openly criticized in these lines: "if humour itself be forced, it loses all the grace; which has been indeed the fault of some of our poets most celebrated in this kind." As for Molière, who comes nearest, Temple says, of foreign playwrights to genuine English humor, he indulges too much in farce—a brilliant hit again, as Molière's admirable technique of laughter, full as it is of the instinct of humor, from the humorist's point of view errs a little, if at all, on the side of explicitness.

Such are the main points touched upon in this essay, a complex of often intuitive and penetrating ideas, along with merely passive ones, which, within its limits, was to remain the most arresting study of humor for some time. Temple's views, of course, are not only patriotic but naïvely nationalist, when he claims that the English have a privilege of humor; he thus starts a fallacy which will pass current almost to our very day. Of French, Italian, German humor, he seems to be ignorant; of dramatic humor before Shakespeare he apparently has no inkling. Of the fact that *humor* is not a native English word, and that the French and Italian languages, notably, had equivalents, he is not aware. But in his general notion of the thing itself he is feeling his way to the truth. He finds its root in the soil of the concrete, which is a shrewd and precocious view; he unerringly places the literary focus of the new manner in the theater, and especially in Shakespeare's work: nothing "excels or equals the humour of our plays."

When all is said, his major contribution is that he raises humor to the level of the approved means of inventive art and makes it a creative activity among the highest. When he declares roundly that nowhere is there "so much true genius as among the English; . . . more sharpness of wit, more pleasantness of humour, more range of fancy, more penetration of thought, or depth of reflection among the better sort," he is voicing the legitimate pride which the England of the Revolution could take in its reasserted greatness among the nations of Europe; but he was as well, although very few of his readers can have followed him so far, throwing the clearest light that had yet shone on one of the deeper traits of English and European thought.

IV. Congreve, Shaftesbury; Steele and Addison; The Decisive Stage

After Temple, Congreve's famous letter "to Mr. Dennis concerning Humour in Comedy" (1695) is somewhat of an anticlimax. His literary instinct is naturally conservative, and although his talent is so different from Jonson's, he too stands under his shadow. On the whole he simply adopts and repeats Temple's views; his description of humor—from a formal definition he says he had rather abstain, thus showing an early sense of the confusion of the subject, and inaugurating a wise policy—remains Jonsonian: it is "a singular and unavoidable manner of doing, or saying any thing, Peculiar and Natural as one man only; by which his Speech and Actions are distinguished from those of other Men." The traditional elements show here very conspicuously; the organic roots of humor in the physical temperament are stressed; Congreve even improves upon Temple when he takes up his cue of the robust individuality of the English: "They have a Proverb among them, which, may be, will shew the Bent and Genius of the People, as well as a longer discourse: He that will have a Maypole, shall have a Maypole. This is a maxim with them, and their Practice is agreeable to it. I believe something considerable too may be ascribed to their feeding so much on Flesh, and the grossness of their Diet in general." The last remark is perhaps the germ of another: "I have never made any observation of what I Apprehend to be true Humour in Women"; a fallacy, again, with a brilliant future. So strong is the link established with the physiological personality that Congreve goes the length of making humor an "unavoidable manner of doing, or saying anything." One wonders whether Voltaire might have caught the hint from Congreve, whom he met, when he later described humor to a correspondent as sallies of wit "qui échappent à un homme sans qu'il s'en doute."[9] This is of course just the reverse of the truth; Voltaire, though not Congreve, must have been deceived by the strategy of the humorist to the extent of mistaking his pretended unawareness for a genuine one. Humor—the spirit, the essence—is inevitably conscious.

[9] Lettre à d'Olivet, 1761.

At the same time, Congreve shows some intuition of the real nature of humor. He is open to the revealing fact that it is alien to farce. He is too much of an artist not to be alive to its comparatively refined method—the self-possessed working of a fastidious taste upon the rough material of oddities. His words, quoted above, "a singular . . . manner of doing *or saying* anything" (italics ours), make room for the whim of the humorist in the modern sense, who is himself odd only in his paradoxical way of putting things. So we may, all told, find in Congreve a sign of the transition and the awakening, but a follower of Temple, rather than a path-opener.

Shaftesbury's *Essay on the Freedom of Wit and Humour* (1709) is of importance to us only in the association which its title emphasizes and of which it definitively makes a set phrase.

The next stage—a decisive one—belongs to the *Spectator* group of essay-writers. Hughes, whom the *N.E.D.* honors with a quotation (*Spectator*, 525, Nov., 1712), plays third fiddle in this matter as in others; his words: "my Opinion of great part of the Writings which once prevail'd among us under the Notion of Humour," voice the desire, common to the whole group, of a better tone of jesting; the saner idea of humor that has become widespread by then is identified with the more decent way of social living that Addison and his friends constantly recommend, after the freedom of the Restoration. The involuntary fallacy lies in this, that the "Notion of Humour" which went along with the coarseness of much of the seventeenth century was a different notion altogether; the semantic change the word had been going through, which by 1712 the vocabulary of criticism had practically registered, is here very imperfectly realized.

Steele's views are more important. His attitude is that of the sincerely repenting rake, who has turned moralist and is somewhat sentimentally inclined. So he points out there may be danger in humor, as in the other modes of merrymaking: "For let any Man who knows what it is to have passed much time in a Series of Jollity, Mirth, Wit, or humourous Entertainments, look back at what he was all that while a-doing . . ." (*Spectator*, 151, Aug., 1711). We are recommended never to allow wit, though not explicitly humor, to be divorced from kindliness (*Spectator*, 422, July, 1712); the first sketch of a doctrine that will grow more and more central in English criticism. Steele's outstandingly suggestive paper, at a time when Addison had written most of his own, is in the *Guardian* (1713). In Number 42 he had shown some lingering confusion of ideas: "Story-telling . . . doth not so much subsist upon wit as upon humour"; and the latter mainly consists in a verve, a gusto that underlines the comic features of a tale by means of appropriate gestures and mimicry. Except that humor has indeed its visible strategy—which is mainly *not* to indulge in gestures and mimicry—this is radically wrong. But in Number 144 Steele makes an interesting synthesis of the Jonsonian and the new notions: "There is scarce an English man of any life and spirit that has not some odd cast of thought, some original humour that distinguishes him from his neighbour." The French phrase "le goût du terroir" is similar to it— a just and illuminating remark. "The shining men among our mob, . . . have an inexhaustible fund of archness and raillery as likewise have our sailors and watermen. . . . Though this singularity of temper, which runs through the generality of us, may make us seem whimsical to strangers, yet it furnishes out a perpetual change of entertainment to ourselves, and diversifies all our conversations with such a variety of mirth, as is not to be met with in any other country." Although Steele next refers to Temple's essay, which he quotes, his words are among the most pregnant yet written; he throws a flash of light on the inner connection of "humors" and "humor," and the passage from one notion to the other.

But Addison's contribution is by far the most essential. As a creator of humor the *finesse* and delicacy of his aesthetic perceptions, the light touch of his art, his naturally shy temper, and his delightfully quiet style make him the heir of the greatest humorists of the Renaissance and the first of the moderns in that line; no one will ever play more dexterously with the subtle shades of implicit raillery. Well can we feel the justice of Steele's discerning tributes to his friend in the Preface to the first edition of the *Drummer* (1716): "The scenes were drawn after Molière's manner, and . . . an easy and natural vein of humour ran through the whole. I do not question but the reader will discover this, and see many beauties that escaped the audience; the touches being too delicate for every taste in a popular assembly." And again, in his Preface to the new edition of the play, after Addison's death (1719): "He was above all men in that talent we call humour, and enjoyed it in such perfection, that I have often reflected, after a night spent with him apart from all the world, that I had had the pleasure of conversing with an intimate acquaintance of Terence and Catullus, who had all their wit and nature, heightened with humour more exquisite and delightful than any other man ever possessed." He speaks further of his friend's "smiling mirth, . . . delicate satire and genteel raillery." Those are not only apt and truthful words, but highly significant from our historical point of view: by then the full recognition of "that talent we call humour," of its genuine essence in nicely, finely shaded raillery, which its reserve will keep within a range of subdued effects, and of its analogy with some parallels in classical literature, was an accomplished fact.

This is not the place to praise Addison's humor in the *Spectator;* especially that of the de Coverley papers, in which his share is paramount. What we have to do is to sum up his views upon our subject. Leaving out his studies of wit, which grow to be a series of disquisitions on literary values in general, his pronouncements upon humor fall under two heads. The first is a plea for good nature in raillery (Nos. 23, 169, 179), a theme in the defense of which he is supported by Steele (No. 422). So we have the best critical authorities on the matter, at the time when humor was coming of age, definitely claiming for it a right to enter into an intimate, almost a binding association with kindness. This is a thesis that will become the staple opinion among English critics; and it is of course of a piece with the improvement of manners, language, and feeling, which the *Spectator* set are promoting with such sincerity and zeal. But it is essential to point out that in Addison's eyes the association is a matter of moral and sentimental preference, not of aesthetic necessity; although it is a feature of "False

Humour" that "his Ridicule is always Personal, and aimed at the Vicious Man, or the Writer; not at the Vice, or at the Writing" (No. 35), which implies that "True Humour" is the truer for avoiding personalities; still, Addison does not go so far as to exclude ill-nature from the domain of humor altogether: "I am very much troubled when I see the talents of Humour and Ridicule in the possession of an ill-natured man" (No. 23). So the founder of the modern school of English humor is aware of the fact that the demand of sympathy from the humorist is a craving of the heart, a preference for a not unkindly though amused picture of life, but is not rooted in the nature of mental things.

The other head is more essential. Here we come upon an intuition which had lain dormant for more than a century, in Falstaff's words ("a jest with a sad brow," *2 Henry IV*, V, i), and to which it is Addison's merit to have given due prominence; a remark indeed that laid the final foundation for the true theory of humor. Number 35 of the *Spectator* is a landmark in the series of critical approximations we have been running through. Like Congreve, Addison confesses to the special difficulty of defining humor: "It is indeed much easier to describe what is not Humour, than what is; and very difficult to define it otherwise than as Cowley has done Wit, by Negatives." The allegory that follows—how Truth was the Father of Good Sense, Good-Sense of Wit, who "married a Lady of a Collateral Line called Mirth, by whom he had issue Humour," is merely fanciful, and of no substantial value, except in so far as the association of humor with "Sense" probably points to its intimate relation with reality and the concrete, a just view. But the author is on more solid ground when he declares that humor should be kept severely apart from farce and explicit comedy, from all the cheap and easy ways of creating broad laughter, "wild irregular Fancies, . . . unnatural distortions of Thought." The breaking of windows, as somebody remarks in a play by Shadwell (*The Woman Captain*, III), is not humor. He comes next to the main point. His first remark is only tentative: as one would expect from its mixed genealogy, humor is "very various and unequal in his

Temper; sometimes you see him putting on grave Looks and a solemn Habit, sometimes airy in his Behaviour and fantastick in his Dress; . . . at different times he appears as serious as a Judge, and as jocular as a Merry-Andrew." But the still somewhat shifting and blurred outline of the notion thus implied is turned next into unerring definiteness and precision: "As True Humour generally looks serious, whilst every Body laughs about him; False Humour is always laughing, whilst every Body about him looks serious." That the unpardonable sin for the humorist is to give away his point by laughing first is indeed the golden clue; and after that remark the consciousness of the peculiar strategy of humor was complete.

In an unidentified paper of the new *Spectator* (No. 616, Nov. 5, 1714), which it seems safe to attribute to Addison, the point is made quite plain a second time: "Cicero hath observed, that a Jest is never uttered with a better Grace, than when it is accompanied with a serious Countenance. . . . Ridicule is never more strong, than when it is concealed in Gravity." It is surprising indeed that for a whole century *Don Quixote* should have been read and enjoyed in England, without this patent conclusion being drawn from the book. Chaucer, Erasmus, More, Shakespeare, Burton—among many others—might have taught the same lesson.

That the characteristic "gravity" of *Don Quixote* was nevertheless being given its full significance we know from Pope's lines to "Dr. Swift," whose range of humor he thus describes: Swift will "take Cervantes' serious air," or "laugh and shake in Rabelais' easy chair"—the latter trait being, one must confess, a singularly inaccurate characterization of the manner of *Gulliver*. Swift himself, who was wide of the mark when he claimed to have "first introduced into these kingdoms the ironical manner of writing," never thought it fit to distinguish irony from humor and to define them. Arbuthnot, like Swift a humorist of the first order, was no less prudent.

The notion of the seriousness of humor, so aptly emphasized by Addison, was thenceforward accepted by many—though not by all. We read in the first edition of Thomson's *Winter* (1726):

Unstudyed Wit, and Humour ever gay. . . . (l. 300)

But in the revised edition (1730) the line has been very happily expanded and corrected:

> Whence lively Wit excites to gay surprise,
> Or folly-painting humour, *grave himself*,
> Calls laughter forth, deep-shaking every nerve. . . .
> (ll. 614-616; italics ours)

Half a century later, William Cowper was to reiterate and emphasize Addison's view with remarkable accuracy:

> Nature imparting her satiric gift,
> Her serious mirth, to Arbuthnot and Swift,
> With droll sobriety they raised a smile
> At folly's cost, themselves unmoved the while.
> (*Table Talk*, ll. 656-659)

And he concludes:

> That constellation set, the world in vain
> Must hope to look upon their like again.
> (*Ibid.*, ll. 660-661)

So the fruitful hint was taken. But from many symptoms it appears that the confusion which had so long obtained was not yet dissipated. Foreign observers would be bewildered by a technique of pleasantry, the like of which, however, they could have experienced in their own country. The difference was that in England their attention was called to it by the now awakened consciousness of the cultivated public and the noise made about that puzzling privilege of the British; whilst the French and the Italians had still to learn that the new-fangled "humor" was an old acquaintance of theirs. We have quoted Voltaire's "sans qu'il s'en doute." Béat de Muralt, a Swiss gentleman who seems to have been rather destitute of a sense of humor, complained of the strange hobby of the English, whose pleasure was to "renverser les idées des choses, tourner la vertu en ridicule, rendre le vice agréable."[10] Worse still: writers eminently gifted with humor would be guilty of egregious errors

[10] *Lettres sur les Anglois et les François et sur les voyages* (Zurich, 1725), p. 64.

when they spoke of it in the abstract. Whilst the *Intelligencer*, No. 3, 1728 (quoted by *N.E.D.*) voices a feeling that was then getting current: "Humour . . . in its perfection is allowed to be much preferable to wit, if it be not rather the most useful and agreeable species of it," Goldsmith thirty years later comes out with a statement that "Wit raises human nature above its level; humour acts a contrary part, and equally depresses it."[11] It might be an explanation that by "depressing human nature," Goldsmith meant using the method of persistent understatement and of realistic concreteness; but this is only a conjecture.

And Fielding, the delightful creator of Parson Adams, will not sufficiently detach the manner from the matter of humor; quoting Pope's lines to Swift, whom he hails as "the greatest master of humour that ever wrote," he goes on to remark: "I do not remember to have seen in his works the least attempt in the manner of Cervantes" (*Amelia*, VIII, v); which of course is true only if the more external elements of the humorous attitude are exclusively stressed. Furthermore, when he tries his hand at a definition, it is still on Ben Jonson's view that he falls back (*Covent-Garden Journal*).[12] As for Sterne, who in his "Invocation" (*Tristram Shandy*, IX, xxiv), addresses the "gentle spirit of sweetest humour, who erst did sit upon the easy pen of my beloved Cervantes"—unexceptionable words these—he never tackled the thorny problem of humor, though he knew more of it, in a practical way, than any man living. But we must agree that a humorist has better things to do than to add one more definition to a long list.

V. Ups and Downs in the Literature of the Eighteenth Century

Meanwhile the professed critics and philosophers were grasping the nettle and duly discussing the tangled relation of "wit and humour"—this being the usually selected approach. Lord Kames (*Elements of Criticism*, 1762) adheres to the traditional view that humor in general is simply queer behavior. He has, however, a correct sense of the strategy of the literary humorist: "This quality belongs to an author, who,

[11] *Present State of Polite Learning* (London, 1759), p. ix.
[12] *Works* (London, 1762), VIII, 297.

affecting to be grave and serious, paints his objects in such colours as to provoke mirth and laughter." But this just intuition is spoilt by the singularly misleading remark that the gift of humor at its best is unconscious: "A writer who is really an humorist in character, does this without design; if not, he must affect the character in order to succeed." What has led Lord Kames to that paradoxical error is probably his clinging, in spite of all, to the Jonsonian view, and an attempt to reconcile the new meaning of "humor" with the old. The facts themselves rise against the distinction which he is trying to establish, and he confesses with much candor to the fragility of his own rule: "Swift and Fontaine, were humorists in character, and their writings are full of humour. Addison was not a humorist in character, and yet in his prose writings a most delicate and refined humour prevails. Arbuthnot exceeds them all in drollery and humorous painting; which shows a great genius, because he had nothing of that peculiarity in his character." It is remarkable that such glaring exceptions should not have destroyed, in his mind, the validity of his imperfect analysis.

James Beattie (*Essay on Laughter and Ludicrous Composition*, 1764, published 1776) only alludes to "that comic exhibition of singular characters, sentiments and imagery which is denominated humour." But he makes the very sensible remark that though wit and humor "do frequently raise laughter, they do not raise it always. . . . Examples of serious humour are not uncommon in Fielding's History of Parson Adams, and in Addison's account of Sir Roger de Coverley." On the stage, in particular, there is "a species of humour, which, if it should force a smile, will draw forth a tear at the same time."

George Campbell's second chapter in *The Philosophy of Rhetoric* (1776) is "Of Wit and Humour"—the two inseparables. His study is hardly satisfactory. Through a long, abstract, and obscure analysis, the conclusion is reached that the "passion" which humor aims at moving is "contempt." There are, it is true, redeeming touches, such as the observation that "humour paints by indirect imitation"—for instance, Addison in the *Spectator* has much "merely graphical" humor—a correct perception of the "objectivity" of the humorist. And among the English dramatists, Shakespeare's "transcendent excellence" is acknowledged in that field.

Lastly, it is a humbling thought that the *Encyclopedia Britannica* should have refused till its third edition to recognize the separate existence of an aesthetic category called humor. The first issue (1771) has the double entry:

Humour: see Fluid
Humour: see Wit.

The second edition follows suit (1783). The third (1797) at last condescends to notice that "Humour . . . is often made use of to express the quality of the imagination, which bears a considerable resemblance to wit." Wit is "more designed, concerted, regular and artificial"; humor, "more wild, loose, extravagant and fantastical"; it "comes by fits," and is not "perfectly consistent with true politeness." One wonders what the concocter of this awed description may have been thinking of! Again, it is "more diverting perhaps than wit, but inferior to it." Our cautious conclusion would be that to the writer humor remained suspiciously connected with the most primitive outbursts of frenzied originality.

VI. Corbyn Morris: The Final Distinction

In order that full light should be thrown upon the historical process itself—on a development of meaning which had bewildered the critics and observers for such a long time—one last link in the chain was missing. The duality of the word *humor* in its two acceptations, one traditional and passive, the other derived and active, must be properly cleared up and emphasized. That was reserved for a forgotten writer, Corbyn Morris, in his *Essay towards fixing the true standards of Wit, Humour, Raillery, Satire and Ridicule* (1744). Although the book was praised by Walpole in a letter (June 18, 1744), the idea which it put forth, and which was too much in advance of the time, remained practically without influence.

At long last Morris makes a distinction between the "Man of Humour" and the "humourist," which goes right down to the essential cleavage between the active and the passive aspects of the notion. It little matters that the labels affixed upon them are misleading to us: the "Man of Humour" here is our "humorist," and the "Humourist" is what Jonson, and a whole century after him, called "a humour." If that entirely conventional question of wording is dismissed, the distinction stands with absolute, unerring precision:

> It may be also proper to describe a Man of Humour, and an Humourist, which are very different persons.
>
> A Man of Humour is one, who can happily exhibit a weak and ridiculous Character in real Life, either by assuming it himself, or representing another in it, so naturally, that the whimsical Oddities, and Foibles, of that character, shall be palpably expos'd.
>
> Whereas an Humourist is a Person in real Life, obstinately attached to sensible peculiar Oddities of his own genuine Growth, which appear in his Temper and Conduct.
>
> In short, a Man of Humour is one, who can happily exhibit and expose the Oddities and Foibles of an Humourist, or of other Characters.

If that illuminating distinction had been properly noted and digested, criticism in the latter half of the eighteenth century, and through most of the nineteenth, would have been spared much ambiguity and confusion. But it was not to be.

That the phrase "man of humour" was not adopted should in itself cause no regret, as "humorist" from that time was being gradually specialized in the "active" sense which it bears today. The last example of its use to denote an odd character in life (the signal instance remaining Donne's "fondling motley humorist"), that *N.E.D.* registers, is dated 1830.[13]

Morris's other remarks are interesting in several ways. He insists that the humorist and the man of humor are united somehow through their inner originality, whether this lies in behavior or thought and expression; now originality is the germ of all the development which the notion and the word underwent from the sixteenth to the eighteenth centuries. He believes that humor is superior to wit, and these are some of his

[13] The phrase "the man of humour" was to be used again by Campbell (*The Philosophy of Rhetoric*, 1776, p. 61), but without attaching any special importance to it.

reasons: it appeals more directly to our humanity, being steeped in the concrete sense of the actual; it shows nature not adorned with intellectual brilliance but as it is; its value to us is lasting, whilst wit is a transitory flash; lastly, it goes along with benevolence, and has not the dryness of wit. The last remark can be traced to the *Spectator;* however we may demur to its absolute validity, these are no negligible additions to a searching analysis.

VII. Conclusion

After Morris, things remained very much as they were; his treatise seems to have been read with profit by very few inquirers. The English instinct, feeling its way to a notion of humor that would end a tiresome confusion and answer its genuine preference for the kindly tradition of Cervantes, fastened on the sympathetic element which Addison and Steele had pointed out—an element frequently to be found in the humorists of the most typical, the most national brand; and so the notion of humor as an essentially genial perception and creation of the comic definitively crystallized. That grew to be the predominant strain in nineteenth-century criticism. Carlyle roundly declares that "the essence of humour is sensibility" (*Essay on Richter*, 1827)—but in this case influences from Jean-Paul and the German *gemütlichkeit* have probably confirmed the native bent of thought. Thackeray, who ought to know, has the same solution ready for the riddle of humor: it is "wit and love" (from a lecture delivered in New York, 1852). C. Reed (*Lectures on English Literature*, 1856) speaks of "the happy compound of pathos and playfulness, which we style by that untranslateable term humour" *(N.E.D.)*. What can the cool stock-taking of the aesthetic elements which go into the making of a special mode of pleasantry do against such an all-but-unanimous verdict? And yet, Fielding, Thackeray's own teacher, had dubbed Swift the "greatest master of humour that ever wrote" (see above, section v).[14]

[14] George Eliot's lucid and objective mind had the privilege of taking stand against an arbitrary opinion which was already popular, but since her time has been even more widely adopted. She points out that the connection between

Be that as it may, on parting from our long-sustained task, it is sobering to think that whatever our effort may have achieved, it cannot have added one jot to the total amount of humor in the world. At the present time, in spite of the stubborn differences in theories and doctrines, a practical realization of what humor is, to an audience or the reading public, is all but universal in cultivated nations; the sense of humor, to give it its proper appellation, is much more broadly diffused than it ever was before; culture and finer intellectual perceptions have soaked down into wider masses of the people, and the raciness of the people has soaked up to the "elite," which they ceaselessly nourish and rejuvenate. As a general result, a much larger number of readers and hearers sense a humorist when they meet one. Humor has become a best-selling label on books, pictures, plays, and films; even on pieces of music. But that limitless diffusion of the name has not actually served the cause of the thing. Turned out most often with only the vaguest and dimmest intuition of its finer possibilities, or hopelessly merged in the crudest kinds of a farcical appeal to laughter, humor is losing its individuality by an extension of its range, in which its proper features are debased and blurred. Its mechanical production has been standardized.

That is all, of course, the abuse of a label that has grown too popular. Genuine humor is not concerned in this degeneracy. Literature still gives us works steeped in its rarest essence. At its best, that peculiar twist of thought and expression remains a way of thinking and feeling, a subtle philosophy;

humor and sympathy is by no means necessary and essential, being due to a set of relatively modern circumstances. "Some confusion as to the nature of Humour has been created by the fact that those who have written most eloquently on it have dwelt almost exclusively on its higher forms, and have defined humor in general as the *sympathetic* presentation of incongruous elements in human nature and life—a definition which only applies to its later developments." And she accounts for the association which has grown almost binding by the instinctive division of labor and the specialization which have taken place, humor gathering unto itself all the trends of sentiment and sympathy, while wit was more clearly assuming a character of dryness and indifference to feeling. "Hence it is, that while coarse and cruel humour has almost disappeared from contemporary literature, coarse and cruel wit abounds. . . ." So the whole trend of her argument is to the effect that originally, and through its aesthetic constitution, humor is free from all inevitable fusion with sentiment (*Essay on German Wit, Henry Heine, Essays,* Collected by N. Sheppard, New York, 1883, pp. 101-2).

at its worst, the poor antics of a tired jester. Of what things human is not this contrast more or less true? But in the present instance, we must own, the proportion of the best is not on the increase.

Whether we lean to optimism or pessimism as to the future of humor, one inference is certain: we should not soothe ourselves with the fond illusion that a plainer comprehension of the historical process which we have been investigating through almost ten centuries has any chance of improving the quantity or the quality of the contemporary product. Once more that elusive sprite, progress, baffles our expectations. And the way our wishes should go is then clear. Let the past of humor remain a hopelessly tangled issue, as it was to the great masters, provided we still are enabled, through a happy unawareness of its whole secret, history, and method, to enjoy the fertile verve of the creative humorists.

But it is time to put a final stop to our inquiry. A survey first of humor without a name, and then of the name and its fortunes, in English literature, from *Beowulf* to Burton and Addison, may have cast some rays of light upon the development of the thing and the history of the word. It may not have added much of substance to our knowledge; but its endeavor will be amply rewarded if it has not been entirely fruitless for the fuller comprehension of that supremely interesting object, the growth of the English mind itself.

INDEX

[All references are to the page, whether text or footnote. Multiple mentions of a name on one page are reported but once. The characters in Shakespeare's plays are indexed separately under his name.]